# ESCAPE

## Carolyn Jessop
### WITH LAURA PALMER

PENGUIN BOOKS

### PENGUIN BOOKS

Published by the Penguin Group
Penguin Books Ltd, 80 Strand, London WC2R 0RL, England
Penguin Group (USA), Inc., 375 Hudson Street, New York, New York 10014, USA
Penguin Group (Canada), 90 Eglinton Avenue East, Suite 700, Toronto, Ontario, Canada M4P 2Y3
(a division of Pearson Penguin Canada Inc.)
Penguin Ireland, 25 St Stephen's Green, Dublin 2, Ireland (a division of Penguin Books Ltd)
Penguin Group (Australia), 250 Camberwell Road, Camberwell, Victoria 3124, Australia
(a division of Pearson Australia Group Pty Ltd)
Penguin Books India Pvt Ltd, 11 Community Centre, Panchsheel Park, New Delhi – 110 017, India
Penguin Group (NZ), 67 Apollo Drive, Rosedale, North Shore 0632, New Zealand
(a division of Pearson New Zealand Ltd)
Penguin Books (South Africa) (Pty) Ltd, 24 Sturdee Avenue, Rosebank, Johannesburg 2196, South Africa

Penguin Books Ltd, Registered Offices: 80 Strand, London WC2R 0RL, England

www.penguin.com

First published in the United States of America by Broadway Books,
an imprint of The Doubleday Broadway Publishing Group,
a division of Random House, Inc., New York 2007
First published in Penguin Books 2008

8

Printed in England by Clays Ltd, St Ives plc

ISBN: 978-0-141-03151-4

www.greenpenguin.co.uk

Penguin Books is committed to a sustainable future
for our business, our readers and our planet.
The book in your hands is made from paper
certified by the Forest Stewardship Council.

PENGUIN BOOKS

# ESCAPE

Carolyn Jessop was born in 1968 into the Fundamentalist Church of Jesus Christ of Latter-day Saints, a group splintered from and renounced by the Mormon Church. At 18 she was forced into an arranged marriage with Merril Jessop, a man 32 years her senior. During her 17-year polygamous marriage to one of the most powerful men in the FLDS community, Carolyn had 8 children, withstood psychological abuse from her husband and his 6 other wives and was denied the right to make any decisions for herself. She eventually escaped in 2003 with all 8 of her children and only $20 to her name. In 2006, her reports to the Utah attorney general on church abuses formed a crucial part of the case that led to the notorious cult leader, Warren Jeffs, being put on the FBI's Most Wanted list and his subsequent arrest. She now lives in Utah with her children.

I dedicate this book to my eight children: Arthur, Betty, LuAnne, Andrew, Patrick, Merrilee, Harrison, and Bryson. My love for you knows no bounds. Even in my darkest days, you always gave me the meaning and reason I needed to go on.

This book is also dedicated to the women and children who may feel as desperately trapped by polygamy as I did and may wonder if they even deserve to dream of freedom and safety. You do.

## ACKNOWLEDGMENTS

I grew up with a love of reading, and I treasured books. When my library of books was seized and destroyed, it was another sign to me of the evil that was overtaking my world.

But if someone had told me then that one day I might write my own book, I would have found that as unimaginable as it was incomprehensible. Nor could I have *ever* believed that I would work with a team of talented professionals who would guide, support, and inspire me every step of the way.

The incomparable Kris Dahl at ICM believed in this project from the very beginning. As my literary agent, her advice, insight, and enthusiasm were crucial in making this book a reality.

Laura Palmer first met me as a reporter, then became my collaborator and, ultimately, a friend. She helped me find my voice and translate it to the page. Her compassion was invaluable as I revisited the most traumatic moments of my life.

My editor, Stacy Creamer, spearheaded a remarkable team at Doubleday who made excellence look effortless day after day. Bill Thomas, the editor-in-chief, and Steven Rubin, the publisher, have had a steadfast and unwavering commitment to this book, for which I am deeply grateful. Attorney Amelia Zalcman patiently and meticulously helped navigate legal issues. David Drake and Joanna Pinsker are so dedicated to publicity that they are the answer to an author's dreams.

Chris Fortunato did a superb job of coordinating the production of the book, recruiting a superb copyeditor, Sue Warga, and the talented Tina Henderson, who designed the text.

I also want to thank Laura Swerdloff at Doubleday and Montana Wojczuk at ICM, whose abilities as "assistants" far transcend their job descriptions. They contributed in immeasurable ways to all that this book is.

But there would never have been a book at all if I had not had the steadfast and unyielding support of friends, family, and strangers who rallied around me immediately after I escaped.

These who provided refuge, understanding, support, and love were Alleena and Dan Fischer, Shem Fischer, Jalleena and Neil Jessop, Saraleena and Louis Jessop, Danica and Daniel Loveridge, Tammy and David Fischer. The shelter and safety they provided for my children and me made everything else that happened in our lives possible. It is not an overstatement to say I could not have survived without them.

Jan Johnson and Laurie Allen made it possible for me to even begin thinking about the book I dreamed of writing. Jan's faith in me and the insight, guidance, and confidence she gave me were what I needed to start the ball rolling. She has my heartfelt gratitude, as does Laurie, who helped me at home when I most needed it so I could begin the long process of writing this book.

My family members—Thelma and Arthur Blackmore, Cathleen and Darrel Blackmore, Linda and Theil Cooke, Annette and Robert Jessop, Karen and John Zitting, Jane and Isaac Wyler, and my good friend Kevin Belt, stood by me without ever flinching. The hope they gave me reinforced my own, and there were times when that really kept me going.

My freedom meant nothing until I felt safe and won custody of my children. Mark Shurtleff, Utah's attorney general, his spokesman Paul Murphy, and attorney Lisa Jones Reading did everything they could to support me and then even more. Words feel too small to express my deep gratitude to all of them.

Audrey, Merril Jessop's daughter, and her husband, Merlin Johnson, were the only relatives from my ex-husband's family who reached out to me in kindness after my escape. Thank you.

I found inspiration and hope from mentors like Jon Krakauer, Crystal Maggelet, and Dorothy and Bruce Solomon. They, too, had faith in me that often felt stronger than my own. A strange new world became less mysterious to me because of the generosity of their spirits and hearts.

My children needed to be stabilized before they could even begin to face a new future, let alone function in it. Connie Crosby, Patty Whittaker, Mitzi and John Magleby, Rhoda Thompson, Lodeen and Paul Peterson, Lee D. Bird, Hill Dalde, Gary Engles, Jean Alport, and Lara and Paul Cox were the people most instrumental in helping them make a positive transition into new lives.

Lorial Mousseau and each and every member of the American Association of the University of Women Wasatch Branch invited me to speak and then took me under their wing to support and encourage me. They believed in this book from the moment it was first mentioned, and their enthusiasm was invaluable. It meant a lot to me to hear them say that I had a story worth telling.

Last, but by no means least, I want to thank the people whose kindness and generosity have made it possible for my family to have Christmases four years in a row. One year a church adopted us; another year a book club made sure we had presents. This helped relieve an annual pressure for me. I remember being so strapped one year I was saving my change to buy laundry detergent. Christmas presents would have been out of the question if it weren't for the kindness of strangers.

The FLDS is constructed on a scaffolding of lies. We were all brainwashed into believing that everyone in the outside world was evil. Every Christmas, when I see the delight in my children as they unwrap presents from people they never met, I realize what a monstrous lie we were taught to believe.

For all the kindness, then, both large and small, that has come into our lives from so many directions I give thanks, again and again.

# ESCAPE

# The Choice Was Freedom or Fear

Escape. The moment had come. I had been watching and waiting for months. The time was right. I had to act fast and without fear. I could not afford to fail. Nine lives were at stake: those of my eight children and my own.

Monday, April 21, 2003. At ten o'clock that night, I found out that my husband had left earlier in the evening on a business trip. All eight of my children were home—including Arthur, fifteen, my oldest, who often traveled on construction jobs. There were two things that had to happen before I could escape, and they just had: my husband was gone and my children were all home. I had to act within hours.

The choice was freedom or fear. I was thirty-five and desperate to flee from polygamy, the only world I had ever known. I came from six generations of polygamists and was part of a sect known as the Fundamentalist Church of the Latter-Day Saints (FLDS). Ten thousand of us lived in a small community along the Utah-Arizona border.

At eighteen, I was coerced into an arranged marriage with Merril Jessop, a fifty-year-old man I barely knew. I became his fourth wife and had eight children in fifteen years. They ranged from Arthur, my oldest, to Bryson, the youngest, who was then eighteen months old and still nursing. The six children in between included my son Harrison, who was almost four and severely disabled with nerve damage from a highly aggressive cancer known as spinal neuroblastoma.

The first thing I did when I realized I might be able to escape was go to my sister Linda's house to use the telephone. I couldn't call from my home because the phones were monitored. My husband's six other wives were suspicious. I had a reputation for being somewhat independent and thinking for myself, so the other wives kept tabs on me. If anyone suspected something, one of the wives would immediately call Merril.

My sister was part of the FLDS community, but she and her husband were not in a plural marriage. She knew from our previous conversations how desperate I was to escape. We both felt the sect was becoming too extreme and frightening under the leadership of its prophet, Warren Jeffs. The running joke between us on the phone was "Don't drink the punch."

Ever since Jeffs had taken over the sect after the death of his father, Rulon Jeffs, he had been preaching that he was Jesus Christ incarnate and that his late father was God. He also started talking in apocalyptic terms about moving his followers to what he called the "Center Place." We feared that meant a walled compound from which there would be no escape. Jeffs did not believe people had the right to make their own choices. My husband was a powerful member of the FLDS community and very close to Jeffs. With his seven wives and fifty-four children, the odds were my husband would be one of the first to be taken to the Center Place. It would be tantamount to a prison camp for me and my children—one where we'd be required to report on others who strayed from or disobeyed the word of God.

When I was growing up in the FLDS, our lives had not been as extreme as they were becoming under Warren Jeffs. The children in the community attended public schools. But that ended when Jeffs took over. He felt that teachers in the public schools had been educated by gentiles and were "contaminated." Jeffs ordered all FLDS children into church-run schools, called private priesthood schools.

Jeffs preached that our children were the "chosen seed of God" and that it was our duty, as God's people, to protect them from all things unclean. In the FLDS-run schools, children were brainwashed, not educated. My kids were taught that dinosaurs had never existed and that men had never set foot on the moon. I could see how fast they were falling behind.

I had been a public school teacher and cherished literature. I had collected more than three hundred children's books. Shortly after Jeffs took over, he decreed that all worldly material—including books—be banned from the community. My husband ordered us to comply. Our home was scoured; all literature was confiscated and destroyed, including my children's books.

It was common knowledge among us that Jeffs was marrying off younger and younger girls and taking more wives for himself. (At last count, he had seventy.) I came home once after one of Harrison's hospitalizations and could not find my twelve-year-old daughter, Betty. My questions were ignored when I tried to find out where she was. I was upset. Someone eventually told me that she was "in compliance with her father's wishes." I finally learned that she and several other young girls had been invited to a sleepover at the prophet's house.

When I arrived at my sister's house, the first call I made was to the police. There was no answer at the Arizona police station at that hour; I got their voice mail. But the Utah police answered. I asked if anyone would be willing to help a woman and her children leave the FLDS community. The police said they had no jurisdiction because even though we were just a mile or so across the border, we were legally in Arizona.

It was getting close to 11 P.M. I tried calling a group that assists women fleeing polygamy. No one there could act immediately.

I felt the trap closing as midnight approached. My sister and I called my brother in Salt Lake City. Arthur had left the sect four years earlier to marry the woman he loved, who was also his stepsister. When our father's third wife moved in with us, she came with her eight children. Arthur fell in love with Thelma, one of her daughters. They were not allowed to marry even though they had no biological relationship. When the prophet at the time, who was Warren Jeffs' father, assigned Thelma to marry someone she didn't want, she and

Arthur fled, quit the FLDS, married, and built a happy life in Salt Lake City.

Arthur was home when I called. "Arthur, if I do it tonight, I can get out. Will you help me?"

"Carolyn," he said, "I'll do everything I can to help you, but even if I leave right now, the soonest I can be there is five in the morning."

"Will you do it?" I tried not to sound as desperate as I felt. We were three hundred miles away. He would have to drive all night.

"I'll be there," he said.

We agreed to meet at Canaan Corners, a convenience store three miles from town on the Utah side of the border. Arthur said he'd bring a trailer to drive my van back to Salt Lake City. It was registered in my name but had expired license plates. (Women in the community could drive—but our cars had either no license plates or outdated ones, so if we tried to leave without our husband's permission, we'd be stopped by the police.) The nine of us could fit in Arthur's SUV, and he said he'd ask our other brother, Darrel, to drive down, too.

I told Arthur my van was almost out of gas but I'd do everything I could to get there. "If I don't show up, come looking for me," I said. "I may have no way out of town, but please don't leave without me."

Now I needed to figure out what to tell my children to get them out of the house and into my van. They would never leave if they knew we were fleeing the community.

My children were terrified of the outside world. We were taught that everyone outside our community was evil. Impending doom is an integral part of the FLDS culture. Instead of playing hide-and-seek as children, we played apocalypse. The belief is that when God comes to destroy the wicked, everyone outside the community will be killed. But those who'd proved their worth would be lifted up to the celestial kingdom and preserved as God's chosen people.

When I was younger I remember being looked at with scorn and disgust when we went into town in the long pastel dresses that we wore over dark leggings. People called us "polygs" and sometimes threw rocks at us. Their hostility confirmed that all the evil people in the outside world were poised to hurt or even destroy us.

It was just after midnight when I left my sister Linda's house. It was quiet when I returned home. I took two black garbage bags from the kitchen and then quietly slipped into my children's rooms to collect clothing—a two-day supply for each. Since I was often up late at night doing laundry, no one would be suspicious if I was spotted carrying my children's clothing from room to room.

My bedroom, in the basement, faced a terraced area. I could leave and enter my room through large French doors. When I came back from my sister's I parked my van in front of my bedroom so it would be easy to pack. I carefully loaded the children's clothing, our family pictures, and Harrison's medications into my van.

I'd been hoarding Harrison's drugs for the past five months so I'd have medicine to give him after we escaped. I didn't know how long it would be until I found a new team of doctors. So I started cutting back on his daily doses—a milligram here and there—until I could accumulate a small supply.

Harrison was almost four, unable to walk or talk, and still in diapers. He couldn't eat food by mouth. He had a feeding tube that sent high-calorie liquids directly into his stomach. To help build up his strength, I began expressing my breast milk—I was still nursing my youngest baby—and adding it to Harrison's feeding tube. I did this for six months, and it seemed to work. Before I started Harrison on breast milk, I was taking him to the hospital about once a week. But in that six-month period before we fled, I didn't have to take him at all.

But I did have to get him to eat food by mouth. Harrison screamed and fought me whenever I put food into his mouth. He hated it. But I knew I couldn't take all his equipment and feeding supplies with us when we escaped.

Pizza saved the day. Harrison loved it. I finally got him to chew and swallow bits of pizza. It took almost four months, but I finally convinced him to eat small bits of other foods.

Harrison was profoundly handicapped, but he helped save us. He needed nearly 24/7 care. I know my husband thought I would never be able to escape with Harrison. How could I? Harrison needed oxygen to sleep. I kept an oxygen machine by his crib so he'd be able to breathe. I was worried about taking him off the oxygen, but it was a risk I just had to take.

At 4:00 A.M. I started getting everybody up. I was very matter-of-fact when I awakened each of my children. I said Harrison was sick and needed to go to the doctor. This was completely plausible—Harrison went to doctors a lot. The younger children thought this would be a great adventure. They didn't get to leave the community very often. I told the older children that since Arthur was home, everyone had to come with me so we could take family pictures afterward at Sears.

My older children were annoyed. They didn't want to come. I insisted.

One of Merril's other wives walked in as my daughter Betty was getting dressed. She was suspicious and started questioning Betty. It was about 4:20 A.M. She then apparently called my husband and reported that I was up and dressing my children. My father told me later that Merril called him about 4:25 A.M. and said, "What the hell is Carolyn doing? She's up and getting all her children dressed." Dad was telling him the truth when he said he had no idea what was happening. I think Merril was caught off guard. I'd been so careful not to arouse any suspicions in him in recent weeks. We'd even had sex two days before.

Merril called the house again, desperately trying to find me. I heard my name paged over the house intercom. I knew if I talked to him I'd never be able to leave. It was almost 4:30 A.M. I had only minutes left.

One by one, I put my children in the van and told them to buckle their seat belts. I was frantic. I was also out of time. Harrison was the only one left. I ran inside, turned off his oxygen, and grabbed him from his crib. I strapped him into his car seat, turned on the ignition, and counted to see if my children were all there. Betty was missing.

I had seconds to decide. *Do I leave one behind to save seven?* No. It had to be all or nothing. I ran inside and found Betty crying and furious in her room.

"Mother, there is something you're doing that's wrong! Why doesn't Father know what you're doing?"

I grabbed her arm. She fought back, struggling to break free. I pulled hard. "Betty, I'm not leaving you behind. You are coming with me."

She kept screaming. I got her into the van, slammed the door, and started the engine. One phone call from Merril to the local police and we'd be trapped. The local police are members of the FLDS and the men whom Merril would rely on to stop my escape. The community also had a watch patrol that drove around during the night. If anyone saw me, I'd be stopped and asked if my husband knew what I was doing.

The night was deathly dark. My eyes locked onto my rearview mirror watching for any other car. If someone started following us, I'd hit the accelerator.

After about two miles, my engine began to sputter. I was almost out of gas. The kids knew something was wrong and were getting scared. I could see Canaan Corners in the distance. My heart was racing. I couldn't breathe. When it felt as if the van was about to die, I pulled over to the side. I told the children we were out of gas but that I saw people up ahead who might be able to help us. I left the van and ran ahead to where Arthur and Darrel were waiting.

I threw my arms around them. But there was no time for excitement or relief. I told my brother that my kids didn't know anything yet, nor could we tell them—the truth would be overwhelming.

When we got back to the van I told the children that these two men were giving us a ride to get more gas. My son looked at my brother, his namesake, and said, "Is that Uncle Arthur?" I didn't say anything. I didn't want to lie, but the others would explode if they knew what was really happening. When I didn't answer, Arthur figured out what was happening. But he kept quiet.

The ride went smoothly for the first twenty minutes. I didn't know where we would hide when we reached Salt Lake City. I knew Merril would come after me. I couldn't stay with family because that would be the first place he would look. I had to find someone my husband would not expect to help us. But who? Maybe I'd knock on strangers' doors until I found someone who would hide us.

Everything changed when we came to a turn-off on the highway and headed toward Salt Lake City instead of St. George, where Harrison's doctor worked. Betty went ballistic.

"You are stealing us! Mother, you are stealing us! Uncle Warren will come and get us." She was hysterical.

"Betty, I can't steal my own children."

"We don't belong to you! We belong to the prophet! You have no right to us."

"We'll see what they say in the courts." I tried to reason with her. "In the courts real mothers have rights to their children."

Andrew, my seven-year-old, turned around to look at us. "Isn't Mom taking us to get pictures after the doctor?"

"She isn't taking us for pictures. She's taking us to hell." Betty was enraged.

"Why are you doing that?" little Andrew asked. "Why are you taking us to hell?"

Arthur was quiet but seething. I had put us all at risk and he knew it.

Finally he began yelling at Betty to shut up. "There is nothing you can do about this situation, Betty. Calm down. Just be quiet." Arthur kept saying this over and over. Betty shouted back that the prophet would condemn me to hell. Arthur did not give up. Exhausted, Betty finally relented.

Five hours later we arrived in Salt Lake City and went into hiding. For the first time in thirty-five years, I was free. I had eight children and twenty dollars to my name. Within hours, Merril was hunting me down like prey.

# Early Childhood

**I** was born in the bitter cold but into warm and loving hands. Aunt Lydia Jessop was the midwife who brought me into the world on January 1, 1968, just two hours after midnight.

Aunt Lydia could not believe I'd survived. She was the midwife who had delivered babies for two generations, including my mother. When she saw the placenta, she realized that my mother had chronic placental abruption. Mom had hemorrhaged throughout her pregnancy and thought she was miscarrying. But when the bleeding stopped, she shrugged it off, assuming she was still pregnant. Aunt Lydia, the midwife, said that by the time I was born, the placenta was almost completely detached from the uterus. My mother could have bled to death and I could have been born prematurely or, worse, stillborn.

But I came into the world as a feisty seven-pound baby, my mother's second daughter. My father said she could name me Carolyn or Annette. She looked up both names and decided to call me Carolyn because it meant "wisdom." My mother always said that even as a baby, I looked extremely wise to her.

I was born into six generations of polygamy on my mother's side and started life in Hildale, Utah, in a fundamentalist Mormon community known as the FLDS, or the Fundamentalist Church of Jesus Christ of Latter-Day Saints. Polygamy was the issue that defined us and the reason we'd split from the mainstream Mormon Church.

My childhood memories really begin in Salt Lake City. We moved there when I was about five. Even though my parents believed in polygamy, my father had only one wife. He owned a small real estate business that was doing well and decided it made sense to use Salt Lake as a base. We had a lovely house with a porch swing and a landscaped yard and trees. This was a big change from the tiny house in Colorado City with dirt and weeds in the yard and a father who was rarely home.

But the biggest difference in moving to Salt Lake City was that my mother, Nurylon, was happy. She loved the city and delighted in having my father home every night after work. My dad was doing well, and Mom had enough money to buy plenty of groceries when we went to the store and even had some extra for toys.

There were soon four of us. I had two sisters, Linda and Annette. I was in the middle—Linda was eighteen months older than I and Annette two years younger. My baby brother Arthur arrived a few years after Annette. My mother was thrilled to finally have a son because in our culture, boys have more value than girls. Linda and my mother were very close. But my mother always seemed very irritated by me, in part, I think, because I was my father's favorite.

I adored my dad, Arthur Blackmore. He was tall and thin, with large bones and dark, wavy hair. I remember that whenever we were around other families I thought I had the best-looking father in the entire world. I saw him as my personal protector and felt safe when I was in his presence. His face lit up when I entered the room; I was always the daughter he wanted to introduce when friends visited our house. My mother complained that he didn't discipline me as much as he did my sister Linda, but he ignored her and didn't seem to care.

We only lived in Salt Lake City for a year, but it was a happy one. Mother took us to the zoo and to the park, where we'd play on the swings and slides. My father's business was successful and expanding. But he decided we needed to move back to Colorado City, Arizona—a tiny, nondescript FLDS enclave about 350 miles south of Salt Lake City and a stone's throw from Hildale, Utah, where I was born. The reason we went back was that he didn't want my sister

Linda attending a regular public school. Even though she would technically be going to a public school in Colorado City, most of the teachers there were FLDS and very conservative. In theory, at least, religion is not to be taught in public schools, but in fact it was an integral part of the curriculum there.

When we returned to Colorado City, my father put an addition onto our house. There was more space to live in, but life became more claustrophobic. Mother changed. When we got up in the morning, she would still be sleeping. My father was on the road a lot now, so she was home alone. When we tried to wake her up, she'd tell us to go back to bed.

She'd finally surface midmorning and come into the kitchen to make us breakfast and talk about how much she wanted to die. While she made us hot cornmeal cereal, toast, or pancakes she'd complain about having nothing to live for and how she'd rather be dead. Those were the good mornings. The really awful mornings were the ones when she'd talk about how she was going to kill herself that day.

I remember how terrified I felt wondering what would happen to us if my mother killed herself. Who'd take care of us? Father was gone nearly all the time. One morning I asked my mother, "Mama, if a mother dies, what will happen to her children? Who will take care of them?"

I don't think Mother noticed my urgency. She had no idea of the impact her words had been having on me. I think she felt my question arose from a general curiosity about dying. Mother was very matter-of-fact in responding to me: "Oh, the children will be all right. The priesthood will give their father a new wife. The new wife will take care of them."

By this time I was about six. I looked at her and said, "Mama, I think that Dad better hurry up and get a new wife."

I was beginning to notice other things about the world around me. One was that some of the women we'd see in the community when we went shopping were wearing dark sunglasses. I was surprised when a woman took her glasses off in the grocery store and I could see that both her eyes were blackened. I asked my mother what was wrong, but the question seemed to make her uncomfortable and she didn't answer me. My curiosity was piqued, however, and every time I saw a woman in dark glasses, I stared at her to see if they were covering strange, mottled bruises.

What I did love about my mother was her beauty. In my eyes, she was gorgeous. She dressed with pride and care. Like my father, she was tall and thin. The clothes she made for herself and my sisters and me were exquisite. She always picked the best fabrics. She knew how to make pleats and frills. I remember beaming when someone would praise my mother for her well-mannered and well-dressed children. Everyone in the community thought she was an exceptional mother.

But that was the public façade. In private, my mother was depressed and volatile. She beat us almost every day. The range was anything from several small swats on the behind to a lengthy whipping with a belt. Once the beating was so bad I had bruises all over my back and my legs for more than a week. When she hit us, she accused us of always doing things to try to make her miserable.

I feared her, but my fear made me a student of her behavior. I watched her closely and realized that even though she slapped us throughout the day, she never spanked us more than once a day. The morning swats were never that intense or prolonged. The real danger came in late afternoon, when she was in the depths of her sorrow.

I concluded that if I got my spanking early in the morning and got it out of the way, I would basically have a free pass for the rest of the day. As soon as Mama got up, I knew I had a spanking coming. Linda and Annette quickly caught on to what I was doing, and they tried to get their spankings out of the way in the morning, too.

There were several times when my mother spanked me and then screamed and screamed at me. "I'm going to give you a beating you'll never forget! I am not going to stop beating you until you shut up and stop crying! You make me so mad! How could you be so stupid!" Even though it's been decades, her screams still echo inside me when I think about her.

I remember overhearing my mother say to a relative, "I just don't understand what has gotten into my three daughters. As soon as I am out of bed every morning, they are so bad that no matter how much I warn them, they will just not be quiet until I give them all a spanking. After they have all gotten a spanking, then everything calms down and we can all get on with our day."

When my mother beat me, she would always say she was doing it because she loved me. So I used to wish that she didn't love me. I was afraid of her, but I would also get angry at her when she hit me. After she beat me she insisted on giving me a hug. I hated that. The hug didn't make the spanking stop hurting. It didn't fix anything.

I never told my father about the beatings because it was such an accepted part of our culture. What my mother was doing would be considered "good discipline." My mother saw herself as raising righteous children and felt teaching us obedience was one of her most important responsibilities. Spanking your children was widely seen as the way to reach that goal. It wasn't considered abuse; it was considered good parenting.

Some of the happiest times for me would be when we would have quilting parties at home. The women from the community would spend the day at our house, quilting around a big frame. Stories and gossip were shared, there was a lot of food, and the children all had a chance to play together. Quilting parties were the one time we had breathing room.

Once I was playing with dolls with my cousin under the quilt when I heard my aunt Elaine say, "I was so scared the other day. Ray Dee was playing out in the yard with her brothers and sisters. Some people from out of town stopped in front of our house. All of the other children ran into the house screaming, but Ray Dee stayed outside and talked to the out-of-towners."

Aunt Elaine was beside herself that her daughter had spoken with outsiders. We were taught that outsiders were "agents of the devil" who wanted to kidnap us and take us away. They were seen as evil people who wanted to destroy the work of God. If they could get access to the children of God's chosen, then they would try to hurt or destroy us.

Our community was so isolated it was rare that we ever saw anyone from the outside. Most of my cousins only left the community to go shopping with their mothers and had almost no sense of the outside world. I still had memories of our happy lives in Salt Lake City, where we even had a TV. (My parents also had a coffeemaker; coffee was strictly forbidden in the Mormon Church.)

As my mother's depression worsened, she spent more of the day in bed. She neglected the house until the day before my father came home and then went into a cleaning frenzy. My father wanted his house spotless. One night he came home and we were all in our pajamas, clean and ready for bed. The house was immaculate. But my father walked over to the refrigerator and ran his finger across the top. It was dusty. He lit into my mother and said she had to do a better job of cleaning. My mother began screaming at my father to go to hell. She'd accuse him of not caring how hard she worked to keep up his home and care for his children. If he didn't like the way she cleaned, then maybe he should take over the job and raise his children by himself.

Our home became a battleground, at least when our father came home. He and Mom would be going after each other within five or ten minutes after he walked through the door. The house was tense, the atmosphere ugly. But the spankings stopped when our father was home, which was a relief. For the most part, Mom avoided hitting us then, although she made it known that our behavior was expected to be perfect.

But there were days when Mom was happy and didn't want to die. She loved to play games with us when she was in a good mood. One of our favorites was the Three Little Pigs. Linda, Annette, and I were the pigs and Mom was the big bad wolf. We'd build our playhouses of sticks and mud and she'd come and blow them all down until we made the brick house, which was stronger than she was. We also spent happy hours listening to Mama read fairy tales. She rarely read us religious scripture and, to our delight, much preferred the fantasy world of fairy tales.

Mother was devout, but she had a frisky side. One time when my father was away she and a friend went to town and came home with a Christmas tree. Imagine! This was completely forbidden in the

FLDS. We decorated it with lights and homemade ornaments. I knew it was wrong to participate in such a worldly tradition, but I was having too much fun to care. Mother beamed. She loved our Christmas tree. We popped popcorn and made garlands for the tree. Before we went to bed that night we hung up our stockings and Mama told us there would be a prize in each of them the next morning. Nothing like this had happened in our lives before. The thought of presents made us wild with anticipation.

The next morning we found not only candy canes and fruit in our stockings but a present under the tree. My father let us have candy once a year—no more. My mother was clearly disobeying our father in giving us sugary treats. And she let us eat them before we had our breakfast!

Linda and I were old enough to realize that Mama was going to have to pay for her disobedience, but we loved feeling so spoiled. We had pancakes for breakfast and then went to the house of Mama's friend, who'd also given her children a Christmas. These children told us Santa Claus had brought them presents, but we said ours came from Mama.

My father came home the next night. I went to sleep listening to them fighting and screaming. The next morning, our Christmas tree was gone. Mama was crying when she fixed us breakfast. When we finished eating, Linda and I went outside to play and saw the Christmas tree lying under the house, stripped of its glittery lights.

My mother was a beautiful person when she was happy. She glowed with delight and laughter the night we put up the tree. During these good times, Mother carried herself with poise and elegance and realized that she was a woman worthy of love. In Salt Lake City, we had been very happy and Mother was engaged in the world around her. In Colorado City, she was locked into a world of constant pregnancies, a loveless marriage, and a rural community strung together with dirt roads.

My father criticized her constantly. The house was never clean enough, her children never well-mannered enough. Even after her babies, Mother was still thin, but my father felt she wasn't thin enough.

Mother sank into a deep depression after our first and last Christmas. She stayed in bed all day and stopped cleaning the house and doing the laundry. After a few days, the friend who had been her Christmas co-conspirator came over and told her to stop feeling bad about herself. If her husband didn't want her to have fun with her kids, that was his problem. Mother rallied, but she never again did something with us in defiance of our religion. I did notice that she became more demanding of us and insisted on more perfection after the Christmas episode. I'm sure she would have preferred to play games with us instead of spanking us, but her own mental slavery prevented her from being who she was.

My grandmother Jenny was one of the buffers between us and our mother's volatility. I learned early on as a child to be a barometer for my mother's mood swings. Her moods could change hour to hour; I always had to pay attention to which frame of mind she was in and adapt accordingly. But Grandma gave Mother some breathing room, especially when the smaller children were driving her crazy. Whatever my mother's mental issues were, she was overall a much better mother than many of the women in the community. Grandma came over almost every day and helped care for us. If she got to our house early enough in the morning, there would be no spankings.

My grandmother was in her mid-sixties. I think she always seemed so much older to me because she was in very poor health. Women age rapidly in the FLDS. Most have hard lives and often a dozen or more children. Women look okay in their thirties and then age dramatically in their forties. My mother was the youngest of Grandma's ten children and was born late in Grandma's life, so my grandmother was very, very old when I knew her. She was heavyset, wrinkled, and worn. Her hair was gray and her eyes were bad, but her spirit was strong and she could tell a story like no one else.

I remember sitting in her lap for hours as she told me stories about the Old West and the southern states before the Civil War. Grandma's husband had died when my mother was two years old. My grandmother—who came from polygamist bloodlines—then was married to an apostle in the FLDS and became part of a plural marriage for the first time. My grandmother believed plural marriage was the most sacred aspect of our faith and told me story after story about how the Mormon Church had been the church of God until it abandoned polygamy.

She told me with great pride that her great-grandfather, Benjamin F. Johnson, was one of the first men whom the prophet Joseph Smith introduced to the holy principle of celestial marriage in the nineteenth century. (Smith was rumored to have had between thirty-three and forty-eight wives himself. It's been said that his youngest wife was fourteen when they married.)

The principle of celestial marriage is what defines the FLDS faith. A man must have multiple wives if he expects to do well in heaven, where he can eventually become a god and wind up with his own planet.

A man has spirit wives in heaven, where he fathers spirit children. (Becoming a spirit child is the first step on the journey in coming to earth.) We also held fast to the belief that our father was once a spirit and then came to earth to get a body and try to prove that he is worthy enough to become a god. Grandma said that the prophet had to be very careful about whom he shared this information with because several men had turned against him when he introduced them to this holy covenant of marriage.

So with deep feeling she told me how my great-great-great-grandfather became one of the first men to live the principle of celestial marriage, which is only given to God's most chosen. It was not for everyone. The prophet Joseph Smith said that this one principle would condemn more men than it would save. But it worked for my great-great-great-great-grandfather, who had seven wives. His sons had many wives, too, and according to Grandma, the principle of celestial marriage had been a blessing to all in our family who practiced it.

I felt like the luckiest little girl to be one of God's elite and a spirit who was the most chosen of all his spirits before I came to earth. Proof of that was that I had been born into a faithful bloodline. I was FLDS royalty. The culture really believes in the value of bloodlines.

Only a spirit who was strong and worthy would be selected to be born into one of the royal lines.

Understand that we were taught to believe we were better than everyone else in the entire world because of our beliefs. Since I had been selected to come to such a royal bloodline, my grandmother told me that I had the chance to become a goddess if I lived polygamy and proved worthy. It was our own version of the Cinderella story. Just having the opportunity to live in a plural marriage was sold to me as a special blessing that few would ever have.

Grandma explained that our family always held fast to the principle of celestial marriage, especially after the Mormon Church issued a manifesto against it in the 1890s. Fearing prosecution, her family fled to Mexico with other Mormons who were devoted to polygamy and determined to keep practicing it. When she was ten years old her family came back to the United States. The official policy of the Mormon Church became, and still is, that those who practice polygamy are not in harmony with God.

But the adherents who believed polygamy was a requirement for their salvation began a fundamentalist movement in the early years of the twentieth century. The grassroots movement slowly gained strength, and it was several years before it became an actual organization, complete with a prophet.

The first fundamentalist prophet claimed his authority through John Taylor, who was considered the third leader of the Mormon Church after Joseph Smith and Brigham Young. It was believed that while John Taylor was in hiding, he was given the keys to the priesthood. As the story goes, he was visited one night by Jesus Christ, who told him that the principle of celestial marriage was to be preserved at all costs. Since there would be opposition to this, the priesthood would have to go into hiding. Christ made it clear to Taylor that the keys to the priesthood were being taken away from the mainstream Mormon Church. Christ told John Taylor that after he died the keys to the priesthood would go to someone other than the next in line in the Mormon Church. They would go to a man who would honor the sacred covenant of celestial marriage and from then on, God would be working only with his most elite children.

Even after the manifesto, the Mormon Church allowed members to live in plural marriage as long as a man did not have more than two wives. Anyone who tried to marry more than two ran the risk of excommunication. That changed in the early 1920s, when the Mormons tried to get rid of polygamy altogether and soon began excommunicating anyone who practiced plural marriage.

Listening to my grandmother talk, I felt like I was being rocked in a cradle of specialness. Grandma made me feel unique, but not in the traditional way. She taught me that I had been blessed by God with an opportunity to come into a family where generations of women had sacrificed their feelings and given up the things of this world to preserve the work of God and prove worthy of the celestial kingdom of God.

I was wide-eyed, thinking of all those women who were now in heaven, reaping the rewards of their earthly sacrifices. I was proud to be part of such an important tradition. As daughters of God, we were bound in a covenant before we came to earth. My grandmother explained that we had pledged to God that we would never do anything to undermine his work and would produce many children. There were thousands of chosen spirits waiting to come to earth. We were the women who would give birth to them. Grandma taught me that my sole purpose on earth was to have as many children as possible. God would reveal the name of the man he wanted me to marry by sending a revelation to the prophet.

To a little girl, this sounded important and thrilling. It was the one way in my life that I could feel special. Nothing explained why my mother beat me or why my parents argued all the time when my father came home. But Grandma made me feel as though I had been singled out for an important life. I didn't question my parents' behavior; it was a fact of life for me. Violence toward children was incorporated into our belief system, and it was very common in the community to see a mother slap one of her children, sometimes very hard. I knew my parents didn't get along, but I didn't really see many other parents who did. This was just the way our world worked; I had no way of making comparisons. But whatever happened at home, I knew in my heart that God thought I was special. I knew that the prophet would tell me whom to marry and then I'd produce as many babies as I could. Because I loved my grandmother so much and because this was presented to me as absolute truth, it would be years before I'd even begin to look at any of the premises my life was based upon.

The most dramatic story my grandmother ever told me was about the raid at Short Creek, Arizona, on July 26, 1953. The way she told it, the women of the FLDS rallied to protect the work of God. The raid is a key focal point of FLDS history. Grandma told us this story over and over, and it always began the same way—with her dream.

Several months before the raid, Grandma dreamed about being with her children in the back of a very old wagon. The prophet, Uncle Roy, was driving the wagon across an old, rickety bridge that was beginning to break apart from the weight of the wagon. Grandma could see that there was a deep ravine below them with a rushing river. She knew that if the bridge collapsed, they'd all be lost forever.

But the wagon made it safely to the other side. She knew, in her dream, that Uncle Roy had saved them and that he was the only man who could have done so.

Grandma said rumors were rampant that a raid was coming. She put my mother and aunt to bed that night in July and went to the schoolhouse to join in a prayer circle, asking God to keep the armies of the devil at bay.

A lookout was posted on the only road coming into town. The young man was supposed to warn the community if he saw the authorities coming by exploding several sticks of dynamite. The blast came. The state of Arizona had launched an invasion. Grandma said the lookout ran into town and fell at the feet of Uncle Roy, shouting, "They are coming, they're coming, and there are hundreds of them!"

Out of the darkness came troops from the Arizona National Guard along with police and other local officials. They moved into

Short Creek (which is now Colorado City) and began arresting men and women who practiced polygamy.

Uncle Roy was urged to flee but decided to stand firm. "My feet are tired of running and I intend to turn to God for protection."

Grandpa Jessop, Grandma Jenny's father-in-law, went out to meet the authorities and said, "What is it that you want? What have you come for? If it is blood you want, take mine, I'm ready." He was an elderly man with a long white beard. Photographers snapped his picture as he stood up to the authorities.

Grandma described the harrowing scene as the troops tried to take babies out of their mothers' arms. The children were wailing, the mothers were screaming, and newspaper photos the next morning captured the terrible images that turned public opinion in *favor* of the polygamists.

By the time the raid was over, 122 men and women had been arrested and 263 children had been identified to be seized from their polygamist families the next day. Everyone except the children was to be transported to Kingman, Arizona, which was four hundred miles away. The men went the first day, and buses came to take the children to Phoenix the next. The women were escorted from their homes, leaving behind bread baking in the oven and laundry hanging on the line. They were ordered to the schoolhouse and not allowed to bring even diapers for their babies. When the buses arrived, they were told they'd be separated from their children. The women revolted. The plan was to not only take the children but make them wards of the state and adopt them out to nonpolygamist families.

Ultimately, the state of Arizona relented. It feared the negative publicity, and it had also underestimated the number of children in the community. They did not have enough adults to care for that many children on the long bus ride to Phoenix, so in the end mothers were allowed to accompany their children.

Grandma had a brother in Phoenix who pressured the authorities into releasing her and her three children into his care. She told me that she stayed strong by remembering her dream. She had faith that Uncle Roy would find a way to save them, and he did.

Uncle Roy traveled to Phoenix and began doggedly tracking down all the children and their mothers. He forbade the women to testify about their marriages and started court proceedings of his own to counter Arizona's action. In a move that perplexed everyone except those who believed Uncle Roy was getting messages from God, Uncle Roy told his lawyers to find the law that said children couldn't be taken from their families without a parent's consent. His attorneys scoffed at the notion that such a law existed. Uncle Roy said it did. Sure enough, a law on the books said just that, and the court case ended.

The Short Creek raid actually turned out to be a boon to the FLDS. It generated monumental sympathy for the cult. Once the court case was thrown out, everyone returned home and the practice of polygamy thrived.

But the sect became more secretive. People were afraid of the government and became much more guarded about their activities. The dress style became more conservative. No one could show any part of their bodies below the neck. Women were forbidden to wear pants.

Marriage also changed. Before the Short Creek raid, women were allowed to choose the men they wanted to marry. The problem was that when women had a say in choosing their own husbands, they chose men close to their own ages. Young women wanted to marry young men. That was bad news for an older man seeking younger wives to enhance his favor with God. The powerful men in the FLDS were older. They knew something had to change because when forced to compete with younger men, they routinely lost out.

They also feared that young men from outside the community would entice young women to live outside once they fell in love with them. The future of polygamy was in jeopardy before the Short Creek raid. Several women were thinking of leaving. Back then many women had family on the outside, so leaving was not frightening. Women had some choice. The men in power didn't like it.

The Short Creek raid sabotaged the trust women had in the outside world. They now felt everyone was against them. They'd seen their terrified babies ripped from their arms. Uncle Roy stood up to the state of Arizona and won. He credited the victory in part to the faithfulness of women who would not turn against the system. The women then believed that they must be even more obedient to the prophet in the future. They were thinking of the terror of losing their children, not of surrendering their human rights, which is precisely what happened.

But change came incrementally. First women were told to change the way they wore their hair and the way they dressed. Several years after the raid, the practice of marriage by the prophet's revelation began. Uncle Roy explained that because they had been so faithful to God, they were ready to receive a more exalted doctrine. Even though the changes were more restrictive, each was seen as a blessing from God.

Obedience had saved them during the raid. Uncle Roy would continue to protect them and act in their best interest as long as they trusted him completely. Freedom was swapped for security.

Each young girl was instructed to pray that the prophet would receive a revelation identifying the man she belonged to. We were taught that men and women made a covenant to marry each other before coming to earth. Falling in love with someone independently of the prophet's revelation was absolutely forbidden, even if it was someone within the FLDS, because that would be a violation of the covenant made to God before birth.

These new restrictions governing daily lives came from within the FLDS, not from without. After the Short Creek raid, everyone was even more willing to be obedient to the prophet in every area of their lives. People were very scared because they knew polygamy was against the law and that the state could come in at any time and arrest them again. Because it was believed that Uncle Roy had rescued them and saved them from losing their children, there was not a scintilla of doubt about his being a true prophet of God. This was when the unquestionable authority of the prophet really took hold.

My grandmother held me in her lap and lovingly told me these stories. It was as if she was handing me maps, charting out the future that she knew I was destined to live.

# Child's Play

Let's play apocalypse!" was the cry that set us off and running through the orchard of my uncle Lee's house. The thrill of playing apocalypse as a six-year-old is unforgettable. It was magic, our version of hide-and-seek.

We grew up knowing a lot about the end of the world. It had been drilled into us in Sunday school that we were God's chosen people. When the end times came, we would be saved, the wicked killed, and the world destroyed. I was too young to question these ideas; they were my spiritual ABCs. Contrary to what most would think, we were not taught that the destruction of the world was a *bad* thing. Not at all. It was a good thing because it would usher in a thousand years of peace.

There was one caveat: before God slaughtered the wicked, he would allow them to try to kill his chosen people. (It should have made us wonder, but we didn't.) We were taught that the government (which was wicked) would move into our community and try to kill every man, woman, and child. But since we had been faithful to God and kept his word, he'd hear our prayers and protect us.

When we dashed into the orchard to play apocalypse, the first thing we did was run around looking for good hiding places. The wicked were coming with a large army and they were going to kill every one of us! They were even going to kill the babies. Our screams would make our young siblings panic. They had no idea what the game was about. To them it was noisy, frightening, and chaotic.

We pretended we'd been sent to the orchard by our parents to hide. I felt safe and secure in my spot until my cousin Jayne blurted out, "I can see you! You're going to be killed!" The other kids were shouting that planes were coming to attack us with bombs. There was more screaming and hiding. Some of the youngest children began to cry.

It was at this moment that the resurrected Indians came to save us.

The resurrected Indians were a uniquely FLDS concept. From what I've been able to piece together, it was a belief that originated with Uncle Roy or possibly one of his predecessors. We'd been taught that a lot of good Indians were killed when America was settled. God had already resurrected them because they were worthy and deserving, but he was waiting until the last day to allow them to vindicate themselves. In exchange for being given a shot at revenge, the resurrected Indians were required to take on the job of protecting God's chosen people. Once saved, we would become the seedlings for a millennium of peace.

But the devil had designs on the end game, too. He wanted to wipe us out so no one would be left on earth to do God's work. The devil would engineer our destruction by using the government and other bad people to destroy us. Then the entire world would be consumed in darkness and he'd triumph.

"Here come the bombers!" we'd yell. But then my cousins, who were playing resurrected Indians, would come charging out and start knocking the bombers out of the sky by aiming their tomahawks at a pilot's head. The pilot would fall dead, crashing his plane to the ground.

When one of the wicked was killed by the tomahawk of a resurrected Indian, he'd fall to the ground, seemingly from a heart attack. But what had happened was that the tomahawk had split his heart in two. When an autopsy was performed, doctors would find the severed heart and be at a loss to explain it. But only a few would know the truth. Most would think that the person hit by the tomahawk had died from a heart attack. No one would know that the resurrected Indians had been our saviors.

Once the planes were knocked out of the sky, my cousins who were playing the role of government agents marched into the orchard. Once again the resurrected Indians came to our rescue without firing a single shot or hurling a single tomahawk. It had been prophesied to us that in the last days, any army that went up against the Lord's people would drop dead for no apparent reason and the armies of Zion would be seen as great and terrible.

In the game of apocalypse, the resurrected Indians protected us from the government. But that wasn't enough. We were being invaded by the Russians in the east and the Chinese in the west. Once again, it was the people of God who turned the invaders back by participating in prayer circles.

We all came out from our hiding places and gathered together in circles, pretending to listen to radio reports about the Chinese invaders, who had made it as far as Nevada. The Russians were poised at the Mississippi River. Women and children had been evacuated from cites. We were informed that the men who'd stayed behind to fight were now dead.

As the Lord's people, we were required to stand in holy places and watch the army of the Lord be made manifest. So we stood in our prayer circles believing that when the last days actually came, the Lord would fight our battles for us.

The war was over, but our game was not. We then faced famine because we had not yet conquered enough land to sustain all the people who needed to live on it. We went back to the orchard, splitting into groups to hide. We had to make sure the food we had set aside for the end times wouldn't be taken from us. Messengers were sent back and forth to communicate between the groups. If we were caught while we were delivering a message, we were killed on the spot.

This part of the game made my baby sister, Annette, burst into tears. The game was fine when the resurrected Indians were fighting our battles, but now that we had to sneak messages back and forth, she was too scared. I loved every minute of it, though. This was a huge and exciting adventure for me. I thrived on being in the thick of things. But my cousin came out and called us all in for dinner.

Twenty of us ran into the kitchen for a dinner of canned peaches and a slice of bread and butter. Those who couldn't fit around the table ate standing up. Afterward we tried to help with the dishes, but it got so chaotic that we were sent back outside.

One of my older cousins, Lee junior, was a mesmerizing story-teller. He built a fire and we all sat close so we could listen. I was captivated by the stories he told us of our religion. He began by telling us about all the gold hidden in the mountains around us. God knew how much was there but he was keeping it hidden until the last days, when he would reveal it to his chosen people.

Gold had a purpose, Lee said, but it was not for making jewelry. God hid all the gold away because he felt it was being misused. Once life was purified in the last days, God would bring the gold out from hiding and we, his chosen people, would pave roads and build houses with it.

My eyes widened at my cousin's saga of the white Indians (not to be confused with the resurrected Indians). One of the earliest funda-mentalist prophets, Lee said, had been taken to the Yucatán so God could show him the army of white Indians that was being trained for the end times.

When God gave the order, the army of several hundred thousand would march out of the jungle. They would decide who would live and who would die by tearing off an individual's clothes. If he or she was wearing blessed garments underneath their outer garb, they'd be spared. But those without the sacred underwear would be murdered.

My cousins looked as scared on the outside as I felt on the inside. Only those who covered every inch of their bodies with blessed garments would be saved and get to live in the millennium of peace. It was sobering—especially to a six-year-old—to think that you could make it through all the different destructions but still end up dead if you didn't wear the right clothes.

My cousin spun out other stories that night around the fire. I was enthralled. It was like listening to fairy tales except that I believed every word I heard. The end times sounded frightening, except that I knew if I survived the destruction I would then live through the thousand years of peace, where there was no death. It sounded like a magic carpet ride that would whisk me away from the disappointments of this life to an enchanted world where life was perfect. I would have listened all night if I could, but Mother arrived to take me and my sisters home.

We kept badgering Mother to let us go back to our cousins' house. We had so much more freedom there to play and explore. In our own home, we were forbidden to play outside unless someone was watching. Mother finally agreed to let us go on a mountain hike with our cousins. When we got to their house they were still making lunches. My cousin Shannon was making sandwiches out of fried potatoes. It looked like food we called "yuck yuck." Shannon said it was something her mother had taught her to make when there was nothing else to eat in the house.

There was great discussion about where to go for a hike. No one wanted to go to the predictable places. We all wanted to go to the place that was off-limits—the ghost mountain, where some said the Gadianton robbers were buried. They were the wicked robbers who hurt the people of God in the Book of Mormon.

We'd been taught that God had the power to change the entire earth at a moment's notice. Uncle Roy used the Grand Canyon as an example of the intensity of God's power. He said God created it on a day when he'd been extremely angry. The wicked city inhabited by the Gadianton robbers had been buried under the mountain in an instant of God's wrath. God just picked up a mountain over in the Pine Valley area and dropped it on top of the evil city.

There were several people in the community who claimed they knew that the mountain was haunted because several evil men had taken a very good man in the community up to the mountain. The mountain was opened up enough for him to see that the city inside was bursting with gold and precious jewels. He was told that if he killed Uncle Roy, the prophet of God, then he would be given all of the gold and treasure buried in the mountain. He refused and the mountain was sealed up again.

My cousins said that their father was a man of God who had a lot of bills and debts. If we could find the gold buried in the mountain, it would be a huge help to him. We decided to take shovels and give it our best shot. We knew we weren't supposed to hike on the haunted mountain, but now that it had been turned into a noble cause, no one felt terribly disobedient.

Ten of us hiked to the mountain—a ragamuffin band of kids ranging in age from four to eight. But our digging didn't produce much. We got tired quickly and it was very hot. Nor did we eat the fried potato sandwiches because they tasted as bad as they looked— yuck yuck. But we did throw them back and forth at one another. As we were hiking, we told story after story of the things that the spirits of the Gadianton robbers had done when they haunted the community before being expelled by the priesthood.

Even evil spirits have to obey the priesthood. The priesthood is the way God acts in us, but the power is given only to men. Boys are initiated into the priesthood at twelve by any man in the FLDS who holds the priesthood and has kept his covenants. We believed that the priesthood was the glue that held the earth together. Without its power, the earth would fly apart.

Because of this, one good man in the priesthood could turn back thousands of evil spirits, who would do whatever he ordered them to do. I'm not sure how this squared with all the destruction that was supposed to rain down on our heads. Couldn't the good men just tell the evil ones to scram? But a six-year-old doesn't put such thoughts together. I took it all in as the grand myth and folklore that it was.

While our fundamentalist faith cast a long shadow on how we played, a lot of the things we did and the trouble we stirred up were fairly typical. It was the consequences that were more severe.

One afternoon we got to go back to my cousins' because Mother needed to do some shopping. It felt like a return to wonderland. My cousin Ray Dee was pushing the family cat around in a small doll

carriage with a pacifier taped to its mouth. The cat was wearing a ruf-
fled dress. Beverly, another cousin, was congratulating her on her
new baby. When we were distracted, the cat leaped out of the carriage and ran for its life. We went looking for it and instead found our
cousin Shannon.

Shannon was sitting in the grass stirring a big bowl of punch. She
had cups and passed out drinks to all of us. We were having a fine
time, savoring our freedom and catching up with our cousins. But it
was short-lived. One of the younger boys came running out with the
news that Shannon had stolen the punch and that his mother, our
aunt Charlotte, planned to spank everyone involved.

Shannon was guilty. She'd gone to Aunt Charlotte and said she
needed a package of Kool-Aid for Aunt Elaine, which was untrue.
Someone squealed on her when we were spotted out in the orchard
drinking punch. Now anyone with punch-stained lips might be
spanked.

Shannon said she didn't care if Aunt Charlotte spanked her.
"Why?" I said. I hated spankings.

Shannon was very matter-of-fact. "Aunt Naomi's spankings are
way too hard. They're so bad, they're ridiculous. Mom's spankings are
so soft you have to pretend that you're crying. But Aunt Charlotte's
spankings are just right."

I didn't think a spanking could ever be just right. So I asked
Shannon what she meant. "It's like this," she said. "You never know
how many swats you are going to get from the other moms, but Aunt
Charlotte gives you two swats for every year old you are. If you
scream really loud, she thinks she's hurting you and doesn't swat
as hard."

Shannon's optimism brought a new mood to the orchard. She got
about a dozen brothers and sisters together and told them they
needed to play the game they always did when they were getting a
spanking from Aunt Charlotte.

She ran through the drill. First they had to act extremely sorry for
what they had done. Then they had to promise that if Aunt Charlotte
would forgive them, they'd never again do whatever they'd done. If

Aunt Charlotte still insisted on spanking them, everyone would act scared, start crying, and beg her not to. This sometimes made Aunt Charlotte feel guilty enough to reduce the number of swats.

When it was time to spank those involved in the punch theft, we all trooped inside. I lucked out. Even though I'd had some punch, I got to stay downstairs with some of the others who weren't being spanked. I was surprised by the volume of screaming coming from upstairs. I said to my cousin Jayne, "I thought that Aunt Charlotte's spankings were just right. It sounds like she's killing everyone."

Jayne told me, "They are just trying to make her think she's killing them. If everyone in the room screams loudly enough, then the person getting the swats has less screaming to do and gets a spanking that doesn't hurt very bad. We always do this to Aunt Charlotte."

"What about with Aunt Elaine?" I asked. Jayne looked at me like I was a little bit crazy. "No, we don't need to bother her because you can't usually feel her spankings. And we don't do it to my mother because she doesn't buy the act."

I nodded. Aunt Charlotte probably thought that day that she was giving everyone a correction. But for those involved, this was just another game. Nevertheless, it was a game I had no interest in playing.

Minutes after the spankings ended, everyone marched downstairs, and shortly all of us were laughing and smiling again. It was as if nothing out of the ordinary had happened, and for us it hadn't.

# School Days

I didn't start school until I was six and a half. Finally! I had watched Linda go to school every day, wishing I could go with her. Kindergarten didn't exist in the FLDS because the belief was that children were better off spending another year at home. It didn't do me any good. I was eager to get going. I wanted to learn.

There wasn't much stimulation at home beyond listening to my grandmother's stories. Fairy tales were frowned upon, and we had no other children's books at home. There was no public library in town, and I don't remember my mother ever buying us books of our own.

In 1974, a few weeks before school started, when I was counting down the days, I met Laura, who would become one of my closest friends. It was a scorching July day, one of those when the air feels too hot and dry to even want to breathe it in. I was playing paper dolls inside with Linda while Mother was sewing new dresses for our first day of school.

The weather shifted suddenly; the sky darkened and then split apart in a downpour. Linda, Annette, and I stood at the kitchen window, listening to the rain pound the roof of the house and smelling its sweetness through the air conditioner.

After the deluge, we begged Mama to let us go outside, and she said we could as long as we didn't get muddy.

The dirt road in front of our house had turned into a large stream of muddy water. I could think of nothing better than to run and splash in it. Linda read my mind. "Carolyn, don't even think of it. We will all get a spanking if you do!"

When my mother got mad at one of us for doing something disobedient or wrong, usually we all paid a price for her anger. What kept me on the porch wasn't my fear of getting a spanking; it was the fear of how Linda would feel if I got her and Annette in trouble.

A moment later, we heard children's voices and suddenly saw the kids from a new polygamous family that had moved into the community. They'd come from Idaho with three wives and what seemed like two dozen children.

A redheaded girl who looked about the same age as me caught my eye. She came running down the street and with a big jump and splash landed in the middle of the muddy water. All her other siblings followed her. They were laughing and splashing in the mud and having the best time. I was dying to join them but knew I couldn't.

Linda didn't envy the mud ducks at all. She looked stricken that they had dared do this. Daring had nothing to do with it for me. I was frustrated that they could do something I couldn't. Linda went over to talk to them, and it was the by now very muddy redheaded girl who spoke to her first. She said her name was Laura, and then she rattled off the names of her little brothers and sisters.

Laura looked over to us and said, "Why don't you guys get in the mud, too?" Linda told her that our mom would get mad at us if we got muddy. Laura seemed perplexed. What we were saying made no sense to her at all.

When the novelty of splashing around in the muddy stream wore off, we asked her if she wanted to play dolls. She said she didn't have any dolls. I couldn't believe it. "You don't have any dolls? What do you play with?"

Laura shrugged. She didn't need *dolls* to play dolls. She picked up a crooked little stick from the ground and walked over to Mama's flower garden and plucked a flower. "See, this is her skirt and this little blossom can be her hat." Next she snapped a blossom off a flower and put it on the stick. Then she found another flower to make a skirt. Now the stick girl had a flounced hat and skirt. I was impressed.

Laura had taken a stick and made it into one of the best dolls I had ever seen. "All I have to do to change her clothes is pick another flower." I certainly couldn't change clothes as much with my real dolls as she could with her stick ones.

Linda, Annette, and I quickly found sticks to make our own dolls. We spent the rest of the afternoon playing with Laura. At dinner that night we talked nonstop about our new friend. In the years ahead, even Mama came to love Laura. She would say that her daughters didn't fight as much when she was around.

The first day of school finally came. My mother took me to my classroom and watched while I picked out my desk. She said she was proud that I was starting first grade. The door to our classroom opened a bit and I saw one of my classmates stick out her tongue at the girl in the doorway, whom I couldn't see. Then I heard her exclaim, "Ooh, she has red hair." Laura came in and found a seat, but I could tell she was shy being around so many new people.

Not only were we in the same class, but we rode the bus to school every day for the entire year. I was so happy! Having her on the bus helped me feel safe.

The bus scared me because strange things often happened there. One day I was sitting next to Linda when Randi, an older girl in the front seat, began whispering to her friend. She rolled up the long sleeve of her dress, and I could see that her arm looked melted and red. Her friend gasped. It was shocking to see. I was standing up, and Linda yanked me down in my seat and said to be still or the bus driver would hit me. It was not unusual for the bus driver to stop the bus when a child misbehaved. He'd walk back and hit a child so hard his or her face would slam into the window of the bus.

When we got off the bus I asked Linda what could have made Randi's arm look so melted and raw. She seemed uncomfortable and said she didn't know. Later we heard Mom telling the story to our dad, and he said that we were never to be allowed anywhere near that girl's father because he'd heard some stories about the man.

The girl with the melted arm had the longest braid I had ever seen. Her braid hung well below her knees. I had never seen anyone with thicker or more beautiful hair. Everyone who rode the bus admired her braid. But what I noticed about her was that she never looked happy. She didn't have many friends and seemed to prefer to be by herself.

One morning Randi got on the bus and was sobbing hysterically. Her face was red and flooded with tears. She was shaking and gasping for breath. Her sobs came like one big wave after another. When she turned around I realized her braid was gone. Her hair was neatly combed, but her braid had been chopped off into stubble. The chatter and noise on the bus stopped as everyone realized what had happened. All of us were shocked by the awful sight.

The bus driver sat there chewing his gum. If he noticed the weeping child who had just gotten on his bus, he didn't show it. The door closed and he pulled away from the curb as if nothing had happened. I felt sick to my stomach. I couldn't even play on the playground that day. Everything went by in a blur.

After school I was waiting in the bus line with Linda when I saw the school's double doors fly open. The principal of the school came running out, chasing his mentally retarded son, Kendall, who was ten. Kendall was screaming and trying to run away from him. His pants were wet with urine. We could all see the wide circle of dampness. The principal caught up with him and grabbed him. He kicked him so hard that Kendall flew off the ground and landed in a heap on the sidewalk. He yelled at Kendall to get up. Kendall started running away again. The principal kept chasing and kicking him. I was so sickened by what had happened to Randi earlier that day that this overwhelmed me. I could not absorb what I was seeing. In the weeks and months ahead, I would see this again and again. Kendall would wet his pants and his father would beat him. Some of the other children on the playground made fun of Kendall for wetting his pants. Others stood still, shocked to witness a father's brutality and terrified because he was the principal of the school.

That day when the school bus pulled up with the same expressionless gum-chewing driver who scared me so much, I said to my sister that I was not getting on his bus, no way. Linda pulled my arm.

"Carolyn, you have to get on this bus." But she wasn't strong enough to pull me past my determination not to ride home on the school bus. Linda gave up. I told her I would run home.

It was about a mile. I thought if I ran fast enough, I could get home before the bus and then maybe Mama wouldn't spank me. I looked at the bus driver again. I wasn't riding on his bus, even if it meant getting spanked. I ran until I couldn't run anymore and then walked until I caught my breath and could start running again.

I dashed into the house just as the bus was dropping off my two sisters. Mother was in the kitchen. "I got home before the school bus, Mama," I said. She said I was silly and asked why I didn't ride home with Annette and Linda. But I never told her.

By now I was in the second grade and I walked to school or ran home for the rest of the year. One day the gum-chewing bus driver hurt Laura's little sister. When Laura got off the bus she said she hated him and stuck out her tongue. She stopped riding the bus after that and walked with me every day.

First grade was the only year I didn't have a violent teacher. It was not until I was in the upper grades that teachers stopped using violence. In the lower school it happened all the time, except in first grade. Most families controlled their children with scripture and a whip. This philosophy extended into the classrooms, too.

I saw teachers beat students with yardsticks until they broke the yardstick. It wasn't uncommon during a school assembly for the principal to kick and slap students around onstage for the entire school to witness. He did this to terrify students so that no one would ever want to be sent to the principal's office. When he singled out a student, he chose one whose parents he knew wouldn't complain. It was common practice at school to make an example of one student so others would comply.

Whenever we walked in lines there would be an adult assigned to monitor us with a yardstick. Anyone who misbehaved in the slightest would be cracked on the head.

Control mattered more than academics in the classroom. Brutality toward children was the norm within the community, but there were different levels of tolerance among families about the level of violence that was acceptable. But families would never judge one another. Even if a family knew there was severe abuse going on in another family, no one intervened. This was part of the religious doctrine that said no man had the right to interfere with another man's family.

We would hear stories about sexual and physical abuse in other families, but nothing was ever done to stop it. As a community, the feeling was that the outside world was our enemy. Its laws and rules did not apply to us in any way. There was no way that someone in the FLDS would report abuse that they'd witnessed or suspected to the authorities for investigation. Anyone who did that would have been seen as a traitor to the entire community.

Many of the teachers at school were nonviolent and would never hit a child. But there were enough violent ones to make me always feel unsafe at school. But I did love learning. No matter how frightened I was by the possibility of what *could* happen, my fears never overrode my desire for knowledge.

The school was a public school that was funded by the state, but it operated as a private school in fact. Virtually every student was a member of the FLDS community. Religion was taught openly in school, and if a subject contradicted our teachings, it was dropped. It was very common to get textbooks with entire chapters missing because they'd been cut out. We were taught things that were patently false—such as the "fact" that dinosaurs had never existed. In some classes, the teachers taught stories from the Book of Mormon. The school got away with this because everyone who worked there back then was part of the FLDS. The state had no reason to investigate because no one ever complained.

I remember learning about sex on the playground when I was in the fourth grade. One of my classmates announced to the rest of us that her brother was teaching her how to have a baby. She had told him she didn't want to learn, but he insisted. He wanted to show her, not just tell her.

She said he pointed to the parts on his body and told her what he was going to do with them on hers. Then he did it. When it was over, he said this was how her husband would make babies with her. She said she hated it and hated him. We all felt repulsed by the story and said her brother was a big liar. We knew our parents would never do anything like that.

But she said we were wrong. This was sex, S-E-X. When we went back into our classroom she got the dictionary and slammed it on a desk. She read us the definition of *sex* and we all felt uncomfortable. Just because it was in the dictionary didn't mean it was true. We felt her brother was wicked, and we talked about this for months. Those with older siblings would come back with more information, so I finally had to conclude that it was true.

We were never taught about sex in the FLDS. When we had health education in the fifth grade, the chapters about reproduction were cut out. Sex was something a husband was to teach his wife on their wedding night. There were women who married thinking babies came from kissing.

One year Linda had a harrowing experience at school. Her teacher was a man with a reputation for not maintaining order well in his classroom. He'd promised Linda's class that they could earn a paper airplane party as a reward for doing something well. Whatever it was, they managed to do it and earn the party.

That afternoon the principal, Alvin Barlow, heard a ruckus coming from a sixth-grade classroom. He didn't know that this was a planned party, nor did he ask. He stormed into the party and began slapping students across the room and kicking them to the ground. The students in the row closest to the door were his first targets and got the worst of his wrath. Linda watched one girl get her head slammed into her desk.

The principal was halfway down the second row of students before he asked the teacher if he'd given the students permission to misbehave. The teacher lied and said he had not. He feared what the principal would do to him if he knew the party was originally his idea.

This increased Barlow's rage. Linda was so terrified she could hardly move. The principal grabbed the hair of a girl sitting in the row next to hers and slapped her face so hard she hit her head on the desk and got a bloody nose. Somehow she managed to run out the door and down the hall to her mother's second-grade classroom. Barlow suddenly stopped. Linda said that if he hadn't, she would have been next.

Then all the students were marched down to his office and forced to listen to his sermons for several hours. He went on and on about the Short Creek raid and how many had sacrificed so these students could learn the work of God. Linda said kids were shaking and crying and had a hard time sitting still. Many of the kids from that class went home with bruises all over their bodies and black eyes. My sister was so shaken that she could barely explain to Mama what had happened.

Brutalizing nearly an entire classroom of students was going too far, even within the FLDS. By late that afternoon, the principal's office was filled with angry fathers. One man said that if the principal touched his daughter again, he'd come and beat him. The school board called an emergency meeting, and the principal was put on notice that if he ever did something like this again, he'd be fired.

He was never reported to the authorities, though. If he had been, the principal could have served time in jail for assault and battery. But in our closed society, he only received a warning. He was not only a member of the FLDS; he was the son of a former prophet and the stepson of Uncle Roy. Uncle Roy protected him and told parents in the community that they should support him in the good work he was doing with their children. The principal's status was untouchable because of his ties to the prophet. Anyone who reported him would have been in serious trouble within the FLDS. (He remained in his job until two years ago, when he retired.)

Children were seen as property, and physical violence toward them was not only permissible but a way of life. It was preached at church that if you didn't put the fear of God into children from the time of their birth, they would grow up and leave the work of God. Abuse was necessary to save a child's soul. The problem with what the principal did, in the eyes of the community, was that he went too far. But not far enough to get fired.

What usually happened when a student was beaten was that the parent assumed the child had done something wrong. The child was then forced to apologize for what he or she had allegedly done. The teacher or authority figure was always backed in his or her claims.

My mother was outraged by the principal's behavior and told us that if anyone ever tried to hurt us in school, we were to come home at once. She didn't make a connection between her abusive behavior toward us and the beatings that happened at school. Mother managed to think that she was beating us only because she loved us and was trying to make us live godly lives. She didn't know that our small bodies were unable to distinguish between the two.

For the most part, I was able to learn what was necessary for my daily survival. I had my operating instructions.

I knew that the consequences were high for disobeying my mother. No meant no, and there was never an exception. Asking or questioning would only lead to more trouble. Sometimes my sisters would tattle on me to get me in trouble, and there was nothing I could do about that but get mad.

I learned in school to walk with my arms folded and never hop up and down in line unless I wanted a very hard smack on top of my head with a yardstick. In the singing group in class, I knew that if I didn't look straight ahead with my chin slightly up I risked getting whacked on the head.

I knew never to ride the school bus because I would see things that would upset me.

I ate all the food on my plate, even if I didn't like it. If I complained, I'd just be forced to eat more of the food I hated.

I knew never to tease or hit my little brother, Arthur, when he annoyed me because he was my mother's favorite. I also learned to listen to my big sister, Linda. She tried hard to keep me out of trouble.

# New Wife,
# New Mother

I was jumping rope outside our house with my sister Annette when Linda came to tell us our father was going to Salt Lake City to get a new wife. We were all very surprised but happy because we knew and liked the woman he had been assigned to marry. Rosie was our cousin and favorite babysitter. Mama and Rosie had been good friends for years. Rosie used to babysit for us before she started nursing school in Salt Lake. We used to look forward to her coming because she was lively and never mean to us. Rosie's father was my mother's brother, so Rosie was my mom's niece.

I was about ten at the time and ran into the house as soon as I heard the news. Mama seemed subdued.

Most men in the community waited between ten and fifteen years before taking on a new wife. It was not uncommon for some men never to get another wife. But the men who got the most wives were the men who had the most power in the FLDS. If a man had more than three wives, it was a signal that he was the son of someone of major importance. It was not at all unusual for sisters to be married to the same husband, and it was certainly not unusual for a niece to share a husband with her aunt.

Rose was pretty and popular in the community. She was a good cook and housekeeper and had a reputation as an extremely hard worker. We hadn't seen her much since she started nursing school. It was rare for a woman in the FLDS to get any higher education while she was still unmarried, and highly unusual even after marriage. Rosie lucked out because one of her father's wives wanted to go to nursing school and my uncle decided that Rosie could go, too, since she'd be under close supervision.

I don't know how my mother really felt about my father taking a second wife. All I'd ever heard her say about the possibility was that if my dad got a new wife, she hoped she would like her. I knew our lives would be changing, but I couldn't imagine how.

We stayed behind when my father and mother went to Salt Lake for the wedding. Oddly enough, they came home without Rosie. She remained in Salt Lake to finish classes and take tests. We thought she'd be back after that, but Dad bought her a house in Salt Lake so she could start working there.

But Rosie came to Colorado City occasionally to visit. When she did, Linda had to move out of her bedroom and sleep with Annette and me so Rosie could have it. Linda seemed the most wary of Rosie and concerned about the situation. Her fear was that Rosie would steal Dad away from Mom. Linda became the watcher, making note of things that Dad did with Rosie that he didn't do with Mom. He spent a lot of time with Rosie in Linda's bedroom when she visited and certainly seemed happier when she was around.

We all knew how tense my parents' marriage had become. Mom seemed to get a lot quieter once Dad married Rosie. Dad had bought Mama a TV several years before he married Rosie, to placate her. She always complained about not being able to watch TV the way she had when we lived in Salt Lake. It was completely against our religion to have a television set, but my father ignored that and just bought one. The reception was terrible; there were only two channels that were even remotely viewable. But when Dad and Rosie went into Linda's bedroom, we all sat with Mom in the front living room and watched TV.

I remember going to visit Rosie when I went to Salt Lake with my parents. I was impressed that she had her own small house and car. She also had her nursing career. Her freedom and autonomy over her own life made an impact on me. Rosie had more independence than any woman I had ever known.

But her freedom was short-lived. Rosie became pregnant shortly after she married my father, and she moved into Linda's bedroom in our house in Colorado City a month before her baby was born. My mother's sixth child, a boy, was born a few months before Rosie's daughter.

The dynamic in our family shifted. Rosie and my mother were competing for Dad's attention. The two babies were compared to each other all the time. We all watched to see which baby Dad seemed to prefer or spend the most time with. My mother could see how happy Dad was with Rosie, so she worked hard to try to outdo her.

If Rosie cooked a lovely dinner, Mom put twice the effort into the next meal she made. Mama had her ways of doing things in the house that she insisted Rosie follow. Sometimes I'd hear Mom saying to her friends that only she, not Rosie, really understood what Father wanted and how to please him. There would be times when my mother would accuse Rosie of being selfish and not working hard enough to please my dad.

Rosie's daughter was born on her birthday, so she named her Rose. We called her Little Rosie. When she was a few months old, Rosie took a job nearby in Cedar City, working in one of her father's nursing homes. She would take one of us along to babysit, and more often than not it was me. I liked going to work with Rosie. My mother and I had never really gotten along well and it was always a relief to be out of her domain.

Rosie was able to earn more money than almost any woman in the community because she had a nursing degree. I saw what an opportunity that was for her, especially in contrast to the rest of the FLDS women, who usually could hope for nothing better than a job in the community sewing plant.

I was shaken by what I saw at the sewing center when our class visited. There were rows and rows and rows of women hunched over machines with endless piles of fabric in front of them. They were making uniforms that were sold to large companies. They looked and worked like slaves on big industrial sewing machines that sewed fast. None of them made much money, and I knew that many of them had more than ten children at home. They made the minimum wage, which was about three dollars an hour, and on top of that were paid for each piece. Any woman who failed to produce enough got fired. The work was deadening, the pressure tremendous, and what they earned was not even enough to buy groceries for their big families, let alone anything else.

I made a vow to myself that I was never going to end up behind one of those sewing machines. No matter what it took, I was going to get an education like Rosie's. I became determined to go to college.

The time I spent with Rosie protected me from my mother's instability. Rosie treated me well and appreciated how much I helped her with her baby. I loved my mother but always had the conflicting feelings of fearing her anger and abuse. Rosie was different. Her stability enabled me to grow. Rosie was deeply religious and believed in plural marriage. She felt that sharing my father with my mother was her only way to God.

I believed in plural marriage then, too. At nine, I believed what everyone else did—that a man learned to love his wives more with each new wife he was given. My mother and Rosie minimized the deep conflicts that arose between them. We saw little signs of the underlying tension, so I had no reason to believe that plural marriage was anything other than something great. My friends talked about how their mothers had screaming fights with each other and threw things. I never saw that at my home. One day I heard my mother say how much better my father was treating her since he married Rosie.

This made me feel good, even though I could tell my father was happier with Rosie than he ever was with Mom. Being so in love with Rosie made it easier for him to be nicer to my mother. Maybe he did even love my mother more now. I didn't know, but it certainly fit in nicely with what I wanted to believe.

The power struggle in my own family paled in comparison to

what was happening within the FLDS. A power struggle that had been brewing for several years broke out into the open in 1978, when I was in the fifth grade. By the time I was in the seventh grade, families were choosing sides and the community was so deeply polarized that we were not allowed to play with our friends if their parents were on the opposing side.

"Are you on the side of Uncle Roy or are you on the side of the brethren?" That was the question, and what was at stake was who would rule the community when Uncle Roy died. It was a power struggle, pure and simple.

My father was on the side that believed that only the prophet should have ultimate power in the FLDS. In a nutshell, it was called the "one-man rule."

Uncle Roy had several stepsons who were the children of the former prophet, John Y. Barlow. Their power was underscored by the fact that they were the nephews of Uncle Fred Jessop, who, as bishop, was in charge of daily life in the community. Because of their ties to the two men at the top, the stepsons had usurped some of the power and authority of the apostles in the FLDS.

Apostles were men chosen by God and ordained by the prophet. At one time in the FLDS apostles as well as the prophet had the power to arrange marriages. They were deeply involved in formulating community policy and were seen as worthy to receive revelations from God, just as the prophet did. The prophet was more powerful—he was the de facto god over the community—but he shared some of his power with the apostles.

If the stepsons could consolidate all power around Uncle Roy, then the apostles would be nearly stripped of their power in the community. Since Uncle Roy had become sick and bedridden, there was jockeying among those who wanted to succeed him.

The rupture was so severe in the community that my mother stopped speaking to her sister because she was married to one of the apostles. I was cut off from my friends, which upset me. Otherwise, I believed what I was told, that the brethren were trying to destroy Uncle Roy and take away all of his power.

It was a time of tremendous accusations. People on the Uncle Roy side started telling stories about the apostles and all the horrible things they had done. Church services became so argumentative that we began to look forward to being entertained by the fights. The theatrics were far more galvanizing than learning the word of God.

It was a strange time. Even though there were people we were forbidden to talk to or associate with, we dropped all those boundaries for holidays. We always celebrated the Fourth of July, as well as July 24. The twenty-fourth was the day when Brigham Young had brought the Latter-Day Saints into the valley and said, "This is the place." It was one of our biggest holidays and we went all out with parades, food, dances, and fireworks.

My family was growing rapidly because Mother and Rosie were both having babies nearly every year and a half. Rosie had a full-time job, so my mother was left in charge of all the children. She depended on Linda, Annette, and me to help take care of our siblings. It seemed like we were babysitting all the time.

But one Saturday night when Linda and I were about thirteen and fourteen, we were given permission to go to a community dance. Neither Mother nor Rosie could go with us, so we were just dropped off at school. At the east of the auditorium was a section for the young unmarried ladies. We always sat there because it was next to the unmarried boys' section.

Linda and I were walking around toward the back of the school, which was the entrance closest to the girls' section. Just as we approached, the doors flew open, unleashing a stampede of girls. "Run for your lives!" they screamed. I did not need convincing and started running with them until the stampede stopped near the south auditorium entrance.

"Oh, yuck," I heard someone say. "He got Laura." Another voice chimed in: "She wasn't paying attention when the signal was given, so she was the only one left in our section for him to pick." Laura, my redheaded friend since childhood! I felt sad for her. We were still close friends. Her father had not chosen sides over the split, so there was no reason we couldn't continue our friendship.

I listened to the girls explain how an elderly man who was looking for an additional wife kept coming to the young ladies' section to
shop around. None of the young girls ever wanted to dance with an
old man.

It was frowned upon for a girl to dance more than one dance with
a young boy. She also could refuse to dance with a young man if she
had no interest. But a girl could *never* refuse the attentions of an
older or even elderly man. This was considered to be one of the most
disrespectful things one of us could do.

These were the rules of engagement. But there was no rule
against a stampede. So when someone saw an elderly man heading
toward our section, she gave a signal and all the girls ran out the door.
If a girl was distracted or not paying attention, she could find herself
left behind. That was what happened to Laura. We all felt so sorry for
her, but thankfully, she didn't have to marry that old man.

We streamed back into the dance hall once we knew the threat
had passed. The young boys would be waiting near the door and we'd
usually be asked to dance right away. The music that was played was
the same music that the saints danced to when they first came to Salt
Lake in the nineteenth century. We danced to waltzes and other slow
music. Dances were one of the most exciting nights in the community for us. This was the only time we were ever allowed to be near
boys our own age. We were closely watched and monitored and
would get into trouble if we danced too much with the same person.
We had to dress appropriately, which meant modest and simple
clothes. Girls could wear some makeup and dresses, but only ones
that were not too tight and didn't have necklines that were too low.
Shiny fabrics and loud colors were unacceptable. Boys wore ties,
dress shirts, and slacks. Jeans were not allowed.

The dances were also another time when the bitter split that had
divided the community was ignored. We were free to dance with anyone. I was beginning to notice boys and realize that there were some
I liked so much more than others. Boys were noticing me, too. Linda
had always been very popular. I became more so in the eighth grade
when I got a big part in a school play.

I think the dances made it possible for us to talk about our feelings in a way we might not have been able to otherwise. One day in eighth grade, several of the girls were talking about the danger we faced in the future. One of my closest friends said, "As soon as you graduate from high school, you are going to be assigned to an old man and you will have to marry him." Another girl said, "Every one of us is doomed! We are all going to have to marry an old man who is so ancient that we'll be forced to take care of him."

I thought of the rest home where Rosie worked and the old men I had seen slumped in their wheelchairs and staring blankly into space. I froze in shock.

"The very thought of marrying an old man is enough to make me throw up," said another friend. For the first time I was confronting a fate I knew I didn't want.

"But wait," I said. "Several girls in the community have married young boys."

The girl who'd started this conversation said that happened only because a young girl and a young boy both went to the prophet and insisted that they be married. "So the only way you are not going to have sex with an old man is if you can get a young boy to fall in love with you. Then you have to insist that he is the only man you are willing to marry. That's the only chance you ever have of marrying someone who's in love with you."

"How do you get someone to fall in love with you?" I asked. We all knew how much trouble we could get in for just talking to a boy. That made the falling-in-love part hard.

This prompted a revelation from one of the other girls in our group. Her sister had been allowed to marry the boy she was in love with because they had sneaked out of theology class together. They'd done it for an entire year without ever being caught.

Suddenly we could see a strategy begin to emerge. We decided to start going to Sunday night theology classes, which were held three times a month. This was something else we could share, regardless of which side we stood on because of the religious divide. We signed up for a class with a teacher on the *opposite* side of the divide from our parents because it was to our advantage to have a teacher who was not on speaking terms with them.

We started going to the classes on Sunday nights to get our parents used to the idea. After a few weeks, one of us let some of the boys in on our scheme. They leaped at the idea of using the theology class as a chance to sneak out to the reservoir.

The plan worked flawlessly. There was a general meeting before we broke up into our smaller classes. The big meeting never lasted very long—someone gave a short speech and a prayer. By the time it was over, our parents had already left. We girls made a beeline for the bathroom.

One girl stood watch at the door, ready to give a signal if someone was coming toward the bathroom who was not part of the scheme. When the coast was clear, we'd line up next to the window, climb up, and jump out. Once we were all outside, we ran to the reservoir, protected by the darkness of the early evening. The boys did exactly the same thing from their bathroom.

Once we were all at the reservoir, we were home free. This was the first time ever in our lives that we could socialize with the opposite sex in an unsupervised way. It was so much fun to be able to relax and get to know one another without any pressure. For the most part, we hung out as a group and just talked. No one tried to have a romantic relationship. Someone always kept a close eye on the time. We knew when class was supposed to end, so we'd run back to the parking lot and stand next to the car of the person who'd brought us. They always assumed our class had gotten out ahead of theirs and were never suspicious.

This worked so well that more girls wanted to join our intrepid group. Boys did, too. Linda and several of her friends were pulled into our newfound freedom. Mother did begin to become suspicious because we were always determined never to miss theology. She had a hard time believing we were that hungry for the gospel because we'd never wanted to go to church to hear the sermons.

Mother told our father that she thought something was up. He brushed her off. Dad was proud that we were so committed to learning how to be more like God.

After the first few months of our unique "theology," some of us had a boy whom we were attracted to and wanted to see more than three times a month. There was someone I liked at the time, but he's still in the FLDS, so the less said the better.

But a year into our ruse, one of the teachers from school was outside the building and saw us jumping out of the windows and making a mad dash for the reservoir when we were supposed to be in class. He went to my father. Another teacher spotted the boys following us. Everyone was scandalized by our behavior. Some were punished severely by their families. My father seemed both furious and brokenhearted.

Fortunately for Linda, he never learned that she hadn't been studying "theology," too. He learned the name of the boy I liked and went to see him to tell him he was forbidden ever to speak to me again. My father gave me the same edict, too. I did not want to get the boy in any more trouble, so we did stop seeing each other. I was more concerned about what might happen to him than to me.

My freedom was not all that was coming to an end. I feared my education was, too. I graduated from eighth grade that spring. The only high school in the community was a private high school that was run by those on the other side of the religious divide from my father. Uncle Roy would not allow us to attend that school. I was devastated. I thrived on school, and all of my closest friends would be going on to high school because their families were on the opposing side of the divide.

Since we had been together since grade school, our friendships had continued despite the controversy. But high school was a dividing line. I wasn't supposed to associate with them anymore. It felt like my happiness was sliding away. Without an education, I was doomed. The thought of losing my friends made me despair.

The only alternative I had was to take a correspondence course. It felt good that there was some recourse for me, but I still hated the thought of being separated from my friends. What made me slightly more hopeful was learning that several girls who were older than me had gone on to community college after finishing the correspondence course. I dug into my courses with a vengeance.

My father had given me a job answering phones at his construction company. I didn't like it, but I was glad to get out of the house and do something other than babysit. When I wasn't working, I stayed in my bedroom and studied. I finished three grades in my correspondence classes in less than a year.

Then the miracle: Uncle Roy decided to let some committed students go to the private high school, despite the split. He wanted us to report back to our parents about what was going on in the school. My father was shocked when the prophet told him to send Linda and me to the private school. Linda started as a senior, and I entered as a sophomore because I wanted to be with my friends.

Everyone welcomed me back with open arms. I had a lifeline back into a world that I loved, and I was overjoyed.

But as I was so often forced to learn, happiness was not something I could hold on to. I had to leave the private high school with my friends after only a year. Uncle Roy started a small public high school for his followers, and I was forced to go. Once more I had to say goodbye to my friends and sever myself from what mattered to me most.

My life felt like it was moving in the wrong direction, but I felt powerless to stop it. But my sister Linda's life had become desperate.

# Linda's Flight to Freedom

Linda had a sense that someone was watching her. He was an old man in the community who was about three times older than she was at seventeen. My father would come home and start asking Linda questions. Why was she wearing a skirt that was too short? Why was she walking down the street in heels that were too high? Why had she combed her hair a certain way before? Dad told Linda who had seen her doing these things.

Linda realized that this man was spying on her and reporting back to my father. When my mother got wind of this she was very upset and told my father that she didn't trust this man. This was highly out of order, and my father ignored her. A woman had no right to speak out like this, even if the goal was protecting her daughter. Linda and I both could see that even when Mother wanted to protect us she had no power to do so. Mother's fear was that he was angling to marry Linda.

Linda feared the same thing. She knew he was a man of power and influence within the community who, if he went to the prophet, could have nearly any woman he wanted. Once he locked onto Linda, there would be no escape. Linda also knew that Mother would drop her concerns about the marriage if the prophet decreed that she should become this man's fifth wife.

These marriages were like live-animal traps. Linda knew her only hope was to flee before the trap snapped shut and there was no escape. She would be eighteen in the fall, which would give her a measure of legal protection.

Linda had a childhood friend in the community who was also desperate to escape. Claudel was terrified that she was going to be forced to marry her stepfather. Claudel had been living with her mother in Salt Lake City for several years. Her mother, who was no longer married to Claudel's biological father, treated her like an indentured servant, forcing her to do all the cooking, cleaning, and babysitting. Claudel feared that if she was forced to marry her stepfather, she would become her mother's slave for life and resigned to a life of bitterness—a living death.

Linda and Claudel began making plans to escape after they turned eighteen. Claudel had made a friend in Salt Lake City who was not in the FLDS and knew about her despair. Having one friend on the outside, one number to call, was huge, especially since Claudel had returned to Colorado City to live.

I had been working at my father's construction company that summer and was being paid $1.25 an hour. But I was saving every dime I made. Mama had gone on a business trip with my father, and Rosie was taking care of the family. Linda had been acting strange for several days, which baffled me.

Elaine, one of Linda's best friends, had come over, ostensibly to help Linda clean out her room. Linda was giving a lot of her things away, which didn't strike me as odd until I realized that she was unpacking her hope chest. Most of us started hope chests in our early teens. Hope chests were status symbols in the community. We filled them with things we'd need in our marriages: pots, pans, linens, and blankets. Some girls made quilts for their hope chests. I did not. But often at birthdays we'd give one another things for our hope chests.

I asked Linda why she was giving away the treasured items she was saving for her marriage and many of her clothes. "I'm sick of everything, so I've given it to Elaine. I don't want to wear these clothes anymore. I'll just make some more."

She wasn't very convincing; her behavior was like jagged pieces of a puzzle that I couldn't put together.

Linda knocked on my door at nine o'clock that night. I was getting ready for bed and was surprised to see her fully dressed at bedtime. Her face was pale. She clutched a large garbage bag of things she hadn't given away.

In a whisper, she said to me, "Carolyn, I am leaving. Some of my friends are taking me to a neighboring community. From there I'm going to disappear. Some people are going to help me escape."

I was stunned. Never, ever would I have guessed that Linda was running away with total strangers. I started to tremble.

"Why are you doing that? How can you trust people you don't even know?"

Linda shrugged again. "Even if they are bad people, I don't have anything to lose. If I stay here, my life is over. I'm not going to do that. Carolyn, do you think I can borrow twenty dollars from you?"

I was numb. I didn't want to lose my sister. I walked over to the dresser drawer where I kept my summer money and handed her the envelope. "Take all of it, Linda—you're going to need it."

Linda resisted. "I only need twenty dollars—that's enough. I can't take all your money."

I refused to take the envelope back. I couldn't bear to look her in the eye. "Take it. You don't know where you are going or even who you are going with. Take the money. Please. It will help me feel better about what you are doing."

Linda grabbed me and we hugged. "Thank you, Carolyn, thank you." She could barely whisper.

Our bedrooms were in the basement, next to the outside door. Linda went into her room to gather her things. Rosie heard her when she opened the outside door and came to see what was happening. When she saw Linda with the black garbage bag she asked her where she was headed.

Linda's voice was as strong as the unshakable will behind it. "Rosie, I am leaving, and there is nothing you can do to stop me because I'm eighteen now."

"Yes, I can," said Rosie. "You are not going to leave."

Linda did not flinch.

"I'm done with this religion! I'm not going to live this way anymore. I am going and nobody can do anything about it." Linda bolted through the door. I watched her run until she was swallowed up by the night.

Rosie was yelling, "Linda, you get back here. You're not going to get away with this. I'm calling your father right now." Rosie soon realized that the more she yelled, the more time she was giving Linda to escape. She quit and ran to the phone.

Rosie raced upstairs and called my father at the hotel where he was staying. Minutes later men appeared at our house. They planned to restrain Linda until my father got home. But she was already gone.

The mayor of the community came and questioned me. Linda had protected me by not telling me of her plans. I told the mayor the truth: I didn't know she had been planning to escape, nor did I know where she was headed.

My father and mother drove all night to get home. As soon as Father arrived, he teamed up with Claudel's stepfather. Claudel and Linda had fled together. Her stepfather had brought about twenty men with him to hunt the girls down. They looked tall and ominous.

My father was tired from driving all night, but I could feel the deeper sadness behind his fatigue and stress. Linda's dash for freedom was a complete disgrace to my father, mother, and entire family. We had lost our status in the community as a completely faithful family. The image my father had nurtured for a lifetime was in smithereens.

I could hear him crying in my mother's bedroom. It was then that I felt the weight of his sadness and the brokenness of his heart. When my father came into the kitchen for breakfast he couldn't eat. He stared at his plate and then asked me if I would ever do something like this and hurt him in the same way.

"Never!"

My fate was sealed.

I loved my father; his love for me was the ballast of my life. It upset me to see how much he was suffering. Both of my parents were worried about Linda's safety. They knew how vulnerable she was, how unsophisticated in the ways of the world.

My mother was crushed that her image of a faithful mother of God was now in ruins. She knew she would never again be complimented within the community for her obedient children. Overnight she had become a mother who'd raised an apostate—someone who had turned against God and the prophet. There was nothing worse a person could become. As an apostate, Linda was now condemned to spend the afterlife in the lowest realm of hell, a place of such torment that it was beyond human comprehension.

Even if Linda was found, we knew she would be out of our lives forever. We would never be allowed to associate with her because she had abandoned the work of God. My father could not risk contaminating his other children by letting them have contact with Linda. Linda's escape was worse than death. She would never be part of our lives on earth again, nor would we see her in the afterlife. I hated the thought of letting her go, but as I watched her disappear into the night, secretly I envied her. What worried me was that I knew Linda didn't have any kind of survival skills. But I certainly didn't think she should be forced to wed someone she didn't want to marry. I said this to Rosie at one point and she said there was no way Linda would be coerced into a marriage; she could always say no. But this was a joke. People said that all the time, but the pressure that was applied to a woman who tried to resist an assigned marriage was crushing.

After several days, my father and several uncles of Linda's friend tracked the two girls to a town not far from Salt Lake City. The posse of men surrounded the house, refusing to leave until the girls talked to them.

Linda and Claudel refused.

The woman who was sheltering them asked the men to leave, but they would not, so she called the police. When the officers arrived, the woman explained that she was protecting two runaways from Colorado City. When the police realized the girls were eighteen, they told the men to leave. The police told them they did not have the power to make the girls return. Nor had Linda and Claudel broken any laws.

My father said he would leave, but he wanted to talk to Linda first. He needed to know that she was all right, and he asked an officer to tell her he was very upset. Linda still wouldn't speak to him. Then my dad said that if Linda would talk to him, he would agree to leave her alone and let her do what she wanted.

Linda relented.

When he finally had the chance, my father asked her why she had done this. Linda said she was finished with the religion and nothing he could say would make her change her mind. Dad tried to talk her into coming back, but she refused. He finally left with the other men.

Linda and her friend knew they had to flee that house before the men came back for them. Someone smuggled them into Salt Lake City. The hunt for them soon became an obsession within the community. It took several weeks, but Linda was finally spotted.

Alma, a boy who had fallen in love with Linda at school, headed to Salt Lake to try to find her because it was the most logical place for her to hide. He was on the opposite side of the religious split and there was no way they ever would have been allowed to marry. By this point, the split had completely severed the community in two. All association between one group and the other was unacceptable. Uncle Roy had kicked three apostles out of the FLDS, and they had established their own church. We no longer went to the same dances or celebrated community holidays together.

After Linda escaped, Alma left the community, too. His father had a house in Salt Lake City, so he moved there to look for her. One day he saw her working in J.B.'s, a chain restaurant, and so he got a job there, too. Alma helped Linda get her sea legs in Salt Lake. She didn't know how to use the city bus system, so Alma taught her how to find her way around town and bought her a bus pass. Though Linda was not in love with Alma or even attracted to him, they spent nearly every moment together because she was so lonely and so fearful of being on her own.

Word somehow reached my father that Linda had been found in Salt Lake City. Dad got in touch with Alma and then showed up at J.B.'s to talk with Linda. She realized she would have to deal with him. There was no way she could spend the rest of her life running from her father.

Dad had one demand: he wanted Linda to speak with the prophet. He promised her that after she talked to Uncle Roy, he would leave her alone. Linda agreed.

When they met, Uncle Roy told Linda that although she had fallen away, she could redeem herself by marrying "a good man." Linda said thanks but no thanks.

The prophet exploded and berated her.

Since Linda had no intention of being saved, Uncle Roy turned to my father and asked if he had any suggestions.

Dad said that there was a young man in Salt Lake who had taken an interest in her. My father said he worried about Linda's safety in the big city and thought it might be a good idea for Alma to marry Linda.

In the prophet's eyes, Linda was now useless to him. But Alma was on the other side of the religious split. If Linda married this boy and managed to convert him to Uncle Roy's side, it could be worthwhile. There had been several marriages already where women were given to men on the other side of the split in hopes of converting the men. If one of the women converted instead, her family condemned her and considered her as dead. But the door was always open to her return. She could renounce her marriage and win back her salvation if she came home and let the prophet assign her to another man.

The boy and his father were subsequently called into Uncle Roy's office. The prophet told Alma he wanted him to marry Linda. The boy's father refused because his son was seventeen and had yet to finish high school. But Alma did not want to lose the prophet's blessing. (I think he realized that Linda could think for herself and that he risked losing her by waiting.)

Linda had fled the community to avoid marriage, and now she was being forced to marry someone to remain free. Poor Linda was exhausted. There was monumental pressure on her to marry Alma. It wasn't what she wanted to do, but it would put an end to the crisis. The hunt would be called off. She could maintain a relationship with our family, but she would not have to move back to Colorado City. It felt like the best of bad options.

Even though she agreed to do what the prophet asked of her, Linda's marriage was still viewed as a marriage of rebellion. She had thwarted the prophet's will by not marrying "the good man" he wanted to choose for her. Linda and Alma would have to have a civil marriage, and then a year later they would be eligible for a priesthood marriage by Uncle Roy.

Dad told me I could go to Salt Lake City and be part of Linda's wedding. This was the first time I had seen her since her escape. We had no time alone and were never able to talk. Linda looked like she'd been run over and was too tired to keep fighting. I thought she looked scared. It was hard for me to see that there had been anything positive for her in the escape. I didn't know how she would survive in the outside world.

Linda was married at the courthouse. My mother and father were there, as was Alma's mother. His father refused to come since he opposed the marriage. Linda wore a simple white wedding dress. The ceremony felt more like a disgrace than a celebration. Linda seemed so unhappy. My father could barely hide his disgust for her. He made it clear that for him, this felt like the lesser of two evils.

Alma's mother didn't look too happy, but to his credit Alma had managed to do something rare within the community: marry someone he was genuinely in love with.

The tension crackled just beneath the surface at the ceremony. But the judge was oblivious to what was really taking place. He talked about what an honor it was for a couple to be married in the eyes of God. In his remarks he told them how important it was to find a way to say "I love you" every day to each other. Marriage was a serious responsibility, he said, one that should not be entered into lightly. If only he knew!

No one smiled when the couple said "I do." They kissed robotically, like a couple on a bad blind date.

When we left the courtroom, I had to say goodbye to Linda again. Neither one of us said anything. I didn't know words that could reach into her unhappiness and make her feel better. She began her new life like a condemned woman, knowing she was a disgrace and disappointment to her mother and father.

It would be several years before Linda and I would see or speak to each other again. It broke my heart. Because she had agreed to a marriage that was ordained by the prophet, she was no longer considered an apostate. But she was still in rebellion to her faith. That meant that she was left out in the cold and could not be included in our lives from that day forward.

Several months later, we heard through the grapevine that Linda was pregnant. Even though she had acquiesced to my father's wishes, he was no longer concerned for her well-being. There was much he could have done to ease the hardships she faced in the next five years, but he didn't lift a finger to help the daughter he had once professed to love, nor did he reach out to his two grandchildren.

I learned a terrible and powerful lesson from Linda's ordeal: escape was not the answer. I knew that if I tried, I'd be hunted down like a fugitive and then forced into a situation that guaranteed misery and unhappiness.

# The Nusses

The moment I saw them, I knew they were trouble. A long line of girls walking two by two turned a corner and streamed into the corridor at the new public high school on the first day of registration. There seemed to be no end to them—and they were all sisters. Their dresses had several layers of flounces that bounced when they walked. Their sleeves, bodices, and necklines were trimmed with yards of lace and frills. They looked like those crocheted pastel dolls that cover up Kleenex boxes, except that they all wore big blue boys' sports shoes and made it clear that they would vaporize anyone who tried to cross them.

I looked at my cousins as if to say, *Who are they?* Shannon started laughing. "Those are Merril Jessop's daughters and they own the school."

"It's obvious that they own the hallway," I said.

My cousin Jayne chimed in, "Oh, they're not as bad as they look. They do a lot of funny things, trying to be so superior and pious."

"Funnier than the way they dress?" I asked, thinking of those blue sports shoes. "Does everyone at school dress that way?"

Jayne and Shannon were giggling again. "No," Shannon said. "Not everyone dresses like that, just the nusses and the wanna-be nusses."

I looked blank. I had no idea what Shannon was talking about. "We call everyone who dresses that way nusses," she said.

Jayne jumped in. "It all started out when we called them *righteousnesses*. People who didn't dress like them or want to be like them were called *hoods*. *Righteousnesses* was too long, so we shortened it to *nusses*."

I could see that the nusses were going to be one of the strangest components to the strange school year of 1984–85.

Registration day was huge for me because I had been out of school for a year. The split in our community was now in its seventh year. One of the consequences was that many families pulled their children out of the private high school so they would not be contaminated by the children of the families on the other side of the divide who supported Uncle Roy. As a result, many boys wound up working on construction jobs instead of going to high school. The girls who were forbidden to go to the private high school were confined to their homes. Most of the girls who were kept out of school were disappointed because they had wanted an education and a diploma before they were assigned to a marriage. They knew their futures were being shortchanged.

I had been working at my father's office during my year away from school, which was at least better than being stuck at home doing babysitting and chores. I was diligent about my correspondence courses but eager to get back into the classroom. I was thrilled when the Colorado City High School opened.

I realized as I stood in the registration line that I didn't have any friends on the Uncle Roy side of the split even though my parents supported him. I had gone against their wishes and maintained friendships with children whose parents supported the brethren, the side that believed that disciples should assist the prophet in interpreting God's word.

No one else looked and dressed like the nusses. Those of us on the Uncle Roy side of the split usually wore only skirts and blouses, as did the girls on the brethren side. Sometimes we'd wear jumpers, and on rare occasions, a dress. I was still wearing my hair piled on top of my head in a granny knot. We'd been forbidden to wear it down at our former school. Even braids were unacceptable.

When I finally sat down with a counselor, I held my breath. I didn't know if all my correspondence courses would be accepted for credit. My fear was that if they weren't, I would be forced to start as a sophomore again, instead of a junior. That would mean I'd turn eighteen before I graduated. If I was assigned in marriage shortly after turning eighteen, as so many girls were, I might not even get my diploma. (By twenty, a girl who was unmarried was considered an old maid.)

But all my credits were accepted, and to my surprise I was told that I was going to begin as a senior. I felt elated. Starting as a senior meant I'd be seventeen when I graduated, and so I'd have a year of college under my belt before I was assigned in marriage. I was beginning to dream about becoming a pediatrician. There were so many children in the community who had no access to comprehensive medical care. Aunt Lydia, the self-taught nurse and midwife, had many practical skills, but she was getting older and soon would have to quit working altogether. I thought that I might be allowed to become a doctor if I worked only with children. But that was a dream in the still distant future. I was thrilled and proud at the thought of being in the first graduating class at the high school. Ever so slowly, my life was starting to feel like my own.

This was shaping up to be an interesting year. It would be lonely being in a school without many of my friends. The majority of my classmates were going to be nusses. Did I really want a diploma bad enough to put up with them? Yes, I did. The trade-off was that I was now a year ahead and would have a chance to get started in college.

On my first day of classes, the nusses were tripping over themselves with femininity. They didn't walk, they pranced on tiptoe. When they spoke, it was in soft and girly voices. When they laughed, it was subdued and modest. "Oh, for heaven's sake" was their all-purpose refrain when anything went wrong, like a book dropping to the floor. Their piety was precious to them but fundamentally fake.

But some of the teachers loved the nusses. They practiced perfect penmanship and were diligent A-plus students. The teachers who loved the nusses looked at me as if I had a righteousness deficiency.

Thankfully, my cousin Lee Ann was in several classes with me, and some of my teachers remembered me from the private school I'd attended before.

By the end of the first week, I realized that for the first time I was embarrassed to be a woman. The nusses sickened me. I knew that I lived in a culture where a baby girl was of less value to her parents than a baby boy, but I'd never thought of myself as "less than." But when I saw the nusses prancing and cavorting through school I felt ashamed and humiliated. Couldn't they see that they were acting like perfect idiots?

Then something snapped inside me. The nusses did not represent women, only fools. Why should I feel disgraced? I knew in my heart that there was nothing wrong with being a woman. I *wanted* to roar like a woman. I knew that would never be allowed, but that didn't stop me from being proud of myself. I was a woman, not a fake!

I grabbed Shannon and Jayne and asked them to meet me Friday after school. I could barely contain myself. "These girls are driving me crazy. Why do they act like this?"

Jayne and Shannon started laughing. "All right, all right," I demanded, "you two have got to let me in on the joke."

Shannon whispered two words in my ear: "*Fascinating Womanhood.*" I pushed Shannon away and loudly said, "What?"

Jayne's voice was very matter-of-fact. "It's a book called *Fascinating Womanhood*. It's all about how to manipulate men."

"But what does that have to do with being an idiot?" I asked.

"Everything," they said. "You have to read the book. It's a scream."

I tracked down a copy and spent the entire weekend reading it. I was stunned. It was a self-help book about how a woman in a monogamous relationship could manipulate and control her husband. The first few chapters were all about why a man loved a woman who could make him feel like a manly man. Men didn't love women who intimidated them. That I could see—no one wants to be made to feel inferior.

But the farther I got into the book, the more I could see how it was the nusses' playbook. *Fascinating Womanhood* was the script that the nusses were following. But what was so surreal was that we didn't even have that many boys in our school. What were they thinking?

There were descriptions about how to pout perfectly when your husband tells you no. The book explained how to stand, how to pucker in anger, and how to stomp your foot in an adorable and feminine way.

The manipulation chapters were outrageous to me. They were also designed for women who were the only wife. What was a plural wife supposed to do, and how could these methods work on a man who was supposed to be obedient to his religion? We were taught not to manipulate our husbands. A woman was supposed to pray for guidance and understanding about fulfilling her husband's desires.

What a comedy. In *Fascinating Womanhood,* acting stupid was one of the most important ways a woman could make her husband feel manly. Installing the Dixie cup dispenser was one example. The husband asks his wife if she needs help. She refuses, insisting she can handle this itsy-bitsy chore herself. She pretends to read the instructions carefully and then hangs the dispenser upside down. Full of pride, she shows her husband what she has managed to do. When her husband explains the dispenser is upside down, the wife acts shocked and disappointed. She should have asked her husband to hang it after all, praising him for his many talents and manly abilities.

"For hell's sake!" I shrieked to myself, not even trying to sanitize my reaction. I could not believe that anyone would believe such a stupid book. Were men so dumb that they could fall for something like that?

On Monday I found Jayne and mocked the book. She chided me about being disrespectful to the nusses' Bible. "They have taken every part of that book to heart and it is going to be their salvation. This is how they will be treated like queens and escape their mothers' fate." I thought I would collapse in laughter. Apparently there was even a younger version, *Fascinating Girl,* which was making the rounds of the nusses' younger siblings.

We began inventing nuss jokes. I came up with one of the first: "Did you hear about the nuss who was really stupid? She hung the Dixie cup dispenser right side up!"

Then there was the joke about the two hoods and the nuss who went on a trip to the Nevada desert. Their car broke down in the scorching heat, and the three girls realized that they would have to hike for help. One hood took a gallon of water from the car, and the other took the sandwiches they'd packed for the trip. The nuss took the car door so in case she got hot she could roll down the window!

There was a clear social divide at school between the hoods and the nusses. If we were in the same room, we never interacted with each other. When something came up at school that forced us to talk to each other, we were deliberately rude. We were divided into two camps, but there was a certain détente. The unwritten rule was that we were going to leave each other alone.

This worked very well until Margaret, one of Merril Jessop's daughters, upset the delicate balance. Margaret was not attending high school. She worked for Merril and was about to turn twenty. She felt bad that she'd not been assigned in marriage yet. Unless something happened soon, she'd be the oldest old maid in town. So she decided to have a party and invite all the unmarried teenage girls. Her plan was to invite only the nusses and exclude all the hoods. That was just fine with us. We really didn't want to go to a nuss party. The nusses were keeping us entertained, which was all we wanted from them.

One prime example of the pure theater they created was watching Merrilyn, one of Merril's most beautiful daughters, flirt with a teacher she had a crush on. One day in class she was standing at the pencil sharpener, loving every moment of looking up into his eyes. The teacher was polite but clearly had a lot of other things to do while preparing for the next class's lesson.

Merrilyn put her pencil in the sharpener and looked up at the teacher with an adoring gaze in her big green eyes. "Will you please turn the crank?" Without giving it a thought, the teacher turned the handle. Merrilyn removed the pencil, blowing on it carefully. "Thank you," she said in her best little nuss voice.

Jayne witnessed the entire episode. Afterward she went up to Merrilyn and said, "So, Merrilyn, how does it feel to have your teacher turn your crank?" The teacher looked pretty sheepish when he realized what he'd been lured into. The nusses were so arrogant it was impossible for them to believe that we were making fun of them. They were so steeped in their own superiority.

The old maids' party was turning into a big deal. All the girls were talking about it at school. One of Merril's more serious daughters, Audrey, seemed bothered that we weren't invited. She approached me in sewing class and asked if I'd come with some of my friends. She wanted us to put together a skit and be part of the entertainment. Other girls would be doing songs. I tried to back out of it—there wouldn't be enough time, et cetera—but Audrey was persistent, and I knew her intentions were good.

Jayne and Shannon thought it would be fun. They loved the idea of performing before a captive audience of nusses and picked a song from *Fiddler on the Roof* that was about arranged marriages. I was sure the nusses would think we were mocking the prophet if we sang this song, and so I opted out of the skit, but my cousins persisted. They did a great job, and I thought if they were allowed to perform it, they'd be the hit of the party.

There was a dress rehearsal before the party, and each contingent of girls got up and did its part. But Merril's daughter, who'd organized the party, hated my cousins' song. A song about an arranged marriage somehow exacerbated the state of misery she was in about being unmarried. She told my cousins that they could come to the party, but they'd have to find another song. Of course, there wasn't enough time for that.

The nusses' old maids' party was the following weekend. The day of the party, my father got a call from Merril Jessop, who was, in effect, king of the nusses. Merril and my father had been business partners for years. He was prominent in the FLDS and very tight with Uncle Roy. Merril wanted me and my cousins to come. Dad explained we hadn't been invited, and Merril went into a whole song and dance about how that wasn't the case. Dad didn't see any reason why we should go to the party and let the matter drop.

Then Margaret, who had been the one to throw us out of the party, came over the week afterward to try to clear up what she felt was a misunderstanding. Rosie, Annette, and I all sat quietly in the living room and listened to her state her case. She had been at the dress rehearsal and said she loved our song. She said the problem was Uncle Fred. He opposed it and had told her to talk to my cousins about doing something different.

She felt bad that we had not been at the party. After it was over, she said, Uncle Fred announced that every girl present at that party would obtain her salvation and make it into the highest degree of the Celestial Kingdom of God—the downtown of heaven. He didn't have the power to make that actually come true. But Uncle Fred was so revered in the community as a godly man that his pronouncements were seen as the next best thing to divine intervention.

I couldn't figure out her motivation. Was she trying to say that because we'd rebelled and not come up with another song, we were disgraced and would never obtain our salvation? I thought she had set up the meeting to apologize. But it seemed like the only point she wanted to make was that she and the other nusses were going to heaven and we were not.

My sewing teacher, Mrs. Johnson, was one of the few who stood up to the nusses. She had no patience for the way they assumed that rules did not apply to them. When it came time for parent-teacher conferences, Mrs. Johnson let Merril's wife Ruth have it when she came up to her and said, "How are our girls doing?" Mrs. Johnson unleashed a tirade against the nusses. She told Ruth that her daughters were rude, none of them obeyed the rules, and she was tired of reminding them day after day of what was expected in class.

After that, suddenly the rules in sewing class applied to the nusses, too. It was the only classroom in the high school where that was true. (But Mrs. Johnson got some serious heat for the way she treated Ruth. In an effort to make amends with Merril's family, she invited one of Merril's other wives, Barbara, to honor our class by teaching us dance aerobics, which was a real hoot.)

I was one of the people the sewing teacher liked. She let me use her personal sewing machine and would allow me to leave class early if I had finished all my work.

Since sewing was my last class of the day, this was a real blessing when Brigham began following me home from school.

I didn't know Brigham at all. We had never been in school together, plus he was a year ahead of me. But at the public school, we had a class together and for whatever reasons, he decided he liked me, so he began to follow me home.

On days when I could manage it, I'd leave sewing class early and run home as fast as I could. The minute I got home I ran to my bedroom, breathless but safe. I always tried to study before I had to help Mama with dinner. One day I had only been there a few minutes when Annette bolted into our bedroom. She was laughing so hard she could barely stand up.

"Annette, shut up, this is not funny!" I said. "I had to nearly run myself into the ground to escape him."

Annette was rolling around on the floor in laughter. "Yes, it *is* funny. The look on his face when he got outside and couldn't find you was the funniest thing that I have ever seen in my life. He was in such a panic when he realized you were gone. He got on his bike and rode as fast as he could. We were dying with laughter."

But this was serious. I said to my sister that I knew I couldn't outrun him every day, and if our father found out that a boy was walking me home from school he'd yank me right out.

Only Annette could think this was so funny. She was slapping her hands on the floor of our bedroom, still laughing. Words were not getting through. I grabbed a pillow off my bed and threw it on her and yelled, "Annette, shut up! I am in terrible trouble. He could make it so I can't go to school. I have fought so hard to get my high school diploma and now this dumb boy could destroy everything."

For the next six weeks he kept trying to follow me home, and eventually someone reported to my father that we were walking home from school together.

My father called me in and said I was disobedient in the ways of God. I should be saving my affections for the man I'd be assigned to in marriage.

I pleaded with my father and tried to explain that I'd been trying to ditch him. Annette came to my rescue and insisted to my father that I was telling the truth. This saved me. My father believed her and told Brigham's father to make him stop bothering me. I felt deeply relieved. Now I knew I was really going to graduate and, I hoped, continue on to college.

I knew my parents wouldn't let me go directly to college. My goal was to start at the community college and then move on. I had been on the honor roll my senior year of high school and had made mostly straight A's.

I was so excited about graduating by the time May arrived. This was the biggest achievement of my life. Since we were the first graduating class of Colorado City High School, nearly the entire community turned out. Our accomplishment was an accomplishment for everyone in the community. Once again, FLDS children were getting a high school education, after nearly a seven-year lapse.

We were told to arrive two hours early for picture taking and goodbyes. As the time drew near, we all lined up to march across the stage. Nothing happened. More time elapsed. Still nothing. I asked someone why. "We're waiting for Audrey."

After what felt like an interminable wait, the teachers decided that we would start the show without her. If Audrey missed her graduation, it was her own fault. Music started to play and we began marching, but then we were ordered to stop and come back.

I felt that I was never going to walk across that stage, never going to graduate. Then I noticed heads turning. Audrey, who had stayed home to finish her graduation dress, walked into the hall in one of the most elaborate dresses I had ever seen.

She looked like an FLDS version of Princess Diana. Her hair was coiffed and every strand sprayed into place. Her gown was a mass of soft, shining blue fabric with yards of expensive lace sewn into cascades of ruffles that floated over her tiny white high heels—instead of the boys' blue sports shoes she usually wore. Her sleeves were puffy and her tightly fitted bodice was smothered in lace. She smiled like she was the belle of the ball, except that there was no ball.

"Carolyn Blackmore." When my name was called, I walked across the stage to get my diploma. It had been worth the fight. Now my sights were set on college and medical school. I smiled, thinking that if I could make it through the nusses, I could make it through anything. Little did I know that in a year I would be forced to marry their father.

# Marriage

After graduation, I worked for a year as a teacher's assistant while attending a weekly class at the community college. It was an exhausting schedule, but I wanted to establish the best academic record I could before I applied to school.

By the time I was eighteen, my secret dream was still to become a pediatrician. I didn't know any woman in the FLDS who had done something so ambitious, but I was determined to try.

I knew the first step was getting into a four-year college that had a good pre-med program. I started by telling my father of my desire to go to college. I left the doctor part out.

He said he'd ask the prophet. Uncle Roy was a comparatively moderate man, and he felt it helped the community if a small percentage of us went on to college and then came back home.

At two o'clock one morning I was awakened from the dead of sleep. It was close to the end of the semester and I'd stayed up late studying. I couldn't imagine why my mother was awakening me or why my father would want to speak with me at such an odd hour. Nothing like this had ever happened before.

Dad was waiting for me in my mother's bedroom. My father acted as though everything was normal. "I had a chance to talk to Uncle Roy about you going to college and he told me you were a smart girl and could go to school to be a teacher."

My heart sank. A teacher? I wanted to do pre-med.

But it got worse.

"Uncle Roy said that before you go to school, you should be married. He wants you to marry Merril Jessop."

I was stunned. My future had just vanished. Even if I continued with my education, I'd have to do so while being pregnant and having babies.

I also knew that although Uncle Roy had given me permission to go to school, my husband could overrule him in this area because he would be the ultimate authority in my life.

Merril Jessop. I knew that name. I'd gone to school with his daughters—they were the nusses. I was now going to be one of their mothers. I knew enough about Merril Jessop to know I didn't like the way he treated his family. He had the reputation within the community of being a jerk. I was eighteen. This was outrageous. Marrying a man who was fifty was like marrying my grandfather. I knew a few boys who worked for Merril on what we called "slave crews." They thought he was an ass. He didn't pay them and worked them like dogs.

I looked at my father in horror. "How does Merril feel about this marriage? How does he feel about marrying a child?"

"Oh, he's done it before."

My father went on to explain that when a directive like this comes down from the prophet of God, it's very important not to waste time. He was stern. "It's very critical that you accept what the prophet has given you. This is a tremendous blessing. You should not question it or allow the devil to interfere and get into your feelings on this issue."

I could barely breathe.

My father continued, "I talked to Merril and arranged for you to marry him this Saturday."

Saturday was two days away.

My life had been swiped out from under me.

What if I ran away? Where could I escape? I had seen what happened to my sister Linda after she fled—she was hunted down like an animal. There was no one I could turn to for help. I didn't know anyone on the outside.

My father wouldn't even let me go back to the bedroom I shared with Annette. My father said I had to sleep with my mother because we were going to take a trip to Bullfrog and meet Merril for breakfast. My parents didn't plan to let me out of their sight until Saturday; they had clearly orchestrated this so I would not be able to escape my fate. They had been deeply humiliated by Linda's bolt for freedom. By taking me out of town, I couldn't tell my sister or anyone else about what had happened.

I told my father I was worried about finishing my classes and taking my final exams. My father said they were unimportant. Doing what the prophet ordered was all that mattered.

We left the house early the next morning and drove to Bullfrog. We traveled through Page, Arizona, on our way there. Merril owned the largest construction company in Page and spent much more time there than he did in Colorado City. Merril was an hour late to breakfast. We had already finished eating. Merril had a cup of coffee with us but spoke only to my father. Merril was only five foot seven, with dark curly hair, weathered and wrinkled skin, blue eyes, and yellow teeth. Merril made a few jokes and then got up to leave.

He knew then that he was marrying the wrong girl. As I later learned, after he asked the prophet for me by name, he went to see my father, who showed him my picture. That's when he realized he'd asked for the wrong daughter. His intention had been to marry my sixteen-year-old sister Annette, who was the family beauty. She was tall and thin with blond hair that fell nearly to her knees. But when he talked to the prophet, Merril got our names mixed up.

Apparently, Merril had gone to the prophet after my father sued him for damages in a business deal. He told Uncle Roy he'd lose millions of dollars if the lawsuit went through. His pitch to Uncle Roy was that if he married one of my father's daughters, he'd be family and the lawsuit would be dropped. He had seen Annette and knew how beautiful she was, but confused her name with mine. Uncle

Roy, in turn, told my father that he'd had a revelation from God about this marriage. Once he said that, there was no turning back.

After Merril left the restaurant that morning, we went to Bullfrog. Mother and I went shopping for fabric for a wedding dress. In the FLDS culture, women make their wedding dresses well before their marriages, because sometimes a girl has only two hours' notice before she's married and the only way a woman can count on having a dress is by making it in advance. The dress is very modest; it's white with long sleeves, a high neck, and a skirt that stops four inches above the ankles. There is no veil or other frills.

It was really important to my mother that I have a wedding dress. When we got home late that Friday night, she stayed up all night sewing. I called my teachers at the community college and said I couldn't take my finals and didn't know when I would be able to reschedule them. I was a conscientious student and my teachers, who knew something unexpected must have happened to me, asked no questions.

My father came into the room shortly after I finished making my calls and said Merril was coming to pick me up. He wanted to take me back to his house and introduce me to his family before we left for our wedding in Salt Lake City. The prophet was living in Salt Lake City and my parents didn't want to postpone the marriage. I think they were worried that with more time, I'd find a way to get out of it or bolt as Linda had. I'm sure that's why I was never allowed to be alone again after I was told about my marriage. My parents could not risk the humiliation they'd face if another daughter rebelled.

When Merril arrived at the house, my younger siblings answered the door and came running to get me. Merril didn't acknowledge me. He walked past me and into the kitchen, where he said hello to everyone. When he left, it was clear that he expected me to follow him, and I did. His truck was parked outside. He didn't even bother to open the door for me.

I got into the truck thinking we were definitely off to a bad start. Neither one of us said a word.

I had no experience with men. I had never really dated a boy. Relationships were taboo in our culture. In theory, we weren't even allowed to socialize with boys, but there were ways around that, as we'd discovered in theology class. My father was the only man I had ever interacted with. I'd never actually met Merril Jessop. I knew who he was because he sometimes came to our house to talk business with my dad.

As his truck pulled away from our house, I felt like I was front and center in a horror movie that was being played out in front of me. Except that the horror was real, and there was no escape.

I wanted to say, *Merril, you don't want to marry me, and I don't want to marry you. Take me home.* But that wasn't an option.

We were silent all the way to his house. Once we arrived, he called everyone together to meet their new mother. Faunita, Merril's first wife, gave me a joyous hug. She said she was absolutely delighted that Merril was getting a new wife because the family really needed one. I didn't know what she meant.

We walked into the living room, and people came from everywhere to give me a hug. I was hugged by at least forty people. I wasn't used to being touched, and it made me very uncomfortable. Merril ordered his two other wives, Barbara and Ruth, to give me a hug. Ruth made the best of it, but Barbara treated me like the enemy. Battle lines were drawn. I was in hostile territory and it freaked me out.

In just twenty-four hours, I had gone from worrying about my finals to preparing for a marriage I didn't want to a man I barely knew. When I got back home, Mom was still frantically working on my wedding dress. She needed me for a final fitting. I was so scared I felt like a zombie bride.

Within hours, Merril's family arrived at my home. He brought his three wives with him and his favored daughters—the nusses. In high school, I'd thought I couldn't get through the year with them; in marrying their father, I'd be stuck with them for eternity.

There had been intense competition among his daughters to get to go to the wedding. The losers had to stay home and babysit. He sent a few of the girls to help my mother finish my wedding dress because he didn't want to wait any longer.

We traveled to Salt Lake City in a small caravan of cars on Saturday morning—less than forty-eight hours since my father had dragged me out of bed to announce my engagement. I rode in the backseat of my father's van. At one stop, Merril got into our van and talked business with my dad for an hour or two. He never once acknowledged me.

It was only much later that I would learn that I was part of a business deal, a way for Merril to get back into my father's good graces after my father filed a lawsuit against him. But at that time, my father truly believed that the prophet, Uncle Roy, had received a revelation from God that I was to become Merril's wife. My father was so brainwashed that he couldn't see the obvious, and I was years away from connecting those dots myself.

I was brainwashed, too. I knew I didn't want Merril to hold my hand or touch me. I didn't even want him to open the car door for me. But I had been conditioned enough to believe that this must be some test from God that Merril and I had to endure and pass.

I had been raised in the FLDS sect and at eighteen still believed that Uncle Roy was a prophet of God. For me to reject my marriage was to reject God's will in my life. I didn't understand the revelation about my marriage at all. But I'd internalized a lifetime of teaching that said God's ways are not man's ways and that there must be a purpose to this that would be revealed in time.

When we got to Salt Lake City, we checked into the Comfort Inn. My father had brought my mom and Rosie with him and reserved two rooms. When I realized there wasn't a room for me, it hit me—I would be expected to sleep with Merril.

Up until this point, I had been too overwhelmed to consider the possibility of sex. The gravity keeping my world in place was gone. I was not only a virgin but someone who had never been touched in an intimate or romantic way. I had been kissed—once—by a boy, but we both got into trouble for it and were made to feel ashamed. The idea of sexual or physical contact with a man thirty-two years my senior was terrifying.

Both of my mothers helped get me ready for the marriage ceremony. Rosie was helping me comb through my long hair, which was ten inches below my waist. It had rarely been cut. My biological mother, Nurylon, was fitting me into the dress she had made. They were laughing nervously to relieve tension. Most girls in my situation agreed to the arranged marriage to protect their families from being disgraced. I felt like I was being prepared for a ritual sacrifice—the proverbial lamb dressed and trussed, readied for slaughter.

Both of my mothers had been involved in arranged marriages and had felt blessed to accept the prophet's will. An arranged marriage was as natural to these women as the sunrise every morning. To me it felt sickening.

When I was ready I got into the van with my father. We were driving to the prophet's home in Salt Lake City for the ceremony.

After we got to Uncle Roy's, Merril went in to talk to him while my father, two mothers, and I waited in the van. My father was matter-of-fact when he spoke to me.

"Carolyn, Merril is a good man, and I want you to know that if you want him to love you and love your children, you should always put his feelings first and find yourself in perfect obedience to him."

Children? I had yet to adjust to the idea of marriage or sex, and now he was talking to me about children?

The shock and horror of the past two days were numbing. It felt like I was being submerged in ice water and every time I came up for air I was pushed down again. *Take that, take this, and take that.* I was gasping for air.

The marriage ceremony was performed in the prophet's office. I was told to stand next to Merril. He took my hand. It was the first time he had ever touched me. The prophet read our vows and we both agreed to a covenant marriage for all eternity.

I felt my life rushing away from me.

We sealed our marriage vows with a kiss. Uncle Roy instructed us in the importance of multiplying and replenishing the earth with children as a way of fulfilling our covenant with God. Everything felt serious, nothing felt safe.

At the end of the ceremony, Merril dropped my hand and walked out of the room without looking back. His family followed him. I didn't know what to do, so I followed my parents into a large dining room where someone was having a birthday party celebration.

When Merril and his family arrived, the partygoers realized there had just been a wedding, and everyone began congratulating Merril. I sat quietly on the opposite side of the room. I was in a wedding dress at somebody else's birthday party while my husband was being congratulated. I knew I didn't belong to my family anymore. Merril's family seemed like a foreign country I didn't want to enter. I felt evicted from everything I had ever known.

One of Uncle Roy's more than twelve wives came over to me with a huge smile. She told me how much God must love me to bless me with a man like Merril. She urged me to come to his table and have some birthday cake.

Merril's wives Barbara and Ruth were on either side of him. When he saw me he told Ruth to go sit somewhere else. But there weren't any other empty places, so she left the room. After we finished eating, my father got up to leave. I followed him and went back to the hotel in his van.

A short while later, Merril arrived at the hotel and knocked on the door of my father's room. He chatted with my father as he gathered up my things. He picked up my suitcase and a box that contained my shoes. I was in a complete panic. As he walked out of the room, I could feel the eyes of everyone else saying, *Aren't you going to go with him?*

Silently, I screamed, *No.*

Merril turned and looked at me. "Carolyn, are you coming? This stuff is kind of heavy." It was the most he had ever said to me.

I must have looked like a miserable wreck standing there in my wedding dress. All I could think of was that my life was really over as I followed him into the hallway.

Merril had forgotten where our room was. I lagged behind him as we walked up and down the halls of the Comfort Inn.

Eventually, we stopped in front of a room, and when Merril put the key in the door it opened.

We were alone for the first time. He put my suitcase down along with the box filled with my shoes. He sat on the bed and turned on the TV. I moved to a corner in the room, sat at a small table, and said nothing. After twenty minutes, he said he was going to check on the rest of the family and left the room.

I got into bed. It had been two days since my father told me about my impending marriage. I had barely slept in those forty-eight hours and I was crushed with exhaustion. When Merril returned a few hours later, he turned on the TV and turned up the volume.

"It would be nice if we talked a little bit to each other," he said.

I told him I was extremely tired and just wanted to sleep.

"That's okay," he said.

He turned off the lights, took off his clothes except for his long underwear, and got into bed with me.

He sat in the bed and stared at me.

I was paralyzed. We didn't even know each other. There was no way I was going to consummate the marriage.

But I didn't have that choice.

He started kissing me. I felt gross. Nothing could be worse. Then he put his hands down the front of my nightgown and began to rub my breasts. His hands were cool and clammy. I had never been that close to a man before and certainly not without my clothes.

I acted as repulsed as I felt, which seemed to feed something in him. He removed my nightgown and underwear and shifted his body on top of mine. I felt even more powerless than I had when my father told me I must marry.

Merril spread my legs apart but could not get an erection. I felt angry, humiliated, and embarrassed. Should I fight him? I began to try to free myself, and after a few minutes he released his hold on me.

I scrambled out of the bed, confused and disoriented, and found my clothes on the other side of the room. I was shaking so hard I couldn't get dressed. I felt myself gasping for breath. I sat on the floor by the foot of the bed. I felt so unsafe.

Merril got dressed and sat on the edge of the bed, saying that he felt it was important to be respectful of a lady's feelings, but in reality he was covering up his own inadequacies.

I said I was tired and wanted to sleep. He didn't seem to care; he just stretched out on the bed and moments later began to snore. I got back into bed and stared at the ceiling until I finally fell asleep.

When I awakened in the morning, Merril was in the shower. He dressed and left the room without saying a word.

As soon as he was gone, I showered and dressed. I was about to leave and find my father's family when Merril returned.

"Come with me," he said. I picked up my luggage and followed him to his van. He moved some things around so there would be a place for my bags. I felt panicked.

We went to breakfast at a place nearby. Merril introduced me to some men there as his new wife. They were happy and excited for Merril. I felt like a complete object. One of the men made some lame joke that compared a new wife to a dog. Merril laughed and said dogs were better because they were more loyal. He made another joke comparing marriage to a bath. "Once you get into it, it's not so hot." The other men laughed. I had never felt so degraded.

After breakfast, we gathered outside in the parking lot. My father started talking to Merril about going to an auction in Oregon. Merril sent the rest of his family home. There was no talk of a honeymoon. We got in his van and headed to Oregon.

I kept thinking about my missing my finals.

# Newlywed

Traveling was a relief because I didn't have to talk to Merril. My father, his wife Rosie, and my father's business partner were traveling with us to the auction in Oregon, which we reached two days later. Merril didn't speak to me in the van. It was business as usual for him. But for me, everything had changed.

The shock from the night before was still too much for me to absorb. I didn't understand anything about sex and had never thought it could be as crude and brutal as it had been. I did think a man should be sensitive to a woman's feelings and that Merril didn't have a right to touch me if I didn't want to be touched. I was so naive, I thought he should at least have asked me before he tried anything on our wedding night. He knew how sexually inexperienced I was, but clearly that didn't matter to him.

My father and Rosie were happy about my marriage, which made it feel even more surreal. If they loved me, how could they have let me go through something so hateful? I knew they thought Merril was a man of God and would never do anything hurtful or wrong in God's eyes. My parents thought that my marriage was a blessing from God because it had been revealed through the prophet. My happiness, in their view, was dependent on my willingness to do the will of God, no matter how painful that might be to me.

At night, when we were alone in the motel, Merril would spend most of his time watching TV or consoling Barbara on the phone.

She was unhappy about being left behind. He kept assuring her that he loved her. I said nothing and in bed tried to avoid any contact with him. Once when he tried to caress my breast I stiffened in terror and he quit.

The next day Merril bought some construction equipment at the auction. I listened to the bidding and selling and felt that I was just another piece of property that Merril owned. Merril called Barbara several times during the day. I didn't want him to pay attention to me, but I thought he'd at least acknowledge my presence or speak to me in the van. I was used to being treated like a person.

We spent the last day of our trip driving through California's redwood forest and shopping in San Francisco's Chinatown. My father had been in real estate and often took us with him when he had to travel. I'd been to San Francisco and the redwood forest with him several times before when I was younger. I was fortunate to have seen as much as I did before I married Merril because it opened my eyes and taught me a lot about the world outside my own. But it felt weird to see these places with a strange man and know that he was now my husband.

Merril made a big point of buying some cheap Chinese fans for his daughters and wives. We drove through much of the night to get back home to Colorado City. Merril stayed with me for an hour or two before heading into Barbara's bedroom.

My first impression the next morning was that the house was immaculate and well organized. I'd soon see that this was a sham.

The first clue that something might be off was when Ruth came out of the kitchen, where she'd been preparing breakfast, to greet Merril, who'd emerged from Barbara's room showered and dressed. He kissed her and said, "It's good to see you, Ruthie."

Ruth nodded stiffly. "It is very good to see you. It was hard not to talk to you all week."

That seemed odd. Merril was always on the phone. I'd assumed when he wasn't talking to Barbara, he was speaking to his other wives, Ruth and Faunita. Merril responded by asking Ruth to gather up his beautiful daughters and lovely wives. He took my hand and led me back into my bedroom. Kissing me, he asked me to get the fans we'd bought in Chinatown.

I dug the fans out of my suitcase and went into the kitchen. Barbara was there, and I noticed her eyes were red and swollen. It looked like she had been crying all night. Merril's ten teenage daughters—the nusses—surrounded him like a tribe of smiling girls. He had four other daughters between the ages of nine and twelve and they were part of the adoring chorus around him. Everyone seemed excited about the fans from Chinatown. It seemed fake and unnatural to me, but not to them.

After the fans were handed out to his wives and daughters, Merril turned and handed me the last one, saying, "This fan is for my lovely wife Carolyn as a memory of our first trip together." He then announced that he and Barbara were leaving that morning for Page and his construction company. Merril told me to help Ruth in the kitchen and spend time getting to know his family.

As soon as Merril left, I went into his office and called my teachers at school. I was desperate to reschedule my finals and relieved when I found out I could still get credit for my classes if I took my exams that week, which I could—the community college was in town and used the same building as the regular school.

I finished all my finals by Friday, came home, and collapsed. The last two weeks had severed me from the only life I'd ever known. I knew Merril would never let me go to medical school, and it was pushing it to even get to be a teacher.

I'd heard he needed a new secretary in Page. Barbara was his traveling secretary. Margaret, Merril's oldest daughter, had been the other secretary who worked in the office, but she'd gotten married and was now living in Salt Lake City. Merril needed help, and fast. I was afraid he might force me to take her job and quit school. Merril had said something about it to me on his way out the door with Barbara earlier in the week.

The next morning I went for a bike ride with Audrey, who was twenty and Merril's oldest unmarried daughter—the nuss princess who had held up graduation. Audrey was graceful and quite pretty.

I'd always liked her, even though she was a nuss, because she didn't put on airs and pretend to be superior to her sisters.

I asked her if she thought Merril might force me to become his secretary. "Barbara has been his traveling secretary. But she has nine children she never sees. It makes more sense for him to start using you since you're a young wife with no children," she said. "This would give Barbara a chance to be with her kids."

"Audrey, do you really think she wants to be home with her children while I'm away with Merril? Your father called her constantly on the trip and spent ten times more time comforting her than he did doing anything else. I can't see how she'd be happy with me taking her place."

Audrey was quiet for a moment, carefully considering her words before she spoke. "Well, maybe she needs to learn what it is like to be the one who has to stay home rather than be the one who gets all the rewards and abuses everyone else."

I didn't know much about the family yet, but I knew I did not want to be involved with teaching someone else a painful lesson. It seemed that if Barbara had really wanted to be home with her children, she could have split the travel time with Merril's other wives.

"Carolyn, right after you married Father, all of Barbara's children were talking about you being the wife to travel with him. They were hoping that she would stay home with them. They all want their mother. They're excited because now they think there's a chance they might have a mom."

I asked Audrey what Barbara in fact did as Merril's traveling secretary. "When I've been in the office, all I've ever seen her do is color flowers and call Father on the radio every two minutes. She'd take him drinks on the job and then go out to dinner with him every night."

I told Audrey that I thought the last thing Barbara wanted in Page was another of Merril's wives. "I haven't gotten one warm feeling or gesture from her," I said. "I don't think she's happy that I married her husband."

Audrey didn't miss a beat. "Of course she's not happy about you marrying Father. She's been his only wife ever since he married her, and you might change that."

I couldn't believe what I was hearing and looked at Audrey in shock. "What do you mean, she is your father's only wife?"

Audrey suddenly looked stricken. "I think I have said too much already. We really should be getting home."

My head was spinning. Why didn't Audrey want to talk to me any more about what was going on in this strange family I'd just married into? For eighteen years, I'd always known where I stood and what was expected of me. Even though my mother was abusive, I grew up in a home that was very structured, and my father was exceedingly well organized. But in less than two weeks, ever since I'd asked my father if I could go to college, my world had turned upside down.

That weekend was tense. Merril spent one night in my bedroom. He didn't interact with the rest of the family at all. He and Barbara went into town on Saturday and spent the rest of the day in her bedroom talking. He didn't say goodbye to anyone when he left for Page on Monday morning. Nancy, one of Merril's daughters, went with him. I was hoping this meant she might be taking Margaret's job. More than anything, I wanted to stay in college. It was absolutely the only chance I had to make something of myself. It was a tiny plot of solid ground on which I would have at least a foothold on a future.

The next weekend was equally tense. Merril spent both nights in my room and on Monday morning asked me to bring coffee to him in his office. Barbara was sitting in a chair next to her desk. Her long wavy hair was a rich auburn. She was only about five foot four, but after nine children she weighed close to two hundred pounds. Merril took a sip of coffee before he spoke. "Barbie, I've decided to have Carolyn come with us to Page this week."

She looked betrayed. Anger swept over her face as she stared at Merril. "I thought you and I discussed this and we both decided Carolyn wasn't coming to Page."

Merril shot right back. "She's not going to be working at Page. I'm taking her on a little trip this week."

Barbara looked like the wind had been sucked right out of her. Her voice was quivering as she looked at Merril and said, "When are you going to take me on a little trip?" Then she fled out of the room in tears.

I wanted to throw up. Merril laughed. He said he needed to check on some paperwork in Barbara's bedroom and left the office. He stayed in Barbara's room for a long time.

I sat in Merril's office and tried to process what I'd just seen. My father made every effort to treat his two wives fairly. There was never any explosive tension between them. Audrey's comment about Barbara being Merril's only wife was unsettling. It was clear that when Merril was home, he spent no time with either Faunita or Ruth. When he was away and called home, Barbara was the only wife he talked to. It was also clear that she saw me as a threat. Every time Merril spent the night with me it seemed he'd spend the entire next day making it up to Barbara. I detested being in the middle of conflict—just hated it.

I went into the kitchen to help Ruth make lunch for the preschoolers. Ruth wore her black hair in a tight knot. She looked unhealthy; her face was sunken and hollow. Merril came in after an hour or so and said I wouldn't be traveling with him after all. He and Barbara had decided that I should stay home and help Ruth with the cooking, housework, and laundry. But there was more. "Barbara has decided that Jackson [her nine-month-old son] is old enough to stay at home now. We both feel that you should be the one to take care of him and make sure he has everything he needs while his mother is gone."

I had never taken care of a baby for more than a few hours. My shock gave way to fury as I realized I was a pawn in their game. Barbara called the shots in this family. Merril pretended to wield power but it was a façade. Ultimately, he kowtowed to Barbara's every demand. If she had her way, I'd never go to college.

They left without saying goodbye or giving me any instructions about Jackson. I went to find him when I realized they were gone. He was careening around in a walker in a drenched diaper when I spotted him. I sat beside him, overwhelmed. What was I supposed to do with him? I knew nothing about his schedule, how many bottles a day he took, or how much solid food he ate. His sister, who was not quite six, was watching him. I couldn't believe Barbara hadn't even said goodbye to them or bothered to change his diaper.

Ruth was on a cleaning rampage. She was tearing the house apart, washing walls, scrubbing corners, and emptying shelves. This seemed to be her response to Merril taking me as wife number four. I assumed she was channeling all her emotions into cleaning obsessively and her daughters were being forced to help. She always acted unhappy around me and often when I saw her I thought she looked like she'd just been crying.

Jackson didn't eat much that first day. I began to worry. His stomach felt as hard as a rock. I tried to get him to sleep, but he wouldn't stop crying. I was worried and called Page to speak to Barbara. Nancy told me they had gone to dinner. I said I needed to speak to her as soon as they came back because I was worried about Jackson.

Barbara never called. I stayed up with Jackson almost all night. He was so unhappy and fussy. At 6 A.M. he finally took his bottle and went to sleep. Merril called around eight and asked how Jackson was doing. I said he'd cried most of the night but had finally fallen asleep early that morning. "Well, it sounds like we left him in capable hands," Merril said.

I ignored the compliment and said, "I don't understand why Barbara didn't call last night to tell me what to do with her baby."

Merril corrected me in a condescending tone. "Carolyn, he is *our* baby and as much your responsibility as Barbara's."

I told Merril that I thought Barbara knew a lot more about what her son needed than I did. Merril continued, "That will change. Barbara and I decided last night that it would be good for you to learn how to care for Jackson on your own without interference from either one of us."

I was angry. How could they be so cruel both to Jackson and to me? Then Merril said I was to come to Page the next day and travel with him to Phoenix and California. I felt blindsided. Barbara had made it clear that she didn't want me to travel with Merril. Who was going to take care of Jackson? "That will not be a problem," Merril said. "I will arrange for his care. All you need to worry about is getting ready to come with me."

I was numb from shock and dizzy from the constant changes. There was no time to adjust to anything. I did not want be alone with Merril both day and night. Jackson was up much of the second night and I slept little. When I finally dozed off I slept right through the alarm. I didn't get to Page until midafternoon, but that didn't matter. Merril was running late. Barbara treated me like ice. I'm sure she hated that I was leaving with Merril.

We drove to Flagstaff, where we were to have dinner. But Merril got a migraine en route and could not continue to drive. We checked into a hotel and went to sleep. It was late the next morning before Merril felt well enough to travel. But it was too late. Uncle Roy and the others we were going to meet had already left for California. We went on to Phoenix, where Merril had some business. But late the next day we turned around and went back to Page and then home.

Merril and I didn't talk much in the car. He seemed preoccupied with business. He was always jotting down notes and stopping to make calls. We didn't know each other at all and he didn't seem interested in getting to know me. The risk for him, I suppose, was that if he started to like me, he'd complicate his life with Barbara.

The tension in the household was always high on weekends, especially after I returned from the trip with Merril. Barbara was sulking and refused to come into the house. Merril spent a long time talking to her in her van. After a while he emerged and told me to put her four daughters and son Danny to bed. Merril said he would sleep with me after he took Barbara for a drive.

Barbara had a small nursery off her room with bunk beds for her four daughters. Danny, who was three, had a small bed of his own on the floor. It took me a while to get the children bathed and ready for bed. By that time, Merril and Barbara had returned and were in her bedroom. The girls had heard their mother come in, but it was Danny who ran into her room before I could stop him.

Minutes later, I heard Danny crying. "Mommy, why did you hit me? Why did you hit me, Mommy?" Barbara had been away from her children for an entire week and now, after just a few minutes, was slapping her son for missing her.

I felt guilty. Even though I had no say in the matter, I felt that if Merril hadn't married me, maybe Barbara wouldn't be slapping her son around. I hated the tension and conflict in Merril's family. Every time he did something with me it seemed that the rest of the family paid a price.

I got into bed and felt sick at the thought that I might never have a relationship with a man other than Merril. There was nothing natural about an eighteen-year-old woman being married to a fifty-year-old man she knew little about and cared for even less. I didn't know much about sexual intimacy beyond duty and baby making. Maybe it could be pleasurable; there had to be more than fear, dread, and panic. Thankfully, Merril never showed up that night and I just went to sleep.

The next morning I found Audrey and asked her if she could go on another bike ride with me. Half an hour later, we were on our way to the reservoir. It was so early the sun hadn't even come up yet. We sat on a big rock that overlooked the water. Audrey was the only person in the family who had been friendly toward me. I felt she could tell me things that might help me survive.

Audrey was Faunita's daughter. She said that after Barbara married Merril, he stopped sleeping with Faunita. Barbara made it clear to him that she would be the only wife with whom he had a sexual relationship.

Merril's first two marriages were disasters, according to Audrey. His marriage to Faunita—his first—had been arranged by the prophet because at the time Merril, who was then in his twenties, was in love with someone else but she was not a member of the FLDS. Her parents were adamantly opposed to her marrying into a religious cult. But Merril persisted. He felt her parents would eventually relent if he kept dating her.

The prophet, Uncle Roy, told Merril this would never work and ordered him to marry Faunita. Merril balked. But several months later he was reprimanded by the prophet for being disobedient about his assigned marriage and told that God was not pleased with his actions.

Audrey said that Merril was forced into marrying her mother, which he did. But he refused to have sex with her. Somehow Uncle Roy learned the truth about their marriage and reprimanded Merril again. He ordered him to be a husband to Faunita and give up the idea of having the other woman. Merril realized he had lost his true love and blamed Faunita. This was the source of his deep aggression toward her.

After several terrible years with Faunita, Audrey said, Merril was forced to marry Ruth. He resisted this marriage as well, until he was reprimanded by the prophet and forced to wed. Ruth had never been emotionally stable. Audrey said she'd had two breakdowns before she even married Merril. She was exceedingly fragile, and Merril had zero interest in having a real relationship with her.

Barbara—who was Ruth's half sister—entered the picture when Merril was thirty-eight and she was eighteen. Audrey said Barbara was hotheaded and thought Merril was a joke of a man. But after two unhappy marriages to women he had no interest in, Merril was ready for something else. Barbara and Merril both loved power and domination and didn't care who got hurt in the process.

Faunita stood up for herself initially and refused to be bullied by Barbara. Barbara accused her of being rebellious and jealous. Barbara said if she really wanted to be in sync with her husband's will, she would not object to his refusal to have sex with her.

I still couldn't understand how Barbara could have so much power over Merril. Audrey said that Merril was captivated by her and fascinated by everything she did, even if it involved bullying his other wives and children. They had a perverse chemistry.

When Barbara came onto the scene, Merril's house was in chaos. She took control and was skilled in manipulating him. In the early years of the marriage, when Merril took a trip with another wife

Barbara would explode and get into a physical confrontation with the other wife who was left behind—or else she'd just disappear.

Audrey said that Barbara had her sights set on me. "She will make it so miserable for father and so hard on him every time he is around you that pretty soon he will cave in and she will be his only wife." In my few short weeks in the family, I'd already observed that Barbara never let Merril out of her sight. She monitored his every move.

"He still sleeps with Ruth, but only enough to keep her pregnant," Audrey said. "Ruth has his most beautiful children, which is why they still have sex." Audrey also told me that another reason Merril tried to keep Ruth pregnant was that she was more stable during her pregnancies than she was at any other time. Then she paused before continuing. "But Barbara uses Ruth as her slave. She orders her around and violently scolds her for the smallest of errors." Ruth was completely subservient to Barbara because she had been so beaten down by her abusive bullying. Barbara would often accuse Ruth of being jealous of her and of not being in harmony with Merril.

The sunrise stretched across the reservoir in colorful stripes. Listening to Audrey made me feel like I'd been sentenced to a hellish world where I might well spend the rest of my life. I couldn't comprehend what was happening to me.

Audrey told me about a time when Faunita had stood up to Merril about Barbara's bullying. Merril locked her in the upstairs of the house and locked everyone else downstairs. Audrey and the other children heard Faunita screaming as Merril beat her. The next morning, Faunita was covered with bruises. She told Audrey, "Your father did this to me. He beat me with a mop." Audrey screamed, "I hate him! I hate him." Faunita grabbed her and said, "Don't you ever say that about your father. He is a good man." There were many more times, Audrey said, when Merril beat her mother; some were so bad that Faunita couldn't see or hear for three days.

In the FLDS culture, a man's wife is his property and he can do whatever he wants to do to her. If a woman complains about violence or abuse, everyone turns on her. The assumption is that she's disobedient. It's always her fault. It's a huge disgrace if your husband beats you. So women rarely speak about abuse because once they do, they're considered rebellious.

Audrey said Merril had not become physically abusive to Faunita until after his marriage to Barbara. Barbara also encouraged Merril to attack his children. Audrey said Barbara had something she called her "beating board" and would lash out at her children when it pleased her. Nor did she have any apparent qualms about physically abusing Faunita's and Ruth's children. Merril never curbed her brutality.

It took Barbara eighteen months until Merril agreed to stop sleeping with Faunita, according to Audrey. Faunita was all of thirty-two. Barbara didn't mind that Merril kept having relations with Ruth because she was her half sister and so their children were blood relatives. This carried a lot of weight in FLDS families because the majority always had an advantage. The majority could be your children and those of your half sister. Merril's family was dominated by Steeds because Ruth and Barbara were both Steeds.

Audrey said every time her mother stood up to Merril, he became violent and beat her down, either physically or emotionally. Eventually Faunita became so defeated she started sleeping all day and watching television at night. It was the only way to escape Barbara's domination. Her older children then took care of their younger siblings, some of whom were still in grade school.

Audrey told me that there were times when she'd find her mother unconscious from an overdose of medication. Audrey would run to her father screaming that her mother was dead, but he refused to even check on her. It was traumatic for Audrey.

Barbara's tyranny had ruled the family for fourteen years. Everyone in the family feared her and no one dared stand up to her. Audrey said the family's only hope was that their father would fall in love with another woman and that the new relationship would strip Barbara of her absolute power. I asked Audrey, "How could your father ever fall in love with a new wife if he's never allowed even to be around her and if she's forced to submit to Barbara's abuse?"

Audrey was silent. She had no answer to that question. But she was sure of one thing: "You have to find a way to get Father to have feelings for you. If you don't, then you will not survive any better than Ruth or my mother."

I was touched by Audrey's willingness to map out the family dynamics for me. At least I had one friend in the family.

But as we pedaled back home from the reservoir I knew I didn't want Merril to fall in love with me. The last thing I wanted to do was be strapped down to a man nearly three times older than I was. In my heart of hearts, I just wanted to go to school. But I didn't say this to Audrey. Despite everything she'd told me, I knew she worshipped her father.

I had to start school as soon as possible. I would see if there were classes I could take that summer at the university in Cedar. If I waited until fall, I might be forced into working full-time for Merril or Barbara, which would be a disaster. My only real hope was carving out some semblance of a career that would enable me to keep my life separate from Barbara and Merril's.

When Audrey and I got back home, Merril was upstairs in his office drinking coffee. When he saw me he said, "Hello, Carolyn. I have been looking for you this morning. Where have you been?" Barbara, who was beside him, stiffened. I could tell by the look on her face that she couldn't stand the idea that her husband was concerned about my whereabouts.

"Oh, Audrey and I went for a long bike ride and stopped off at the reservoir for a while." Merril nodded.

I was determined to talk to him that weekend about school. Sunday night was my first opportunity. He came into my room and said he would be staying there that night. This was my moment. I told Merril there was a two-week course at Southern Utah University. I could stay at my uncle's and everything would be safe and simple.

Merril was uncomfortable with the idea. He said he hadn't had a chance to really get to know me and wasn't sure I should go to school this soon. In fact, he said, he wasn't sure I should go to college at all.

My heart sank. He could see the disappointment in my face. I looked stricken when he said that there might be a better way for me to fit into his life than by going to college. The sex between us was as empty and meaningless as always.

But by the time Merril was ready to return to Page the next morning, the situation had completely reversed itself. I think that Barbara's jealousy might have worked to my advantage. She wanted me out of the house. Suddenly Merril thought school was a fine idea. He gave me a check to sign up for classes.

When Merril came home the next weekend, he called several of his daughters into his office. I later learned that he told them he was afraid I might get into trouble if I went there on my own. Several daughters volunteered to go with me and report what I did back to him.

I learned this the next morning from Audrey. I was furious. "How dare he talk to his daughters about what I should or shouldn't do! It's none of their business." Audrey agreed with me. "But I don't think my sisters who volunteered to monitor you at school really want to be involved with tattling on you. They just want to get a chance to go to college. If they agree to keep tabs on you, this is a ticket to school for them."

I hadn't thought of that aspect. Audrey continued. "Carolyn, we all want to go to college, but there is just no way Father would ever allow any of his daughters to do it. But he would under these conditions. I heard he is thinking of buying you a car and talked about letting you register for the whole summer quarter."

"Did he really say that?" I asked. I had only talked to Merril about the two-week course. I was so happy. But I hid my joy. I wasn't sure how Audrey would interpret it, nor did I know how realistic this option really was. Audrey said it was her other sisters who'd encouraged Merril to let me go for more than just the two-week course because they were eager to go to college, too.

Late that afternoon, Merril came home and asked me to come into Barbara's bedroom. I noticed a new picture on her wall of a sad puppy. They asked me to sit down on a stool beside the bed. Barbara caught me looking at the picture. "I purchased that picture the week you married Merril. When the two of you were gone on your trip I felt like the puppy does in that picture."

I had no response.

Merril began by saying, "Carolyn, I guess you are wondering why I sent for you. I've been thinking about that class you talked to me about last weekend. When I gave you permission to take it, I gave no thought to what you would do for a car. I'm embarrassed to say that my family doesn't have a decent car, except the one I'm driving."

I listened, barely breathing in anticipation of what might be coming next.

"It doesn't make sense to buy a car for a two-week class. So, if you like, I'll buy you a car now, and you can take the course and start college in the fall, or, if you are eager to get started, it's all right for you to start this summer."

I smiled, trying to contain my emotions. I was so excited! Few women in the FLDS at that time had their own cars, and even fewer were allowed to live independently of their families. But apparently Merril was willing to do that, too.

"I guess we'll have to find you an apartment in Cedar. In considering the expense, I realized it is going to cost me nearly the same amount to send you to college as it would to send two of my daughters along with you. So I've decided to use this opportunity to give two of my daughters an education."

We then went into town and bought two cars—one for me and one for Merril's daughter Nancy, who worked at Page. I would have a week more at home before school started.

As Merril and Barbara were leaving on Monday morning, Barbara's four small daughters asked him if they could sleep with me while they were gone. Millie, Barbara's four-year-old, already did. Now her sisters wanted to, as well. The girls pleaded, and Merril relented. But I didn't have enough space in my room for them, so Merril asked me to sleep in Barbara's bed that week with her daughters. Seven days and counting. I agreed.

I was elated and sleeping better than I had since my marriage two months before. Relief had swept over me and my future did not feel as terrifying or claustrophobic.

A few days later, I was deep in sleep when someone shook me. "Carolyn, wake up. I have to talk to you." I sat up in bed. I recognized Audrey's voice but couldn't see her because the room was pitch black. I flipped on a light by the bed. Audrey looked shaken. Her face seemed tense, her body, stiff.

"Audrey, what's wrong?" I said in a whisper. "Has something happened?"

"Yes, something is terribly wrong. Oh, Carolyn, I have been assigned to marry someone. Father called me early today and told me."

This was shocking news. "Who are they making you marry?"

Audrey looked at me with desperate eyes. "It's someone I don't really know and he's younger than I. Maybe he's a nice guy. But I'm in love with someone else. I've been trying and trying to get Father to take me to see the prophet so I could ask to marry the man I love."

I didn't know how to comfort Audrey. She was speaking forbidden words. It was not allowed in the FLDS for a young woman to get her heart set on marrying a man of her own choosing. Occasionally a young girl would tell the prophet that she felt she belonged to a certain man, but she would always also insist that what she wanted most was to do the Lord's will, saying something like "I want to be by this man's side in marriage if it is where I belong."

Marriage in the FLDS was always a divine revelation. The prophet received the news and then told the lucky couple. Audrey's love for a man she didn't belong to was something that could get her into a lot of trouble and bring disgrace to Merril's family.

A woman could only see the prophet with her husband or father. It was impossible for a woman to see him alone—even someone like Audrey, who was already twenty. Merril had agreed to take her to the prophet, but he never came home in time to make it happen and the meetings kept getting cancelled.

"I feel like my whole life is ending. If I could have had one opportunity to talk to the prophet I would feel different about what is happening," she said. I could certainly relate—my world had collapsed when I was forced to marry Merril, even though I wasn't in love with someone else. "I have to do this. There is no other option now." Audrey paced around the room. "If I refuse this man there is no way I'd be allowed to marry the other man, anyway. I will only bring disgrace on Father's family."

Complicating matters was the fact that the man Audrey was in love with already had one wife. She could marry him only if the prophet assigned Audrey to him, which was unlikely since he now had plans for her to marry someone else. She would be seen as being in rebellion if she made her wishes known now.

Her husband-to-be came to the house a day or two later and took her on a hike. (He had Merril's permission to do so.) His name was Merlin. When Audrey returned home she found me and we went into my bedroom, where she cried. "He was really nice to me, but every time I look at him, I see him as the man who is stealing my future happiness." I listened but knew there was really nothing to say. The trap had closed on her, too. The once-radiant nuss princess now felt she was condemned to marry a nobody.

On Sunday, I left for college. Audrey was married during the week. Merril didn't attend the civil marriage. Faunita was sick, so she missed her daughter's wedding. Ruth went but told Audrey she had to accept the prophet's will.

The next day was the religious wedding, when Audrey and Merlin were married by the prophet. All of her parents went except me. (Even though I was two years younger than Audrey I was considered one of her mothers.) When I saw the wedding photos, Merlin and Audrey both looked miserable.

At the reception, everyone from the community brought gifts and Audrey's sisters sang songs. These big parties were great fun for everyone else, but not for the couple, especially the bride. Audrey had tried to cancel the reception because she didn't think she could be around so many people celebrating her marriage. She was traumatized, humiliated, and in despair. But Merlin wanted to celebrate his marriage, and the reception went ahead as planned.

When I came home that weekend, Audrey told me everything when we went on our long bike ride. She didn't think she could ever learn to love Merlin. As we pedaled toward the reservoir she said, "If I have to live my entire life with a man who I can never love, then why couldn't I have at least married someone of importance, as you did? Why did I, the daughter of an important man, get stuck marrying a nobody?"

"Audrey," I said, "I would have loved to have married a nobody who was my age or someone younger. I envy what you have. At least Merlin acts like he does love you. You can have a relationship with him if you decide to. I will never have a relationship with a man in my entire life and this will never change. Even if I wanted to, Barbara would never allow it. At least no one is trying to sabotage you and make you a bad person."

Audrey couldn't see that her marriage was more desirable than mine. Word got around the community that she was mistreating him because she was in love with someone else. The rumors didn't seem to bother Audrey, but they brought disgrace to Merril's family, which he could not abide. He let her know that she had to do whatever it took to stop the rumors.

Pregnancy seemed like the quick fix. Audrey told me that if she had a baby, it would stop the rumors. She told me that she thought if she had a baby with Merlin, she might learn to love him. She thought this even though she knew that once she had a child with Merlin she'd be trapped forever as his wife.

But a few weeks after the pregnancy push began, Merlin got a job with a construction company out of town. Audrey asked me if she could go to school with me in the fall.

School had given me a good focus. I'd finished my two-week class and was about to start the summer quarter. I told Audrey I thought it was a great idea. Her little sister Lenore was going to be living with me, but more as a spy. The idea of living with a friend seemed almost too good to be true.

Audrey told her husband that this was something she'd always wanted to do, and moved ahead without getting his consent. He wanted Audrey to be happy and didn't give her a hard time.

Merril was another story. He had somehow learned that after her marriage Audrey had been writing letters to the man she really loved. He was outraged. Once he'd driven by the man's house and saw Audrey standing next to her bike and talking to him. Merril told her God had chosen a good man for her and she needed to give up her idea of running away to college.

But Merlin saved her. He told Merril he had no objections to her going to school and thought a little space might help her. Merlin was basically a very decent guy who seemed to genuinely care about Audrey. Merril's opposition dissolved, and Audrey made plans to start college with me in September.

I still had to survive the summer. Lenore was making my life difficult. She monitored everything I did and would report back to her father, hoping to score points with him.

We lived about five miles from school, and one of the things Lenore did to pick fights with me was to "forget" to pick me up even though we were sharing my car. The first few times it happened I was annoyed. Once I saw that it had become a pattern, I realized it was deliberate and abusive. I told Merril that Lenore was trying to hurt my grades. He said my accusations were unjust.

Merril and I had several more heated discussions about this over the phone. Conflict between Merril and me created glory for Lenore in the family. When we went home on weekends, Barbara would reward her by taking her shopping and treating Lenore like her best friend. Lenore now had status in the family. She'd gone from a nobody to someone special.

Lenore soon started bragging to her sisters about how she had been treating me at college. They envied the attention she was getting from Merril as a result. Merril seemed obsessed with the idea that I'd get in trouble at school and damage his reputation within the community.

After a few weeks I changed my strategy. Complaining about Lenore was backfiring. It gave Lenore attention she craved and gave Merril a reason to scold me and say I was a bad person. Instead, I put on a happy face, and when I spoke to Merril by phone I told him everything was fine, just fine.

Once I stopped complaining about her, neither Merril nor Barbara had reason to congratulate her. I acted as though she didn't exist. I found some cousins who were also taking classes and they agreed to give me a ride home. I explained that Lenore and I had scheduling conflicts and they were happy to help out.

That night, Lenore told Merril I refused to ride home with her. When she finished speaking to him, she pranced into the room and told me to come to the phone. Merril demanded to know what was going on. I said I'd simply made other arrangements since Lenore had been unable to pick me up. This seemed easier, and I thought everyone would be happy.

Merril exploded. "You're the only one that is happy about this! Embarrassing me like this is terrible. I want you to ride home with Lenore and nobody else." I was perfectly acquiescent. I started having my cousins drop me off a few blocks from the apartment so Lenore would think that I had walked. I was too embarrassed to tell my cousins what was really going on. I would always wait at the arranged place and sometimes Lenore would come to pick me up. If she did not, I knew my cousins would come for me within forty-five minutes.

Merril called every night. I told him that everything was fine. This drove Lenore right up the wall. How could she be rewarded for abusing me if I didn't complain?

Her grades slipped. I had cut her out of my life and found other friends. Lenore was isolated and very unhappy. One day I heard her call Barbara at Page. "Carolyn thinks she's so much better than I am. She treats me like I am total scum and refuses to talk to me." Listening to Lenore's meltdown, I almost felt sorry for her. She was a pawn in Barbara and Merril's game. They were using her to do their dirty work and betraying her in the process.

A few hours after her teary call with Barbara, Merril called and talked to Lenore for several hours. The next day, several of her sisters arrived to spend the rest of the week with us. This worked to my advantage because Lenore took a break from torturing me to enjoy her sisters.

But in the long run, nothing changed. Lenore complained to them that I was mistreating her and that she was all alone. Her grades were suffering because I was so mean. She was only going to school to assist Father. Poor Lenore.

Where she succeeded was in changing the dynamic at home. Merril's other nine teenage daughters now aligned themselves against me. They were rude to me and demanded explanations from me for my actions. Their stance was that they knew their father and what he wanted. I reminded them that I was, in fact, one of their mothers and it was their job to answer to me, not the reverse. They didn't care. What they wanted was the kind of preferential treatment that Lenore was not getting, and they also wanted Barbara's approval.

Before I married Merril, they'd competed with Barbara for Merril's attention. Now by turning the tables against me, they were Barbara's allies, not her adversaries.

What confused them, though, was that when Merril came home for the weekends, he still wanted to spend time with me. Once I settled into classes at Cedar, he made it a point to get there on Mondays. He'd come when Lenore was at class so he could have sex with me and then take me to dinner. Lenore would return and realize we were gone.

Merril's daughters soon saw that despite their abuse of me, I was still getting rewards from their father. So there was a shift in tactics. His daughters started reporting to Barbara. She would listen intensely, praise them, and see that they got special treatment or a favor.

There was little that I did that they could fault, and I refused to fight with them, so they began to make things up. They also rifled my bedroom at home and stole my sheet music and country and western tapes, turning them in to their father.

When Merril approached me with the evidence, I went through the roof. I think he was shocked at my anger. I told him that allowing his daughters to invade my privacy was going too far and he had to put a stop to it.

"It's up to me to decide who can go through your things," he replied. "If there is something inappropriate, it should be brought to my attention."

I shot back, "If those are the conditions of living here, then maybe I will have to leave this house. I am not willing to live this way."

Merril showed no emotion. The last thing he could do would be to act as though I had any impact on him. "You are to do what I say. If you are doing the things I want you to do, then there should be no problems with other family members going through your things because there will be nothing to find."

I turned and went into my bedroom. I decided to go through my belongings and give everything that might create conflict with Merril to my friends. He hated turtleneck sweaters because they showed the shape of my bust, so I never wore them around him, but I'd kept them. I also had several sheer blouses that I never dared wear around him. But rather than risk having them confiscated, I gave them away to friends. I also began to lock my bedroom door.

This was like adding kerosene to a smoldering fire. Soon there were flames. Merril asked me why I was locking my bedroom door. "Your daughters need to respect me enough to give me some privacy."

Merril said he'd given his daughters permission to pick the lock on my door. "No one in my family has the right to hide things from me," he said.

I told him there was nothing in my room to find. But invading my privacy was abusive. Merril accused me of not being in harmony with him. I surely was not, but I kept my mouth shut.

The following weekend when I came back from college, I found that some of my personal items were missing from my room. They were nowhere to be found. I went to Merril and said they'd been stolen. "Carolyn, saying things have been stolen is a strong accusation. There is nothing that you have that doesn't belong to me. If someone in my family needs something, you should not begrudge their taking it."

I couldn't believe what I was hearing. He was giving his daughters a free pass to rob me blind. I left Merril's home that morning and spent the entire weekend at my father's house. I returned to Merril's to sleep, but nothing else. I refused to go to church with Merril's family, and late Sunday told Lenore I was going back to school. She could come with me that night or make other plans. She stomped off.

Merril called me that night in Cedar and asked where I'd been all weekend. He complained that I hadn't checked in with him before going back to school. I made light of his concerns and told him that I'd gone back early to study for exams.

After that first weekend, I made it a habit to leave on Sunday night for college. I spent as much time away from Merril's family as I could. I stopped cooking on weekends. I stopped coming home and trying to help Ruth clean house. I continued to lock my bedroom door. It improved my life immensely. I was out of Barbara's line of fire, which reduced the pressure on me. If I was doing something in the house, she would find any reason to correct me. "Father wants the chairs put up on the table before the floor is swept." "Father wants you to improve X." "Father likes it when you do Y this way." It was all about power and domination. I opted out, which was seen as outright rebellion. Now Barbara could go to Merril with further proof of my unworthiness as a wife. For her it was a win no matter what I did. When I realized that, I just did what was going to be best for me.

What Audrey had told me on our first bike ride to the reservoir was true. Barbara would do anything she could to undermine me. Ruth eventually came to me and asked me why I wasn't helping her more on weekends with the cleaning. I told her it was because I had a lot of studying to do. She said I should do it during the week and help the family when I was home. Her complaints were soon echoed by Merril's daughters. I was purposely not studying during the week at Cedar to avoid helping out around the house on weekends.

Merril's daughters retaliated with one of the few weapons they had left: wash time. It might not sound like much to someone on the outside of our world, but in a large family, wash time was sacrosanct. When I would go to use a machine at my allotted time, I'd find one of Merril's daughters doing her laundry. There would be a lame excuse—she'd missed her time and had no clothes. I knew if I complained, Merril would side with his daughters, so I didn't.

Audrey came to my rescue. She was coming home to wash her clothes, and she shared whatever time she had with me. By stepping in and protecting me, she made the other girls disdainful. They began making fun of her and said it was no wonder God had cursed her. She had been a disobedient daughter, and that was why she'd been given to a man of no importance. Audrey had never participated with the other girls in abusing me and or hurting others. But for her to actually *protect* me was seen by them as an outright betrayal.

One Saturday morning Merril called everyone for morning prayers. When I didn't show up, he sent one of his daughters to find me. My bed was empty because I'd gone for an early morning bike ride. But she lied and told Merril I was still in bed and refused to come to prayers.

Merril said it was obvious that I had no interest in doing what my husband wanted, and he berated me in front of his family.

After prayers, he walked out of the house to go to breakfast with some other men. He saw me ride my bike into the yard. When I went to put it away, he approached me. He began laughing. "I was told this morning you were sleeping and refusing to get up. I just told the entire family you were a lazy pig with no interest in doing what your husband wants."

I didn't know why he was telling me this. Was he trying to intimidate me? He'd smeared me to his family and now was making it into a big joke.

I told him it was too bad he felt this way toward me.

I walked toward the house without turning back. I was beyond disgusted with Merril and his family. I had figured out, though, that if I wanted to be able to smart off to him, I had to start right from the beginning of the marriage. I'd never get away with it if I waited and started later.

I knew that when Merril attacked me, it was like dumping blood and chum in the water and that the sharks would soon swim around. But how much worse could it really get?

I was in my bedroom for a few minutes when I heard a knock on the door. It was one of Barbara's daughters asking me to come to the kitchen to meet with her. I told the child I'd be there in a moment. Two minutes later she was back. "Mother wants to invite you to help her and all of the girls in cleaning the kitchen." I told her I had a few things to finish first.

I locked my door and climbed out my bedroom window and went to my father's house, where I remained for the rest of the day. I knew there would be repercussions for my misbehavior, but it was better than being the family scapegoat. My family knew how unhappy I was in my marriage but offered little consolation. My parents didn't like to see me upset, but they also believed that my marriage was a revelation from God.

When I came home that night Merril stormed into my room while I was getting ready for bed. He began hounding me about why I'd refused to help Barbara with cleaning the kitchen. I said I hadn't refused. I had explained I had a few things to finish before I could help. Merril tried to provoke me into an argument with him. But I kept thinking of Audrey's stories of how he'd attacked Faunita, and I resisted getting drawn into any confrontations. He finally left, and I closed my bedroom door, relieved that he hadn't slapped me.

Thankfully, he didn't stay with me that weekend or visit me in Cedar after the weekend. I was relieved by the absence of stress. The next weekend, he came and spent a night with me, but never again would we spend Saturday and Sunday nights together as we usually had. There were times when he would sneak into my room in the middle of the night and have sex with me while Barbara was asleep. He returned to her room right away and she never even knew.

But even though Merril was spending less time with me, it didn't decrease the pressure on me or the abuse directed toward me from everyone else in the house except the children.

# Tragedy

**F**our months after my marriage I was finishing up my final summer classes at Cedar and feeling reasonably grounded. While Merril's family seemed dark, strange, and complicated, I knew that if I could stay in college and carve out a place for myself in the world, it would offset the other realities I had to deal with as wife number four.

In the middle of my final week, Lenore got a phone call from home with the news that the prophet had decided her sister Rebecca would marry Rulon, a young man in the community who was in his early twenties.

Rebecca, at nineteen, was a year older than I, and now that she had been assigned in marriage, all of Merril's remaining unmarried daughters were my age or younger. Lenore got permission from Merril to go home for Rebecca's marriage, which was taking place the next day. I stayed at school to keep studying, relieved that I didn't have to change my final exams again as I had to do when I married.

Even though I wasn't there, the stories reached me about Rulon and Rebecca. He hadn't met her before he found out she'd been assigned to him. When he went over to Merril's house for the first time, all of Merril's daughters waited in the office. Rulon arrived, not knowing which daughter was to be his bride.

Rulon, who was shy and apparently almost stuttering, said, "Is Rebecca here?" One of the girls said, "Yes, she is, and she is right there." She then pointed to the youngest sister in the room. That girl quickly exclaimed, "It's not me, it's her!" before pointing to someone else who looked way too young for marriage, even in the FLDS. Rulon looked red and embarrassed when he realized the game that was being played at his expense. Finally Rebecca stood up laughing and said, "Yes, I am here. I'm the one you have come for."

Rebecca was one of Merril's and Ruth's most beautiful daughters. She had long black hair and green eyes. She had a vibrant and engaging personality. But she was stunned by her arranged marriage, I later learned. She simply told Rulon that her sisters were heartbroken that she was leaving the family and couldn't resist giving him a hard time. They were married the next day.

I went home, eager to settle into the few quiet days of August that remained. When I had free time I would try to go over to my father's home and help out with the children. Ever since my marriage, it had been difficult for my mother to adjust to having less help around the house. There were still nine small children at home.

One slow, sultry day in August, my sixteen-year-old sister, Annette, offered to take the children on a picnic to a place we called Indian Bathtubs. It was about five miles from town where big rocks with holes in them caught the rainwater. It was peaceful and safe, the perfect place for a picnic with a lot of little children. My cousin Bonnie brought six of her siblings and Annette brought nine of hers. All fifteen children were loaded in the back of my father's pickup truck and left for the day.

The kids loved riding in the truck, even though the hot, dusty wind that blew across the desert plateau we lived on kicked up sand that stung their eyes and made a mess of their hair. Annette was driving, and Bonnie kept her eye on the children through the open window that faced the back of the truck.

Suddenly the truck came over a crest on the road and hit a bump. Even though it wasn't going too fast, the truck flipped when it hit an embankment of sand and landed with an enormous thud on top of several children.

The children trapped under the truck were panicked and

those who had been thrown from it were screaming in terror. The truck was smoking. Annette told me later she knew it was going to explode.

She and Bonnie ran to the truck and lifted it so the other children could pull their siblings out. Some of the children were injured themselves but nevertheless tried to do what they could to extricate their siblings from the wreckage. Most of the children were under six but still tried with all their might to do what they could.

Annette thought she had everyone out from under the truck when she saw Nurylon's lifeless body. Nurylon was my two-year-old sister and my mother's namesake. We looked like identical twins, even though we were sixteen years apart. Annette grabbed Nurylon and took her to the side of the road, away from the truck, and frantically began doing CPR, trying to breathe oxygen and life back into her body. She heard a gurgling in her lungs and thought it might be a sign of life, so she breathed even harder into the limp child.

The truck exploded. The children screamed in terror. The heat from the blast radiated back toward the injured. The fourteen children watched as flames consumed the truck and as Annette kept up her desperate efforts to save Nurylon. She finally quit when she realized she was having no impact. Nurylon's limp body held no signs of life.

Annette and Bonnie had to get help for the fourteen surviving children. Some seemed to have serious injuries, even though they were breathing. But what to do? No one had cell phones in those days, and they were also no longer on the main road. Help would come only if someone ran for it.

Christopher, my six-year-old brother, did not seem as injured as the rest. One arm seemed to be broken, but despite that he had managed to pull his siblings out from under the truck with the other one. Christopher volunteered to go to town for help. "I will run there as fast as I can and tell someone what happened!"

Annette wasn't comfortable sending a six-year-old child on a five-mile run for help, but she and Bonnie had to stay with the injured.

Christopher was a capable little boy, but he was still very little. Annette told him to watch out for cars and stop the first one he saw.

Christopher ran most of the way. My father had a business at the edge of town where he built modular homes that were shipped to different housing projects. A man there spotted Christopher and listened to him blurt out his story. One of the other men on the job radioed for help, and the volunteer fire and ambulance crews headed down the road, unsure of what they'd find.

Christopher told them that the truck had blown up and that Nurylon was dead. A radio call went out for another ambulance crew.

While waiting for help to arrive, Annette saw four-year-old JR, who seemed to have a broken arm and collarbone, huddling over the body of his dead sister. He was trembling from pain and trauma, tears making tracks down his dust-covered cheeks. He was Nurylon's full brother—a shy and introspective child who seemed to live for his little sister. From the moment she was born, she'd seemed to belong to him. He got her up every morning and wouldn't eat unless she was next to him or sleep unless she was beside him. He taught her how to walk, and then to run.

The first ambulance that came screaming down the road was from Hurricane. Someone had seen smoke in the distance and called for help. The ambulance crew was overwhelmed by what it found: fourteen injured and terrified children and the body of a little girl.

The paramedics examined Nurylon first. When they realized there was nothing more that could be done, they covered her with a small blanket. The paramedics said her injuries were so massive she probably died instantly. The ambulance left with Nurylon's body and the two most seriously injured children.

The ambulance radioed ahead to the hospital about the number of children arriving. The hospital in St. George had a small ER and not enough doctors to treat fourteen kids with an array of injuries. Off-duty docs were called in to lend a hand.

My father got to the hospital before my mother arrived. He was taken to see Nurylon's body. The hospital had called the mortuary. My father refused to let anyone else take her there. My father insisted on doing it himself. The hospital staff helped him to his car and he put Nurylon in the backseat wrapped in a blanket. When my father carried her into the mortuary, his face was flooded in tears.

My mother was told about the accident by someone from the volunteer fire department. She went immediately to the hospital.

My mother held herself together at the hospital. She was in shock. Her daughter was dead and eight other children were injured, some of whom were hers and others who were Rosie's. At one point when a doctor was working on Karen's leg my mother made a comment about how hard this was, and the doctor exploded, "You think this is hard on you!" The stress of seeing so many injured children was overwhelming, and all of this had happened because they were riding in an open truck. Miraculously, no one needed to be hospitalized overnight. There were some broken bones, bad bruises, and cuts that needed stitches, but nothing that was more severe or life-threatening.

That night Annette gave JR a bath. He was still shaking from trauma. He looked at her with his luminous brown eyes and said, "Why did you do it? Why did you kill Nurylon?"

Annette fell apart. She had managed to make it through that hellish day by doing each next thing that needed to be done. JR's question slayed her. She began to sob and could not stop. Her pain exploded with the guilt that all of this was her fault. Her sister was dead, her siblings were injured, and she was sure that she was the one who deserved the blame. No one would ever offer her any solace or commend her for staying calm and rescuing children from under the truck. No one would ever tell Annette and Bonnie that they'd saved lives by making the children move away from the truck before it exploded. Annette's valor and determination in trying to save Nurylon with CPR would never be acknowledged. No one ever said that it was an accident—as random as a bolt of lightning across an evening sky.

I was in one of my last classes when I saw that my cousin Valerie was standing outside the classroom. I couldn't imagine why she'd come. Her sister Lee Ann was in the class with me and went out to the hallway first. Lee Ann turned away when she saw me approaching. Valerie just looked at me and said, "Carolyn, there has been an accident and your little sister Nurylon was killed." Lee Ann was crying when she turned around. Six of her brothers and sisters had been in the accident.

My mind went blank. I was shocked. I could not find words to assemble into sentences. My face asked the questions I could not.

Valerie spoke calmly. She told me a few details of the accident and that all the children were safe except for Nurylon. "God was definitely there, protecting them. It was a miracle that Nurylon was the only one killed. Everyone else will make a full recovery."

The death of my beloved sister didn't feel like a miracle to me. It was fortunate that the other children survived, but I was blindsided by the news that Nurylon was gone.

Nurylon and I were far apart in years but indescribably close. Everyone said that she was a carbon copy of me. I found her death incomprehensible. No one close to me had ever died before. Nothing seemed crueler than the loss of a child.

I went back to my apartment and packed a few things for the ride home. Someone volunteered to call my professors and explain that I would need to reschedule my exams.

When I walked into Merril's house, no one said anything to me, even though everyone knew about the accident. Rebecca had been married earlier that day and her sisters were sad that she was gone. I felt so alone. I didn't belong in this family, and this family didn't belong in my life. My loss seemed to widen and deepen the gulf between us.

Merril and Barbara had gone to dinner to celebrate Rebecca's wedding. Ruth, Rebecca's mother, was left behind to fix dinner for the rest of the family. I didn't offer to help her cook. I just wanted to go to my father's house. I needed to feel his strength and his protection.

When I walked into the house, my brothers and sisters came to greet me. Some had casts on their arms, others on their legs, and all had bruises in various shades of black and blue.

That night a family arrived from the other side of the religious divide with loaves of freshly baked bread. I invited them in, and they hugged my mother and offered us all words of consolation. The communal pain we all shared transcended our religious differences.

The outpouring of sympathy ran like a strong river. The next day our yard was filled with families raking, hoeing, and cleaning every corner of the yard. Windows were being washed, both inside and outside our house. The kitchen counters were laden with food. People brought soup, roast beef for sandwiches, and rolls for the freezer. It was touching to see how much people cared and how generous they were in reaching out to my family.

I returned home that night to Merril's house. He never said a word to me about my sister's death. Never.

We believed in the FLDS principle that death, like everything else, was God's will. It was God's will that Nurylon was taken and that the other children survived. There was no such thing as an untimely death. Sadness was acceptable during the immediate aftermath, but questioning God was not.

God had the right to give and the right to take away. We believed that Nurylon was too pure for this world and that God had taken her back. She had known she would be with us for only a short time. For any of us to mourn in a prolonged way would be detrimental to her progress to celestial glory. We believed that the dead go to the spirit world, where they remain until they are resurrected. If our family held on to her in our grief, our attachment to her spirit would hold her back because she would have too many ties to earth. I had been raised to believe that the death of a family member was actually a blessing because it gave our family a representative on the other side who would try to protect us. That, at least, was the theory, but it gave me no consolation. I wanted my baby sister back—not some special advocate in heaven.

Hundreds came to Nurylon's funeral. It was held in the school-house auditorium, which we used for worship services. After the funeral we walked to the cemetery and, after the grave was blessed, saw Nurylon's small casket lowered into a dark hole in the ground. We stopped talking about her after a week or two. Mourning for any length of time was considered inappropriate.

JR's broken bones healed and the bruises on his face faded. But he was changed forever. He became a reclusive child and didn't interact with anyone in the family very much. He never seemed to bond to any other of his siblings.

Several months later, we were at the cemetery again. My father stood next to another tiny casket with a wife on either side to bury Lehigh, Rosie's infant son, next to Nurylon.

Lehigh was a full-term baby but had been born dead a few days before. The doctors said the cause of death was starvation. I don't know if the placenta failed or how much the trauma of the accident might have affected Rosie's pregnancy. But we were staggering in sorrow once again. The dirt on Nurylon's grave was still fresh.

My mother had lost a daughter who would never see her third birthday. Rosie had lost a son who never took a breath of life. Fall was slowly surrendering to winter. I had never felt more alone as I stood there in the windswept cemetery.

Annette's face looked lifeless as she stood before Lehigh's grave. I stared at her as our baby brother's casket was blessed. I had no sense of how emotionally obliterated she was by the accident. But within a year, she fled the community for the party scene in nearby Mesquite, Nevada. Annette's long blond hair and exquisite blue eyes made her look like a beauty queen, masking her despair and making her popular with those who were just out for a good time.

She disappeared for a few years. It was the only way she felt she could cope with her overwhelming guilt. In time, Annette was able to remake her life and is a loving and excellent mother to four beautiful children.

# Cathleen and Tammy
# Marry Merril

**M**y semester ended in December and I arrived home late on Friday night. I was extremely tired and delighted to learn Merril would not be returning from Page until later Saturday. The next morning I learned that Merril and Barbara had come home during the night. When I saw them in Merril's office that morning, they were drinking coffee and talking. Their suitcases were packed. They were heading to Salt Lake City.

Merril's wife Ruth was with them. It seemed odd that Merril would take Ruth, too. She and Barbara were sisters, but they had a tremendous rivalry. I was suspicious but didn't ask questions. It was a relief to see their van pull out of the driveway and know that I had the weekend to myself—or, I should say, to myself and about four-teen children. Merril had thirty-three, but the rest were older or away for the weekend. I was in charge of everything, but that was still relaxing for me because there was no tension—at least not in the form of confrontations with adults. I knew Merril's daughters would take advantage of his absence to ditch all their chores and hang out with boys on the volleyball court. They knew I wouldn't report them.

Faunita, the other wife who was left behind, was a total recluse. She had ten children, but five were grown and gone. She slept all day and stayed up all night watching television or some of the hundreds of movies she'd recorded on video. She loved Shirley Temple and John Wayne movies. Merril had long since lost interest in her. He never treated her like a wife and they never had sex anymore. She talked about that openly and to everybody.

I spent much of the day doing laundry, which was slow going because we had an old-fashioned industrial-size washing machine. It didn't rinse the clothes. I had to take each load out, rinse them, and spin them in a spinner. Then I hung them on the clothesline to dry. This was very labor-intensive. We had an automatic washer and dryer, but with the volume of clothes that had to be cleaned it was too time-consuming to do dozens of loads of laundry.

Once the children's laundry was on the line, I vacuumed the house, mopped the floors, and dusted. The toddlers tagged along behind me. I loved to cook and was looking forward to making a good dinner and baking cookies for the kids. During the week, when Merril's daughters cooked, we'd eat only what could be thrown together in a few minutes—big bowls of pasta, or rice and raisins with cinnamon sugar and milk. We cooked with little meat. It was mostly used for flavoring sauces or gravies. Nutrition was abysmal. After dinner, I told the children we'd pop popcorn. I looked forward to getting to bed early.

The phone rang just before I started dinner. Merril was tense and abrupt. I was startled because he never talked to me this way. He told me that as soon as he arrived in the city, the new prophet, Rulon Jeffs, sent him to pick up one of the former prophet's wives, Cathleen, and marry her.

Rulon Jeffs had succeeded the prophet Leroy Johnson, whom we called "Uncle Roy." He'd died three weeks before, on November 25, 1986. He was beloved within the FLDS community, which he had led since 1954.

The late prophet had about fourteen wives, and Cathleen was the youngest. She had dark hair and green eyes and was thin and attractive. I immediately thought that Merril would probably want to develop a relationship with her, which meant he might ignore me. Even though I hadn't wanted to marry him and didn't love him, let alone like him, I still believed in the FLDS doctrines and wanted to uphold them. I still believed Merril was the revelation the prophet had received for me. I was destined to bear his children and love and serve Merril Jessop without question until the day he died.

I knew that the only way I could protect myself in my marriage was by remaining of value to Merril. Like every other polygamist wife, I had no say in whom I would marry and no way to divorce my husband if it did not work out. Sex was the only currency I had to spend in my marriage—every polygamist wife knows that. Once we are no longer sexually attractive to our husbands, we are doomed.

A woman's value is assigned in marriage, not earned. We all knew that a woman who is in sexual favor with her husband has a higher value than his other wives. This has enormous significance because a woman's sexual power determines how she will be treated by other wives and how she will be respected by her stepchildren. And because of this, our sex lives were not our own. People knew when you were in favor, and everyone spoke about who was and wasn't sleeping with her husband.

A woman who possesses high sexual status with her husband has more power over his other wives. This means he will listen to her complaints more seriously and will discipline wives she might be angry with. Knowing her husband will enact retribution for her is an enormous weapon for a wife to wield.

Sexual power also will often exempt a wife from physical labor or other family responsibilities. She can make sure that the wives she dislikes or feels might be sexual competitors are assigned the worst jobs and made to work the hardest in the family.

A woman who is no longer physically attractive to her husband is stranded on dangerous grounds. She often winds up as a slave to the dominant wife. She has no voice to report on any shortcomings or abuse in the family. The sexually favored wives will often recruit the children of the less powerful wives and reward them for turning on their biological mothers. It is nothing short of ruthless vengeance.

Every member of a polygamous family knows which wives hold power. When a new wife enters a family, it is imperative for her to establish power with her husband sexually. While there are exceptions, most men routinely change their favorite wives and don't remain loyal to any woman indefinitely.

A woman without any sexual currency to spend may find it difficult to have children. This undermines her future completely. Without children—or with even just a few—a woman has little long-term value to her husband or status within his family. Children are a woman's insurance policy. Even if her husband takes a new and younger wife, a woman who has produced a bevy of beautiful children for him will have respect and status within the family.

The news that Merril was marrying Cathleen made me *fear I'd never become a mother*. Merril had been having frequent sex with me in the seven months we'd been married and I'd not become pregnant. There was no chemistry between us. Sex between us was always cold and devoid of feeling. Merril never removed his long underwear when we had sex. Mine stayed on, too. The bedroom was completely dark. In my seventeen years of marriage, Merril only saw me naked a few times. I never saw him completely unclothed.

He would come to my room late at night after I was asleep and climb on top of me. The sex was perfunctory—without either passion or intimacy. I thought the problem was that Merril was not attracted to me. The news that he was marrying Cathleen so soon after our wedding only confirmed my undesirability.

When the phone call with Merril ended, I sat down on the steps and stared blankly at the wall. I felt as shocked and powerless as I had when I was pulled out of bed at 2 A.M. to hear my father tell me I was going to marry Merril. It felt like my life was at another dead end. Children were the only happiness I could count on.

I knew Merril was lying when he said he hadn't known about the marriage before he went to Salt Lake City. He'd known. Now I understood why Barbara had been so nervous and upset before they left that morning. She must have known about the upcoming nuptials and hated the thought that her husband was marrying again. She had great power with Merril, but not enough to stop him from pursuing his plans. Ruth was too unstable to be suspicious or register what was going on.

It was customary in the FLDS to have a man's wives witness his other weddings. This was called the Law of Sarah, after Abraham's wife, who gave her slave, Hagar, to her husband after she failed to conceive. The presence of the other wives is a way of demonstrating—or pretending—that they are willing to give their husband to another woman.

There is tremendous prestige in marrying a former prophet's wife. It demonstrates to the community that after his death, the prophet sent a divine revelation about whom his wife should marry. For a prophet of God—even a deceased one—to have enough confidence and love for a man to give him one of his wives indicates a man of exceptional character.

In fact, what was beginning to play out was the power grab between Merril and his cousin Truman Barlow. They knew they could enhance their prestige and status within the FLDS by quickly marrying several of Uncle Roy's wives after his death.

Uncle Roy had led the community for thirty-two years. His stepsons preached that he would never die. According to them, he would be at the Second Coming of Christ, when he'd turn over the keys to the priesthood. Uncle Roy had a better grasp on reality and had told my father that he would die and that all men had to as part of the earthly process. Uncle Roy proved to be correct. After his death, Rulon Jeffs took over the sect. He was, at that time, the only one who could do so. He was the only living apostle who had not been excommunicated. The mantle of leadership could go only to him.

Merril and Truman were no fools. A quick marriage to several of Uncle Roy's widows could catapult them into leadership roles in the FLDS hierarchy by signaling that these were the men Uncle Roy loved and trusted most. If they acted fast, his wives would still be in shock and not have a chance to think of whom they might like to marry. As if their wishes mattered!

A prophet's widow generally is not allowed to remarry below the status of her husband. She's usually married off to the new prophet. This tradition goes all the way back to Joseph Smith, the founder of the Mormon Church. When he died he left an abundance of young wives. Those who were willing to do the will of God were remarried to the new prophet, Brigham Young.

Uncle Roy was adamantly opposed to a son marrying one of his father's wives. If his son had taken over the sect, Merril and Truman would have been legally entitled to marry Uncle Roy's wives. But his successor, Rulon Jeffs, was no relation to Uncle Roy. Jeffs was so new that he'd not yet focused on his predecessor's widows. Merril, who'd been Uncle Roy's nephew, and Truman, his stepson, were violating FLDS tradition and practice when they made their move.

As I would soon learn, when Merril and Truman arrived in Salt Lake City, where Uncle Roy had been living, they gathered up the widows they planned to marry and took them to the new prophet, Uncle Rulon. They said the widows wanted to marry them, which was not true. Truman had been the late prophet's right-hand man and insisted he wanted these marriages to happen. Truman had so much credibility because of his close connection to Uncle Roy that Rulon Jeffs sanctioned the marriages.

Merril insisted on the phone that I come to Salt Lake City the next day. He said he'd already made arrangements for my father to drive me there. I balked and said I didn't want to go.

He exploded and said I had no right to challenge him, the man who was my priesthood head. "Do you want to have your way or do you want to be in harmony with your husband? I would think you would want to do the will of the one you belong to! I won't allow you to insist on something else. It will cost you heavily if you do. Falling out of favor with me is not something you want to have happen." When he calmed down he pretended that it was a compliment from my loving husband to include me in the celebration of his newest marriage. He said that as an obedient wife I surely would want to come and please him. I felt like he was tightening the chains around me. I also realized that if I didn't go to Salt Lake City, it would appear that I was angry that my husband had married another woman. One of the worst sins a woman can commit in the FLDS is to resist the will of the prophet in giving her husband another wife. Even *appearing* to be unhappy about the new wife could reflect badly on me.

After Merril's explosion on the phone, I didn't want anything to do with him ever again. I could not have imagined that we would have eight children together. Not then.

The peace of the day was shattered. The relaxing evening at home that I'd looked forward to was ripped apart.

Merril's daughters came home just as I was sitting down to dinner with the small children. We were having soup and rolls that I'd baked. Sheets of unbaked cookies were ready to go in the oven. They noticed the shining house and the children's clothes and bedding hanging on the line. Several of them said God must have inspired me and something wonderful was about to happen.

When they heard that their father had taken a fifth wife they were thrilled. The world had just rotated in their direction. The girls had hoped that their father would marry again. They couldn't stand being dominated by Barbara, and now her reign of terror might be over. This new marriage had the potential to tip the balance of power in their direction. All I did was get in the way of their relationship with their father.

They made it clear to me that they knew their father hadn't fallen in love with me. I came from a family of no importance. They felt it was a pity that their father had had to marry such a dud. I had intruded on their lives without bringing a solution to their bondage. A widow of the late prophet was a woman of real stature. Surely she would come into the family and improve things. What delight it gave them to think of how upset Barbara would be at being replaced by a woman who was younger, prettier, and more powerful than she! The girls hated Barbara not only for her meanness but also because her ascendancy in Merril's life had driven their mothers, Ruth and Faunita, into oblivion. Cathleen could spell an end to her supremacy.

As I listened to Merril's daughters prattle on I began to rethink my situation. Merril was much older than my father, and I'd always known the chances of our ever having a real relationship were almost nonexistent. In my heart of hearts, I'd always known that there would never really be love in my life. This was a grief I'd already contemplated.

But I despaired at this new possibility of never having children—not that I was certain I wanted to create life in such a loveless environment. If Merril became consumed by his new marriage, I could go to sleep at night knowing I would never again awaken with his torpid, clammy body over mine. His abuse would be less humiliating if I wasn't also having sex with him. I would just concentrate on college and becoming a teacher. That was the most I could hope for.

Merril's daughters delighted in what looked to be my demise. I was now consigned to the pile of wives who no longer were in favor.

My father and I made the five-hour trip to Salt Lake City that Sunday morning. Merril told my dad not to bring me to the hotel. We met somewhere else for lunch. When we finished eating, my father left Merril and me alone. Merril looked at me and told me he'd married yet another wife late on Saturday night.

Merril said he was back at the hotel when the call came from Uncle Rulon to marry Tammy, another of Uncle Roy's widows. He acted as though it had come as a bolt out of the blue.

In the coming days, I'd learn the truth. Merril had been planning to marry Tammy and Cathleen at the same time. But Tammy had balked and refused to come to Salt Lake City. He married Cathleen Saturday morning and kept the pressure on Tammy to relent.

Tammy, as I would later learn, had gone to her father shortly after Uncle Roy died and demanded that she be allowed to marry an FLDS bishop who was living in Canada. The Canadian FLDS community was far smaller than our community in Colorado City. It had fewer than a thousand members. It began with a small group of converts who left the mainstream Mormon Church to live the principle of plural marriage.

Tammy had been in love with the Canadian bishop. When he came down to Uncle Roy's from Canada, he'd spend a lot of time in the evenings talking to her. Tammy's father didn't like him at all. Her father refused to let her think of marrying him and said there was a good man in Colorado City whom she belonged to and with whom she would fulfill the work of God. Tammy was incensed. After a decade of marriage to Uncle Roy, she was now twenty-eight and had never had sex, let alone children. If she was sealed for all eternity to the prophet, why couldn't she make a life with the man of her dreams?

In the end, Tammy buckled under the pressure, was whisked to Salt Lake City, and married Merril late Saturday night. Even though she had been to college and was a teacher, she never mastered the ability to stand up for herself. She had a mouth and would often complain about things no one else would, but Tammy also felt the need to please people.

I felt blindsided by the news and said little. Merril took me back to the hotel. Barbara was prancing around, trying to appear as though she was in complete control. Ruth was veering into a nervous breakdown. She blinked uncontrollably, her eyes seemed not to focus, and they danced when she talked. There was little coherence in her words. Her jaw shook with palsy as she spoke. When I arrived, she gave me a hug and in slurred speech said, "For our husband to be given this honor of marrying two new wives is a blessing to us all." But it was clear she didn't believe a word of what she was saying.

Cathleen was sitting by herself on the bed, her eyes so red from crying they were almost swollen shut. The tension in the room was pulsating.

I was eighteen and Cathleen was about twenty. I knew exactly how she felt.

Merril announced that he had business to take care of, and he and Barbara left together. I was left with the mess his marriages had created.

I said a few gentle words to Cathleen and she opened up immediately. She told me she'd had no warning that she was about to marry Merril. The order came out of the blue. She'd been told that all of Uncle Roy's wives were going to be married off to two men. The late prophet didn't want his family separated. Truman was her uncle, so she couldn't marry him. That left Merril.

She hadn't been allowed to call her father or consider other options. She told me that she'd said over and over to anyone who would listen that she didn't want to marry Merril Jessop. But she was told her feelings didn't matter—only the will of her late husband did.

Cathleen ran to her room and wept until she had to get in Merril's van for the ride to her marriage.

She was taken directly to the prophet's home to stand before Rulon Jeffs and marry Merril. Cathleen was demolished by sadness.

Barbara and Merril soon returned and insisted we all go to dinner. Afterward we returned to the hotel and Merril announced that I was to come to his room. I thought Cathleen had slept with him on her wedding night and that he didn't want to sleep with her again because she was so upset. I later learned he hadn't slept with her at all. Barbara was apparently so upset after his marriage to Cathleen that Merril slept with her.

I hoped Cathleen and I could become friends. We were both mired in a weird and disturbed world. I would try to help her if I could. Maybe if we grew close we could find ways to help each other survive Merril's oppression.

Sunday night, Merril insisted I have sex with him. As always, I complied and went through the motions.

When we returned home from Salt Lake City, the dysfunction within our family escalated. There was not enough space in our house in Colorado City for Merril's six wives.

Tammy and Cathleen had yet to sleep with their new husband. This infuriated Tammy, but to Cathleen it felt like an answered prayer. She had been praying to the late prophet to rescue her from this debacle, and her hope was that if her marriage remained unconsummated, she might have a chance to have it annulled.

When we first returned from Salt Lake, Tammy went back to Uncle Roy's. I was in Merril's office with Merril's other wives when Tammy called and asked when she should come over to meet her new family. Merril told her to wait until the next morning. Then he turned to me and said, "Carolyn, I will have Cathleen sleep in your room with you until I can make another room in the house available for her."

It felt strange beyond words to be sharing my bed with someone, especially my husband's newest wife. Cathleen could barely talk, she was so frustrated and upset.

It was highly unusual for a man in our culture to ignore his new wives. The first wife was often unloved, mistreated, and ignored. Most men believed they would have an abundance of wives, so they didn't put much effort into their first marriage. It was the later wives, the women who ended up marrying men twice their age, who were usually more valued and better treated by their spouses.

Tammy tried to cajole Merril to sleep with her at Uncle Roy's. He refused. Finally, after several days, she marched over to our house and commandeered a room. Merril had given Cathleen one of his sons' bedrooms and sent the younger boys to share a room with their older brothers. Tammy took one of Merril's daughter's rooms, so it meant five of the girls would have to sleep together.

Before I went back to college, I helped Cathleen bring some of her furniture over from Uncle Roy's. As soon as she entered her former home she burst into loud sobs. The other wives hugged her and tried to be consoling, but she was too distraught to be comforted. Everything about her life was coming undone.

She was giving up a large and beautiful bedroom and a private bath at Uncle Roy's. In our house she had a room barely large enough to hold her furniture and sewing machine. She also had to share the four bathrooms in the house with dozens of children and Merril's other wives.

Cathleen had been forced to marry Merril without her father's knowledge. He was enraged when he found out what had happened. But there was nothing he could do. Once a marriage is sealed by the prophet nothing can be done to take it apart.

Cathleen told me she knew this marriage was not inspired by a revelation from God. It was put in motion by a power play of her Uncle Truman's. She tried to pray and stay full of faith, hoping for divine revelation to get her out of her marriage.

Cathleen had married Uncle Roy when she was seventeen and he was ninety-six. They never had sex, she told me, but he kissed her a lot and said he wanted to make love to her. She felt honored to serve him. Even though she did a lot of housecleaning as a younger wife, the house was so orderly it did not feel like the slave labor she was slammed into at Merril's.

Because Merril and Barbara took off for Page, Cathleen was left as the only stable adult in charge of twenty-eight children. I was spending the week at college, Faunita slept all day, and Ruth was descending deeper into madness.

Ruth's breakdowns were cataclysmic and frightening. When we came back from the weddings Ruth began watering the shoes in her closet and treating them like plants. She put her clothes on backward and would dance with the dishes in the kitchen while the children watched and laughed. Ruth had a beautiful voice when she was well, but she sang out of tune when she was mentally ill. We always knew she was getting sick when she began singing off-key. She'd shut herself up in her room and sing song after song.

Cathleen got up every morning at five. When she first married Uncle Roy he asked her to get up that early, and she felt it had a religious significance and was something she would have to do for the rest of her life. So at five o'clock she began to get the children ready for school and prepare their breakfasts. Then she spent the day cleaning our house, which was so overcrowded it was usually filthy. When Merril called home, his teenage daughters would pretend that they were doing the work and everything was running smoothly.

The next weekend when I returned home from college she told me that she'd grabbed the phone and said, "Merril, this house is total chaos. I don't know why you are asking your daughters what is going on here. None of them has been in this house since you left."

Merril had chided her. "Cathleen, you don't need to worry. My daughters have everything under control. Since you are the newest member of my family, you should learn from them about how I like things done."

She'd shot back, "I'm up at five o'clock in the morning, getting the children off to school, fixing all the meals, doing all the family laundry, trying to clean a house that refuses to stay clean. I've never worked so hard in my life." Merril told her maybe she'd feel better if she took a nap and that she should be careful not to misrepresent things to him. Cathleen told him that Ruth wasn't even able to care for her baby. Merril said he knew she wasn't feeling well and he'd take care of that, too.

After two days in our home, Cathleen was beside herself. Merril was due home the next night, Friday. It also was the day Tammy would officially move into our house. All she could talk about was getting Merril to finally sleep with her.

When Merril returned, Cathleen went up to his office to find him. Two of the toddlers followed in her wake. When she sat down, they flopped in her lap. Ruth joined them, eyes dancing, jaw shaking. Merril acted oblivious to her. She took off her shoes and began smelling the bottom of her feet. She got up and put on one of Merril's jackets, buttoning and unbuttoning it.

Cathleen became even more distressed at the way Merril ignored Ruth. Why would a man of God allow his wife to behave in such a manner? In the FLDS culture, people believe that the mentally ill have invited evil spirits into themselves. Cathleen could not fathom why Merril would allow a wife who'd been taken over by an evil spirit to be running around his home and scaring his children with her bizarre behavior.

Poor Cathleen. Here was a woman who felt she had been worthy enough to marry a prophet of God. Now she was married to a man who seemed completely ungodly and who allowed a contaminated woman to interact with his children.

It got worse. Merril continued to ignore Ruth until she pulled out all the stops. She announced that she was pregnant. Merril congratulated her.

"This baby I am pregnant with is not your baby," she said.

Silence.

Ruth was confessing a sin unto death: adultery. Surely, thought Cathleen, this must be at the root of the evil that had overtaken her.

Merril looked at her and said calmly, "Ruth, if you are pregnant, then the baby is mine."

"I can assure you that the child I am carrying is not yours because this child is God's."

Merril told her that all children were of God.

"I have proven worthy enough to carry the child of Jesus Christ. He has come to me and I am pregnant with his baby," she said in a strange, trancelike voice.

Cathleen could not sit in Merril's office any longer. Adultery, but with Jesus Christ! Ungodliness was rampant. The devil had inhabited Ruth's body. Cathleen fled.

Ruth's mother had been mentally ill, and because of that, her father was allowed to enter plural marriage—his ticket to the celestial kingdom. Ruth, when she was stable enough to have a semblance of coherent thoughts, saw mental illness as a sacrifice for God. The ravages of her mother had helped her father on his path to celestial glory. Ruth always had grandiose fantasies when she was most disturbed. If it wasn't Jesus' baby, she was carrying the child of Joseph Smith or God.

When I came home with Tammy after helping her move from Uncle Roy's, I saw Ruth in the kitchen and realized she was sicker than I'd ever seen her before. She was crying because one of the children had left a pair of socks on the floor. What frightened me was that I sensed that she was on the verge of violence.

She stormed off into her bedroom. I followed her and found her on her knees, begging for God's mercy between sobs.

"Ruth, are you all right?"

"No." She looked at me blankly. "I haven't been able to sleep all week, and even when I lie down and try to, I can't sleep." Her speech was slow and her words seem to lurch out.

I kneeled beside her and put my arm around her and helped her get up. I guided her to a chair, covered her with a blanket, and offered to get her some hot tea. I came back with a mug of peppermint tea for her and placed it beside her easy chair.

Then I went to find Merril. Merril was in his office with his adoring teenage daughters around him. They were laughing and giggling. I stood by the door until Merril noticed me.

"There's my Carolee. How are you doing tonight?" Carolee was Merril's pet name for me, which I never liked. But it was better than when he accidentally called me by one of his daughters' names.

I looked at him and replied, "I'm doing great, but I can't say that for all of your wives."

"What concerns could my lovely wife Carolee have?"

"Merril, have you seen Ruth since you've been home?"

"Yes, she came up here and talked to me a while ago."

"Then you know she's extremely ill and somebody needs to do something for her. I found her downstairs, crying and shaking all over."

He was dismissive. "I will look into it, and thank you, Carolee, for your concern."

I went back to her room, but she was gone. The peppermint tea was untouched.

Then I heard the shrieks and ran to the kitchen. Ruth was throwing different things around and breaking some glass bowls. "I am going to get the devil out of you if I have to break you to do it."

Several of the smaller children were watching her and laughing.

When she paused I said quietly, "Ruth, do you think you've gotten the devil out of enough of the dishes now?"

She seemed to snap into reality. "Yes, I think I can get the devil out of the other dishes later."

I reminded her that she hadn't drunk her peppermint tea. She thought she had. I suggested we go back to her room and she could try sipping it through a straw. I made her half a sandwich. It was tedious work coaching her to eat and drink, but after two hours she finished the sandwich and tea. I rubbed her shoulders until she seemed to be asleep.

Cathleen and I were both up the next morning at five. She told me how ghastly the past few days had been and how upset she was about Merril's reaction to Ruth's madness. "The way I'm being treated is completely unacceptable," she said. "There is no way I'm going to stand for it. Uncle Roy and his other wives always treated me like I was their little princess. I have been a princess to a prophet of God and I will not be treated as something lesser by people who are nobodies."

I listened as she catalogued her disgust. "The preschoolers in this home do not have a mother willing to care for them. Barbara is only interested in supervising Merril every minute of the day. Ruth doesn't love her children because if she did, she'd never allow herself to be inhabited by forbidden spirits. Faunita only comes out of her room at night when everyone is asleep."

Cathleen lowered her voice. "One night I woke up and heard Faunita slamming things around. I got up and listened at the bottom of the stairs. I could hear her talking to herself and complaining about Merril. I think she hates him." I told her that I knew Faunita and Merril had a lot of problems in their relationship.

The two of us made breakfast for the family: stacks of toast, two gallons of orange juice, and a large pan of scrambled eggs. I took a plate to Ruth's bedroom.

Ruth and Merril's daughter Merrilyn was there. She was my age—the former nuss who'd shyly flirted with our teacher at the pencil sharpener a few years before—and looked exhausted. She'd been assigned to sit with her mother all night and scowled when I entered the room. I encouraged her to urge her mother to eat. She shot back, "I know how to take care of my mother. I have been doing it all my life." As I turned to walk away I saw her stick her tongue out at me.

Back in the kitchen, Cathleen had gathered the preschoolers around the table for breakfast. She was brushing their hair while they ate, yanking and pulling at the snarls. So much for her pristine sense of order and tidiness, I thought. I saw that Millie, a sweet four-year-old, was next in line. I knew she had a sensitive scalp so I took her into my bedroom, which was downstairs near the kitchen, and carefully combed her hair.

When we returned to the kitchen, Merril's teenage daughters were streaming in. They were annoyed about having to give up one of their bedrooms to Tammy and Cathleen. They had been so eager for additional mothers to counterbalance what they perceived as Barbara's tyranny, but now they were starting to see the consequences. Tammy was vying for their father's attention all the time. The house was more crowded. But above all, Barbara seemed to have a lock on Merril's attention. With three wives waiting in the wings, they were more shut out now than ever before.

Merril walked past the kitchen after sleeping with Barbara again.

He sent one of the children in and asked that I bring coffee upstairs to his office. When I returned, Tammy was in the kitchen, her cheeks flushed with anger.

I asked Cathleen what was wrong. "She knows," she said.

"Knows what?"

"She knows Merril hasn't been sleeping with me, either. He hasn't slept with anyone but you and Barbara."

I was shocked. I told Cathleen I'd thought she had slept with him on her wedding night.

"No, I have been married to him for a week now and he hasn't stayed with me at all."

Tammy had not been badgering Merril as much in recent days because she thought he was sleeping with Cathleen. Now she knew the truth and stormed right up to Merril's office. I followed, curious to hear what would happen.

Barbara was with Merril. Tammy entered and said, "I guess for some men when they get a new wife it is off with the new and on with the old." Merril started to laugh.

Barbara chimed in. "Father, I think it would be good if you took Tammy and me on a drive to look at the Saturday work projects. Maybe Tammy would be interested in learning about her husband instead of you listening to how she feels."

I left the office as fast as I could. I didn't want to get stuck driving around all day with the three of them listening to Merril's sermons about all his good work. When they got back that night, Barbara said they'd decided Ruth needed to go to Hildale and have Aunt Lydia give her a vitamin $B_{12}$ shot.

This was ridiculous. Ruth had barely slept or eaten for a week. She needed major medical intervention, not a vitamin shot. Barbara went searching for her half sister and found her at the table, crying. "Ruth, you are to come with me at once. Merril has had enough of your nonsense. We're going to Hildale for a $B_{12}$ shot and then all this crying can end and you can straighten up and be some use to your husband." Hildale was the clinic where we delivered our babies.

Aunt Lydia was the wife of the bishop and acted as nurse and midwife. She had no degree, but her years of experience made her very reliable. She did most of the basic medical care in the community.

Ruth lit into Barbara. "Get away from me right now. I am not going anywhere with you. You are all puffed up with pride and filled with the devil."

"Ruth, you are in rebellion to your husband and you are to stop this at once. I command it. If you rebel against me, then you are rebelling against your priesthood head and God will not be able to help you." Barbara grabbed Ruth by the arm.

Ruth found energy I didn't know she had to push Barbara off her. After she did, she seized her by the throat and began choking her. She pushed Barbara back against the stove until the other woman was nearly lying on top of it. "I am going to kill you. You deserve to die for what you have done to me." Ruth was enraged.

Barbara managed to push herself free momentarily. She screamed, "Go get Merril!" before Ruth lunged again at her and pinned her down.

I ran outside to the van and banged on the window. Merril could see that something was really wrong and he opened the door. I just shouted, "You have to get downstairs now." The fear in my voice sent him running.

By the time he got in the house, Ruth had retreated to her bedroom and was crying. Barbara was in her bedroom. Frightened children were huddled in the corner of the bathroom next to the kitchen, crying.

Merril stormed into Ruth's room and started screaming at her. His words were muffled by her loud crying. I felt so dizzy I suddenly found it hard to stand. Several of Merril's teenage daughters came running. When they saw the small children crying they looked at me in shock. "What happened? What's going on?"

I looked at them blankly. What was I supposed to say—*I just watched your mother try to kill your aunt?* I merely shook my head and walked away. Someone else could fill them in. I was too depleted.

Barbara and Merril slept together again that night. Cathleen and Tammy were still shut out. Tensions kept rising.

# Honeymoon

Two weeks after Merril's two weddings, he decided it was time for a honeymoon and that all of his six wives and thirty-four children would go.

For years, Merril had been promising the family a trip to the San Diego Zoo. His construction company was working on a major project in Yuma, Arizona. In a maniacal moment of multitasking, he opted to combine a honeymoon, site visit, and trip to the zoo into a five-day ordeal.

Merril rented a Greyhound bus from a friend who lived in the community. It was old and had been out of service for several years. Merril assigned his twenty-year-old son Nathan to drive the bus. Five wives would ride with Merril in his van. Faunita was assigned to travel in the bus with the children.

Tammy had finally spent a night with Merril. She was so excited afterward that she couldn't talk about anything else. She told Cathleen that she felt like she would count every breath she breathed until he slept with her again. But Cathleen still had not slept with Merril. Faunita remained sequestered in her bedroom. She was angry about not being invited to the double wedding and now rarely left her room. Ruth was still in the throes of madness. Aunt Lydia had prevailed upon Merril to let Ruth take some potent sleeping medication, so at least she now slept for a few hours every night. But it had been weeks since she'd been able to care for any of her fourteen children.

Cathleen broke the news to me about the trip one morning when I walked into the kitchen for coffee. She was washing the breakfast dishes and motioned for me to sit down. "We are going on the largest family trip I have ever been on in my life, and we're leaving in less than a week." She looked dazed and stricken. The full horror of our family life was becoming increasingly obvious to her every day.

"No one has even started talking about how we are going to take care of the children on this trip. If Barbara and Ruth treat them on the road the way they do at home, then you and I will be doing everything." I knew she was right. She said we could expect no help from Tammy, who had been completely spoiled and pampered by Uncle Roy's family.

I told her that I didn't see why we should be made to be responsible for Barbara's and Ruth's children.

"Carolyn, it's not about right or wrong. It's not about fair." Her voice was firm. "You and I are the only ones in the family fixing meals, combing hair, doing dishes, changing diapers, and cleaning. The trip won't be any different. We can spend the next few days working around the clock trying to get ready, or we can find the responsibility dumped on us at the last minute with no way of making any provisions to care for the kids—a sad place for both of us."

I started to tremble from nervousness. I'd never had this kind of responsibility before. Cathleen did not seem scared. Nor did she ever mention the word *honeymoon*. I think she still held out hope that she might be able to escape from her marriage to Merril.

We quietly made preparations. Forty-one people—thirty-four of them children—was too large a group to eat in restaurants. We would have to take all our food. Cathleen and I began baking bread and cookies. We packed cereal and lots of snack food such as raisins, pretzels, and gigantic bags of chips that we separated into small zip-top bags.

Merril had a charge account with the local grocery store, so after Cathleen and I did five days' worth of menu planning, we went shopping multiple times.

But food was only half the battle. We had to pack clothing, bedding, and other supplies for all the children, four of whom were still in diapers. Planning and organizing were overwhelming. But the worst was yet to come.

A day or two later, Cathleen and I were placing dozens of loaves of homemade bread into boxes and plastic bread bags when Barbara marched into the kitchen and said in her authoritarian way, "What kind of arrangements are you girls making for food? What plans have been made for the children's clothing?" None of our answers were satisfactory. "Father has given me the job to see to it that you girls get things together in the way he wants them handled. It's clear neither one of you is in harmony with him or you would have been checking in with me before you started this project."

Barbara was adamant that everything we had done so far was wrong. But she was unable to tell us what to do to fix it. When I said to her, "Barbara, how much sandwich meat do you think we will need for one lunch?" she looked clueless. I told her we were doing the baking first and would get the items for the cooler last. She stammered as she said, "I think that the amount of meat is of no importance. The thing that is important is if you girls are packing the kinds of meals that are agreeable for Father's children to be eating. I will be telling you what to do from this point on."

If the look on my face could have spoken, it would have said, *I don't think so.* Instead, I quietly said, "Barbara, maybe Merril needs to come and talk to us. Cathleen and I will gladly explain what we are doing. We'll listen to anything he has to say. Rather than complaining, maybe you could offer some input about what we've done right rather than nit-picking everything we've done so far."

Barbara stiffened. I was surprised by my candor. I usually didn't talk back to her, but this time she'd really pushed me. I had to push back. I clearly caught her completely off guard. "I will talk to Father about the way you girls have treated me. I only want the trip to be prepared in a way that will be of comfort to my husband. Both of you have enough jealousy and hostility toward me that we will never be united behind our priesthood head."

Cathleen now had one more reason to be shocked and upset.

After Barbara left, she said, "Uncle Roy would never have allowed one of his wives to treat another wife the way we were both just treated. I don't care what she accuses me of if I don't suck up to her abuse."

Barbara returned to the kitchen the day before the trip. The tables and countertops were covered with sweet rolls Cathleen and I had baked the night before. We'd made over a hundred and left them out overnight to cool. Barbara went to Merril's office and reported on us. Tammy was always coming to Cathleen and me and reporting on what Barbara was saying to Merril. Either Barbara would tell her or Tammy would eavesdrop outside Merril's office. "Father, I have a concern that Cathleen and Carolyn are making too much food. I have spoken to them several times about this. It's an enormous expense and a huge amount of food will be wasted. They have also packed almost all of the clothing in the children's closets. This will all have to be cleaned when we get back. I also don't understand why they are packing any bedding because we'll be in a hotel. Things seem out of control and they need to be disciplined."

Merril was realistic and told her that disciplining us at this stage wouldn't fix anything, especially since the food was purchased, packed, and baked. His attitude was that we'd have to live with the consequences of our actions.

Barbara didn't give up easily. "I had no input into what they prepared for the children. I would have far preferred that the children eat bread sticks instead of sweet rolls," she said. "These girls have no concern for the health of your children."

We were both summoned to Merril's office. Neither of us was surprised by Merril's interrogation. It was clear to us that since we had bypassed Barbara and not asked her permission for everything we were doing to get ready for the trip, she'd see to it that we were in trouble with Merril. There had been many episodes before this where she'd been complaining about us to Merril and Tammy came to give us the full report.

Merril's interrogation began as soon as we sat on the couch. "I am getting information that you girls haven't prepared anything healthy for the children to snack on during the trip. I'm also concerned that you've made too much food and there will be a lot of waste."

Cathleen jumped right in. She was not intimidated by Merril, but she stopped short of defying him. "Merril, we've purchased several cases of apples and oranges for the children to eat on the way," she said. "We have sandwich bags with vegetables and carrot sticks. Most of what we've prepared is healthy."

"Sweet rolls are not healthy."

I interrupted Merril. "We only made enough for each person to have two. After that, the rest of the snacks will all be healthy."

Merril seemed confident that he now had the upper hand. He laughed nervously. "I think you should work with Barbara on making something healthy. Barbara has always been a wife who is interested in doing what her husband wants."

My spirits sank. I did not want to prepare one more thing for this awful trip. I knew Barbara would do something now to make us miserable.

"Father, I think that bread sticks would be a good thing to make for the children. Instead of two or three apiece, why don't we have these girls make enough for each child to have ten?" Barbara now seemed pleased.

Bread sticks were a ton of work. Cathleen and I would be working all day and into the night. I spoke up. "Merril, if you are so concerned with there being too much food, it would seem like ten bread sticks per person is way too much."

"Why don't you make as many as you can. We can always bring them back and eat them afterward." Merril was matter-of-fact. I knew he'd never overrule Barbara but felt compelled to try. She smiled, secure and satisfied in her complete dominance over Cathleen and me.

Cathleen and I spent the rest of the day in the kitchen. Neither one of us said much. We were hot, exhausted, and robotic in our efforts.

Tammy spent the day before our departure strolling around with Barbara and praising her every move. She had figured out that her success as Merril's wife depended on winning Barbara's favor. Cathleen and I both knew that Barbara would drink up the flattery and stab Tammy in the back whenever it suited her needs. "I have never in my life met a woman as selfish and cruel as she is," Cathleen said. I nodded in agreement.

I slept through my alarm the next morning. Cathleen shook me awake at five-thirty and said my alarm clock had awakened everyone else in the house except me. We were due to leave at eight o'clock. We got everyone dressed and fed, then cleaned up the kitchen.

The children were excited. Going to the zoo was a huge event for them. It was beyond imagining. Merril's teenage daughters were smiling and laughing, upbeat and eager to be going on a trip. Nathan said the mechanic had checked out the bus and it would not break down. Faunita boarded the bus with the children. Thirty-two would travel with us and the two smallest babies would come in the van with the other wives. Barbara's son Jackson was about sixteen months old and Ruth's daughter Ruthie was just under a year.

It's nearly five hundred miles to San Diego from Colorado City. But with so many children, we had to stop in every small town and at every highway rest stop for someone to go to the bathroom. It was tedious travel. We'd drive for forty-five minutes and then stop for fifteen or twenty. Several children would jump off the bus and run inside. No one took roll call before we got started again, and in Flagstaff, one of them was left behind at a gas station.

Truman was Barbara's talkative nine-year-old son who was a grade behind in school. When he returned from the bathroom, the big Greyhound bus was gone. He tried not to attract any attention and sat alone on the sidewalk. After a while one of the cashiers inside noticed him and wondered if he might have been part of the busload of kids dressed in strange clothing that had stopped by earlier.

Truman told her he'd been on the bus. The cashier took him inside and called the police. When the police arrived they began questioning him. (Truman recapped this for us after he was rescued, and it was a story told and retold in the family for at least five years.) As he told us the story, Truman said that when he was asked where he lived, he said, "At the creek." He told the officers, "My dad's name is Father, and sometimes I hear people calling my mom Barbara." The police asked if he was on a school trip with other children. Truman told them, "Of course not. It is only my father's family. We don't take other families with us." He said he had fourteen brothers but he didn't know how many sisters, except that there were more girls than boys.

At the police station the questioning continued. Somehow the officers figured out that Truman's father owned a construction company called General Rock and Sand, in Page, Arizona. With that information as a starting point, police were able to get the license number for Merril's van. When the police officer asked Truman why his family was taking a vacation, he said, "It's because father just married two new wives and he is taking them on a honeymoon with the whole family."

An alert went out with the license number of Merril's van. We had driven several hours beyond Flagstaff without Truman. I was thinking what a relief it would be to finally get to Phoenix and sleep when I heard sirens from a police car and saw the flashing lights. Merril's van pulled over and so did the bus. The officers spoke to Merril, who then boarded the bus.

When he got back in the van he said, "Well, I guess we left Truman at one of the rest stops in Flagstaff. I've sent the bus on to the hotel and Nathan will get everyone settled in for the night. We are going to drive back to Flagstaff and get Truman."

Even though we didn't have to stop at every rest stop, it still took nearly two hours. Once we got there we all stayed in the van while Merril went into the police station to find Truman. Barbara was disgusted that the people on his bus had not taken better care of him, and she seemed very moody and irritated. She wasn't at all consoling to Truman when he rejoined us. He acted as if nothing special had happened. Truman came out of the police station walking behind Merril. Merril rarely touched his children or held their hands. They got into the van and we started driving back to Phoenix. It was around one in the morning when we finally arrived.

At the hotel Merril began assigning rooms to each wife. He told Cathleen she'd be staying with him. This was the first night they spent together since their marriage. They'd only have five hours together since we were getting up at 6 A.M. I felt so sorry for Cathleen. She'd been hoping this would never happen.

When I opened the door to my room I saw that both beds were filled with sleeping children. I picked up one of Barbara's daughters and placed her in bed with her small sisters. Relieved and exhausted, I collapsed into the other bed.

The next morning we tried to organize breakfast in the parking lot. We took coolers out of the bus and put them on the ground. With no adult in charge, it spun into chaos.

Cold cereal spilled everywhere. Children were grabbing paper bowls from one another and splashing milk all over the sidewalk. The smaller children were crying because they were hungry and too little to fend for themselves. No one was supervising the kids. Everyone was pushing and shoving. I tried to pour some milk into a bowl and someone bumped into me. I went crashing into Merril's daughter Merrilyn and accidentally tipped most of a gallon of milk onto her dress. She screamed at the sudden shock of cold milk. She raised her hand and was ready to hit someone, but when she saw it was her new mother who had drenched her, she stopped. I apologized. Her other sisters were laughing at her. She trudged off to change clothes.

Cathleen and Merril arrived. He ordered the children to stop grabbing food. Cathleen became a drill sergeant at this point and started making kids sit in the grass until it was their turn. She ordered them to stop shouting and pushing one another. Barbara and Tammy soon made their appearance on the scene. Barbara said to Merril, "Let's go over to that restaurant and have some real breakfast and some coffee. Cathleen and Carolyn can handle things here." Cathleen seemed quiet and remote. She had just spent her first night with Merril but seemed not to want to discuss it. I suspected that she was upset because Merril was ignoring her and not treating her like a wife. She'd finally slept with him and the next morning he was eager to take off with Barbara and Tammy to eat breakfast while leaving Cathleen behind to babysit. Faunita was the next wife to surface. She complained about having to put thirty kids to bed by herself and said they needed more hotel rooms.

Ruth came down to breakfast with Nathan's wife, who was trying to take care of her. Ruth couldn't walk straight. She went over to a shrub with some purple flowers and picked a ridiculously large bunch for her hair. We tried to get her to eat some breakfast, but she refused. Then she decided she wanted to run around the parking lot for some exercise before we started driving to Yuma. Nathan's wife tried to dissuade her but had no luck. Ruth took off, running in circles. We could follow the big bouquet of purple flowers as it bobbed around the parking lot.

I felt that I was part of something so strange it belonged to another realm. We were a traveling road show of freaks and noisy children. Before I married Merril, my life had been relatively normal with moments of strangeness. Now it was surreal, with occasional bursts of reality.

Merril, Barbara, and Tammy came back from breakfast. They were laughing and acting so righteous. They told us we were not "keeping sweet," a religious phrase we said to one another to remind us not to react to things that made us mad. We had been taught to believe that reacting in anger could cause a person to lose the spirit of God.

The children piled back into the bus for our departure to Yuma. Faunita took a roll call and made sure no one was missing. Merril and his five other wives loaded into his van. He planned to check on his construction job in Yuma, hardly a big attraction for the rest of us. The mood in the van was chilly. We didn't talk very much. At every rest stop, Ruth would get out and run around in circles. She progressed from running to skipping, then singing, and finally dancing. Merril made her take the big bunch of purple flowers out of her hair. I was so mortified by her behavior I stayed in the van.

But her acting out was less frightening than what happened inside the van. Ruth's baby, Ruthie, was about a year old. At one point the baby became fussy and started crying when she was hungry. Ruth decided she would breast-feed her. She had no milk since she'd stopped nursing her seven months before. But that didn't faze her.

Ruth started stripping in the van and was topless in moments. Then she tried to remove the rest of her clothes, but Tammy and Barbara were trying to put her clothes back on her as soon as she took them off. When Ruth asked for her baby, Tammy started to give the child to her, but then Merril ordered her to halt. Everything was chaotic. Poor Ruthie was crying and distressed and her mother was trying to take off her clothes to nurse her with breasts that had no milk.

Merril couldn't ignore Ruth's behavior this time. He pulled over and became extremely angry, shouting and scolding her. He insisted she put her clothes back on, and she did.

Cathleen was ready to throw herself out of the van. Tammy, the late prophet's little princess, was also taken aback. Neither of them had ever seen anything this strange before. After seven months of marriage, I was more numb than shocked. *Oh, well, Ruth stripped naked today and tried to nurse the baby she hadn't nursed for months. Whatever.*

We stopped at the construction site in Yuma. For Merril, this was a photo op. We took pictures of Merril with all his wives on the job site. He spent time walking around and talking to men working on the job. We waited for him in the van and drove on to California. It was late at night when we arrived. Merril announced that I would be sleeping with him.

He said goodnight to Tammy and Barbara and arrived at our room with five little children in tow. There were only two beds in the room and the five kids couldn't fit in one. He told me to make a bed on the floor and two of his children slept there.

I went to sleep thinking that this weird night would be finished by morning. The next time I opened my eyes, I told myself, it would be over. I was wrong. In the middle of the night, I felt Merril pulling up my nightgown and then straddling me. I realized that he was going to try to have sex with me, despite the fact that his children were sleeping on the bed and floor beside us. The room was pitch black. I hated, just hated, having sex with the children around us.

After it was over, Merril rolled over and went to sleep. I stared into the darkness, feeling like I had been raped in front of his sleeping children. I did not, could not, sleep for the rest of the night. I was in complete shock. Ever since I was married it had been one shock after another. I felt numb. Not anymore. This was a new low. I was shaking.

The bright light of morning did nothing to banish my utter disgust and revulsion at Merril. For the first time in my marriage, I realized how much had been stripped from me. When I saw myself in the mirror I felt like I was looking at the shell of a human being—my spirit and dignity had been stolen from me.

Merril decided to take all his wives to breakfast and left his daughters in charge of the thirty-four children. Barbara and Tammy were clearly annoyed that Merril had spent the first two nights of the trip with Cathleen and me. Cathleen was still reeling from Ruth's naked nursing fiasco. Faunita used our breakfast time to educate Merril's two newest wives about the abuses he'd committed against her.

Ruth would not put food directly into her mouth. She tried instead to throw food in by the forkful. Her head was bobbing around to catch it and of course she missed every time. This was uproariously funny to her.

Faunita continued her nonstop catalogue of the horrors of her marriage, telling Cathleen and Tammy that Merril had put her away ten years earlier. "Putting someone away" is shorthand in the FLDS for what happens when a man stops having sex with one of his wives. Faunita said he announced he'd never sleep with her again and that he'd not even given her a kiss since.

I really didn't want to listen to a diatribe about whom Merril was sleeping with or having a relationship with and whom he was not. I was still so traumatized from the sex the night before, I felt remote and numb. I couldn't engage with anyone and didn't want to participate in anything.

When we returned to the hotel we found unbelievable chaos. The children had been poorly supervised by Merril's daughters and food was slopped over everything. Milk and juice had been spilled on the carpet and upholstery. Wet cereal was all over the bedspreads. It was shameful and disgusting. The kids never should have been allowed to take food into their rooms. When Cathleen and I had been in charge the day before, we'd made everyone eat outside and clean up afterward. No garbage was left behind.

Cathleen now refused to ride in the van with Merril because of Ruth's behavior the night before. She got on the bus instead, determined to endure the screaming and crying of the young kids and the arguing and commotion of the teenagers.

When we arrived in San Diego we checked into the hotel and then the entire family ran to the beach. We didn't change into bathing suits because we didn't have any. Swimming was considered immodest. The children were overjoyed to see the ocean for the first time. The kids were jumping and splashing in the waves in their long underwear and layers of fundamentalist clothing. It's a miracle to me that no one drowned.

Merril, swept up by romance, decided to walk down to the beach from the hotel with each wife, one at a time, and kiss her at the ocean's edge. This seemed to be the pinnacle of romance to him, and even Faunita got kissed, which made the children jump up and down because most of them liked her a lot. I was happy for Faunita but felt the whole ritual was stupid.

Back at the hotel, we were hit with the onslaught of wet, sandy clothing from the beach escapade. We tried to find a way to dry the garments instead of hurling them into garbage bags to ferry home. Clothes were hung from every railing outside the rooms and on every chair inside.

The next morning was the long-awaited arrival at the San Diego Zoo. Merril bought the tickets and we all entered the park. The older children split off and no one was assigned to watch the younger ones. Barbara and Tammy shadowed Merril; Ruth was in her own crazy orbit. Faunita tried to keep up, but with so many children, it was impossible. Ever since Truman had been left behind she conscientiously tried to stay on top of everyone's whereabouts. Cathleen and I tried to help by taking some of the younger girls around with us.

At one point, Merril stopped at an ice cream stand and began buying cones. The children rushed to him like a flock of ducklings. Cathleen and I stopped and sat by the monkeys' cage. I turned just in time to see one of the monkeys picking his nose and eating the mucus. I said to Cathleen, "Oh, gross, why did we have to sit here?" Cathleen said it was less gross than conditions on the bus. She didn't understand how women such as Barbara, who had nine children, and Ruth, who had fourteen, could take no responsibility for them.

We rode on a train that circled the zoo. We could see the larger animals from a distance in their natural habitats. Afterward we saw some of the big apes in their cages. One was carrying a small baby on his foot, and Merril said that was how he felt with his kids. The kids started calling each other "apes" and "baboons" as they slapped one another around.

After a full day at the zoo, we herded the very tired but mostly happy children back to the hotel. We were due to start the two-day trip back to Colorado City in the morning. There was no talk about staying another day, although the kids would have loved it. One day was allotted for the zoo and four days for driving and that was that.

Breakfast was simplified: there was no food. We'd run out. Merril sent his son Nathan out to buy fast food for the masses. None of the kids had any interest in eating the zillion bread sticks Cathleen and I had baked for the trip.

As we were leaving San Diego, we became separated from the bus. Merril continued driving. This was in the days before cell phones, so for hours Merril would have no idea that the bus had broken down just outside San Diego. The younger children were tired and hungry from not having had enough to eat. The teenagers were cranky.

Nathan left Cathleen and Faunita on the bus and went to find an auto shop. All he could do was call ahead to Merril's construction company and leave a message about what had happened. A mechanic came and after a few hours, the bus was ready to roll again.

The children were forced to eat bread sticks for their lunch and then for dinner. The small amounts of water and milk that remained were rationed.

When Merril checked in with his construction company, he learned what had happened to the bus. He decided that we'd check into a hotel and wait for them. The place where we'd stayed on the trip west wouldn't take us because of the way we'd trashed the rooms at breakfast.

Merril found other lodging, but there were not enough rooms for his thirty-four children. He decreed that they would sleep in the bus. Merril left word at his construction company for Nathan when he checked in so he'd know where to find us.

In the middle of the night, Merril brought Cathleen to my room. The bus had arrived. She recounted the day's horrors and said how fortunate it was that we'd made so many bread sticks.

The next day was grueling. The children ate fast food, but there was no food for snacks in between meals. We were all physically and emotionally drained.

So much for a honeymoon. Cathleen had spent the night with Merril, but I didn't know if they'd even had sex. I wondered if her first experience with him had been as crude as mine. Even Tammy, who had spent so much time and effort cozying up to Barbara, seemed discouraged.

Ruth was medicated with a very strong tranquilizer as soon as we got home. After a few weeks, she began to recover. Faunita went back to sleeping all day and staying up all night.

Cathleen and I spent several days doing laundry after the trip. I then returned to college, as thankful as I ever had been for the opportunity to be a student.

I was so grateful not to be pregnant. I wanted children, but I was determined to get through school first. Maybe the family would stabilize by the time I had my degree. What I was experiencing seemed like an aberration. I wasn't questioning my faith, but I was questioning Merril. If people knew what was really going on in our family, I thought, Merril would be condemned. We weren't living in accordance with FLDS values.

# Accident

Eleven months after my wedding, I became pregnant with my first child. I was violently ill for nine months; the morning sickness that some women complain of laid siege to me. I lost weight, looked pale, and felt weaker than I'd imagined possible. I knew that by marrying, I had lost control of my life. With my pregnancy, I lost control of my body as well. I had barely any prenatal care. Worse, my pregnancy created even more problems for me within Merril's family.

Within the FLDS, any personal problem is seen as the direct result of sin. Serious emotional or physical problems were considered a curse from God. It was also dangerous for a woman to show any incapacitation related to pregnancy because it was viewed within her family as a sign of rebellion—unless, of course, you were Barbara, for whom the double standard applied with regard to her crying bouts during pregnancy.

The other wives would discuss whether or not they thought I was really suffering or just seeking attention. I was accused of putting on a show to gain more status for myself. Producing large numbers of faithful children was a way for a woman to gain favor not only with her husband but with God. It wasn't uncommon for a woman in the community to have as many as sixteen children, and most had at least twelve.

My worst enemies in Merril's family were, more often than not, his other wives. They had no tolerance for a woman who did not fit the perfect little polygamist mold. A woman who does not accept her powerlessness and complete submission to her husband's will is targeted by the other wives as a troublemaker. She's treated with disdain, often verbally abused, and assigned the grunt work in the household.

Even in the deeply repressed fundamentalist culture, sexual status determines class and power. A woman who refuses her husband sexually is seen as rebellious. Word gets around and the other wives treat her with scorn, but it can work the other way, too. If a husband spends a lot of time at night with one wife, the other wives become jealous because she's now more powerful. Pregnancy is also a status symbol because it is a sign that your husband considers you worthy to father his children. It's common in these plural marriages for a man to favor some wives to the exclusion of others. The rejected women are consigned to a life of emptiness and disgrace. The rejected wives also become an example to the others of what can happen if they displease their husband.

Even though my pregnancy was making me miserable, I was determined to finish the two years I needed to graduate. I was majoring in education with a minor in business and reading. I had taken the summer off from school and just managed to finish the fall quarter before giving birth. Arthur was born on December 20, 1987, after only six hours of labor, which impressed the other wives. Aunt Lydia, the elderly midwife who had delivered both my mother and me, brought Arthur into the world.

I fell in love with him the moment I saw him. He was a beautiful baby and gave my life a purpose it had never had before. I mattered because Arthur mattered. My future was important because he was now part of it; I wanted the best for him. I never felt alone again after Arthur was born. Marriage had separated me from my younger siblings, which filled me with acute loneliness and longing. My roots felt like they'd been yanked out of the ground. But with Arthur I forged a new connection to life. Merril drove back from Salt Lake City the day he was born and was excited when he first saw him.

Three months after Arthur's birth, I panicked when I began menstruating again. I knew my body couldn't handle a pregnancy so soon, but I also knew I didn't dare refuse sex. My world clearly centered around Arthur now, and I could tell Merril was feeling threatened. Merril would cut off my money if I stopped having sex with him. Money was a prime means of control for Merril, as it was for some men in the FLDS. Women who worked were required to turn over all their income to their husbands as well as any money gotten from welfare.

Merril had plenty of money, but that didn't mean we had enough food. Merril gave us $500 a week to feed at least thirty people every night and more than fifty on weekends, when relatives joined us for Sunday dinner. But Merril let his teenage daughters do the shopping. They would squander the majority of the money on other things. Merril would be traveling many nights with Barbara, but those of us at home often would have nothing more than a bowl of soup or some beans. Some nights we'd have something like a few cans of cream of chicken soup mixed into a big pot of rice. (One of the reasons I had easy deliveries was because my babies were small.)

Complaining was out of the question. While I could tell my mother that I was hungry and not getting enough food, if I became at all critical of Merril, she'd refuse to hear any more and would stop listening to me. A man has the absolute right to control his house in any way he chooses.

I returned to college after Arthur was born and took him with me. I had a relative there whose husband was in school, and she watched Arthur while I went to classes for that first year. I didn't want more children right away but was too intimidated to ask any of the women at school about birth control. I felt insecure among them. When I walked into a classroom everyone looked as though they were afraid I might sit next to them. In my long dresses, I stood out as strange, someone from a distant century, if not a different planet. No one made any effort to associate with me, and I lacked the confidence to try to connect with them.

When Arthur was seven months old, Merril started pressuring me to get pregnant again. We were driving somewhere together and he said that Arthur was old enough for me to have another child and we should start trying to make that happen. I felt sickened at the thought because I was still so exhausted. But I knew most of Merril's other wives became pregnant three months after giving birth. I was still nursing Arthur and weak when I conceived again in October, and I became violently ill. It felt like my body was allergic to being pregnant. My weight plummeted. I lost about twenty pounds and looked anorexic.

Wives targeted one another constantly, but when I was so sick, it felt like I was in the bull's-eye. They attacked my character and made fun of my illness. They didn't understand why I hadn't repented after Arthur's pregnancy so I wouldn't continue to have the same problems. Merril finally realized how sick I was and, to my amazement, bought me vitamins. He bought them because I didn't have enough money of my own. I could charge things only where we had an account, so anything I bought came from the grocery store, which usually didn't carry vitamins. After a few months, I began to feel myself getting slightly stronger. But I still had massive headaches and sometimes vomited nearly every hour. It was hard to keep anything down, but some days were better than others, and on those I might vomit only three times.

Since I had not been able to find a babysitter for the whole week and I couldn't bear being apart from Arthur for more than three days, on Wednesdays I would make the one-hour drive from Cedar back to Colorado City to pick him up and bring him back to school. If I didn't have someone lined up at school to watch him, I'd bring one of Merril's daughters back with me to help out.

A light snow was falling when I got into the van to head back to Colorado City. In the three years I'd been at school, I'd traversed many snowstorms without a problem. I hadn't been listening to the radio that day, but there was nothing unusual about the snow that was falling. But fifteen miles outside of Cedar on Black Ridge, I found myself in the middle of a whiteout. Even with the headlights on I could barely see more than a foot or two in front of the van. I slowed down to a crawl of just a few miles an hour. Because I was going so slowly and hugging the side of the road I felt reasonably safe. The van didn't have snow tires because it was rare to have storm conditions like this in southern Utah. I thought this was a freak occurrence and that it would clear soon.

I made it to the top of the ridge without skidding. Then I hit black ice. The van started spinning out of control. I could feel it moving in a clockwise direction. It hit something and then began spinning the opposite way. The steering wheel was spinning, too, and I grabbed it, thinking I could get some kind of control, but that was impossible. I could see the road coming up against me in the windshield and knew that the van was about to roll. I also knew there wasn't enough protection to keep the van from rolling over the cliff and onto the northbound highway. *Oh,* I thought in slow motion, *I will probably not survive. This is not the way I thought I would die.* But then the van hit something and changed direction, spinning backward and out of control until it crashed into the opposite side of the road and the side of the mountain. The back end of the van absorbed most of the impact of the crash.

When I opened my eyes, I could see snow, rocks, and dirt out the window on my side of the van. Every other window in the van was broken except mine. Frozen air rushed in. My teeth started chattering. I was not dead. I was freezing to death. The blurry image of the spinning van took hold in my mind. I tried to focus. The van was on its side. My book bag had come undone and books were everywhere. I thought I should gather up my books and make sure I had everything I needed for my classes. I maneuvered my way around inside the van and found all of my books. After neatly repacking my book bag, I realized I was trapped inside the van. By using the seat on the passenger's side as a foothold, I boosted myself up and managed to open the door by pushing it straight out. I walked along the cliff I'd almost hurtled over, looked at the northbound highway below, and realized what I had been spared. But now what? The van was totaled, every side smashed in except the driver's. I'd been driving Merril's luxury van because the other car was in the shop being repaired. I was afraid Merril would be furious.

But I had bigger fears than Merril's wrath. I was trapped in a world of snow and deathly silence. I was wearing only a light jacket, and there were too many smashed windows in the van for it to provide me with any warmth. Now I would slowly freeze to death. And if I died, my baby would, too. I thought of walking down the highway, where a number of other cars that had been involved in accidents because of the weather had been abandoned, and seeing if I could crawl into any of the smashed cars for protection. But from what I could see in the distance, those cars were as wrecked as my own. And there was no active traffic—apparently the bad weather had led the authorities to close the highway, and there was no way of knowing how long until it reopened. All I knew was that I was stranded on the mountaintop until it did. I huddled against the side of the van that was closest to the mountain. I was protected from one side against the wind. But I knew I couldn't survive that way for long. My feet were frozen, and I couldn't feel the tips of my fingers. I knew I didn't have any broken bones, but what about internal injuries? I was overwhelmed with grief. I had destroyed Merril's van, killed my baby, and would now freeze to death before help arrived.

*Stop it.* I couldn't let myself think like that. Merril be damned. I couldn't worry about the van. I wanted to stay alive. I started to jump up and down to generate a little warmth and keep my circulation going. The snow kept falling. The silence felt oppressive. I would jump up and down, then stop, then start again. But I was too tired. I wanted to crawl back into the driver's side of the van and go to sleep. Maybe there would be help by morning. I leaned against the van. Maybe I wouldn't sleep if I kept standing up. I could rest against the van, close my eyes just for a little bit . . .

*No!* Awareness hit me with a slap. If I stopped moving, I would freeze to death. Arthur would never see me again. I would never see him again. *Jump*—I had to make myself jump up and down to stay warm. Five minutes on, five off. I did it and did it again. Five minutes. Then five minutes more and five minutes after that. I lost my sense of time. It felt like only an hour had elapsed since the accident, but I had no way of knowing.

Suddenly, in the distance, I heard a noise. It had to be a snowplow! I saw the plow coming up the ridge with snow spitting in every direction. I ran across the road, jumping up and down to get the driver's attention. I screamed and hollered but was drowned out by the snowplow's grinding roar. The snowplow drove right past me. I ran down that road screaming and waving my arms. But it was no use. I was back in my frozen, silent crypt.

As despair began closing in around me again, I heard something else. It was coming from the northbound highway below me. Two people were standing next to a car, waving. "Hey, are you all right?"

"Yes!" I answered as I started to maneuver toward them, cautiously making my way down that cliff and toward the two strangers.

The two turned out to be college students from California who were traveling to Brigham Young University in Provo. One of them had rolled his car. His girlfriend, driving behind him, had stopped. Her car was packed with what seemed like everything they owned, but the driver's seat was clear. The two of them took turns staying warm by trading places in the car. When they saw how frozen I looked, both of them told me to sit down and warm up. I didn't argue. The car was cold, but it was a relief not to be battling the elements.

While we waited, we talked about the damage we had done to our vehicles. I couldn't tell them that I was burning up with the fear that I might have killed my baby.

When another snowplow appeared on the highway, the three of us jumped up and down and got it to stop. He had a radio and called for help. I told him my van was on the southbound highway. He called the police and a patrol car met me at my van.

The officer walked around the smashed van. "You were in that when it crashed?" he asked. I nodded. "And you're still standing? That must have been one hell of a ride."

I sat in the warmth of the patrol car and tried to fill out an accident report. But my fingers were still too stiff, so I dictated and the officer wrote down what I said. The snowplows had made the roads passable, and while I was still in the patrol car, one of Merril's friends stopped by the van. The officer said he looked like someone I probably knew because he was dressed in typical FLDS clothes. I realized the man was Merril's brother. While the two men were talking, another man from the community arrived. He stopped, too. After a brief consultation, he decided to take me home, and my brother-in-law said he'd wait for the tow truck to arrive.

Merril had heard about the storm in Page and knew I was driving home. He'd called my apartment in Cedar and talked to his daughters there, who said I'd left a few hours before. Then he called my parents to see if they had heard from me. No one had. Merril told my dad there had been a lot of accidents on the road. Dad decided to look for me. He had to make his way through the storm, which was still wreaking havoc in the area. He started following the route he thought I'd have taken and spotted Merril's van in Hurricane, where it had been towed. He was stricken by the sight of the damaged van. He flagged the driver down and asked if he knew what had happened to me. But the driver of the tow truck had no idea of my whereabouts. Ambulances were coming in from everywhere.

My father got back in the car and told my mother that they'd just have to go home and wait for a phone call with news. When my parents got home at midnight, they learned I was safe and had called about an hour before.

The first thing I did when I got home was hold Arthur in my arms. He was now just over a year and nothing on earth was more precious to me than him. The warmth of his small body against mine began to melt some of my awful fear. It took me more than twenty-four hours to feel warm again. But I still didn't know about my pregnancy. I hadn't started bleeding, which I thought was a good sign. Maybe, just maybe, the baby had been spared. When I was stranded, I'd prayed and prayed to God to save my baby.

I went back to school and started studying again. College gave me a focus. The days were fine, but I started having terrible nightmares. I would see the steering wheel spinning out of control and feel the van skidding out from under me. The terror was unshakably alive in me.

I stopped driving, but I just didn't tell anyone about it. I made up excuses about why I didn't want to drive. In large families, there is *always* someone who is willing and eager to drive. I was too traumatized, but no one ever suspected the real reason I never drove. There would be times when I had to drive between school and Merril's house, but they were few and far between. Once I graduated, I never wanted to drive again.

No one knew how hard I had worked for my degree or how much it meant to me. This was my shining moment. Merril and my father came to my graduation but got there late and missed the beginning. I smiled when I walked across the stage to receive my bachelor of science degree. Marriage to Merril had ended my dream of becoming a doctor—he'd never have allowed it. But I was proud that my marriage had not compromised this moment, and I was grateful in the deepest part of my being that my pregnancy had survived the accident.

I wasn't sure what the future held. Now that I had my degree, I would have to move back to Colorado City and, for the first time since my marriage, live a day-to-day life as Merril Jessop's fourth wife.

Morning sickness continued to plague me. It finally stopped the day before my daughter was born. Merril came to her birth; thankfully, no one else did. She was a beautiful baby. She weighed seven pounds and was in robust health. I was as exhausted as I was relieved.

Merril was captivated by the baby from the moment he saw her. When she was three weeks old, he decided her name would be Betty. It was his favorite name and he had been waiting to give it to a favorite daughter.

Merril played favorites with his children. It was always clear who they were. A favorite child always had more status over his other children. They were held up and honored before the entire family. It would be years before I realized how exalted Betty's status would be in our family and how it would impact on our lives.

When she was born on July 2, 1989, I was simply grateful that she was alive and healthy. Now I had a son and a daughter. Arthur had a baby sister. Within my chaotic world, I had an island of love. I was twenty-one years old.

# Move Home

**A** week after I moved home from college, Tammy and I sat down for a long talk. In nearly four years of marriage, I'd grown closer to Tammy than any of the other wives. Tammy played both sides of the family. She'd flatter Barbara and Merril but often used her power to protect others. In the early years of my marriage her backstabbing was kept to a minimum.

Merril had always been financially stable, but a dispute with the state over land he leased for a gravel business that was not resolved in his favor sent him into a financial crisis. He was hit with a $90,000 fine, which left him on the verge of bankruptcy. The repercussions for our family were terrible.

We were no longer able to participate in the community's barter system because of Merril's financial problems. We had been trading cement credit for goods, but lost that purchasing power when Merril was no longer able to provide cement because of his company's problems.

We paid cash for everything. But there wasn't enough of it. Merril gave us only a hundred dollars a week to purchase food for a family of six wives and thirty children who were eating at home. (At this point he had ten more children who were married and gone.) Tammy and I were now doing most of the family shopping. Merril's daughters were only too glad to let us take over the chore. Everyone else in the family would give us their lists of personal items, from shampoo to toothpaste. But we didn't have enough money to feed the family, let alone purchase extras.

Tammy and I talked about the chaos that had engulfed the household. It had always been bad, but now that we were hungry it was worse. Merril's teenage daughters, those fabled nusses, were not living fairy-tale lives. Instead they were Cinderellas who were forced to stay at home cooking, cleaning, and babysitting.

They were sullen and resentful. They were also responsible for making the meals, baking bread for the family, doing most of the children's laundry, and washing all the dishes. What compounded their hostility was that when Merril came home with Barbara on weekends he'd gather his wives around him for a steak dinner. He basked in our adoring attention while we sipped red wine. None of us ever drank more than two glasses—some, barely a half—but it was still a treat.

Drinking alcohol was a point of departure between the Mormon Church and the FLDS. There is a principle in the faith called the "word of wisdom" that bans all alcoholic beverages and hot drinks. I was taught as a child that the mainstream Mormon Church did not start adhering to the "word of wisdom" until after it renounced polygamy and celestial marriage. Those of us adhering to the tenets of the FLDS practiced the older beliefs and felt following the "word of wisdom" was optional. Many of us in the fundamentalist faith drank coffee, tea, beer, and wine, all of which is strictly forbidden in mainstream Mormonism.

The only way Merril's daughters could express their resentment over being treated like maids was in the careless way they did their work. The house was cleaned sporadically; most of the time it was filthy. The dishes usually got done because one of the wives would get so fed up she'd do them herself. We rarely had enough bread because they never baked enough. With nearly twenty children in grade school and younger, it was almost impossible to keep up with the laundry. It had to be done on a schedule. But that never happened. The children's bedrooms were a mess. Dirty clothes were strewn everywhere. The house looked like the dumping ground it was.

Despite her pandering to Merril and Barbara, Tammy hated the chaos we dealt with every day. We decided to tackle what we could to bring more order to our lives. "I like to get up in the morning," Tammy said. "I'm usually up by five, so there is no reason why I can't fix breakfast every day. I can also bake a batch of bread the night before. When there is no bread in the house, it feels like there's nothing to eat. While I'm waiting for the bread I'll mop the kitchen floor."

"The thing that is driving me crazy is dinner," I said. "The babies are crying and I can't feed them because someone is cooking dinner in the kitchen and won't let the babies be fed until that's finished. We never eat until after eight and sometimes not until midnight, which is unacceptable." I wasn't eager to take on the responsibility, but said I'd make dinner every night.

We still had the issue of money. There simply wasn't enough cash. Tammy and I decided to triage the shopping list and purge it of all personal items. People would have to go without. We had children still in diapers, which took a big bite out of our budget.

I planted a huge garden that summer and we managed to eat every meal from its harvest. We bought flour for bread and had some beans in the cellar, bottled vegetables, and fruit. But despite our best efforts, the tension at home because of sheer want kept building.

Rather than appreciating our efforts, Merril and Barbara were offended. Merril made it clear that Tammy and I should have checked with Barbara before we implemented changes in the daily household routine. Merril once refused to eat dinner because I hadn't checked with Barbara before preparing it. I could not believe the ego of that man.

I didn't think of him as my husband, a gift from God. I thought of him as "that man," an egocentric bully whom I had been forced to marry, someone who had control over my life and my body. I hated depending on him financially. I still believed in my religion, but I knew Merril wasn't following it the way he should. I knew the way he treated me and his other five wives was wrong, and yet he was a powerful man in the FLDS. I felt frustrated and confused.

The breaking point came after a few months of running on

empty. We had been out of things such as shampoo, toothpaste, and soap for weeks. Once winter came and the garden froze, the only food we had left in the house was cracked wheat, which we ate for breakfast, and the makings of tomato sandwiches, which we had for lunch and dinner. We'd picked the green tomatoes just before the frost and let them ripen in buckets. Every day we'd sort through them looking for some that were ripe enough to eat. I thought that once Merril realized we couldn't feed ourselves from the garden now that it had frozen he'd be more attentive to the family. I was wrong.

Merril and Barbara were still living large in Page. Whatever money Merril did make fueled their lifestyles and appetite for dining out and drinking wine. Barbara never had to scrimp or save. Barbara was so selfish, I thought she probably enjoyed eating in fancy restaurants while we were struggling at home.

I was nursing Betty but very worried about Arthur. He was losing weight from lack of food. I also feared that if I didn't get enough to eat I'd be unable to produce enough breast milk for Betty. I knew there was absolutely no money for formula.

When Merril came home that November we had been in a deteriorating crisis for two months and our food supply was dwindling. Merril called all six wives into his office for a meeting. He decreed that only Barbara could implement changes in family policies or assign jobs. Merril was enthusiastic in explaining that now Barbara would preside over every detail of family life.

"I have one question," I said when Merril finished. "How can every one of us check in with Barbara before we tie our shoes if she's rarely at home? I need to understand how this is going to work at a practical level."

Merril's neck reddened and his face hardened. He was angry and started scolding me for questioning his decision. Merril hated to be challenged.

None of the other wives spoke. But I knew they were as fed up with the abuse and degradation as I was.

When Merril finished his tirade against me I looked at him and said, "Well, maybe since all there is to eat in this house are tomato sandwiches I will call Barbara while she's eating a steak dinner with you and ask her for permission to make tomato sandwiches for dinner. That way everything can be done just the way she wants it."

If Merril had a gun he would have aimed it at me. I was scared of him, but I'd been pushed to the point where I didn't care. Merril was seething. "Don't you accuse me! You act like a tomato sandwich isn't something that is good to eat!"

I'd touched the untouchable and spoken the unspeakable. They were feasting while we were nearly starving.

Everyone else in the room was so quiet I thought they were holding their breath. I was undeterred. I rarely stood up to Merril or Barbara, but when I was pushed too far, I had no fear of confronting them. I was fed up with their cruelty and constant put-downs. Merril's other wives would complain once in a while, but he always belittled them and made it so painful they were disinclined to do it again. I think what was starting to crack open in me was my authentic self. I had been in survival mode. In a cult, you have two identities: your cult identity and your authentic self. Most of the time I operated from my cult identity, which was pliant, submissive, and obedient. But when I was pushed to the point where it felt like my survival was at stake, my authentic self came to the fore. The worse life became in Merril's family, the more confidence I found in my authentic self.

In a steady and sure voice I said to Merril, "If tomato sandwiches are so wonderful, then why aren't you and Barbara eating them for lunch and dinner like the rest of us?"

That was the shout that brought down the avalanche. The other women piled on in what became known as "the famous tomato sandwich fight." My courage enabled the other women to find their own. They told Merril how unfair it felt to them to turn over whatever income they had and not receive anything in return. Their children were hungry, and they were, too. How could we be asked to sacrifice while Barbara and Merril lived like royalty? Barbara looked appalled and disgusted by what we were saying but let Merril do the talking.

Several wives complained that most of the young children in the

home were Barbara's and that she needed to be more engaged in raising them. In short, she needed to start acting like their mother. Cathleen said she was finished combing out the long, tangled hair of
Barbara's daughters before school each morning. Tammy demanded
to know why Barbara only gave orders and never did anything to help
around the house. We made it clear that she was not a good example
for the rest of the wives.

Barbara started crying when she came under attack from the rest
of us, and got up and left. Merril was incensed and scolded us for
humiliating her.

He berated us for quite a while until we all just stopped talking.
Finally he demanded to know what we thought the answers were if
we weren't going to do what he wanted us to. We said we had to have
money to feed the kids and we couldn't go on indefinitely without
being able to buy personal items. Merril finally agreed to give us
more money for groceries, but he made it clear that we'd be paying a
price down the road for what we had done. His threat was meaningless, however. Merril knew he had pushed us too far; he also knew
we needed money to live.

Our morale improved when we were able to buy food again.
Sometimes we'd get money for personal items, but often not. It
became a running joke among us.

I knew Merril was terribly angry at me for sparking the insurrec-
tion. I also knew that he held grudges and when the right moment
came he'd lash out at me. I wasn't proud of what I'd done. We had
been reduced to fighting for food. I thought it was completely hypo-
critical that Merril would let a large family like ours go hungry while
he and Barbara were indulging themselves in Page.

I had been substitute-teaching for four months when a permanent job opened up teaching sixth grade. The following year I was
transferred to the second grade. There were other, more qualified
teachers on the list for openings, but I got it because of Merril's high
standing with the prophet, which was derived from his father's
prominence. His father, who was known as Uncle Rich, was the
apostle who was next in line to the prophet.

I loved finally having my own classroom. It was the one and only place in my life where I was in control of my environment on a daily basis. But I hated leaving my children at home in mediocre care. Merril's teenage daughters were watching Arthur and Betty, but I knew their hearts weren't in it. Worse still, Merril's daughters treated my children as second-class citizens, and that upset me. The girls were often belligerent when I asked them something about Betty and Arthur, which increased the anxiety I felt about the overall situation.

Merril had several older daughters—former nusses—who were my age and still unmarried in their early twenties. Tension was building in FLDS communities in Colorado City, Hildale, Salt Lake, and Canada because there were so many girls who were getting older and were still unmarried. The prophet usually arranged hundreds of marriages for girls every year. But when Uncle Rulon became head of the FLDS he fell behind in arranging marriages. Part of the problem was that he'd always lived in Salt Lake City and didn't know most of the families who lived in Colorado City and Hildale.

Parents feared that if their daughters weren't assigned in marriage they would begin to think that they could choose someone for themselves. When complaints were made to Uncle Rulon, he told fathers to place their daughters in marriages themselves. We all knew this was what was happening, but no one spoke of it because it was against the precepts of the FLDS. A man could receive revelations from God about his family, but only the prophet received divine revelations about matchmaking.

Merril took several of his wives with him to Salt Lake City when he went for the priesthood meeting on the third weekend of the month. Tammy and I were sharing a hotel room. The night of the priesthood meeting she came into our room in a daze. Tammy sat on the bed and stared at the wall, trancelike.

"Tammy, is something wrong?" I asked.

She walked over to a table and cradled her head in her hands. A few moments later she pounded her fist on the table. "Yes! There's something wrong and I'm a bad person for feeling this way."

I was perplexed and could not imagine what might have happened.

Tammy turned to me with tears streaming down her face. Uncle Rulon had just married Bonnie, who was Barbara and Ruth's little sister. Bonnie was in her early twenties; Uncle Rulon was in his early eighties.

Tammy grabbed a Kleenex and wiped the tears from her face.

"Carolyn, I can't stand this! This is what happened to me and I hate to see it happening to another girl. I know what it is like to have to marry a man who is so much older. You don't have anything in life to live for anymore." Her chest was heaving with sobs. All the grief in her life from having had to marry Uncle Roy when she was a young girl overwhelmed her. Tammy's life had been stolen from her just as Bonnie's was being stolen now.

Tammy had been eighteen and Uncle Roy eighty-eight when she was assigned to him in marriage. She told me that Uncle Roy was so old he had only slept with her a few times in the decade that they were married. During most of their marriage he was sick and bedridden. Tammy never felt she had any kind of relationship with him at all.

Being the wife of the prophet of God is a very public position, and every move a woman makes is monitored. If you are a younger wife, that scrutiny is compounded by the fact that all of your sister wives, who are old enough to be your mother, act superior, if not out-right disdainful, toward you.

When Tammy stopped sobbing she said, "It feels like her parents took her like a lamb to slaughter and sacrificed her purely for the purpose of having a daughter married to the Prophet of God." With that she left the room and said she was going outside for some fresh air.

I saw Bonnie a few times in public after her marriage to Uncle Rulon. The light was gone from her eyes. She was wearing even more restrictive clothing and looked distressed. It was as if her being had been evacuated. My stomach began churning and I felt sick. Bonnie was a year younger than I was and had always been a beautiful girl who sparkled with life. Now she looked so alone and forsaken. I knew how difficult it was to marry a man thirty years my senior, but the thought of being assigned to someone who was sixty years older was as horrifying as it was incomprehensible.

Word was moving around the community now that fathers were arranging most of the marriages. The prophet had hardly any involvement with where girls were going or to whom. Our lives were currency for other people to spend.

I remember my surprise one day about nine months later when I heard that Loretta, one of Merril's daughters, was going to be married, because he had several who were still unmarried and older than she. When I asked him whom Loretta was marrying, he turned to me with a smile. "Well, it's Uncle Rulon."

I sat down, too shocked to stand. I didn't want to make a scene because marriages were supposedly arranged by God, so I quickly threw the switch to erase any emotion from my face. I did not dare let Merril know what I was thinking. But I knew in my bones that he had arranged this marriage. Tall and thin, with a mane of jet-black hair, Loretta had striking features and was one of Merril's most beautiful daughters.

My first memory of her was seeing her in high school as a staunch member of the nusses. She lived and breathed *Fascinating Womanhood* and was well-versed in the art of manipulating a man. Now she was about to marry the most powerful man in the FLDS who, at eighty-two, probably wouldn't even notice if the Dixie cup dispenser was right side up or not.

Loretta seemed to accept her fate without much enthusiasm. She began making her wedding dress as soon as she learned about her imminent marriage, which was to take place within days.

Merril decided that the entire family would go to Salt Lake City—all six wives and some thirty children. The wedding was that night, and we set out in the morning in a caravan of six or seven cars and trucks. Merril had been promising his children a trip to a fishing farm en route to Salt Lake City. He decided this was the time to do it.

This was idiotic because there weren't enough older children to help the younger ones with their lines and poles. Within minutes, there was a tangled blur of lines both in the water and out. Hooks were caught in clothing and hair. It was mayhem. The farm was well stocked with fish, but we caught only two.

After we left the fishing farm, one of the cars in our caravan broke down, which slowed us even more. Loretta was beside herself. This was not just any wedding. Uncle Rulon was obsessed with punctuality. He had no tolerance for people who were late, and now Loretta had missed her own wedding and felt disgraced.

Merril performed the marriage the following evening at Uncle Rulon's home. As an elder in the FLDS, he had that power. It was a huge event, with about a hundred people in attendance. Loretta looked stunning in a modest white wedding dress with elegant lace trim. Uncle Rulon wasn't strong enough to stand for the wedding. He sat in an armchair. Loretta sat in a chair beside him. His wizened old hand held hers in the patriarchal grip, which is symbolic of the way he will hold her hand when he resurrects her into heaven after death.

Merril was beaming. Now he had direct access to the prophet. I had always known Merril was hungry for power. But I had never understood how voracious an appetite he had or how much human sacrifice it would require.

# My Patriarchal Blessing

**A** woman's destiny in the FLDS is handed to her in two ways. She is assigned in marriage by the prophet who's told by God the name of her husband-to-be. But even before that happens, usually sometime in her early teenage years, a woman is given a patriarchal blessing, which explains her purpose in life.

When Merril's younger daughters were getting their patriarchal blessing I realized that, for whatever reason, I'd never had one. I asked Merril if he'd arrange for me to have one. He was surprised that I hadn't and agreed to ask one of the three patriarchs in the community to schedule an appointment for me. A patriarch ranks third in the FLDS hierarchy, after the prophet and his apostles.

The prophet receives revelations for people at large or for the entire community. While the prophet will tell an individual whom God wants him to marry, he doesn't get involved in revealing the futures of each young person in the community. That responsibility is divided up among the patriarchs. In our community, there were three patriarchs who gave blessings.

Women never talked too much about their blessings. The information was supposed to be kept private because we believed that if you talked too much about it you could compromise the blessing. From what I'd heard, most young women were told that they would become a faithful wife and a mother in Zion, raising faithful children up to the Lord.

My blessing was much different.

It was bestowed on me by Joseph Barlow, a son of the former prophet. Merril took me to his home and we went into a private room. I sat in a chair and the patriarch put his hands on my head. In a deep voice he began by saying, "The purpose of this blessing is to learn the will of God concerning his daughter Carolyn, the daughter of Arthur and Nurylon Blackmore."

He told me I was a direct descendant of Abraham, Isaac, Jacob, and Jesus Christ. "The pure blood of Jesus Christ runs through your veins," he said in a sober tone. I was surprised but not quite sure how to feel. I had heard that this was told to some people in their blessings. It seemed like a privilege, but I had no idea why.

In my preexistence, I'd been one of the choicest spirits, held in reserve for the last days to be part of ushering in a thousand years of peace. In my mortal lifetime, I would see Christ live again on earth. The patriarch told me I'd been selected for this gift because in my preexistence, I had been an enormous influence in casting the devil out of heaven. I was an intelligent spirit before I came to earth and my intelligence had been put to good use during the war in heaven against the spirits who stood against God.

I listened intently. I was expecting to hear a lot about marriage and children. This felt much bigger.

My intelligence was the reason God had chosen to use me again on earth. Apparently one of my talents was discernment. The patriarch told me I could look at people and know when I met them if they were good or evil.

Because of my gifts, there were many spirits on the other side who were watching over me. These spirits would give me opportunities to see things and would make me aware of dangers. The reason for this was that God intended to use me to protect his people in the last days. I was also going to be put to work in the temple and be responsible for many people receiving their priesthood training.

There was more. I was told that I'd be working with the ten tribes when they returned to earth and many of them would be personally trained by me. It was a great honor to live until the time of the ten tribes, and being engaged in their education was a rare privilege.

As if these responsibilities weren't enough, I was told that some of the most precious spirits from the other side were waiting to come to earth as my children. The blessing continued as the patriarch told me that educational opportunities would continue to come my way and that I would end up as a valiant member of God's chosen.

These blessings were contingent on my remaining faithful until the end of my life. In return, I had the promise that I would be lifted up on the last day and protected.

After my blessing was over I felt confused. Not many women in the FLDS had ever lived lives that were valued as having an impact on others in their community. My blessing sounded like a destiny I wasn't really seeking.

Merril never asked me about my blessing. I'm sure he assumed it was nothing special.

# Hawaii: Seven Days
# but Only Two Nights

The moment I heard that Merril was planning a trip to Hawaii I knew there would be trouble in paradise. But I underestimated what an unmitigated disaster it would turn out to be.

I was upset when I heard about the trip for the first time at my father's house. My dad and Merril had become business partners again after my marriage. They'd worked together before on a deal that turned out badly and my father decided he was never going to do business with him again, but after my marriage their partnership accelerated. They were investing in motels, rest homes, and a restaurant or two. They would often travel together to check on their businesses. Six months before, they'd gone to Washington, D.C. Merril took Barbara with him. He usually always traveled with Barbara because she was the love of his life.

But now he had three more wives and the pressure was on him to include more than just Barbara on his trips. Merril had an image to protect. In the FLDS culture, a man is supposed to treat each of his wives equally. There's always favoritism, but in theory a family is supposed to be united behind the husband, who's called the priesthood head. A woman's only avenue to God is through her husband. We were raised to believe we could not receive direct revelations from God on our own. Whatever God had to communicate or reveal to a woman could be transmitted only through her husband. This doctrine was unassailable and had been so for generations in the culture I was born into.

If a man shows favoritism or appears not to be in control of his family, it damages his image in the community and opens him up to accusations that he does not have the spirit of God within him. One of the reasons Merril tried to keep us all pregnant was that it created the illusion that he was having a relationship with each of us. But that was a myth. The reality was he loved Barbara and no one else. Merril was a polygamist in body but a monogamist in soul. He enjoyed the power polygamy gave him, and as a narcissist, he craved the attention. But Barbara was the only woman he ever loved.

When I heard about the Hawaii trip, I knew there would be no way Merril could take Barbara with him so soon after their trip to Washington. At my father's I heard that my father had paid for extra tickets so Merril could take three wives. I was furious. No one ever traveled with multiple wives. It never worked. It was an insult and humiliating to think that Merril was even considering taking three wives. I told both my mothers I didn't want to go. My mother accused me of being ungrateful and said I didn't know what my father had gone through to see that I was included on the trip. I still didn't care. My father knew Merril was unfair to his wives but he didn't know to what extent. He sensed my unhappiness but not the depth of it, and I think he believed the trip might give me hope that things would get better.

I was twenty-two and thought this would probably be the only big trip I'd ever have in my lifetime. Merril was unfair in doling out rewards in his family, and Barbara was so clearly his favorite wife I knew that he'd continue to travel with her as often as he could. As women, we had no right to travel by ourselves. I didn't want to share what would most likely be the only major trip of my lifetime with two other of Merril's wives.

Tammy got wind of the trip within days and confronted Merril immediately in his office. Like me, she was outraged that he was taking three of us.

"If Carolyn's father is paying for this trip, then Carolyn should go. Anyone else who comes along is just an intruder," Tammy said.

Merril was unfazed. "This is my trip and I can invite whomever I choose. If I choose to invite my lovely wife Tammy, I would think she would be honored to accept the invitation."

Tammy shot back in a rare burst of self-assertiveness, "How can you say that like a compliment? You are inviting me on the trip to destroy Carolyn's opportunity to have a trip with you. How is that a compliment?"

Merril was furious. "This is *not* Carolyn's trip. You, Tammy, are out of order for trying to tell me what I can and cannot do with my family. Carolyn has a right to go with me alone only if that's what I want her to do. You have a responsibility to be obedient to your husband, but you do not have any right to ask questions!"

Cathleen was equally incensed when she found out that one of the tickets was in her name. She called Merril at his office in Page and said she should be the sole wife traveling with him to Hawaii. Cathleen called from a phone in the house that was very public and was talking so loudly we all could hear. She felt entitled to go alone because she had only ever taken short trips with Merril. There was no logic to her argument—she was just angling to get a trip for herself. We all had been married to Merril for about four years. If the trip had been based on seniority, then I should have been the one to go alone because I'd been married to Merril seven months longer than they.

By the time Cathleen finished talking to Merril she was in tears and stormed off to her room.

I was furious, but I knew confronting Merril would be unproductive. We'd already had several major fights in our marriage and I knew there was no way to reason with him or refuse to acquiesce to whatever he desired. I was in the early stages of my third pregnancy and in the throes of morning sickness so severe I'd vomit several times a day. The thought of getting on an airplane and leaving my children, Arthur and Betty, behind made me feel even worse. Nor would I have any say about their care while I was away. I couldn't even ask my sister or a friend to watch them. I had to leave them at the mercy of the wives remaining at home.

Quiet and resigned, I started making preparations for the trip. I knew I couldn't miss more than a week of school without making arrangements for my class, so I started doing lesson plans in advance. I bought some fabric and started sewing some lightweight dresses for the trip. Tammy saw me working on my dress and felt threatened. She had a closet full of beautiful clothes but now felt she needed seven new dresses for the trip. She bought fabric and then asked her sisters to make her new dresses.

Tammy was on the warpath. She'd tell anyone who'd listen that she was being forced to go on a trip to Hawaii with me. In an about-face, she'd managed to turn me into the villain, even while knowing I had no desire to go. She started obsessing about everything I did. If I bought something for the trip, she needed to buy five of them. Cathleen, who was also pregnant, stayed in the background and out of the line of fire.

I tried reasoning with Tammy, but she wanted no part of it. I said that since it appeared that the trip was a fait accompli, why didn't we all just make the best of it? If we tried, we could have a good time, or at the very least not make things any worse or stranger than they already were.

Tammy was dismissive. She had a new mission: pregnancy. Tammy was the only one of Merril's wives who'd never had a baby. This was a disaster for her, especially since her mother had twenty children and was the wife who had substantial influence over her husband's entire family. In comparison to her mother, she was nothing. Without children, a woman had no power or status. None of us in plural marriages had even remotely normal relationships with men, but Tammy's was unique, even in our bizarre culture.

At eighteen, she had been married to the prophet Uncle Roy. He was eighty-eight. In ten years, they'd never had sex because he was too old and incapacitated. Even though she'd been married for a decade, she was still a virgin when she married Merril shortly after Uncle Roy's death.

She was upset when I gave birth because she'd been so unsuccessful in getting pregnant. She'd had an ectopic pregnancy before I gave birth to Arthur. Tammy had been taking Clomid, a fertility drug. When Merril found out that one of the side effects of Clomid was ectopic pregnancy, he was furious and told Tammy to quit the drug. She refused. Merril stopped having sex with her. (I knew this because she told us. We also had heard her screaming at Merril for three years that it was his priesthood duty to get her pregnant.)

Her desperation for a child kept escalating. Before the trip she went to the doctor again for more Clomid and began taking a double dose. She was determined to conceive in Hawaii. The more she focused on pregnancy, the less of a threat I became. Tammy stopped attacking me and suddenly became enthusiastic about Hawaii.

There was never a moment when Merril sat down with us and told us we were all going to Hawaii and explained the plan. Our lives were never that logical. We heard about the trip, and then learned that tickets were purchased with our names on them, and each of us began making our own unilateral preparations.

The morning we left, Tammy was the only happy one. Cathleen was still sulky and quiet. I was resigned but told myself I might see some good sights. If this was the one trip I was ever going to take, I wanted to see and learn as much as possible.

We all had breakfast before driving to the airport. Barbara was sitting next to Merril and seemed totally heartbroken about losing him for seven days. It was the longest separation they'd had in the four years since I'd been married to Merril. Merril seemed filled with dread. But there was no way out for him. If he took just Barbara, his image within the community would be damaged. He had to at least feign commitment to his other wives. When he kissed Barbara good-bye, she began to cry.

We piled into the car for the drive to the Las Vegas airport. There was so much luggage that it had to be crammed in around Cathleen and me in the backseat. Tammy had claimed the front seat to be next to Merril. She talked nonstop. Tammy was a geyser of gossip and kept spewing. Merril said almost nothing during the three-hour drive.

When Cathleen tried to engage in the conversation, Tammy cut her off and accused her of being rude. According to Tammy, this was her trip and the conversation should focus only on her. She told Cathleen not to interrupt. Cathleen began to pout.

Merril was despondent over leaving Barbara. I was upset about leaving Arthur and Betty and weak from morning sickness. Cathleen was sullen and self-pitying. Tammy was manic and agitated on her double dose of Clomid and completely obsessed with getting pregnant.

We were traveling with about six other FLDS couples. It was not uncommon within the community for members who could afford it to take several vacations a year to places like Cancún or California.

We were quite a sight in the airport in our long dresses and long underwear. It's a safe bet that we were the only ones traveling to Hawaii without bikinis, shorts, or T-shirts. The men were casually dressed in slacks and shirts while we were all shrouded in our multiple layers. People stared at us, but we didn't care.

The strange looks we got didn't bother me because I still believed we were God's chosen people. I was only twenty-two and my childhood faith continued to be absolute. Even though I didn't want to marry Merril, it didn't challenge my belief system in any way. I never doubted the central tenet of our faith, which said that in order to come to earth a spirit must be worthy to incarnate into a priesthood home. We had to prove ourselves worthy before we could inhabit the spirit of a child.

The fact of our birth meant we were precious spirits—one in a million—and when the last days came, we would be the ones who would be lifted up to heaven in the rapture. So by the time you're born into the FLDS culture, you've already won a lottery of sorts. You're a spirit chosen to do God's work on earth, which is priceless. When God gives one of his children so much, it carries a lot of responsibility. Over and over we're told, "Where much is given, much is required."

So while I thought it was strange and uncomfortable when people stared at me, I did not feel embarrassed. I was one of the pure and select. I looked down on the people who thought I looked strange. They were wicked and less evolved.

Tammy insisted on sitting next to Merril on the flight from Las Vegas to Los Angeles. Cathleen and I sat two seats behind them. We changed planes in Los Angeles. Merril had two empty seats on either side of him, and after Tammy grabbed one, I took the other. This infuriated Cathleen, who took an empty seat next to Tammy. But she felt like the outsider and started pouting and sniveling. Merril made some snide remark and Cathleen stormed to the back of the plane where there were empty seats. Soon we could hear her sobbing.

The other passengers stared at us and tried to fathom our strange behavior. The several other couples from Colorado City pretended nothing was amiss out of respect for Merril. Tammy felt victorious now that Cathleen had been reduced to tears and exiled to the back of the plane.

Then Tammy took aim at me. How could I abandon my sister wife? How could I be so selfish and inconsiderate? I ignored her until that became impossible and then I blurted out that I had no intention of babysitting Cathleen. Merril started to laugh. It was the first time he seemed engaged with any aspect of the trip since his tearful parting with Barbara.

It was a long flight. The drama continued almost nonstop. I put on my headphones and watched the movie. During this era in the FLDS, some people had TVs in their homes, and it was not uncommon to occasionally go to movies in theaters. While I had contact with the outside world in some limited ways—mostly through school and college—being on a plane was unusual to me. But when we finally touched down in Honolulu I was exhausted.

Merril and I walked off the plane together and someone came up to us and threw leis around our necks. A tourist photographer took our picture. Tammy barged in and said that she and Cathleen were also part of the couple. She insisted that another picture be taken of the four of us together.

We took the shuttle bus to our hotel. I sat next to Merril, which sent Tammy into the stratosphere. She started badgering him. "Father, are Cathleen and I part of this trip, too?"

Merril was unresponsive. Tammy continued, "Father, who are you planning on sleeping with tonight?" Her questions got more specific. "Why are you sitting by Carolyn again? Are you only going to have sex with her? Do we get to be included?"

The other tourists were trying not to stare at this freak show. I was mortified. Even the other couples from Colorado City seemed to be embarrassed. My father was blushing. I knew Tammy's bizarre talk made him uncomfortable. Merril acted as though he were somewhere else. He did not react as Tammy dredged up all of our dirty laundry and flung it in his face.

When we got to the hotel, Merril said he had a bad headache. He told Cathleen and me to take one of the two rooms and kissed us both good night. Tammy felt like she'd just been crowned queen.

Cathleen was in a terrible mood, still frothing mad about the way she had been treated on the plane. I tried to talk to her, but she refused. Not much time had passed before Tammy was knocking on our door. She was extremely upset and agitated. Merril had told her he had a headache and went right to sleep. He refused to have sex with her. She wanted our sympathy because we were both pregnant and she was not.

But she did not get it. She was maddening, manipulative, and mean. Cathleen and I ordered dinner from room service. She refused to speak to me, so we ate in silence.

Welcome to paradise.

Early the next morning, Merril knocked on our door and asked if we were ready for breakfast. We followed him to an exquisite garden restaurant overlooking the ocean. I was awed by the beauty surrounding us. The air smelled salty and the breeze, silky. I wanted to drink in the intense colors, but the day's first fiasco was already launched—who would get to sit next to Merril?

Tammy had taken one seat and I the other. In the confrontation that ensued, Cathleen ended up refusing even to eat at our table. Tammy continued her rant: "You sat next to him on the plane and on the shuttle bus. . . ." The waitress came to take our order, but she had to wait until Tammy's tirade subsided.

We finally ordered, ate, and left for our first day of sight-seeing. The other couples rented snappy convertibles to zip around Oahu. But Merril rented a van. I think he was determined that none of us would enjoy the trip. It was his way of retaliating for not being able to bring Barbara along.

The fresh air in a convertible would have helped with my terrible morning sickness. I vomited several times a day. The winding roads didn't help, either. I had to ask Merril to pull over so I could throw up. I felt wretched. In the tropical heat, my long dress and long underwear compounded my misery.

Merril noticed how awful I felt and stopped to get me some food. This drove Cathleen around the bend. She was pregnant, too, but Merril paid no attention to her at all. She couldn't fake nausea, but she did start complaining of a headache. Merril stopped to buy her some aspirin and then kept paying attention to me. I didn't want attention. I just wanted to quit throwing up. We stopped for food, which seemed to help me.

After a few hours of this, Tammy announced she'd had enough of my behavior. I was ruining her trip. Why didn't I stay in the hotel if I felt so sick? I told Tammy that it was good for Merril to take care of his pregnant wife, and if that was too much of an inconvenience, she could ride with one of the other couples.

We finally returned to the hotel and went to dinner. I opted to sit with my dad and his wife Rosie. It was wonderful to have a lovely meal without having to listen to any whining or complaining. But the respite was short-lived.

When I returned to the hotel Merril said to bring my things and spend the night with him. He told Tammy she'd be staying with Cathleen. She was annoyed.

"Father, all you ever do when you stay with me is sleep. You've already gotten Carolyn pregnant. It isn't right for you to be having sex with her." Merril's failure to respond angered Tammy more. "You had a headache last night, so we didn't have sex. Carolyn and Cathleen are already pregnant. I'm not."

Merril didn't react. Tammy wouldn't quit. "I know you feel better tonight and you are going to have sex with the person you stay with. That should be me. You already made me come on this trip with them. I have to share you all day, but I don't think I should have to share you at night." I was appalled but didn't engage with her. I took my suitcase and went to Merril's room, relieved not to have to be sharing a bedroom with either Tammy or Cathleen.

Merril turned on the TV. Within moments, the phone was ringing. Tammy was still on the attack. Merril enjoyed the attention. It fed his narcissism. He loved that his wives were fighting over who would have sex with him. He didn't care if Tammy was unstable. I'm not sure he even noticed. She called a few more times that evening. I learned later that she told Cathleen that part of her rant was that Merril had sex with me when I was pregnant, which was a sin within the FLDS.

Part of the FLDS doctrine is that a man should abstain from sex with his pregnant wife. But there's a loophole. A man who has attained priesthood is believed to have the spirit of God within him. His "inspirations" are seen as being transmitted from God. If he's "inspired" to have sex with his pregnant wife, it's within his rights since it comes from God.

Pregnancy was a turn-on for Merril in a way I never understood and he never tried to explain. We never talked about sex, either before, during, or afterward. In seventeen years of marriage, I never saw him naked because we had sex in total darkness. It was rudimentary and over in minutes. Merril remained mute throughout. Afterward he'd lie on top of me for a long time. I felt crushed and sometimes almost suffocated. Eventually he'd roll over like a dead animal and sleep.

What made it even more bizarre was that every time we had sex with each other we did it while clothed in our long underwear—except that night in Hawaii when we had sex completely naked. I was shocked when he took off my long underwear and began touching my skin. It felt different and far more enjoyable. But I didn't let myself respond too emotionally because I knew it would probably never happen again.

Every woman in a plural marriage knows that her only power in life will come from her relationship to her husband. I felt hostile to Merril. I hadn't wanted to marry him and never wanted to sleep with him. But I knew that my survival and the caliber of life I could provide for my children depended on my forging a relationship with Merril. Pleasing him—or at least not aggravating him—was a skill I was determined to master no matter what it cost me at a personal level. Sublimating my needs to his felt natural to me at twenty-two. I knew this was how generations of women had lived in my family.

In order to have power in Merril's family, I had to make myself important to him. That gave me status over his other wives and protected me and my children from their attacks. It's an insanely competitive environment. Only the strong survived. No one in our family ever tried to look out for a sister wife.

Cathleen and Tammy felt threatened by my access to Merril. They felt that any attention he paid to me came at their expense. The angry bickering resumed at breakfast the next morning about who would sit next to Merril. There would be moments when I'd think how weird it was that the three of us were competing for a man none of us loved, desired, or had ever wanted to marry.

After breakfast we flew to the island of Kauai. It was the most spectacular of all the islands we visited. It looked like a mock-up for the Garden of Eden. I had never seen so much vegetation. It was green beyond all imagining. Plants grew from crevices in jagged rocks. Flowers in bright Crayola colors seemed to be ablaze in bloom. Treetops were dense with tropical birds. The blue of the Pacific seemed to mirror the sky and added a pulse and vitality to the landscape it encircled.

Our condo was only a few feet from the beach. I took off my shoes and tried to find someone to walk along the water with me. Tammy and Cathleen insisted on staying in the condo with Merril, who wanted to take a nap. Merril had indicated that he wanted to be with Cathleen that night.

Rosie, my mother, agreed to take a walk with me. It was peaceful. The ocean was warm, my bare feet sank into the wet sand, and sparkling water washed over my toes. The breeze was gentle and the air felt pure. But swimming in the ocean was unthinkable. I didn't own a bathing suit and never considered swimming in the ocean or even a pool during the week we spent in Hawaii. FLDS members are usually not allowed near water because it's considered the devil's domain. We're taught that if you put yourself in a place where the devil has sole power, he can take your life. But this belief was often ignored. People swam in the FLDS, but only completely clothed. If your body is covered, swimming is considered daring, but not evil or wrong.

The beach was so tranquil that I didn't want to leave. I felt joy amidst such beauty and experienced a pervasive sense of calm. The absence of anger, tension, and rivalry centered me. Rosie and I had a comfortable but superficial relationship. I never told her what I was really feeling because she wouldn't be able to hear what I needed to say. She was my father's second wife and his favorite. He never got along with my biological mother. If I talked honestly to Rosie about my life, she'd tell me to stop whining and complaining. In her eyes, Merril was a man of God and I needed to honor him with my life.

On the way back to the condo we picked up some coconuts that had fallen from the trees. When we got inside, we sliced them open and put the fresh coconut on plates. Merril thought it was delicious—so delicious, in fact, that he decided to send dozens to his friends as gifts.

Instead of spending time relaxing or sight-seeing on Kauai, Merril had us pick coconuts and ship them via UPS to his friends. Tammy, Cathleen, and I spent the rest of the afternoon at UPS in our own mini-shipping department. Once we were in a work environment with Merril giving us orders, the tension among us subsided. Work was something we understood. This was the least contentious moment of the entire trip.

After sending the coconuts, we had dinner at a steak restaurant that sat high up over the ocean on a big rock. The roaring surf echoed around us.

The waves on Kauai seemed more massive than they had on the other islands. Every time a wave crashed on the rocks I could hear the spray splashing. I loved the steadying rhythm of the waves. It was powerful but not at all frightening. I felt small, safe, and protected, which was a rare feeling for me and a distraction from the tawdry soap opera that was being played out all around me.

Tammy was infuriated that Merril was planning to sleep with Cathleen that night. She screeched again about the unfairness of it all, but Merril tuned her out. I refused to share a room with her and slept on the sofa in the condo. After three hellish days together, having a sofa all to myself felt like a prize.

Cathleen was in a happy mood the next morning, which helped the overall atmosphere. My morning sickness abated and I felt better than I had since we'd arrived. We spent the day sight-seeing on Kauai, traveling to the highest point, where we had a magnificent view of the entire island. A lighthouse there seemed to be a magnet for thousands of birds that would sweep in and off the cliff on waves. When we weren't high above the Pacific we ambled along beachside roads that were shaded by palm trees.

Tammy knew it was her turn to sleep with Merril that night, so she was in a reasonable mood for most of the day and not on the attack. We capped off our day of sight-seeing with dinner at one of the island's most famous restaurants. When I ordered shrimp, Merril threw a fit.

Merril doesn't eat shrimp, which meant I couldn't either. It was wrong for me to like something he didn't. As his wife, I was to become one with him in every way. In the FLDS, a woman is supposed to be in complete harmony with her husband. A devout wife would never even desire to eat something her husband disliked. The only fish Merril liked was halibut. It wasn't on the menu. I ordered steak.

Tammy spent the night with Merril, so there were no bedtime theatrics. The next morning, we headed to Honolulu after changing planes in Maui. When we claimed our luggage, one of Cathleen's suitcases—the one with her long underwear—was missing.

She began sobbing uncontrollably. I thought she was lucky not to have to wear it for the rest of the trip. The underwear always made me feel clumsy, but in the tropics it was worse because of the three pairs of socks we wore over them—a light support stocking, followed by a heavy dance sock capped off with a heavier support stocking to keep everything in place.

Tammy and I both had extra underwear, but sharing was not permissible. Cathleen was out of luck and she was inconsolable. Merril offered her a thousand dollars to replace whatever was in her missing suitcase, but the money didn't matter to her. She wanted her garments.

The drama resumed at the hotel when Merril announced that he wanted to spend the night with me. Tammy went ballistic. She had spent two nights with Merril and made it quite well known to Cathleen and me that they hadn't had sex either time. She launched into Merril again about his sinful behavior, calling him immoral for not getting her pregnant and for having sex with me while I was.

Tammy called the room soon after we got there. Not only had Cathleen locked her out, she'd barricaded the door with the furniture in the room. Cathleen was screaming as loud as she could, "I'm totally done with you! I don't want to see you ever again!"

Merril listened to Tammy's play-by-play account of the fight and said he'd take care of it. He called Cathleen and berated her. Why had she come on the trip if she couldn't behave? After a barrage of Merril's disparaging and humiliating remarks, Cathleen relented and let Tammy back into the room. Merril and I had sex. The snaps were unsnapped, but our long underwear stayed on.

No one spoke at breakfast. Afterward we headed for the van and another day of sight-seeing. Even though Cathleen was only in the early stages of her pregnancy, she began wobbling like a woman on the verge of delivery. It was her way of trying to show what a sacrifice she was making for Merril—even though he mistreated her, she was hobbling along and carrying his child.

Oddly enough, the day was relatively relaxed. The other couples went their separate ways. Tammy seemed to have accepted defeat, Cathleen was quiet, and I sat near a window in the van to try to keep from throwing up.

During the afternoon drive, I did something I'd rarely done before: I told Merril that his teenage daughters were constantly abusive toward me and my children at home. When I'd complained about this in the past, he'd always said it was my fault. He felt his daughters were in complete harmony with him and said that if they were correcting me, I must be doing something wrong. Now I accused him of using his daughters to discipline me, and said I'd fight back to defend myself and my children.

Tammy and Cathleen listened attentively. Merril's daughters were actually more abusive to them than they were to me. Tammy would try to butter them up, even if it meant agreeing with the accusations they were making against her. Cathleen, who was nonconfrontational, would storm off and sulk in her room.

I usually avoided talking to Merril about my feelings because he'd always explode at the mention of something being wrong. But the week in Hawaii had been so explosive that I think I'd lost my fear of violent outbursts. Merril told me to be quiet. I said I wouldn't shut up.

I brought up a recent episode between me and one of his daughters. Merril roared back in rage: "Carolyn, if you were willing to do what your husband wanted, then my daughter wouldn't have any reason to treat you that way. You shouldn't respond with anger to a correction from someone who is trying to do what I want; you should thank her for the correction and express sorrow that you are not more in harmony with me. I know you are in the wrong because you never came to talk to me about it."

This infuriated me. "I never talk to you about it because you refuse to listen. I am automatically in the wrong no matter how bizarre the abuse toward me is. I learned a long time ago that going to you would only get me more abuse, not justice."

Merril tried to silence me by saying, "If I am not home and a member of my family is aware of something that they know is in concurrence with my wishes, then you have no right to interfere in any way."

I insisted that I did. "If they say or do something abusive, I have every right as a human being to protect myself and use whatever it takes to defend my children. If you and your daughters want to wage war with me, you should know I will fight back."

To my complete surprise, Tammy chimed in at this point. "Merril, it's wrong for you to use your daughters against your wives and encourage them to be hurtful and mean to us and your other children. If you have a problem with something we're doing, why can't you handle it directly and stop hiding behind your children for protection?"

This angered Merril as much as anything I had said, if not more. He struck back. "If either of you was willing to be obedient to me, then there would be no need for this conversation. You and Carolyn are saying things that, I assure you both, you will be paying for and regret."

Merril's threats drew Cathleen from her silence for the first time that day. "I think someone who encourages his children to act inappropriately like you do is sinning against God and the prophet," she said. "A man is supposed to teach his children to love all of their mothers and to overlook their faults. Children should not judge or take action against one of their mothers. Your actions are destroying your family." Once Cathleen got going, she revved up fast. "Tammy and Carolyn may pay for what they say to you today, but it doesn't change the fact that what you're doing is wrong."

I could not believe what I was hearing. The three of us were united against Merril. No one was backing down. He became quiet.

What a change! For five days we'd been battling one another, and now we were standing up to our mutual husband. If Merril was upset, he didn't show it. He was cornered and forced to listen. He didn't like our accusations of abuse. Even though he had no intention of intervening to stop the abuse, I think he knew what was happening was wrong. But he also knew that ultimately our protests would lead nowhere.

After dinner, one of the other couples took Tammy and me for a ride in their rented convertible. I loved feeling the wind against my face and skin. It was a freedom I'd never experienced before. The wind ripped my hair out from under layers of hair spray and whipped it around my face. I loved feeling that there was nothing separating me from the outside. It was sensual and elemental—an unusual but delightful feeling for me.

We stopped at some tourist shops and I picked up presents for my children and the other wives at home. Tammy saw me pull out a hundred-dollar bill and freaked out when she realized Merril had given me additional money. I was finished with her bullying. She followed me around, complaining to the other women about my purchases. When we got back to the hotel she ran to Merril with her tattling tales, but he didn't care.

Merril was spending his last night with Cathleen. After Tammy finished berating me in her call to Merril, I said that maybe she had managed to interrupt him during sex with Cathleen. She screeched at me and said she hoped they *were* having sex. I said, "Tammy, that is so immoral. Do you really want your husband to commit those kinds of heathen sins?"

"Yes, I do, because he commits those sins with you!"

"You have no idea what he does with me," I shot back. "And it's none of your business."

"But you're pregnant and I am not. I think we all know he is committing heathen sins with you."

Breakfast the next morning was tense and angry. Cathleen was still upset about her missing long underwear. Tammy attacked Cathleen for being too emotional. Then she told Merril about our fight and how rude I had been to her in the conversation about heathen sex. Tammy was relentless. Merril could have told her to knock it off, but he never did. I think he tried to ignore our bickering because he prided himself on being a martyr to his rebellious wives.

When we left the restaurant we gathered up our piles of luggage and headed to the airport. None of us had had a good time. It had been six days of nearly relentless arguing broken up by long periods of tense silence.

On the flight back, Cathleen sat by herself, so there was no competition about who got to sit next to Merril. We changed planes in Los Angeles. I almost missed the connection because I went to buy some water and Merril got on the plane with my boarding pass. When I didn't show up, he realized what had happened and rushed off the plane to find me.

After the short flight to Las Vegas, we piled into the van for the three-hour drive back to Colorado City. Cathleen and I sat in the back and didn't speak. Tammy was up front with Merril and tried to engage him in conversation, but he wanted nothing to do with her. After a while, Tammy offered to drive and Merril let her.

He put his seat back as far as it would go and asked me to rub his shoulders.

I did. The car was quiet. I was exhausted. I'd survived my six days in paradise and, thankfully, only two nights with my husband.

# Giving Birth
# in the FLDS

**W**hen I returned from Hawaii, I wasn't as panicked about my third pregnancy. In part it was because I knew all I would ever have in my life that mattered to me would be my children.

The intimacy and tenderness I felt in caring for Arthur and Betty was boundless and unparalleled by anything I had ever felt in my life. My two children had shown me a depth of love that I never knew existed.

Being pregnant, sick, and a second-grade teacher was not nearly as stressful as being pregnant, sick, and a college student. I spent much of the day running down the hall from my classroom to vomit in the bathroom. Sometimes I didn't make it and I threw up in the nearest garbage can. The other teachers worried about me and urged me to go home and rest, but I was committed to my second graders.

As it had in the past, pregnancy seemed to make me more desirable to Merril, although I was still so malnourished that I never looked very big. Even though it was supposed to be taboo in our culture, Merril continued to have sex with me while I was pregnant.

Now that I had children, they had become fair game for the other wives when they wanted to create conflict for me. Arthur was targeted as a toddler because he was very cute and looked a lot like Merril. The other wives were threatened by this because they were afraid Arthur would be more favored than their own children. There wasn't a move Arthur could make without being chastised for being a bad baby. They'd insist Arthur was full of rebellion and condemn me for being a bad mother.

The pressure was unrelenting. Any wife could discipline another woman's children. When a woman in the FLDS wanted to sabotage a rival wife, she'd attack her children by exaggerating or inventing bad behavior so they could be punished.

Wives were endlessly jockeying to become the favorite wife and gain as much power as they could within the family. In our family I had some protection because the other wives knew Merril liked to have sex with me and they were slightly intimidated about attacking my children. I think they feared that Merril might side with me if I protested.

They never dared hit my children when I was home. If anything happened, it was when I was out of the house or teaching school. I always retaliated when I heard about it by confronting the woman who did it. She would say the children were Merril's, not mine, and that if I wasn't willing to raise them correctly, she was obliged to step in.

One of the few ways I could protect my children was to please Merril sexually. As long as I remained in Merril's favor, the other women knew there was a good chance that he might side with me in any confrontation. So even though I never desired my husband, I trained myself to go through the motions that would satisfy him sexually. I knew if I quit having sex with him, the abuse toward my children would escalate. I learned to protect myself by studying and analyzing behaviors. I knew I was powerless in my environment. But I also knew I could gain some power by figuring out who was predatory and sadistic. I had concluded from my position as wife number four that Merril was a creature of habit. I paid close attention to what provoked his abuse. He attacked the same people repeatedly. In time, I learned to outsmart him by reading his facial movements and understanding his tone of voice. This was a survival skill I learned in childhood to survive my mother's abuse.

By May 1991, I was two months away from delivering my third child. The school year was ending and every moment I wasn't teaching I spent working in the garden with Arthur and Betty tagging along behind me. The garden was a peaceful place for me, a time of deep quietude and escape from the chaos of Merril's household. Often I would work in the garden until early evening and watch the sinking sun paint the sky in flaming colors. Arthur was three and a half and Betty nearly two. They played happily beside me, digging in the dirt and helping me pull up weeds and plants.

One night we came back in from gardening and Merril and Barbara had arrived home unexpectedly from Page. I always tried to avoid Merril when he first came home because he was usually in a very bad mood. I grabbed Betty and Arthur and scooted them off to my room to give them a bath, get them ready for bed, and avoid any confrontation with Merril.

Once they were tucked away, I came upstairs to the kitchen and found Tammy and Cathleen deep in discussion. I got a glass of water and sat down. Tammy seemed angry and Cathleen, very frustrated. I asked them what was going on.

"We're both tired of Merril and Barbara excluding us," Tammy said. I looked puzzled. "From what?"

Tammy explained that as soon as Merril and Barbara got home, they left again and that Barbara was carrying the small suitcase she took to the hospital with her whenever she gave birth. Barbara, Cathleen, and I were all pregnant, and our three due dates were all a month apart. Barbara was due in May; Cathleen, June; and I, July.

Tammy and Cathleen were upset because they didn't get to go with Barbara to watch her give birth to Samson, her twelfth child. It was a well-established tradition in the FLDS that sister wives were supposed to attend one another's deliveries. It was believed that since all the wives were going to participate in raising the child, they should be at the birth to bond with the baby and support their sister wife. That was the belief; in practice it was something else entirely.

I, like Barbara, loathed the idea of turning the birth of my baby into a communal event. Wives were competitive with one another and conniving. Those intense feelings and complicated relationships were not left outside the delivery room door.

When I gave birth to Arthur, Ruth was the only one of Merril's wives present. I hated it. It felt like an invasion of my privacy and she certainly didn't treat me any better after Arthur was born. I'd had a relatively easy delivery, and afterward Ruth began telling everyone in the family that it would be good for the unmarried daughters to watch me give birth in the future.

Women in the FLDS gave birth in the local clinic. Aunt Lydia, the midwife, delivered the babies. A doctor was never present, nor was pain medication ever used. Women were expected to be perfectly silent during childbirth. If a woman screamed or made loud noises she was criticized for being out of control. Sometimes she'd be reprimanded by her husband during her delivery.

Tammy and Cathleen felt outright betrayal by being excluded from seeing Barbara give birth. They felt that all six wives should be present at the delivery and chastised me for holding a completely different view and rebelling against our traditions.

"Carolyn, you don't have a right to impose your selfishness onto your baby," Tammy said. "If you're excluding the family from the baby's birth, it's as if you're trying to exclude them from the baby's life."

Cathleen said that Barbara had insisted on being present when she gave birth to her first child and she didn't understand why she insisted on privacy for her own deliveries.

Tammy piped up that Barbara was still upset that I hadn't allowed her to be present when I had Betty and Arthur.

"I didn't stop her from coming," I said. "She just didn't make it to the delivery room on time, so I see no reason for her to be angry."

When Arthur was born, everyone was out of town except Ruth and Barbara. Ruth came, but Barbara was sulking because I'd called my mother instead of her when I went into labor. She refused to come to the clinic at first, and when she did, Arthur had already been born. Betty was born so quickly that only Merril had been there.

"I really don't care if Barbara's upset with me," I said to Tammy. "If she wants privacy when her babies are born, she can allow me the same."

Little did I know I'd launched a war. Tammy went to see Barbara at the clinic the next morning. She told her I didn't want any of my sister wives coming to the birth of my babies and that I felt none of them had the right to invade my privacy. Exactly.

Barbara was furious. She said the only reason she had private births was that Merril felt it was required in her situation but not for any of his other wives. What right did I have to say who could be present when my babies were born? Tammy came back intending to continue the argument from the night before. She said Barbara felt I was in outright rebellion and needed to be disciplined. Barbara said that if I was uncomfortable with just a few people in the delivery room, then she would ensure that many people were there as punishment. Once Merril sanctioned this, she said I'd have no right to object.

A month later I heard Tammy paging me on the intercom. She said Cathleen, who was due to give birth any day, had gone to the clinic in Hildale. Merril wanted all the wives to come and visit her, but Tammy said she wasn't going to give birth until the next day.

When I got to the clinic I was surprised not to find anyone in the waiting room. One of the women who worked there approached me. "Oh, there you are. Everyone was wondering when you'd get here." I didn't understand what she meant at first. "They are back there in the delivery room." Then it hit me. I'd been tricked.

She led me back to a small room in the clinic. It was crammed with people staring at Cathleen, who was in anguished labor. Merril smiled when he saw the shock on my face. He offered me his chair, which was right next to Cathleen. I sat down because my head was spinning.

I'd never witnessed another woman give birth and didn't want to. I was eight months pregnant and terrified by what I was seeing. Cathleen was writhing in pain and grunting and groaning with each intense contraction. People looked at her with disdain. The small room was crammed with Merril and his six wives, plus five or six of his unmarried daughters. It was difficult for Aunt Lydia to move around because the room was so packed.

I hated seeing Cathleen humiliated. This felt like a total freak show. We were part of a tradition that insisted on covering women's bodies from head to toe when they were in public. But now the most intimate and vulnerable moment of a woman's life was stripped of its dignity and privacy. Cathleen was wearing a nightgown with white leggings and her legs were spread apart in the stirrups. More than a dozen people were not only staring at her, but judging her. She was sweating profusely and seemed emotionally and physically exhausted. Merril was there but seemed nonchalant about the drama that was unfolding around him.

Cathleen's baby finally pushed his way into the world, wet, slimy and screaming. Aunt Lydia cut his umbilical cord and handed him to Cathleen, who immediately handed him to Merril. Merril didn't want him and handed him to me. Everyone wanted to see this child born, but no one wanted to hold him! Johnson was a beautiful baby. I was so anxious and upset I was afraid I might drop him. I took some big breaths and tried to calm down by staring at this sweet and innocent child. After a few moments, Aunt Lydia came and said he needed to be put in the incubator before he got too cold. I got out of there as fast as I could.

I was still too upset at home to concentrate on any of the things I needed to do. I decided to find and confront Merril. I intended to make sure he knew that what had been done to Cathleen would never be done to me. I found him working in one of his alfalfa fields. Raising alfalfa was one of his hobbies.

"Hello, Carolee, what can I do for you?" He knew by looking at my face that I was upset.

"I want an explanation about what happened today."

Merril pretended he didn't know what I was talking about. "What do you want your loving husband to explain?"

"I thought what happened to Cathleen today was inexcusable. You need to understand that I will not be treated that way. You will show me respect when I have this baby."

"Cathleen and I were in perfect harmony about the birth today."

My silence demanded more and he knew it.

"But of course I will show you respect. You will want the people at the delivery who I decide should be there."

"Merril, wake up. You're dreaming if you think I'm going to make a freak show out of the birth of my baby. I won't let you deny me my dignity."

Merril laughed the way he did when he wanted to sound superior. "What are you going to do to prevent it? Have your baby in a closet? If you have the baby in a facility that is in harmony with the prophet, then the family members I decide on will be there for the birth."

I looked at him with what felt like fire blazing from my eyes. "Don't flatter yourself with all the abundance of your power. I don't have to have this baby at Hildale. I may choose a more private place, like on a public highway, off to one side!"

I turned and walked away. I would not be humiliated by him.

My due date was a few weeks later. I decided I would tell no one when I went into labor. I knew that Rosie, my father's second wife, knew how to deliver babies because she was a nurse. I asked her if she would be there when I gave birth, but explained nothing else. She agreed. My plan was to call her when I went into second stage later. She'd come and pick me up. I knew that even if I had the baby in her car, it would still be better than starring in one of Merril's freak shows.

Merril and I had not spoken about my delivery since that angry confrontation after Cathleen gave birth. As my due date drew near, he did not return to Page after the weekend as he usually did. I felt my labor was imminent but tried to will it away for a few more days so he'd have to return to Page. It worked.

The night he left I knew I had my chance. I walked for several miles after dinner, willing my labor to begin. In the middle of the night, it did. I could feel the first of the contractions begin, but they were faint and far apart. It was July 24th, or Pioneer Day, our biggest Mormon holiday.

It was the day the entire community turned out for a parade through town. As soon as our house emptied out, I called Rosie. I sent Betty and Arthur to the parade with the family and told them I didn't feel up to going.

Then I called Merril in Page and got the answering machine. What a miracle! Now I knew that I had time to have the baby in private.

Rosie came right away and had already alerted Aunt Lydia to meet us at the clinic. She and one of her assistants were waiting for me in the delivery room. The other woman said, "We're supposed to be on the float in the parade. If we deliver this baby, we'll miss the parade."

Aunt Lydia told me to push and turned to her whining assistant. "We can deliver this baby and still be in the parade."

"Not unless she has the baby in the next ten minutes," she said.

"This baby is going to be here in ten minutes," Aunt Lydia said. She was right.

LuAnne was a screaming, beautiful baby with a thick mass of dark hair. I smiled when I looked at her exquisite features. She was a triumph, and her birth, for me, a small victory for me over Merril's oppression.

# Marrying into the Jeffs' Family

Loretta was the first of Merril's daughters to be married off to the prophet, but she was not the last. Paula was next. She was as beautiful as her sister, Loretta. They looked almost like twins. Her wedding gown was princess style, but for the former nuss, this was hardly a fairy-tale wedding. Uncle Rulon was at least sixty years older than she. Her still smile barely hid her despair. She was very disciplined and determined to keep her feelings in check.

I kept thinking of that day in school when we joked about having to marry an old man who was a rest-home patient. Rulon Jeffs was sitting in a chair because he wasn't strong enough to stand. He had a palsy, so when he took her hand in his patriarchal grip the shaking was visible from quite a distance. The marriage was grotesque to me. Merril, of course, had no reason to hide his feelings. He was proud and overjoyed. Merril's status within the community was enhanced when he married off Loretta to the prophet. But his obsession with power would soon make him want more.

Merril was now considered one of the most exalted men in the community since he had married two daughters to Uncle Rulon. I noticed how differently we, as Merril's wives, were treated in the community. We rarely had to wait in line at the grocery store or at the fabric shop. It was considered a privilege by other families to associate with us. No one wanted to offend Merril or anyone in his family since he now had a firm and direct connection to the prophet.

Most people in the community usually only ever saw Uncle Rulon at church. Those who were able to make an appointment to see him usually found the meetings were kept short. There was time to make a tithe, but not to exert any influence.

Merril's inroads into the Jeffs family did not stop with Uncle Rulon. Several of Rulon's sons started marrying Merril's daughters. The one who married the most was the favorite son among the prophet's seventy children, Warren Jeffs. Warren was gaining influence in the community, and often spoke for his father in church when he was too weak to attend. He was on the verge of becoming a rising star with the potential to take over the FLDS when his father died. I think Merril saw it as a shrewd move to marry as many daughters as he could to Warren.

Warren was now in his late thirties. His three wives were churning out children; there were now about fifteen. My opinion of Warren had never changed since I had first met him shortly after marrying Merril. I thought he looked like a big nobody but also felt there was something creepy about him.

Warren was at least six feet tall, and seemed even taller because he was so thin. He had zero charisma, but was polite and well-mannered and chose his words carefully. Warren was the principal at the private school on his father's property. What disturbed me most about him were the stories I heard about his brutality.

Warren thrived on brutality and seemed to love hurting people. He'd pull some kids out of their classroom and beat them on an almost daily basis. Warren targeted the kids from bad homes whose parents wouldn't make waves even if their kids told.

Warren also taught brutality. One day he brought one of his wives into the auditorium, which was packed with boys. Annette had a long braid that fell past her knees. Warren grabbed the braid and twisted and twisted it until she was on her knees and he was ripping hair from her head. He told the boys that this was how obedient their wives had to be to them.

This incident was widely reported in the community because so many of the boys went home and reported what they had seen. Uncle

Rulon was also reported to have said that the only thing Warren had ever done to displease him was study books on Hitler. Stories like this were in wide circulation about Warren before he took control of the FLDS. Once he did, though, the stories stopped because people feared his wrath.

After Merril's daughter Paula was married off to Uncle Rulon, he sent her to teach in his school. Paula had a college degree and was a certified high school teacher. She told me that Warren saw her as "contaminated" by worldly education and insisted she bring all her college books to school and throw them in the dumpster. "If you're going to teach in this school you cannot bring worldly contamination into the classroom." Paula complied because she had no other choice.

The daughters Merril married to the prophet and Warren tended to be the ones he had used to spy on his wives and keep us in line. They eavesdropped outside our doorways and told their father everything they heard. Even after they married, they felt like we were still a threat to them. They'd call home and pump their younger siblings for information. But now they would tell the prophet, instead of Merril, what was going on in our home. This became a huge embarrassment for Merril because on several occasions, the prophet called him in to reprimand him for not having more control over his family.

We routinely made the trip to Salt Lake City with Merril for the priesthood meeting on the third weekend of the month. Merril never missed a meeting because he got to drink in the personal time this gave him with Uncle Rulon.

After the meeting was over, there would be a pizza party at the home of Rulon's son, Leroy. Leroy was the one we thought had the greatest likelihood of becoming the next prophet after Uncle Rulon's death. The first one I went to sent my head spinning.

There was pizza, to be sure, but there was also fried chicken and lots of junk food. But people didn't go for the food, they went for the alcohol. Men sat in the dining room around a large table and the women stayed in the living room.

Vans of women would arrive about forty-five minutes before the men. These were the wives of the most respected men in the FLDS, those in the priesthood. Many came carrying babies in their arms. But that didn't stop them from hitting the beer—not even the nursing mothers. I was disgusted watching women drinking beer and nursing their babies at the same time. They rarely ate because there was a rigid rule in the Jeffs family against becoming obese.

When the men arrived, they sat down in the dining room and expected to be served food. I was taking orders for pizza or chicken and bringing them drinks. I went into the living room to see if any of the other wives would be willing to help me, but they were too drunk. After several bottles of beer, they were laughing and preaching the gospel about keeping sweet and loving your sister wives. When they arrived at the party they'd seemed nervous and irritable, but not now. I thought maybe that was why their husbands let them drink.

After a few beers, the men's mood changed, too. Now they started complaining about their wives. Even Uncle Rulon joined in. He started bitching about one of his wives who was obese after having sixteen kids, which he felt was a sign of pure rebellion toward him. The other men jumped in, ranting and raving about their fat wives, too.

I was disgusted by what I was seeing. These were the elite in the FLDS. It shocked me to see those who were held in such high esteem within the community exalting in things they all knew were punishable by excommunication.

This was something new to add to the list of ugly realities I had seen within the faith I once prized.

# Tammy's Failed Rebellion

**C**arolyn, I'm pregnant."

Tammy and I were in the kitchen. I was getting a quick cup of coffee before heading back to school.

I was shocked by the news. Was this for real? Tammy had been trying to get pregnant for six years. Fertility drugs hadn't worked. Her desperation had increased to the point that rarely a day went by that she didn't say something to me about it. I knew she'd finally abandoned the Clomid and for the last few months had been taking an herbal tincture a friend recommended.

"It's true," she said. "I am really going to have a baby and I hope it will be a girl."

I thought Tammy would be overjoyed, but she seemed subdued.

"Maybe if it's not a girl then you'll get one next time."

"Barbara was the first person I told, then Merril. I've waited a few weeks before telling my sister wives."

"Tammy, I'm so happy for you," I said.

Tammy and I were not close at this point because I no longer felt I could trust her. She was always tattling on her sister wives to Barbara. We'd barely been on speaking terms, but this broke the ice between us.

Conceiving was never a problem for me, which made Tammy envy me. But now we were on even ground again. A few months later

I became pregnant for the fourth time and was vomiting daily from morning sickness.

Tammy gave birth in January. She wanted her delivery to be a big production. Not only did she invite Merril's six wives, but she also wanted all of her sister wives from her marriage to the late prophet, Uncle Roy, to come, too. There were at least a dozen people in the delivery room. Thankfully, I was too sick to attend—one of the only gifts morning sickness ever gave to me.

But Tammy's baby became stuck in the delivery canal during labor. She had to be moved into several different and awkward positions to try and free the baby. I was told later that the mood at the clinic was tense because Tammy's baby was in real trouble.

Merril left the delivery room at that point. He was uncomfortable with the situation and found a place at the clinic to take a nap. Barbara went with him and rubbed his head, neck, and shoulders trying to help him relax and sleep.

Tammy seemed to have been abandoned and betrayed in her hour of need. She had been blindly loyal to Barbara and Merril and was very upset that they had not stayed by her side during the traumatic birth. Her newborn son started having seizures after birth. Merril wouldn't let her take him to the hospital, but she was allowed to see a doctor.

Merril named Tammy's son, Parley, without consulting her. Tammy had another name picked out for her son, and she wanted to include her family at the naming ceremony. But for whatever reason, Merril prevented this from happening. We had a family Sunday school in the living room. Tammy was there with Parley. After Sunday school ended, Merril took Parley away from her and asked his sons to help him name him.

I had never been able to choose any of my children's names or even participate in a discussion with Merril about them. This was just the way we did things in the FLDS, and I was used to the idea.

Parley seemed to outgrow his seizures by the time he was a few months old. I gave birth to Patrick, my second son and fourth child, on July 6, 1993. I was spared an audience because he came so quickly. Patrick was my healthiest baby, at 7 lbs., 15 ozs. Compared to my first three, he was jumbo-size. I was twenty-five.

For the first time since I'd known her, Tammy was not resentful about my having a baby because she had one, too. Tammy was excited because she hoped our boys could grow up and be close brothers.

But after giving birth Tammy seemed to become increasingly upset by the mean, hurtful things that Merril and Barbara had inflicted on her. For years, she'd been trying to repress her feelings by pasting on a perfect smile. But her façade cracked. I don't know if she had postpartum depression or if she just was too exhausted to play games, but something snapped and she lashed out at Merril, which was completely out of character for her.

This happened multiple times. Sometimes I was in Merril's office and heard everything, other times Tammy recounted everything in great detail.

At one climactic moment, Tammy took off her wedding ring and told Merril he wasn't being a husband to her and she was finished pretending otherwise. This infuriated Barbara, who accused her of trying to stir up conflict in the family. Barbara demanded that Tammy be more discreet and warned her not to create a scandal for the family.

Tammy's behavior changed. She stopped acting as Barbara's shadow and Merril's spy. She no longer called Barbara every day at Page and reported every wrong move that anyone in the family had made in the past twenty-four hours.

Tammy told me that Merril and Barbara had put her on notice. We were having coffee together one morning before school. Tammy taught seventh grade. "I am in big trouble with Barbara and Merril," she said. "I didn't spend any time with Barbara this weekend and I didn't call and check in with her once last week."

This was so out of character for Tammy I was shocked.

"Is it now your responsibility to report to Barbara?"

"I have been calling Barbara every day and reporting on the family for several years. Merril put me on notice this weekend that if I stopped doing it there would be consequences."

The change in Tammy had been so radical, I wondered if it would last. It didn't. Tammy soon caved in to their pressure. After thirty years of never standing up for herself, I did not expect her to suddenly change. Once again, Tammy became Barbara's loyal supplicant. I was sure her spirit had been quashed once and for all.

But I was wrong.

Tammy exploded a few months later and told me all about it the next morning when we were having our coffee.

Tammy had waited up for Barbara and Merril, who came back from Page late on Fridays. Merril came into her room and asked her to massage his feet. He did this often, and would hint that maybe he'd spend the night with Tammy, but then decided to sleep with Barbara.

Tammy had been massaging Merril's feet for an hour when he got up and said he was going into Barbara's room and also planned to take her to Salt Lake City in the morning.

Tammy snapped.

She accused Merril of being a "true monogamous" and said he had never lived plural marriage. Barbara was the only woman he treated as a wife and her children were the only children he cared about. Tammy told Merril that he treated the rest of us as his property or slaves.

Tammy spoke the truth that none of us dared speak.

Merril's abuse was well-known among his wives. But none of us had ever found the courage to stand up to him because we were afraid of the consequences.

Merril said nothing when he stood up. He washed his hands in Tammy's bathroom and left her room.

The next morning Tammy went into the kitchen and tried to apologize to Barbara and Merril before they left for Salt Lake City. Neither of them spoke to her. She had crossed every boundary, and now she would have to pay.

Merril stopped speaking to her altogether. Tammy begged for his mercy and forgiveness. But she was an outcast. A few weeks later, Merril told her that he would never have sex with her again under any conditions. It was Tammy's fault. Because of her rebellion Tammy would never bear another child of his.

This devastated her. Tammy had been celibate during the ten years of her marriage to Uncle Roy because he was in his eighties when she married him while still in her late teens. It had taken her six years to get pregnant with Parley. Tammy wanted more children. Her mother had twenty children, and while Tammy knew she'd never come close to that number, she felt embarrassed and ashamed to have only one. Children reflected a woman's sexual status with her husband and social status in the community.

Tammy tried to get Merril to reconsider, but even though he would sleep in her room, he'd never touch her.

Merril once took Tammy and me on a trip to Salt Lake City. He slept in Tammy's room the first night of the trip. The next morning he called me on the phone and asked me to come to their room.

I knocked on their door, and when Merril answered, he pulled me to him and gave me a kiss.

Tammy started sobbing. Merril completely ignored her. I asked, "What's wrong?"

"He slept with me all night and didn't kiss me once, not even this morning. You walk through the door and he's grabbing you and kissing you the minute he gets his hands on you."

Tammy was so distraught and her pain so real, but I didn't know what to say. Tammy had humiliated Merril to his family and children. Her future was the price Merril would make her pay.

I told Tammy I was sorry and wished there was more I could do. But we both knew there wasn't.

Tammy stopped talking to Merril, but did not give up on trying to win him back. She waited on him hand and foot and, once again, began following Barbara around. I think she thought if she could win Barbara back as an ally, she might urge Merril to have sex with her again. But nothing changed.

Merril and Barbara knew she was now an example of what could happen to someone who challenged their authority. Tammy was refuse—another body added to the scrap heap along with Faunita and Ruth.

Several years later, Tammy went to Merril and told him she could no longer live without physical affection. How could he expect her to live that way forever?

Merril was reading while she talked. He turned to her when she was finished, took off his reading glasses, looked across his desk, and said, "I always knew you had a weak character!"

Tammy stood up and walked out of Merril's office. As far as I know, this was the last time this matter was ever discussed.

# Resound of Music

**M**y sister Linda had moved back into the FLDS community with her husband because they were broke. She was pregnant with her second baby and didn't have a lot of options. Linda also missed her family terribly.

Linda was having a hard time in her marriage, which made her precarious life even harder. My father said he would help her financially, but there were strings attached. Linda had to agree to leave her husband, since he had refused to swing to our side of the religious split. She also had to agree to be reassigned in marriage by the prophet to another man.

Linda had no other cards to play, so she agreed. She was assigned to marry a man with three children. Linda was told that if she kept herself in harmony with her new husband, then her life would be perfect in every way and God would bless her with everything she needed.

This philosophy of "perfect obedience produces perfect faith" began sweeping through the community. Warren was assuming more control of the FLDS, claiming he was acting for his father. He began promoting the doctrine of perfect obedience. He preached it and talked about it on tapes, and laminated handmade signs proclaiming it were hung in nearly every home. We were told that every problem a woman faced was because she was not being perfectly obedient to her husband. Women were being instructed to listen to the whispers of God and pray to know their husband's hearts. A wife's goal was to be able to meet his every need without ever being asked. If she asked questions when her husband gave her an order, it was only because she still had contamination in her heart. If she was in harmony with him, God's whisper would have made it precisely clear what was expected of her.

But even if a woman did *exactly* what her husband demanded, he could still find fault with her and accuse her of still not being in perfect harmony with him, because otherwise she'd have understood what he *really* meant.

Linda and I had grown close again after she returned to the community. We'd had almost no contact for nearly five years. Linda was now twenty-seven and was raising five children—her own two and her new husband's three. She'd managed to get a nursing degree but had to quit working to take care of five preschoolers.

Linda's husband traveled a lot and she began inviting women over for coffee some mornings to break up her loneliness. These became rare forums to talk about what we felt was happening within the FLDS. Had it been known that we were meeting, we would have been reprimanded and seen as being out of harmony with our priesthood training. We kept our coffee parties secret.

This was a radical departure for me. For the first time I had women friends outside my family. Compared to Merril's other wives, I was running in a rowdy crowd and was being exposed to new viewpoints and controversial ideas.

All of us, myself included, believed that Uncle Rulon was the true prophet of God, so we would never dream of criticizing anything he said or did. But that still left us room to talk about how people interpreted his teachings and how the new religious doctrines that were coming to us via Warren Jeffs were playing out in people's lives. These women weren't afraid to make fun of what they were seeing.

"Perfect obedience" was very much on our minds. I remember the morning when one of the women said, "Remember *Fascinating*

*Womanhood*? We don't have to be fascinating anymore! The prophet has given us a new answer and we will never have to be abused again. The new answer is obedience!"

I chimed in, "So, are you trying to tell us that all we have to do is be obedient and we'll never be abused again?"

"Yes, I am," she said, "and do I have a story for you about obedience." The story she told—which was true—held everyone in a trance about a large polygamous family that went on a picnic in a small car and a large van.

The car began to have problems and wouldn't start. The father told one of his wives—a first-grade teacher I knew—that she needed to help him get the small car going. He instructed her to get in the van and use it to push the car slowly up the hill. He said when it got to forty miles an hour it would start.

The wife was somewhat confused but didn't dare ask a question. If she wanted the blessing of perfect faith, she must be perfectly obedient. The wife got behind the wheel of the large van and her husband got into the car. He waited, but there was no push. When he turned around, the van was gone and he couldn't figure out what had happened. After a few moments the van appeared in his rearview mirror, bearing down on him at forty miles an hour. He leaped out of the car just before she pulverized it.

Everyone at the coffee roared with laughter.

"Yes, the prophet's answer is far more efficient," I said. "Killing our husbands through perfect obedience is a lot more practical than trying to woo them by being fascinating." The women laughed again. We were being dangerously honest with one another and we knew it. I realized how much freedom I had lost since I'd been married. I hadn't had such fun with other women since high school when my friends and I joked about the nusses.

I was wary about a lot of the new ideas that were circulating in the community, but I didn't have any sense of how fast they could take hold. Even if Warren Jeffs seemed to have some weird ideas, Uncle Rulon was still the prophet, and I had complete faith in him.

Merril continued to marry his daughters off to Uncle Rulon to enhance his own prestige with the aging prophet. Merril's need for power was insatiable. His daughter Merrilyn was also assigned to marry Uncle Rulon in 1992. She cried and pleaded with her father in protest. Merrilyn said it was impossible for her to marry Uncle Rulon because she was not as strong as Loretta and Paula. Merril didn't care, nor did he realize that she was telling him the truth.

Merrilyn was Ruth's daughter and was also gorgeous. She was thin with long, dark hair, and like me, she was still in her early twenties. When forced to do something she didn't want to, Merrilyn would pretend to comply but then somehow find a way to rebel. Merril insisted she must be obedient to the will of God.

Merrilyn wanted a life with a man. She wanted love and children. Being married off to a man six decades her senior terrified her. Merrilyn knew it was unlikely that she would have children with him because he was so old and feeble.

But there was no way out. The wedding was in Salt Lake City. Merrilyn had been making wedding dresses over the year, thinking that she'd be married any day. She had three dresses by the time she married Uncle Rulon. The one she wore was the least fancy of the three. Merrilyn looked stunning. Uncle Rulon's younger wives were telling Merrilyn how happy they were she was coming into the family and how much she'd love it. As for the prophet, he was again too feeble to stand, and his hands shook with palsy as he held hers.

Merril was now one of the most exalted men in the community since he had married three daughters—Loretta, Paula, and now Merrilyn—to Uncle Rulon.

Merril was still abusive to his own wives, but I was more skilled in navigating around him. He was not as predictable as my mother, but I had studied him so closely for so long, I could usually tell when he was ready to explode and would find a reason to leave the room, one that wouldn't make him suspicious. When he did blow, he'd accuse any wives who happened to be around him of being rebellious and having weak characters—a terrible insult. Merril decided the worth of each wife: Barbara was a goddess. Faunita, the lowest of low.

I knew that when he had two wives crying it was safe to return.

What made Merril different from my mother was that she would quit after beating one of us. Merril, unlike my mom, seemed to crave more. Humiliating just one wife was never enough.

As strange as it might sound, I'd adapted to my bizarre environment and was, by 1993, feeling more grounded than I'd been in years. My world consisted of children: my second-graders at school and my own four at home. Arthur, Betty, LuAnne, and Patrick were bright and loving.

I drew strength from activities and events in the community. We had a huge Harvest Festival that would consume the family for days in preparation. One year we made four hundred pies in the week leading up to the three-day event. The Harvest Festival was our version of a county fair. Large families were assigned booths; our booth was for pies. There were games and other activities for kids. The children loved it, and I was always happy for any focus beyond Merril's family.

But the reality was that despite my success in making a reasonably stable life for myself and my children, I knew I was walking a tightrope and was never more than one step away from danger.

Barbara still felt that I was the only one of Merril's wives who had never completely submitted to her, which was true. Faunita, defeated and broken, stayed in her room watching movies. Tammy spent her time flattering Barbara and Merril. Cathleen had given up and did what she was told without complaint. When Ruth was not in the throes of madness and watering the shoes in her closet, she obsessed about being in perfect harmony with Merril and following Barbara's orders.

My strategy was to ignore Barbara and live around her. But by late 1993 she and Merril had decided to try to make me surrender to her one-woman rule.

Money was the weapon they decided to use against me.

Merril cut off every account in town and then informed us that if we needed something we had to come to him directly and ask for it. I was still teaching and turning over my entire salary to him, which, after taxes, was about $500 every two weeks. I had no money of my own, but in the past this had not been a problem because we had charge accounts everywhere in town. Merril seemed to think that if he denied me the basic necessities for me and my children I'd submit to Barbara's rule.

Merril told me he was having financial problems again. I believed him initially and tried not to ask him for money. But then I discovered everyone else in the family was still spending at the same levels. When they went to Merril, he instantly gave them the money they needed.

The first time I went to his office I told him I needed a few items. He ignored me and didn't even speak. I left, suspicious.

The next week I went into Merril's office to turn over my salary check. When I did, I asked Merril for five dollars to buy Arthur a pair of shoes. He ignored me again, refusing to respond. I sat down in his office. I wanted an answer.

Barbara came in and asked Merril for money to pick up pictures in town. He wrote her a check that was almost equivalent to the paycheck I'd just handed him. When Barbara left I said, "It looks like you have plenty of money if you can spend nearly as much as I make in two weeks on pictures. Surely there must be money for shoes for your son."

Merril's face turned crimson. "There is money for those who do the things I want."

I knew that was the opening for an argument. But I also knew he held all the cards. If I challenged him, he'd berate and humiliate me. I walked out of his office determined to never again ask him for a dime.

I vowed never to surrender to either Merril or Barbara. I quietly began to figure out a survival strategy. I filed my tax return without telling Merril. I'd never done that before. I started to do a few extra things on the side to make money. I began selling NuSkin cosmetics. Merril knew about my venture but had no idea of my success.

There were months when I sold $5,000 worth of cosmetics in a community where makeup was strictly forbidden. A banner month could net me $1,000. There was so much competition in the community among wives that when a man took one wife on a trip, the others would come and blow a few hundred bucks on cosmetics to stay competitive. I could even accept credit card payments by calling the number in to NuSkin. No one in the family suspected how much money I was making. It was one of the most empowering experiences I'd ever had. I was able to do it because I was married to Merril. Merril paraded me around town as his young trophy wife. Men would give their wives permission to buy cosmetics from me.

Doing my own taxes and hiding money was the first time I'd ever gone against the teachings of the prophet. I didn't care. I felt no guilt, no shame. This was the beginning, the fragile, tentative beginning, of mentally breaking free from the control of my "religion." I still basically believed in the FLDS but thought Merril was corrupting and distorting its values for his own selfish and narcissistic ends.

While I began putting energy into staying ahead of Merril and Barbara's dirty little games, the rest of the family was intent on pampering Merril's ego.

Every year around Merril's birthday on December 27 the family would perform a play or put on a program in his honor. His daughters usually took charge and orchestrated everything. For Merril's birthday in 1994 one of his daughters did a new version of *The Sound of Music*.

In those pre–Warren Jeffs years, we still watched movies and listened to the radio. Some families had TVs and their children watched videos. We were all familiar with *The Sound of Music*. Our extravaganza was going to be staged, in honor of Merril, at the community center, which could hold a thousand people. Margaret's version of the musical was based on several polygamous families. She wrote parts for every child in Merril's family, and by then there were more than forty. Margaret called it *The Resound of Music*.

I was pregnant with my fifth child and was too weak from morning sickness to take part. In our version, Maria was a nanny sent from one large polygamous family to another. Captain Von Trapp was not a widower but a married man with a large family. He had recently been introduced to the principle of plural marriage and was thinking about joining the FLDS. He hired Maria because he respected her father and knew he needed her to take care of his very large family.

These two large families created parts for many of the children. But then Margaret needed parts for sons and daughters-in-law. So there were characters in the script that seemed to wander in and out from nowhere.

Margaret dreamed of having an orchestra provide the music, but the reality was she was stuck with our little FLDS band. She dressed them up in formal wear so they looked like a professional orchestra, but when the band started playing the score from the real *Sound of Music* the audience laughed because they sounded so amateurish.

The gist of the plot was that everyone was trying to escape the Nazis and flee to America to join the work of God. The play ended with a musical talent show while German soldiers stood guard. Merril's sons-in-law played the Germans. After each talent number the actors pretended to flee to the mountains to escape. When the show ended everyone was hiking through the mountains to safety.

But then the German soldiers came frantically searching after them. Uncle Rulon's sons, Leroy and Warren Jeffs, who had married into Merril's family, appeared in full Nazi regalia and were the last to march across the stage.

The audience was laughing, unaware of the shadow falling across our community. It was the shadow of a totalitarian society that would one day consume every aspect of our lives and be under the control of Warren Jeffs.

# Warren's Rise to Power

All my pregnancies had been awful, but my fifth pregnancy was the first that was life-threatening. The pregnancy began with the same severe illness and vomiting. But this time I continued to menstruate. Shirley, the nurse practitioner I saw, said it was not unusual for a woman to have one period after becoming pregnant. She listened to the baby's heartbeat, said it was normal, and sent me home.

Two nights after Shirley told me not to worry about the bleeding I awoke because I was soaked. I turned on the light and saw that I was covered in blood. There was a pool of blood in the bed. I was hemorrhaging. I panicked and got in the shower, and the bleeding stopped.

I taught my second graders the next day, thinking that I had probably miscarried and that my pregnancy was over. But my morning sickness continued. I saw Shirley a week later and she ordered an ultrasound.

The test showed a healthy baby but a placenta that had abrupted—torn away from the uterus. Only 50 percent of the placenta was functioning. I was only thirteen weeks pregnant. Shirley consulted with the other nurse practitioner now working in the community and the two agreed that I needed to spend the rest of my pregnancy in bed. The half of the placenta that was abrupted would continue to leak blood into the uterus and that would produce cramping that could potentially tear more of the placenta away. The nurses warned me that there was a high probability that my baby would not survive.

Who would care for my four children if I was confined to bed? Patrick, the youngest, was still in diapers, and I knew that no one would bother to change him more than once a day. I knew the other wives wouldn't bring meals to me in bed or see that my children got enough food. I also hated the thought of leaving my second-grade classroom. I'd become very attached to my students. But this was a matter of life and death.

I asked Merril what I should do. He accused me of trying to make this into something it wasn't and said to stop pitying myself. "What mother wouldn't give her life for her baby?" He told me to quit my job and go to bed. In his view, this pregnancy was a test required by God.

I continued to hemorrhage off and on for the next six months. I was so weak it was difficult even to stand. One morning after waking up in a pool of blood again I felt that I was dying and feared this might be the last day I would have to spend with my children.

I called for my two youngest, LuAnne and Patrick. They hadn't had a bath in weeks because I had been too weak and sick. I gave them a long bubble bath in the tub. They played joyfully together while I lay on the bathroom floor. I dressed each child in clean clothes. My head was pounding so hard it felt like a sledgehammer was battering my brain. I sent LuAnne and Patrick to find their older brother and sister. I saw no reason to stay in bed any longer because I was sure my baby and I were dying.

When I had all four children together, we walked to the park near our house. I sat on a bench and wept as I watched my children swing and play. I wanted to be their mother. I wanted to watch them grow up. I was angry thinking how much of their lives I would miss by dying. Leaving them alone and motherless stabbed me with sorrow. But I ached in sorrow for myself. My unborn baby and I were dying and no one really cared. My husband wouldn't miss me. My sister wives would be glad I was gone. My death would be seen as God's will and there would be no questioning, no mourning. The only tears that would be shed for me were those I was shedding for myself. My children were exuberant and it felt as unbearable to watch them as it was to turn away.

Shirley learned of my deteriorating condition from Tammy. Tammy and Shirley had been sister wives of Uncle Roy. Tammy was having coffee with her and condemning me to Shirley. Shirley knew how grave my condition was and went through the roof. For Shirley, this was a medical issue, not a religious one. She immediately called Merril and insisted he take me to the hospital. He made light of it and Shirley could tell he wasn't going to act. The next day when she saw Merril at a community function she spoke to him in front of people she knew he was trying to impress. She told him I needed to go to the hospital immediately and if I didn't he'd have a dead wife and a dead baby.

I could not go to the hospital on my own. My husband had to authorize it. The volunteer ambulance drivers in Colorado City and Hildale were all members of the FLDS. Because of this they were under enormous pressure not to interfere with another man's family. And so they would not take a woman (or her child) to the hospital unless her husband had given his approval.

Shirley shamed Merril into sending me to the hospital, and I was en route an hour later. The doctor didn't want to deliver me because the baby was still small and his lungs undeveloped. By now I was thirty-three weeks pregnant. I stabilized in the hospital quickly with adequate food and hydration. I stayed there for four weeks and then Andrew, my fifth child and third son, was born by Cesarean section. Andrew was small, but he nursed heartily and gained weight quickly. His survival was a miracle. Shirley said she'd never thought I'd carry Andrew as long as I did. Thankfully, only Merril was allowed to be present in the delivery room.

On a follow-up visit, I talked to Shirley about my fears of getting pregnant again. She said I didn't meet any of the risk factors for another abruption and assured me it would never happen again. She was wrong. I had three more life-threatening pregnancies.

My pregnancy with Andrew changed my sense of security in the world. I had five healthy and beautiful children whom I cherished, but I was terrified of becoming pregnant again. I wanted birth control but had no access to it. The FLDS believed that if a woman used birth control to keep life from coming into the world, she would pay for it in her next life by being a childless servant to her husband's other wives throughout eternity.

The instability I felt in my personal life was mirrored by increasingly strange changes taking place in the community. By 1995, Warren Jeffs was becoming a subtle but more powerful presence in our daily lives. This struck me as odd because there were many other men who were more powerful in the FLDS than he. But he was Uncle Rulon's favored son, and the prophet would often say that Warren spoke for him.

Warren spoke in other ways. He began teaching special priesthood history classes in Salt Lake City, where he still worked as the principal at a private FLDS school. The classes were taped, and Tammy's sister came to our house one day enthusiastically talking about how much information they contained. I wondered why anyone would care about whatever Warren Jeffs had to say. Tammy's sister said that these tapes were not available to just anybody. Only the privileged could purchase them.

Some people who heard them found them disgusting and said they were little more than Warren's racist rants. He claimed that the black race had been put on earth to preserve evil.

I decided to listen to them myself. Warren based his talks on foundational FLDS doctrine. He spoke in a strange, trancelike voice that seemed deliberately aimed at hypnotizing the listener. One set of tapes described how God would destroy everyone on the North and South American continents. Then he recited a lengthy list of things a person would have to do before he or she could be lifted off earth.

Anyone who hoped to ascend had to live with a burning in their chest at all times, and this burning was the spirit of God. The tapes were becoming so popular that there was a frenzy among those who were trying to get them. Their exclusivity gave them great status and everyone wanted to get hold of a set.

Warren spoke at church and elaborated on how the burning in our chests would presage being lifted from the earth. Those who didn't have it would be destroyed along with the wicked.

It was around this time when Warren banned the color red. He announced that it was inappropriate to wear the color red or have red items in our home because it was reserved for our Lord and Savior, Jesus Christ. He preached that when Jesus Christ returns he'll do so in a red robe, and that wearing that color prior to the second coming is unholy.

He made the pronouncement one Sunday in church, and those wearing red went home immediately and changed clothes. Other families got rid of every red item they owned. This was a hardship for families without much money. Children lost a lot of clothes, coats, and boots. Women with red in their dresses had to get rid of them; for some this meant throwing out a sizable percentage of their wardrobes. Some families adapted to this with a more moderate approach: when the red clothes, toys, or household items wore out, they would abandon them. The more extreme families discarded all red items immediately.

One teacher told her students red wasn't a bad color, it was beautiful. The students reported her rebellion to their parents. The parents complained, asked that the teacher, who was not a member of the FLDS, respect their beliefs, and demanded that red be removed from her classroom.

Merril had always liked red. In our family we went through the closets and eliminated most of our red clothes. That evening I watched the sunset—a blaze of orange and red. If God wanted red preserved for Jesus Christ alone, why did he spread it across the sky in such abundance?

When some of us gathered for coffee later that week at Linda's, the topic of having a burning in our chests as a proof of righteousness came up again. Jayne, my high-spirited cousin with whom I'd played apocalypse as a child, kicked off the discussion. "Ladies, I have one question. What the hell is this burning in your chest all about anyway? I always thought that burning is mastitis." (Mastitis is an infection common to nursing mothers.) Everyone laughed. Someone asked Jayne how she dared question the requirements about being lifted up. "Well," she said, "if I have to have a breast infection to be lifted up, then no thank you! I would rather die with the wicked!"

The discussion then became more serious, about what felt like a new extremism taking root in the community that felt more radical than anything that we'd known in the past. One of the women recounted a harrowing story about one of the police officers in the FLDS. (All of the police officers in our community were FLDS members, which complicated matters if a woman tried to escape, because she'd get no help or protection from police. It also made reporting domestic violence almost meaningless because the police would always side with the husband.)

I had rarely heard a story as disturbing as I did that morning. The FLDS police officer wanted to take his wife up to the Steeds ranch to teach her a lesson in obedience. He put her in a pen with a bull and then tied a rope to the neck of the bull. He told his wife, who was pregnant, that she had to control the bull with the rope on orders of her priesthood head. She tried to hang on to the bull, but he ran off and she ended up being dragged until she let go of the rope.

Her husband got into the pen and handed her the rope again and told her she had to hold on. But the bull pulled away from her and her husband became enraged. This time he took the end of the rope and tied it around the neck of the bull and told her she better hang on this time. But it was impossible. The third time he tied the rope to her so she could not let go. She was dragged around the ring again and so badly injured she lost the baby—which then became her fault because she was so disobedient.

When I heard it I told the group I had a burning sensation in my chest—I wanted to kill the guy. The others agreed, and we talked about what we'd do if he ever pulled us over. The story was well circulated in the community because the man's stepmother became aware of what he'd done to his wife and was so incensed that she started talking about it. No one went to the authorities because we knew the woman would deny the whole thing. We all knew we were powerless when it came to protecting ourselves. I feared that it was an example of hysteria that was manifesting itself in extreme ways. This police officer had carried the notion of "perfect obedience" to a criminal level.

The obedience Warren preached was a woman's complete submission to her husband. He said women should not work outside the home and should not even leave home unless allowed to do so by their husband.

We'd always kept our coffee meetings quiet, but now we knew we had to be even more careful. We began to be much more circumspect about what we were doing as changes swept over our community. As women were required to leave the workforce because of Jeffs' new doctrines, it became harder for some families to make ends meet.

The changes Warren Jeffs mandated were obeyed because it was believed he was the voice of the prophet, Uncle Rulon. People did not resist the more oppressive policies he advocated. Instead, it was widely believed that we were being called to a higher way of living the gospel. This wasn't oppression, this was grace. God was giving us a new and better way of being more faithful to him via the prophet and his mouthpiece, Warren Jeffs.

People who feared these changes and sensed danger, like me, kept quiet. It wasn't safe anymore to talk about what you were feeling. Women now were not even supposed to go into town without the company of a man. Our husband was our lord and supreme master, holding exclusive power over our lives. It was seen as no longer acceptable for a woman to enter the same room as her husband without first saying a personal prayer asking God to put the same spirit on her as on her husband.

I saw this as a real dilemma because most of the time when I entered the same room as Merril he was in a very bad mood. If I had the same spirit that he had, one of us might get hurt. This doctrine was one I decided to ignore.

# Charter School

There was no aspect of our lives that Warren Jeffs left untouched. Education was one of the first areas where his imprint was punitive and spiteful.

Warren's father had put a stop to higher education after he became the prophet. The only exceptions were those of us who had been given permission to attend college by his predecessor, Uncle Roy, before he died. So a few of us were allowed to go on to college, but most could not. This created a population that was even more isolated by its lack of exposure to reading, critical thinking, and the arts. It also meant there was a real shortage of trained teachers.

We couldn't hire teachers from out of town because no one was willing to work for such low salaries. Teachers made, at most, twenty thousand dollars a year. Some families were home-schooling their children because they felt public schools were too contaminated with worldly influence. The education the home-schooled got was abysmal. But the number of kids being taught at home did not have any impact on the teacher shortage. Classrooms were overcrowded, teachers overwhelmed.

Several of the second-grade teachers talked about this problem at our monthly meeting. We knew families were getting bigger, not smaller. Our brainstorming produced no answers. But the next week I heard about charter schools that were starting in Arizona.

The state was accepting proposals for additional schools that would open in the following years. I started doing research to see what a charter school might mean for us, and it was breathtaking.

If the state funded a charter school, it would do so based on the school's total number of students. The rate per student was the same as it was in Phoenix. This meant that we could generate enough income from a charter school to hire competent teachers from outside the community. Win-win, it seemed to me.

I told the school superintendent, Alvin Barlow, that if we used computers in the classroom, we could make them more efficient and actually help decrease class size. Some teaching could go on in the computer lab, but it could be done by a lab tech instead of a teacher. This would free up teachers to spend more time in the classroom. Kids could do math and reading drills in the computer lab that would support their classroom studies.

I had taken several courses in computer programming and writing HTML—hand-coding Web sites. I knew I could develop software specific for our curriculums. Barlow was impressed. He wholeheartedly supported my idea for a charter school.

I was a well-respected teacher because I had a talent for teaching any child to read. Parents whose children had reading problems would go to Barlow and ask for their child to be put in my second-grade class.

Merril also thought the charter school plan was a good idea and gave me the go-ahead. I asked Merril before I started writing the proposal if we needed to run it by Uncle Rulon first. He said he'd talk to the prophet about it but didn't see any problem. I don't know if Merril ever did have that conversation, but several of the prophet's wives knew I was writing the charter, so I think he knew what was going on.

I worked on the proposal night and day. My cousins, Jayne and Lee Ann, both teachers, also pitched in. We got our proposal in the night before the deadline and then took a big breath. We were proud of what we'd accomplished and now had to wait and see what happened.

A month later, we were invited to Phoenix to present our charter. There had been a hundred entries. Most of the presenters were school administrators or superintendents with much more experience than we had. Jayne and I felt like kids.

Of the twenty proposals presented before ours, only one was given the green light. The stakes were high. Our turn finally came. We were questioned repeatedly.

One of the women on the board finally put a halt to the questioning. "I want this school. It contains the best assessment plan I have ever seen." One of her male colleagues concurred. He liked the innovative ideas we had in our proposal and wanted to see how they'd work in practice.

The board had concerns about whether we could build a school the size we'd proposed over the summer. I said that would be no problem. The community was used to building things fast.

We were approved! Jayne and I were elated. I'd never done something so empowering. I was proud and determined to make this school work. When the Arizona State Board of Education reviewed our charter, we were told it was one of the best assessment plans they'd ever seen.

Merril was impressed with our accomplishment and said he'd tell Uncle Rulon. Word got back to Warren Jeffs in Salt Lake City about our triumph. Warren was still running the private FLDS school there and handling a lot of the day-to-day running of the sect for his ailing father. Warren's teaching style consisted in beating students with yardsticks. Only two teachers in the school had teaching degrees. The rest had, at most, high school degrees. Their only qualification was their loyalty to the FLDS and to Warren.

Warren heard that our charter school proposal had a big computer program. He had banned computers from his school. He knew I was developing my own reading books to complement my reading program, which was also threatening to him. Well-educated children might one day think for themselves. I think Jeffs knew this could ultimately undermine his leadership. So maybe I should have been better prepared for what happened next.

Merril went to talk to Uncle Rulon about the school. He told

Merril it wouldn't happen. I have no idea if Merril even tried to change his mind.

All I was told was that the prophet was opposed. There would be no charter school. Alvin Barlow, the superintendent, was upset. Merril forbade me to do anything more with the charter school. I had been the backbone of the entire operation.

I was furious. My anger touched a core in me that burst into flame. Nearly everyone in the community wanted this school. For the first time, I began to see how religion could suppress something positive and life-giving. Failing to educate our children was unconscionable.

What was also maddening was that I was not allowed to present my case to Uncle Rulon before Warren turned him against the school.

Pieces were beginning to come together, but I had not yet added up the sum of the parts. I was too upset. I stopped eating for a week.

We told the state of Arizona that we couldn't pull the building together in time and that we were canceling the charter. This was a lie. (The state called us every year afterward asking what it could do to help get the school built. Jayne kept coming up with excuses but said sooner or later she'd blurt out the truth: the prophet opposed the school and would not allow it to happen.)

I was too distraught over the crash of the charter school to continue teaching. I quit when the school year ended. There was no future for me in education, at least not while Warren Jeffs was the de facto prophet. I didn't think about what might happen after his father died. No one really expected Warren to become the next prophet. I certainly didn't. He was too much of a nobody.

# Merril's Heart Attack

After the demise of my charter school, I knew I could never go back to teaching. The thought of going into a classroom again was heartbreaking. I wanted to move before the public schools were closed in the community, which I was sure was going to happen. I told Merril that I could make more money as a Web site designer, and he agreed to let me try.

Merril gave me some office space and I began developing simple Web sites for local businesses and selling health food over the Internet. Within a few months—the fall of 1996—I was pregnant with my sixth child and was sick again.

Life was changing, and not in good ways, as Uncle Rulon began exerting more control on the community. He had built a house in Colorado City, and he and Warren were spending more and more time among us. Our freedom was increasingly disappearing. We were now under strict regulations that prohibited us from going to the movies. Television and the Internet were also completely off-limits except for business purposes.

Even our clothing requirements changed. It was now forbidden to wear large prints. In the coming months and years, as our lives became more severe, plaids were banned and we were limited to wearing only pastel clothing in a few styles.

The other new and completely bizarre commandment from the prophet was that now we were all required to wear long underwear—

including all children who were old enough to be potty trained. This created frenzy within the community as we all struggled to comply immediately. Until Warren's edict, wearing long underwear was optional. Only about 20 percent of the families chose to wear long underwear on their own—but they never tried to make toddlers wear them. I had to buy and sew underwear for us all. Then I had to buy more clothes that would cover up all the long underwear, which was not supposed to be visible. Like all the changes, the only reason that was given was that God believed his people were now ready to live by a higher law.

One afternoon I went with several of Merril's other wives to take a baby gift to one of Warren's wives who'd just given birth to a son. I'd heard that she delivered at Uncle Rulon's house and could not understand why she hadn't gone to the clinic.

I asked her what happened.

"Warren didn't want me to go to Hildale," she said. "He decided I'd have the baby at home. We had to improvise a bit, but everything worked out okay in the end."

She looked like she'd been through hell.

"What do you mean, 'improvise'?" I asked.

"I was given an episiotomy with sewing scissors and then stitched up with dental floss," she said in a weak and flat voice.

I was speechless. How could someone put his wife and child at risk and treat her in such a barbaric way?

But I knew I had to keep my mouth shut. Many of Warren's wives were in the room, and if I reacted, it might get this one in trouble—and me. It was hard to contain my shock. She had already said too much.

Later I heard that Merril's daughters who had married Warren defended his actions. They thought she was out of order for even talking about what had happened to her. No one questioned Warren's beliefs.

Months after the baby was born, word got around that Warren had stopped having sex with this wife. I'm sure it was because he was angry that she told the truth about her episiotomy and it reflected badly on him. But Warren had always been mean to this girl and he might have rejected her for other reasons.

What frightened me now was that as word got around about how Warren Jeffs treated his wives, other men would start emulating his extreme behavior. At Linda's coffees we talked about how domestic violence had increased after the release of Warren's tapes calling for even more obedience among women toward their husbands.

Warren's expanding influence over our lives spread into the bedroom. He took sex away from the community by decreeing that it could only be used for procreation. We had to keep track of when we ovulated and sex could occur only at that time. Then we had to wait a month to see if we were pregnant before we could have sex again.

Merril just ignored this new decree and continued to have sex with me whether I was pregnant or not. He was in such a high position in the FLDS that none of his wives would ever report his lack of compliance. Some men didn't abide by this new ruling about sex, but they knew that was risky. This new ruling gave Warren Jeffs more power over them. If their wives complained to Jeffs that they were being disobedient, their husbands could be kicked out of the FLDS.

But there was a catch: even if a woman told on her husband, it could still backfire. If Warren liked her husband, he could take his side through a loophole Jeffs called "the power of inspiration." God could act directly in a family by inspiring the husband. So if a husband was inspired to have sex with his wife when she wasn't ovulating, then Warren would argue that God knew this was best for that man's family and the woman could be seen as being in rebellion and face consequences. The bottom line was that Warren was gaining complete control over our lives; he could make the rules but also manipulate them to his advantage.

The women who suffered most were those whose husbands didn't like to have sex with them. Their husbands would say they were not worthy to bear their children and quit having sex with them altogether. This freed up men to just have sex with their most favorite wives. He'd tell the other wife that when she was worthy enough he would give her a baby. It was as crass as that.

It wasn't long after this decree went into effect that there was an upsurge of women in the community seeking antidepressants. Pregnant women started losing it because their husbands stopped having sex with them. (Since women were pregnant almost all of the time, they expected to continue having sex throughout their pregnancies, otherwise they rarely would have it.)

Women would go into the clinic pregnant and distraught. The two nurse practitioners had the power to prescribe antidepressants. Pregnant women were put on Zoloft; everyone else got Prozac. This was not a secret. I heard about it both directly and indirectly from Shirley, one of the nurse practitioners, who worried that some of these pregnant women would have nervous breakdowns without the drugs. She said that at least a third of the wives in the community were on medication. (After several years of this, the Health Department was alerted to the number of prescriptions that were being written for antidepressants, looked at their charts, and said that women could not be on these medications for an extended period of time without seeing a therapist or a doctor. But if any serious action was taken as a result, I never heard about it.)

Sex was power in the FLDS. If a man stopped sleeping with his wife, she was cut off at her knees. She lost power and status within her family. We always knew which wife in a family was like Barbara, the favorite. The woman having the most sex won in the intense sexual competition played out in polygamous families. Her husband treated her like a queen and she used that power to lord it over her sister wives.

But children got caught in the crossfire of these sexual wars. Husbands tended to become more abusive toward the wives they no longer had sex with. They also mistreated the children of those wives.

Barbara was typical of a woman exalted in her status as the favorite wife. She genuinely believed she was superior to us all. As a favorite wife, both she and her children were untouchable. Her children looked down on their half siblings as inferior, which was also common in these large polygamous families.

The caste system in Merril's family was entrenched before I even arrived. But in that our family was an exception. Warren's new decree meant other families would now become more like ours. Many men in the FLDS tried to be fair to all their wives. They felt it was their religious duty *not* to play favorites. There were schedules for sex in the home so no one felt hurt or left out. If a man had three wives, each woman knew that according to the schedule, she would sleep with her husband every third night.

But this new sex policy gave men a freedom they never had. There was no longer any obligation to sleep with a woman unless he wanted to have a child with her. So expectations about decency were off. Once free from sleeping with a wife, most men singled out their favorites and locked in a caste system in their families. Caste systems in families are breeding grounds for family members to harm one another. As the months and years wore on, Warren would underscore this by preaching that a man had the right to treat one wife better than another if she was more worthy of love.

Sex was the only hope a woman had in this life. If she pleased her husband sexually, she and her children would be protected by him. Since he was her passport to eternal life, she could not risk displeasing him sexually. So it was emotionally destabilizing to women when their husbands only had sex with them once a month or stopped altogether when they were pregnant. Their chances to seduce, impress, and satisfy their husbands were so drastically limited it threatened their very being.

But, like everything else, this new decree was done in the name of God. Warren was preaching that Christ would come to our community because we were pure and abstained from sex except to create children. He preached that we were now living at a higher spiritual plane, but to me, it felt that we had crossed a new and dangerous threshold.

One morning when I was in the bathroom vomiting, Tammy came and pounded on the door. "Carolyn, Merril had a heart attack this morning. The ambulance is here to take him to the hospital. Barbara's going with him and the rest of us will meet them at the ER."

Tammy drove the small family car and I sat in the backseat, upset and so sick it was hard to stop vomiting. What if Merril died?

I was terrified. Women I knew in the community who were assigned to marry other men after their husbands' deaths always ended up in more drastic situations. I honestly did not know how I could survive in a family if I was treated any worse.

Not all—but many—big polygamous families were similar to lions' prides. When a new lion takes over, it kills off all the cubs from the previous lion. I had seen situations where the new husband chased off all his new wife's sons and then married her daughters or married them to his sons. Girls can stay in the new family as a commodity, but the boys are often outcasts.

If Merril died, I'd be forced to remarry. There was no way around it. I prayed hard for Merril to live. My children were so young, and I was pregnant with another; we would be completely vulnerable if we were moved into another family.

Barbara became the spokesperson for the family. She stayed with Merril around the clock, but she was very secretive—at least with the other wives. She confided more in Merril's daughters. His condition was not good. His heart had been permanently damaged from a massive attack. It was touch and go for several days. When he failed to improve, he was transferred to University Hospital in Salt Lake for bypass surgery. He went on a life flight. We made the five-hour trip the next day in a caravan of cars.

Merril did not do well in surgery. There was concern that he would not make it through the night.

What a strange scene we were. All six wives, Merril's married children, and several of his friends sat outside the surgical ICU. Many were in tears. The head surgeon returned to the hospital at about 3 A.M. After spending several hours at his bedside, he told us Merril had stabilized and we could all go and get some sleep.

The next week was a nightmare. Merril got a staph infection and became septic. His kidneys started shutting down and he was put on life support. I was sure he was going to die. I couldn't stand being away from my children, but we had no choice. All of Merril's wives were required to keep a vigil while he was hospitalized. When I went in to see him I was convinced he was dying. Machines were keeping him alive.

Linda and I are sitting on the doorstep of our home in Colorado City. I'm on the right and about three years old. Linda is five. *Below:* Here I am with my two sisters after we moved back to the community from Salt Lake City. I'm on the left, Linda's in the middle, and Annette is to her right.

*Above:* This is my beloved sister Nurylon at two, a few months before she was killed in an auto accident.
*Right:* Here I am at fourteen.
*Below:* This is my high school graduation in 1985. I'm holding my newest brother, Carl.

My college graduation in 1989, a proud day! I am also pregnant with my second child. *Below:* This is my father with his two wives. Rosie is on the right and my mother, Nurylon, is on the left. I'm third from the right on the back row and pregnant. This was taken four years after I married Merril.

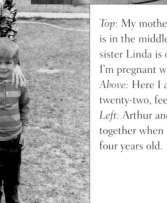

*Top:* My mother, Nurylon, is in the middle. My sister Linda is on the left. I'm pregnant with Betty. *Above:* Here I am at twenty-two, feeding Betty. *Left:* Arthur and I together when he was four years old.

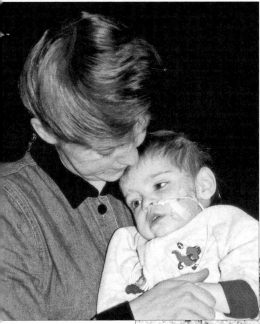

*Left*: Harrison and I had just come home from the hospital with his feeding tube. *Below*: Betty, LuAnne, and Merrilee at the motel in Caliente.

*Right:* My first child, Arthur, holds his baby brother, Bryson, my eighth child and my last. *Below:* My karate crew after we escaped. From left to right: Andrew, Merrilee, Patrick, and LuAnne.

Betty (on the left) and LuAnne skiing in Salt Lake City.
*Below:* Princess Merrilee's first birthday party ever.

Betty, at seventeen, on a hiking trip we took to Donut Falls.
*Below:* Here I am with Brian, the love of my life. This was taken during
the intermission of *Hairspray,* the first Broadway musical I ever saw!

People stared at us in the hospital; I felt like an alien when I went into the cafeteria. Rumors were circulating that a polygamist was in the ICU. I heard two janitors talking in the hallway saying, "Six wives—what does he do with them?"

Ruth was unhappy. She wanted to go home. Cathleen just left one day and went back to work. Barbara insisted we all had to stay. Tammy was marching in step, but I was desperate to get home. The conflict between Ruth and Barbara escalated. Several of Merril's daughters reported this to Uncle Rulon, and he assigned another man to be responsible for Merril's family until he recovered.

This man had more power than even Barbara, and she hated being usurped. He took us all out to dinner, but Barbara's open hostility toward him made the meal tense. I didn't engage at all with either of them. I just needed to get back to my children. We'd been apart now for nearly three weeks.

One of Merril's daughters brought Arthur and Betty to stay with me for a week. That helped, but there were still the three others I yearned for. I talked to them every day, but it wasn't the same.

LuAnne had sent a present to her father. It was nicely wrapped— I assumed someone had taken her shopping. When Merril opened the present there was a wilted flower along with a few scraps of fabric. Everyone in his room roared with laughter. I ached for LuAnne so much; I knew what she had sent her father were treasures in her five-year-old eyes. Merril was so sick I'm not sure he understood what was going on, but I hated that everyone else was mocking my sweet little girl.

Merril had improved enough after a month to return home. We flew back to Colorado City on Uncle Rulon's private plane. As we touched down, I could see that a crowd of people had gathered on the tarmac to greet us.

I scanned the crowd looking for my children. I finally saw a small redhead popping through the crowd. Merril reached out for her. "Well, how is my Betty baby doing?"

Moments later I was hugging the rest of my children.

# Ruth's Nose

**W**arren's preaching touched every area of our lives. We were used to Uncle Rulon's admonitions. Children no longer got immunizations because he prohibited them. Arthur and Betty had theirs, but none of the others did. Uncle Rulon said the immunizations were engineered to make our children sterile. The government was behind it, he said.

But we still took our kids to doctors when they needed treatment. It seemed to me that Warren's views were always an extreme departure from his father's. He began preaching that anyone who needed medical help to heal was a person of little faith. A person in harmony with God could heal him- or herself with fasting and prayer. Before I saw this play out in our own home, I knew of several people who nearly died and children who became severely ill before they were taken to the hospital as a last resort.

In 1997, Ruth was diagnosed with skin cancer. The spot was on her nose. Merril had sent her to our local clinic because she had a sore there. At the clinic, she was sent to see a dermatologist, who diagnosed her skin cancer. But he said the good news was that the cancer had been caught at an early stage and could be eliminated with a few treatments.

Ruth wanted to try Warren's way and began fasting and praying. I tried to convince her that God could send answers in many ways and maybe the dermatologist was one of them. She felt that if she continued to see the physician it meant that she had little faith.

Ruth went to a health food store and asked for an alternative way to treat her cancer. She was given some herbs along with a chemical to burn the cancer out.

I came back from the office and my Web site business one day and found Ruth mixing up a big batch of herbs and chemicals for her nose. She said God had answered her prayers and revealed to her a new way to heal her skin cancer. When I saw the enthusiasm she had for the witch's brew she was concocting, I kept my mouth shut.

When Ruth told me she was only supposed to put a drop on her nose the size of a pinhead, I asked her why she was making such a big batch. "Oh, I guess I've gotten a little too excited."

I thought that her enthusiasm for the glop in the bowl would die down quickly once she saw how ineffective it was. I knew it was impossible to talk sense to her and I didn't think this would be harmful.

But when I saw her later that night the whole end of her nose was green. I asked her about the pinhead-size treatment she'd described earlier. "I started putting a tiny bit on the cancer and then I decided to put on more. I really think it's important to get rid of this. After I put a big amount on the cancer, I saw another sore on the other side of my nose and I thought that might be a cancer sore also."

"Ruth, the doctor would have told you if he'd seen more than one cancer."

"Carolyn, doctors don't know everything, and I have been fasting and praying to God for the answer about how to get rid of this. God can inspire me with how to care for what is wrong with my body."

"But why did you cover all the areas in between those two spots on your nose?" I asked.

"I thought there might be cancer sores there that I could not see," Ruth said before marching off to her bedroom, confident that she was curing her cancer with some green gook.

I was up early the next morning and went into the kitchen to make coffee. Ruth was sitting there, crying, her nose still very green.

"Ruth, what's wrong?"

"I was in so much pain last night I couldn't sleep. It felt like great big balls of fire were on my nose. It was so bad I got on my knees to pray to God for mercy."

"But Ruth, why didn't you wash it off?"

"I'm not washing this off. If this is what God wants me to go through to be healed from my cancer, then I will do it with a humble heart."

"Ruth, you have to listen to me. This could be damaging your nose if it's hurting that much. You have to wash it off." It took some wrangling to get her to agree, but she finally did.

But when I came home from the office later that afternoon, Ruth's nose was still green and she said she was in a lot of pain. She had tried to wash off the herbs but still had a green nose and great discomfort.

I told Ruth that this was an emergency. She had to call her doctor. But that to her was tantamount to admitting defeat and she refused.

The next morning I found her in the kitchen again crying from pain. I didn't even try to reason with her. When she still refused to call her doctor I said I was calling 911 and the National Guard if that was what it took to get her medical care.

Ruth said other people would get into trouble if she went for help. I had no idea what she was talking about and asked her to explain. She went to her room and brought me a big jar of chemicals. I thought it would be empty because she'd made such a large batch, but Ruth told me she'd used only a tiny amount. The jar was so full I realized how toxic these were. "Ruth, you have enough chemicals here to burn off the Statue of Liberty's nose!"

I told Ruth that if she hadn't done something by the time I got home at lunch I was taking action. When I came home Ruth told me she'd called the clinic in Hildale but was told to go to the emergency room. I said I'd take her to the ER in St. George. I knew she would go only if Merril agreed, so I called him in Page.

Merril said he saw no reason to rush to any conclusion. "You are only assuming that she has damaged her nose."

"Merril, I am not assuming anything. I took the jar of chemicals she used to do it with away from her. Plus her nose is beginning to stink."

Merril said there was no reason to get bent out of shape about this. He would handle it that evening when he came home.

What could I do when everyone insisted there was no problem? Nothing. I went back to the office. When Merril came back that night he told Ruth to make an appointment with the dermatologist, even though part of her nose was breaking away from the burned area.

When she finally returned home she was extremely upset. The dermatologist said she'd burned her nose off with the chemicals, which would continue burning until she neutralized them with vinegar. The doctor had demanded that Ruth tell him who had given her the chemicals. But she refused. The doctor said they could only be obtained illegally, and he'd seen several other cases of severe burns in people who tried to treat their own skin cancer.

But the dermatologist also told Ruth that she did burn off the cancer along with everything else. He made an emergency appointment for her to see a plastic surgeon in Salt Lake City to begin to reconstruct her nose. It was a cheap job and looked terrible. The side that was burned so badly was very misshapen. I felt bad for her.

Ruth's nose was bizarre. But I knew I never would do something so mindless. I'd also continue to take my children to the doctor at the first sign of serious illness, Merril be damned. I felt that in this area, I was immune from Warren's extremism.

But it frightened me when I realized how pervasive extremism was becoming in ways I could not have anticipated.

I was in the kitchen one night making dinner and I overheard Merril's daughter Merrilyn say, "When Dee took that pig's heart out it squealed so loud you could hear it for blocks."

I shuddered, then left the kitchen to find out what Merrilyn meant. Information was power to me. If I knew what was happening, I felt reasonably confident I could figure out a survival strategy. Merrilyn was talking about the survival classes Warren was holding at his private school in Salt Lake City. Dee Jessop was Ruth and Barbara's nephew and just a few years older than I was. He'd been making regular trips to Salt Lake from Colorado City and killing animals in front of students. He did this to show students how many different ways an animal could be killed. Very few people talked about what they had seen. I think the children were too traumatized. The parents who knew what was going on also knew to keep their mouths shut. No one stood up to Warren, even then.

This was happening under Warren's orders. I knew him well enough to know that there was always a reason behind his actions. He never did things on a whim. But I couldn't fathom how torturing animals fit into the picture.

Warren's power began to be solidified when Uncle Rulon had his first stroke in 1996. The community was informed when he was taken to the hospital, and there was deep concern. After his release, we were told that he had his full mental capacity but was still very ill. He had to be mentally with it in order to remain as the prophet. But since no one was allowed to see him after his stroke, I began to think that something was up. Now I'm convinced that he was kept out of sight because he wasn't competent enough to continue in his leadership role.

Throughout 1997, Warren Jeffs moved to solidify his hold on the community. He made it clear that he was speaking for his father. People accepted this because before he got sick, Uncle Rulon had made it evident that Warren spoke for him.

At one of the priesthood meetings shortly after he'd moved his father to Colorado City, Warren announced that his father had decreed that there would no longer be immorality among his people. Any man who had been involved with immorality would have to leave his family and the community.

Men were given pamphlets that spelled out the new moral code. All sex in marriage was forbidden except that which was for procreation. Immoral acts for which there could be no forgiveness were also named. Any person who committed these sins, such as fornication and adultery, would have to pay for them with "blood atonement."

I had never heard of blood atonement before. Blood atonement is a murder. Warren claimed the ordinance of blood atonement dated back to the beginning of the Mormon Church. But he said that blood atonement could only be practiced in a temple that he said we would build in the near future.

Dee Jessop began to teach "survival class" in Colorado City. But he upped the ante. Word went out that a survivalist demonstration was going to be held in Cottonwood Park. This was a class open to all, including children. No one suspected anything very dramatic would take place because children had been invited and it was sanctioned by Uncle Fred, who was the FLDS bishop responsible for Colorado City. I didn't go because I was too busy and I'd heard Merrilyn talk about what Dee had done to animals in Salt Lake. There was no way I'd risk letting my children attend anything done under his auspices.

Dee decided to demonstrate that a woman could take care of herself if she didn't have a husband. Since I was a little girl I'd been taught that a time would come among the Lord's people when all the men would be gone. No explanation was ever given for why that might happen. But I remember being told that men would be so scarce that if a child ever saw one she'd go running home to her mother screaming because it would have been such an unusual sight. So maybe Dee was trying to play into that kind of scenario.

Dee's class drew a large audience of parents and children. No one suspected anything when they first got to the park. Dee's wife was tying down a cow with ropes. But once the cow was restrained, she took out a handsaw and began sawing off the cow's head.

The cow's screams sounded like a woman's. Children shrieked in terror. Those closest to the cow were sprayed by its blood. Stunned parents grabbed their kids and started to run away. Some stayed, frozen in shock and unable to move.

People were furious. Everyone was talking about it. People were disgusted by what Dee had done and blamed him. No one dared criticize Warren Jeffs or Uncle Fred. The community was united against Dee alone and wanted to see him slammed.

That happened a few months later in a way none of us expected.

Ruth was in the throes of a breakdown. She'd stopped sleeping and was close to spinning completely out of control. Her oldest daughter, Rebecca, came home for the weekend to care for her. Merril was ignoring her condition, as he usually did.

By Monday morning, Ruth was babbling nonstop about being late. She said she was supposed to play her accordion at the Monday church meeting. She was parked in Merril's office, waiting for him. He came in and put on his shoes, and when he sized up Ruth he told her she wasn't well enough to perform.

Ruth said she couldn't neglect her duties.

"Calm down, Ruthie. You know your duties are to your husband," Merril said.

Ruth waited until Merril left the office with Tammy and several of his children. Then she grabbed her accordion and took off.

I was worried about her because she was so unstable, and went to find Merril. I told him she'd escaped. "Oh, don't worry. She'll be heading for the meetinghouse and we'll pick her up along the way."

Dee Jessop was Ruth's nephew. He saw her running crazily on the road and stopped his truck. He told Ruth to get in and he'd take her home. Ruth wanted nothing to do with him.

He did what all of us knew never to do: touch Ruth when she was crazy.

Ruth ripped into him, smashing him in the face with her accordion. She kicked him everywhere her legs could fly. Cars coming down the road slowed down to watch.

But no one intervened. Most of us in the community felt that Ruth could not have picked a better person to brutalize. When Dee managed to break free, he got into his truck and drove home. The rest of us felt that justice had been served.

But Ruth continued on her downward spiral. Word reached Uncle Rulon that she was out of control, and he sent Merrilyn to help take care of her.

But Merrilyn hated being in charge of her mother. One morning Tammy came down for breakfast and heard Ruth screaming like a child. She walked into Merril's office and saw Merrilyn beating her mother. Ruth finally sank into the corner of the office, sobbing and hugging herself.

Tammy was shocked. "Why are you slapping your mother like that?"

Merrilyn shrugged. "That's the way Father handled her ever since I was a little girl. When she gets out of control, he beats the hell out of her until she comes to her senses."

Ruth was finally hospitalized for two weeks.

# Patrick's Abuse

**O**ne of the moments I'd do over in my life if I could is this: Patrick, my four-year-old son, was trying to wake me up at ten-thirty one weekend night. Merril had called family prayers and we were all to assemble upstairs in the living room. One of his older children had tried to rouse me from sleep. When that failed, he sent Patrick.

"Mother, Father wants you to come pray," Patrick said. I rolled over and said that I was too tired. Merrilee was only a few weeks old and I still had not recovered from her birth. I was so depleted and wiped out that I'd fallen into bed after tucking in my children. But apparently Merril had called for prayers, and all my sleeping children were dragged from their beds. I was sick from exhaustion and told Patrick I could not get out of bed to pray.

There had been a period of relative stability in our home after Merril's heart attack. Barbara continued to cause problems for the five other wives, but we were making a determined effort not to engage with her in hopes of minimizing stress at home while Merril recuperated. After a few weeks this strategy seemed to set Barbara off. She thrived on tension and on reporting on our shortcomings to Merril.

To stir up trouble, Barbara encouraged the children to act up to get us to respond abusively. One day I lost it with several of Merril's daughters. They'd been making my life miserable by being argumentative and resistant. When I overheard them acting shocked about a girl who was being bullied and sent dog food as a symbol of her worth, I lit into them.

"You girls are such hypocrites after the way that every one of you has been treating the mothers in this family. If any of you allowed me as much respect as dog food, I would be overjoyed." After I said that, I walked across the room and said, "I think I'm going to throw up. Every one of you is a self-righteous, disgusting little hypocrite."

The room began boiling with anger. I had spoken the truth and they knew it. But standing up to abuse in Merril's family threatened the power structure and was unacceptable to Barbara. I knew I would be disciplined. But I didn't care.

I didn't know she would target Patrick.

I never knew what happened that night until three and a half years after our escape. I was driving Patrick home from karate when his story spilled out and he told me about the night he'd tried to wake me up for prayers.

When Patrick returned to the living room, he told Merril that I was too tired to come to prayers. Barbara became enraged. The family was on their knees in the living room. My refusal to come caused something of a commotion. Patrick's older brothers began questioning him about my absence.

Patrick remembered Merril saying something to Barbara, who then came over and asked him to follow her. He thought they were going to my room, but she took him to a room across the hall and shut the door.

Barbara began drilling Patrick with question after question about me. He tried to answer her questions, but she still slapped him. He started crying, which infuriated her even more. Then she picked him up and threw him several feet across the floor. He was shaking visibly when Barbara came and grabbed him and threw him into the metal bars at the foot of the bed. The first blow knocked the air out of him and he said it was hard to breathe. She slammed him into the bed again and again. He was crumpled in a heap. When he made an effort to stand, Barbara, who weighed nearly two hundred pounds, kicked him in the stomach. Patrick was not unconscious, but he couldn't breathe at all for a few frightening moments.

Patrick was still shaking. Barbara said to him, "Patrick, hush up. If you tell anyone what I have done to you, it will be far worse the next time." Patrick was sobbing uncontrollably. Barbara grabbed his face. "Patrick, look at me. I don't want you telling Merril or your mother about this. Do you understand?" Barbara shook him again. Patrick finally said, "Okay, okay, I won't tell anyone."

Barbara sat in the room with him, handed him a Kleenex, and told him to blow his nose. She didn't touch him again. Patrick feared that if he kept crying, she'd keep hitting him. He stopped, but he could not stop shaking. Barbara told him to return with her to prayers.

Prayers were over. But Merril and a few wives and children were in the living room. One of the other children said, "Patrick, what did she do to you?"

Merril jumped in and told Patrick to go to bed.

Patrick came into my room. The lights were off and I was asleep. I had taught him how to put my La-Z-Boy chair into a reclining position. He climbed into the chair and sobbed himself to sleep.

Patrick was too afraid to awaken me or tell me about the attack the next morning. It would take nine years before he was able to speak about what happened—nine years.

The next morning I was getting Patrick ready for his bath. I saw bruises all over his back, bottom, and legs.

"Patrick, what happened to you? Who did this to you?"

Patrick's face went white with fear. "Nothing, Mama, nothing happened to me."

"Patrick, someone hurt you and I want to know who it is."

"Mama, I promise that nobody hurt me. I was playing with Parley and Johnson and we were roughing around. No one was supposed to get hurt."

I knew he was lying. I could see how traumatized he was, but I didn't want to push him into telling me the truth. I thought someone might have hurt him while I had been at work.

There were few options, all bad. If I went to Merril and complained, he would scold me and say nothing had happened. I did not want to get trapped into playing someone's sick game—my child was hurt, and if I told Merril and he didn't believe me, my child could be hurt again, perhaps even more, in retaliation for my protest. Whoever had hurt Patrick might hurt him even more.

I couldn't go to the police. The community police were all members of the FLDS. They would never investigate. The police would tell me to go home and be obedient to my husband. Merril was too powerful in the FLDS. No local police officer would ever make waves against him.

I could report the abuse to state child protection agencies in Utah or Arizona, but they had poor track records of protecting women and children in Colorado City. Victims routinely got sent back to perpetrators.

I decided my preschoolers were never staying at home again without me. Though my children could see how upset I was that morning, I told them it was a special day. We were going to breakfast and then to see their grandmother. I would buy them some new books and papers because from now on, they'd be coming to work with me.

Over the next few months I never let my children out of my sight. I stopped taking them to family meals and fed them in my bedroom. I told my mother that I had found bruises on Patrick's body and that I didn't feel my children were safe in Merril's family. She began sending food home with me that I could keep in my bedroom.

Warren Jeffs was now living in his father's house in Hildale with his family. He decided to start a religious school and picked a few "elite" families to participate. Our family was one of them, which meant that Betty and Arthur were yanked out of public schools in the fourth and fifth grades in the middle of the academic year.

I was upset and worried because they were both doing well and getting a solid education in the public schools. I knew that in the private school Warren ran in Salt Lake, science, health, and social studies weren't taught. I shuddered to think how far behind Betty and Arthur would now begin to fall.

Barbara was beginning to notice that she had lost power over me and my children. She rarely saw us on weekends when she came home with Merril. I was deliberately doing nothing to provoke conflict. She had lost control over me, and that was intolerable to her.

So I was not surprised when she asked to see the records of my business. Merril insisted that I report to Barbara and explain what I was doing with the small Web site design business I had started. Barbara was a master manipulator, but she was utterly clueless when it came to business. I told Merril I'd be happy to oblige and copied all my files onto a disk and brought it home to be downloaded into another computer.

I knew that Barbara would not be able even to turn on the computer, let alone download something to her hard drive or navigate the financial programs. Merril said I had to provide handwritten records. I told him that was impossible and offered to show Barbara how to operate the computer, knowing she'd be incapable.

I wasn't selling enough over the Internet to do more than clear my operating costs. I thought I could do more if I had some help, so I talked to my cousin Jeremy about joining me. Merril offered to pay him, knowing that if he did, he could use Jeremy to keep tabs on what I was doing with my business.

Jeremy and I began putting in long hours together. After a few weeks, Merril decided he wanted more bang for his buck with Jeremy and decided that we should go to Caliente, Nevada, and manage a motel that he owned. He said we could work on Web sites at night when we weren't cleaning rooms or managing the motel by day.

Merril's motel was in financial trouble and he was afraid he'd lose it if he didn't take drastic action. I wasn't sure Jeremy would be willing to make the move to Caliente; this was more than he'd bargained for when he agreed to work on the Web site business. I told him exactly what Merril's motivations were, and to my surprise Jeremy agreed to work with me there.

I had an ulterior motive: if I ran the motel in Caliente, my children and I would be out of the house for substantial periods of time. I knew Merril and Barbara were thinking that if I went there it would get me away from my children. But I'd never agree to that. They thought I'd never take my children with me. But they were wrong.

The first week that I went I packed up everything for my four youngest. Betty was refusing to come, but I knew no one would touch her if I left her at home because she was clearly her father's favorite. Arthur was going to be working on a farm during that summer of 1998, so I knew he'd be safe. I drove out there with Patrick, Andrew, LuAnne, and Merrilee.

I hadn't been there for two hours when Merril called and scolded me for taking the children without checking with him. "Having your children there is unnecessary," he said. "If you are interested in what your husband wants, you won't do this." I didn't argue with him, nor did I agree. The conversation ended.

Three weeks later, he came to see me and size up the progress we were making with the motel. He came with several other children and three of his wives. The next morning he announced that he was taking my children home with him. I told Merril I couldn't send my nursing baby and that I needed LuAnne to help me watch her when I worked. Andrew was one of Merril's favorites and would be safe. I worried about Patrick.

I had to figure out how to outsmart Merril again. If he ordered the children to go with him, they'd be in rebellion if they stayed with me. I let the boys go. The moment Merril left, I began telling Jeremy that he had been working so hard he needed a break that weekend.

Jeremy had left his family in Colorado City and was eager to comply. I told him he didn't need to come back until Tuesday. I knew Merril would have left for Page by then. I asked Jeremy to bring Patrick and Andrew with him, which he did.

Merril was furious when he found out, and called to scream at me. He came back to Caliente ten days later and said my children were going home. Again, I kept the baby, Merrilee. LuAnne was bored and wanted to go home. So I kept Patrick with me and let LuAnne and Andrew go back.

I didn't have many cards left to play. I couldn't have Jeremy bring my two children back to me. That had already been tried once. I began calling my friends to see if I could find someone who'd make the three-hour drive out with LuAnne and Andrew. I offered a night at the motel and said we could also hang out in the mineral springs. Two days later, LuAnne and Andrew returned.

Merril was livid. He told me that there would be consequences for my behavior. "Carolyn, if you are going to insist on doing things the way you want, then you're not someone I can have confidence in. You're throwing your future away only to satisfy yourself."

I tried to be calming and told Merril I was so sorry and had no idea he would be so upset. But secretly I was pleased because I had outmaneuvered him to keep my children safe.

Jeremy and I worked nonstop on cleaning up the motel, which was infested with roaches and scorpions. The linens were filthy and the rooms needed repainting, but I didn't care. We were safe and out of Colorado City.

After two months, I think Merril began to notice that I wasn't begging him for time off and didn't act as though I missed being at home. Merril ordered me to start coming home every other weekend, which I did.

Betty missed us and—with Merril and Barbara's approval—came to spend a week at the motel. I think they encouraged her to report back to them about me. It was an awful time. Betty was nine and came with her two half sisters. All three of them were deliberately rude and refused to clean up any of their messes.

I had no control over Betty because whenever there was a conflict between us she went running to her father and used him to sabotage me. Warren Jeffs had strictly forbidden television and movies once he took over. Betty told Merril that I let the younger kids watch TV, which was true. It was the only way I could keep them occupied while I was cleaning rooms. I would turn it on, and when Betty came into the room she turned it off and the kids would get into trouble because they then had nothing else to do. It was madness. She was out to sabotage me whenever she had the chance

Arthur was eleven and came to see us during the summer. He was tanned and getting taller. I was proud of the way he was developing. Arthur was the classic type-A personality who always did well in school and prided himself on being a hard worker. Like many firstborn children, he was highly motivated and very determined to do whatever was necessary to reach his goal. He had a quiet but steadfast ability to persevere. I always marveled at him because even as a little boy he'd known which way he was headed.

But Arthur got into trouble with his father because he watched *Scooby-Doo* on TV when he stayed with us. I was always tense when Merril came to see us because I feared one of my kids would talk about watching cartoons on TV. I warned them not to but was always nervous until Merril and Barbara left.

Merril and Barbara were coming more frequently. I had them over a barrel. The motel was running well. Jeremy and I had worked really hard and made it a financial success. Barbara absolutely hated our success—no one was supposed to be happy outside their orbit, and I had made a life independent of them.

My newfound freedom energized and stabilized me. I felt happy in a way I had never been since I married Merril. I was alone with my children, or four of them at least, and we were making it. I was exhausted, but I was not under Merril and Barbara's domination and control.

Both of them did things to make my job even harder. Barbara stopped paying the motel's phone bills. Then she stopped paying utilities and the gas got turned off. Jeremy and I scrounged up the money to pay the bills. This angered Merril. Why hadn't we asked Barbara to deal with this?

I was not going to tell Merril the real reason. Jeremy and I kept coming up with end runs around whatever obstacle they would put in our path. We were running a business and running it well. Merril tried to turn Jeremy against me. But that backfired. Jeremy saw through his tactics and refused to be intimidated by him.

Both of us knew the enemy was Merril Jessop.

# Turning Point

Jeremy and I were an outrageous success in running the motel. We started there in April 1998, and by the end of that summer there was a net profit of $60,000 that enabled Merril to pay off past-due bills. The motel was shining, the tourists were happy, and it was clear that the momentum we'd generated for the business was going strong.

It was a joy for me to wake up happy every day. I knew my children were safe and I was in control of my day-to-day destiny. Now that Jeremy and I had the motel up and running, we were going to focus on our Web site business. That would be impossible for Merril or Barbara to sabotage. It would truly be our own.

As summer ended, Jeremy left for a two-week break and my sisters came to stay with me. We were going to clean the motel from top to bottom in preparation for the slower fall and winter season.

I was cleaning the north buildings when a man walked over to me. I didn't like the looks of Jason the moment I saw him. There was something creepy about him. He told me he needed a place to stay on a long-term basis. I said we hadn't anything available.

Jason told me his girlfriend had kicked him out and he was desperate. He was tall and muscular and willing to work in exchange for any kind of lodging. I sent him away.

He was back the next day and asked to speak to the owner. His eyes were shifty and his manner abrasive. I told him the owner was out of town. But Jason kept hanging around, driving back and forth past the motel. It seemed like he was sizing things up. I didn't trust him.

When he saw Merril's truck outside three days later and saw Merril talking to me, he put two and two together and decided Merril must be the owner. He asked to speak with him.

Jason had a real sob story. He told Merril he'd been sleeping on a bench in town but got so dehydrated that he ended up in the hospital. He was willing to do anything if Merril would give him a chance. Merril found a broken lawn mower and asked Jason to fix it.

He did—and then went on to mow the lawn around the motel. Merril was pleased, hired him, and told me to give Jason a room. I protested. I told Merril I didn't like his looks and didn't want to be alone with him at the motel. That was a mistake—and it was the kind I usually didn't make with Merril because it was like throwing blood in the water for sharks.

Merril now had something that made me uncomfortable. He reveled in it. He told Jason to call him each day and discuss with him the jobs he was going to do.

I was pregnant with my seventh child and wretchedly sick again with morning sickness. I knew Merril cared little about me, but seemingly he cared nothing about his unborn child.

A local police officer showed up at the motel the day Jason was hired and asked to speak to Merril. His voice sounded urgent. He had seen Jason at the motel and told me he needed to speak to Merril about him. They talked for a few hours.

When it was over, I asked Merril what it was about. Merril acted nonchalant. "Oh, he's concerned that Jason is working here because Jason is a criminal and is bad news." My suspicions about Jason were confirmed. He was dangerous.

But it made no difference. The next morning, Merril was walking around the property with Jason discussing the various projects he wanted him to tackle.

Jason began to act like a stalker. He was always looking for me. He wanted to have supper with me and my sisters. I refused and brought a plate of food outside for him. There was always a reason, in his mind, that he had to get into our house. I rebuffed him.

When Jeremy returned from his break, I left for the weekend. He let Jason go into the laundry room to do his wash. This created problems because it gave him access to our house. Things started disappearing right and left, like towels. I had fought hard to keep the motel well-stocked with towels and when large numbers started to disappear I was suspicious. I called Merril and told him my suspicions.

Merril said I should not blame an innocent person. He said we were short on towels because of my laziness and accused me of using Jason as a cover-up. I slammed the phone down.

Jason started making incessant demands on my time. He would come into the motel nearly every ten minutes with a question or a complaint about the job he was working on. He'd always have an excuse for why he couldn't start or finish a project until Merril got back.

Again, I turned to Merril and asked him to deal with Jason. He made light of the problem but said he'd talk to Jason.

Nothing changed, except that Jason's advances became bolder. Once when he came into the lobby on some pretext he grabbed my hand as I was handing him an item.

"I don't know what to do with my girlfriend," he said. "She's jealous because I spend all my time with you."

"Well, why don't you spend more time with her?" I asked. The minute the words were out of my mouth I knew I'd regret them.

"I don't like being around her because she isn't nice like you," he said.

The next weekend it got so bad I called Merril. Jason was harassing me at every turn. If I was scrubbing the bathroom, I'd look up and see him standing behind me. He'd follow me to the laundry room and watch me move clothes from the washer to the dryer. I told Merril that I was as sick as I'd ever been during a pregnancy and that I had all I could do to get through the day. Jason was making a bad situation intolerable.

Merril told me the only reason Jason was following me around was that I was encouraging him. If he was abusing me, it was because I asked for it. He accused me of using my pregnancy to try and get his sympathy.

I was infuriated. Merril had let a criminal into our midst and put our lives and business in jeopardy. Again I knew what I had always known: Merril would never protect me. I would have to defend myself and my children.

I told Jason he could talk to me only once a day, at 6 P.M. We would make arrangements then for any supplies he needed for his various jobs. I locked myself into the lobby and locked all the doors to the house. He would stand outside and ring the bell relentlessly. I disconnected the bell.

When Jeremy came back from a weekend away I told him what was happening and asked him to keep a log of Jason's behavior for a few hours. I told him to write down every time he banged on the window or knocked on the door. When the phone rang and it was Jason, I nodded to Jeremy and he wrote it down.

Within three hours, Jeremy logged thirty interruptions.

The next time Merril came to Caliente, Jeremy told Merril that Jason was out of control and that the situation was unsafe. He showed Merril the log he'd made of Jason's actions. Merril scanned the report. When he looked up he said, "Well, you have to realize that Jason has burned his brains out on drugs and is a little bit daffy."

I could not believe what I was hearing. I hadn't thought Merril still had the capacity to shock me, but I was wrong. Not only did he know of Jason's criminal past, he knew that he was dangerous because he'd fried his brain on drugs.

Jason had been on the premises for about six weeks when his foul-looking friend showed up. Even though it was cold he was wearing only ripped brown shorts, a chain around his neck, and earrings in his nose and earlobes. The stench that emanated from him filled the lobby.

He asked for Jason and then sized me up with a frightening glint in his eye. The two of them went off. The next time I saw Jason he stank with that same nauseating odor.

I told Merril I couldn't stay at the motel with Jason and a man who acted like his drug dealer. Merril ridiculed me. "Carolyn, I finally get a man who can get a little bit done and you're insisting I get rid of him!"

Word was out around town that Jason was living at the motel. He had a reputation as a lowlife and we heard that people were starting to stay away. No one felt he was safe to be around, least of all James.

James lived in a trailer on the property. The previous managers had hired him for security. Now in his seventies, James claimed he had been a member of the Mafia in his younger days and had stories about killing people and burying them in the desert.

James did twenty years in prison because of a plea bargain. He kept rattlesnakes as pets and stuck to himself.

I liked James and I liked the fact that if I hit a button on the front desk he'd be in the lobby in minutes. James knew how to handle a gun. No one wanted to mess with him.

James never complained. But after several weeks, he came to me because Jason was harassing him. He warned me to stay away from him because the police had told James that Jason had raped several women in the area. None of the rapes had ever been prosecuted because the women were too terrified to press charges.

No one in my life had ever worried about me until James did. "I have talked to Merril several times about this and have told him you should not be out here alone with Jason on the property." I nodded in agreement. He was exactly right.

"Why are the men from Colorado City so abusive to their wives?" James said, his face red, his speech quickened. "You're in danger and your husband knows it. The police have told him and so have I."

This tough guy we called "Rattlesnake Man" touched my heart. He was strange in some of his ways, but he was far kinder and more concerned about me than Merril Jessop had ever been.

Jason was not satisfied with just his one room. He soon commandeered the one next to it. I told him that was unacceptable because the motel was sold out for the upcoming weekend. He was furious with me and told James' son Jimmy that he was going to dump acid in our well water. I told Jimmy to change every lock on every door that led to the shed where our well was.

So Jason called the police, making wild accusations about Merril. When the police called Merril for his side of the story he finally stopped making excuses about Jason's behavior and came to the motel a few days later to fire him. Merril would not stand for attacks on himself.

The police came for the confrontation with Jason, which was stormy. He accused me of being abusive, hurtling accusations one after another. But no one was buying it. Dale, the police officer, finally insisted Jason leave the property.

Then he turned to Merril and told him he needed to take me somewhere else. It wasn't safe because Jason was directing all of his anger at me. James, who'd been in on the meeting, turned to Merril and said, "You have to get Carolyn out of here tonight. He might kill her if you leave her here."

Merril made light of James' concerns. My world was so surreal that an ex-con who'd done twenty years for murder was more protective of me than my own husband.

James went ballistic at Merril's cavalier attitude. "Damn you, Merril. You don't know what the hell you're talking about. The man is dangerous. I'll fucking kill him before I let him hurt your pregnant wife."

Dale turned to James and said that while his feelings were noble, he was looking at life in prison if he killed him.

James was too angry to be intimidated. "Merril, you need to wake the hell up. Don't put me in this position."

"I don't see any concern in this situation," Merril said in the strange and stilted way he had of speaking.

James would not quit. "If you don't take her home tonight, will you stay with her?"

Merril said he would.

"Do you have a gun?" James asked.

"Of course not."

"If you don't have a gun, you better take a hammer to bed with you. You don't know what you're dealing with here. Jason is the kind of person who's likely to put gasoline in a bottle with a rag, light it, and throw it through the window."

Merril assured James there was nothing to worry about.

James and the police left. A few moments later, Merril did, too. He took a key to a room he planned to stay in with Barbara that was out of Jason's reach.

I was almost too terrified to move, but I had to do something. I couldn't stay in my room because Jason knew exactly where that was. My sister, little Rosie, was sleeping in the office, and I decided to stay with her. She was asleep when I got there. I knew she'd be frightened if I woke her up and told her what was going on, so I didn't. I had sent my children back to Colorado City three weeks after Jason started working at the motel because I felt he was danger-ous. I think that was another reason Merril wanted Jason at the motel: he knew that if I felt threatened, I'd leave my children at home and not bring them to Caliente.

I locked all the doors but left the bathroom door open so I could see the lights on the shed. They were on sensors and turned on in response to movement. For the next two hours, I lay in bed, watch-ing the lights flip on and off. Someone was out there.

At 1 A.M. the motel phone rang. A voice I didn't recognize asked to be transferred to Jason's room. I said we didn't put calls through that late. I was paralyzed by fear. I was sure the caller was checking to see if I was still awake.

I was so exhausted that I finally dropped off to sleep. But at 2 A.M. I was jolted awake by a scraping sound on top of the roof. I could hear what sounded like footsteps and something being dragged across the motel roof. Then came more footsteps. It wasn't just one person. I tried to wake Rosie, but then the footsteps stopped.

I called James. In less than a minute he and his son Jimmy were in front of the motel with flashlights and guns. They called me to say they didn't see anyone. James was firm on the phone. "But just because we didn't find anything doesn't mean that everything is all right. Stay awake. If he's going to do something, it will probably be around now."

I thanked him and sat stiff in my bed. The phone rang again. It was James. "Carolyn, I have a bad feeling. We are coming down and staying. What you heard on the roof might have just been the first step of something. If we keep a presence there for a few hours, it will be too close to morning for Jason to do anything."

James and Jimmy spent the next few hours right next to the motel lobby. At regular intervals they circled around the house with their flashlights and guns drawn. They might have saved my life. I know they saved my sanity.

The next morning I told Merril I was sure I'd heard people on the roof during the night and that James was on patrol to make sure nothing happened. Merril was furious and told me I'd blown everything out of proportion. He accused James of playing into my paranoid behavior. After he gave me a tongue-lashing he left for home with Barbara. I told them I needed to clean the laundry room before I returned to Colorado City. The last thing I wanted to do was travel with them.

By the time I got back to Colorado City, Merril and Barbara were gone. I was a nervous wreck. On top of everything I still was sick and vomiting from being pregnant. The trauma hit me hard when I got home and I started crying so hard I couldn't stop. The next day I felt desperately sick and broke out in hives. I was so weak it was hard to stand.

I had never felt so sick in my life before. I had to crawl to the bathroom to throw up. The hives were all over my body.

Merril called and wanted to talk to me. I told him that I was terribly ill and that I'd broken out in hives. "Well, that's good," he said.

I thought he was joking. "Good?"

His rage shot through the phone. "After the way you've been acting, I think so."

I said goodbye and hung up the phone.

I knew I needed help. I couldn't go back there without protection. My sister Annette was married to Merril's half brother Bob. They had managed the motel for over four years in the past. I was betting they knew Jason.

A week later I went to see them. The hives were gone and I was feeling a little better. I didn't tell anyone where I was going. I got in my van and drove to St. George, which was about forty-five minutes away. I hadn't seen Annette and Bob for years, but I knew they were still at the same address.

They were glad to see me, and after catching up a bit I asked Bob if he knew Jason. He told me he knew a lot about him, and wanted to know why I was asking.

When I told him Jason had been living at the motel he leaped to his feet and said, *"Get him out!"* Bob was shaking his finger at me. "That man has been involved in murder. He's involved with a drug operation in Las Vegas. He's done time in jail, but the police haven't been able to convict him for the serious stuff he's been involved with."

Annette looked shocked. "I can't believe he's still there," she said. "When we left the police had a rap sheet on him and were going to take him down."

I told Bob that Jason was moving out; Merril was getting a no-trespassing order to keep him off the property and a restraining order to keep him away from me.

Annette shook her head. Bob spoke first. "Carolyn, a restraining order isn't going to protect you. This man has a sick mind. He belongs in an institution. The worst part is he's hooked up with people who are very evil. He's kind of a coward. I don't know if he'd come after you himself, but he knows a lot of people who'd be happy to take you out for a few drugs."

I told them I wasn't going back for two weeks—and that I didn't think there was any way out of it. Annette couldn't believe Merril was making me return to Caliente if it was so unsafe. "He insists that I'm paranoid and that my fears are out of control," I told them.

Bob was getting angrier by the moment. "I'll tell that son-of-a-bitch husband of yours what you are involved with in Jason. I know the area and I know the people."

"It's not going to change him just because you talk to him," I said. "I know Merril."

"You're going back there with a gun," Annette said. "You can take mine. Bob and I will take you out to the gun range and teach you how to shoot it."

I didn't argue with my sister. She came with me when I returned to Caliente the following week and made sure I knew how to use the gun. I kept it under my pillow. But Jason wasn't the only trauma I was dealing with.

I was having trouble with preterm labor. Each contraction frightened me because I was afraid the placenta might abrupt again. I was on medicine to stop the contractions. But it did nothing to diminish the stress, which was certainly not good either for me or my baby.

I told Merril that I needed to be closer to a hospital because of the complications from my pregnancy. He growled at me, accusing me of using my pregnancy as an excuse for my laziness.

Jeremy could see how sick I was and insisted I stop cleaning rooms. I stayed in the office and did computer work. For several days, Jeremy talked about having an eerie feeling as he cleaned. Finally he spotted Jason's red car. A few days after that, Jason walked into the lobby and wanted to talk to me. Jeremy told him to leave and called the police, who did not get there for forty-five minutes. Jason was gone by then, but the police tracked him down and gave him a warning.

A few weekends later my cousin Lee Ann was with me and the power went out at 9 P.M. That meant the phones were cut off, too, and I couldn't call James for help. I locked the doors and grabbed my can of Mace. Lee Ann and I went to find James. I had that same eerie feeling Jeremy had talked about; it felt like Jason was watching and waiting, but I didn't know where. James and Jimmy walked us back to the house.

He checked the breaker boxes and found nothing wrong with any systems in the motel. He quickly restored power to the main house. But he said he was alarmed because usually when a breaker trips from a power overload it only flips partway. This breaker had been flipped all the way off, which said to James that it had been flipped deliberately. Jimmy put a key lock on the breaker box before leaving us. James promised us that they'd patrol around the house again that night with their flashlights and guns.

Several days later James caught Jason on the property. He put a loaded gun to his head and told him he was going to blow his brains out. Jason dropped to his knees and pleaded and whimpered for mercy. James told him to get the hell off the property and that if he ever caught him again he'd enjoy the pleasure of killing him.

I found this out two weeks later when I was visiting James in his trailer. James said he felt confident that he'd scared Jason away. "He knows from the police that I have killed a lot of men and I have nothing against killing him if I need to." James had a beer in one hand and a cigarette in another. He offered me a beer, but I told him I didn't drink when I was pregnant. "With a husband like that, you should," he said. I couldn't stop staring at the rattlesnakes in cages over his bed.

Then James went on. "You know, sweetheart, that Jason is a small problem for you in comparison to that bastard you're married to. You are nothing to that man but a piece of meat. You need to do whatever it takes to get yourself away from him." He stopped, turned off the TV, and sat back in his chair.

I knew what he said was true. But it was still a lot to take in.

"James, you know I can't leave Merril. I have nowhere to go and no one to help me get away from him. Not with six children and another on the way."

James was undeterred. "You are a very smart girl. You've been to college, but there was one class you should have taken."

I looked perplexed.

"You should have taken a class on domestic violence. You are in over your head in a domestic violence situation."

Now he wasn't making sense. I told him Merril had never hit me.

"Doesn't matter. It doesn't have to be physical abuse. Emotional abuse is just as bad. I've never seen a man more emotionally abusive than your husband. He's dangerous."

This was all new to me and not easy to process.

"You girls from Colorado City think you're only going to heaven if your husband lets you in. But that ain't true. You don't need your husband's permission to go to heaven. No man's going to keep you out of heaven."

I'd known Merril was dangerous from the moment I met him. But I'd never had the right words for it until I heard James describe it.

I felt like the gravity had been stripped from my world. What James was saying undermined a main premise of my faith: that only my husband could determine whether or not I was worthy enough to enter into heaven. James did not comprehend what I knew in my bones to be true.

James wasn't finished. "I know the kind of man your husband is. I have seen his like before. You're going to end up dead if you don't wake up and get away from him."

I didn't know how to respond.

"Men like him start out with abuse but they will eventually kill their victims."

I thought of how Merril used to beat and brutalize Faunita. I knew Merril was scared of my father, but that certainly didn't preclude him setting me up to be hurt by someone else. James had gotten rid of Jason, but how much longer would it be until Merril found some other criminal to work in the motel?

I walked up the hill back to the motel. James' words had burned into me.

Life with Merril had always been painful and I hated it. That I knew. But now there was another element: danger. I'd never thought of myself as the target of domestic violence before. Was I?

I lived in such an isolated world—one that since Warren Jeffs had taken over the FLDS, which he'd done within the past year, was now without television, newspapers, and magazines.

James, who lived with rattlesnakes and stayed up all night and slept all day, cared more about me than anyone else in my world. No one else saw my situation with his clarity. No one else would dare suggest that I leave Merril. My parents knew I was unhappy, but both still believed my marriage was based on a revelation from God.

Merril called a few days after my conversation with James and asked me to come home for a wedding. He was about to marry his seventh wife, Lorraine Steed. There was no way I could refuse. But I didn't understand his urgency. His last two weddings had been top-secret.

When I got home Tammy told me that Merril's daughters—the ones he had married off to Uncle Rulon—had arranged the marriage because they wanted their father to marry someone nice.

I felt revolted. Merril's daughters weren't supposed to be arranging marriages. I realized that my daughters were not going to be safe. How could I ever tell one of my girls that her marriage was the will of the prophet when, in fact, it was the will of her older sisters?

My mother and grandmother had raised me to believe in the beauty of polygamy. I was taught that not only was it a more natural lifestyle, but a privileged one because it meant living a higher law of God, which always brought more happiness. A woman's sister wives were her best friends who would always be there for her in sickness and in health. The love shared for the same man extended to the love wives shared for one another's children. I grew up believing in the myth; my life proved it a lie.

I knew I didn't want to condemn my daughters to polygamy. But if I didn't want them involved in polygamy, why was I staying?

Merril's wedding was full of pomp and grandeur. He was now in his mid-sixties; Lorraine was twenty years old. She went through the motions as robotically as I had, stiff, scared, and resigned.

After the wedding I gathered up my four children and we drove back to the motel. Jason was out of the picture and I felt confident he wouldn't be back. I wasn't going to be separated from my children anymore. My cousin Jayne and her children came, too.

When Jeremy got back to the motel after his vacation he told me Barbara had been badgering him about me. She was questioning him about all sorts of bizarre behavior she thought I was involved in. Why weren't the daily reports longer? How much did I spend on cleaning supplies? Did I charge everyone who used the bathhouses? Did I give rooms free to my family? Was I underreporting room rentals and keeping the money for myself?

Jeremy was disgusted. "All of this time I thought I was working for Merril and keeping him from losing his motel. But Barbara is the one running this family. I'm not scrubbing toilets and making beds for her." Jeremy said he'd told his wife he was going to look for another job. Four weeks later, he was gone.

I had one weekend at home before he quit. I was riding home in a truck after church with Tammy and Merril's other wives. Tammy made a point to tell a story about a teacher she knew who'd celebrated his anniversary with his wife in Caliente. He was there when I was managing the motel alone, pregnant, and overwhelmed with work.

When he saw Tammy at school he said, "How can Merril send one of his wives off miles away from home to be in a rank area like that?" (*Rank* was a word we used all the time to refer to something bad.)

She said Merril replied, "You tell him that I sent Carolyn to Caliente because I'm trying to get rid of her." Everyone roared with laughter.

Merril was bragging about putting me in danger. I could not believe what I was hearing.

Tammy couldn't get enough of this story. When we had guests over for dinner after church she told it again for their benefit. Merril and his wives thought it was just as funny the second time.

I felt stricken. The guests weren't sure how to react.

That was the turning point. James had pointed me to the door. Now I was ready to walk through it.

I took my plate into the kitchen and went to my bedroom to get away from Merril and his sickening wives. I started packing my things to return to Caliente.

Thoughts were coming fast. If Merril wanted to get rid of me now, why would he take me with him into the kingdom of God in the next life? I realized I could spend the rest of my life enduring his abuse so I would not have to go to hell and then find myself sent there anyway by him after I died.

When I realized that either way I was going to hell, I thought that I could at least escape from the hell of living with Merril in this life. Even if I didn't end up in hell, I knew I did not want to spend eternity with someone I hated as much as Merril.

I hadn't rejected my religion. But I knew that all it could offer me was hell in this life and beyond.

I did not even bother to say goodbye. I strapped my children into the van and we headed back to Caliente.

In the coming weeks, I asked my sisters to come and help. Each time I had a chance to go back to Colorado City I moved some of my things back home. I didn't want anyone to realize I was quitting Caliente. But my bedroom had an outside door and I deliberately moved things in after dark.

I was finally ready to leave Caliente for the last time. I walked to James' trailer to say goodbye. Again he told me that I had to leave Merril. I said I understood his concerns but still didn't know how I could.

My seventh child was due in a few weeks. I told Merril I would not be going back to the motel. He sent Barbara to run things, which was a disaster, and then sent Tammy. The rest of the family thought I was worthless for staying at home. But I didn't care. My life with Merril had ended. I was finished with his family and its sick games. I didn't know how I would ever escape or where I would go. Leaving seemed impossible, but staying wasn't an option.

My obstetrician did not want me to go into labor naturally because I was too high-risk. He felt it was safer to induce labor and deliver the baby on a day when he knew he could set aside the time to monitor things properly. The only date that fit his schedule turned out to be on my thirteenth wedding anniversary, May 17, 1999. I didn't care. My marriage was never something I celebrated.

When Merril heard the date, he insisted on being there. I was upset. I would have much preferred having one of my friends accompany me. But this was not a time to say no to Merril. He was driving down from Salt Lake City. I agreed to meet him at a hotel the night before in St. George since I had to be at the hospital at 6 A.M.

As soon as we were alone in our room, Merril started kissing me. I was revolted. Everything about him repelled me. His cell phone started ringing. It was Barbara. He quit kissing me to talk to her. But as soon as the call ended, he was all over me again. Thirty seconds later, Barbara called back and they talked for twenty minutes. I crawled into bed welcoming the last night of a difficult pregnancy.

Merril joined me. The kissing began again. But within minutes, Barbara called back and I finally fell asleep.

We were at the hospital by six the next morning. I was taken into the labor and delivery area and was put on a drip to induce labor. Merril stayed for an hour and then left. He said Barbara was bringing his truck back from St. George and he was going to meet her at the hotel and get some rest.

After six hours I went from active labor to transition. I knew the baby would be born soon. The nurse wanted to know how she could get hold of my husband. She was worried about him missing the birth of his son. (We knew it was a boy from all the ultrasounds I had during my pregnancy.)

I lied and said Merril would call in a few minutes. The truth was he'd called a short while before and I told him nothing was happening. I didn't want to deliver my baby alone, but I certainly didn't want him with me.

Contractions took over my body. The nurse told me not to push and called frantically for the doctor. He ran into the room and Harrison was born minutes later.

The doctor handed me my beautiful baby boy. He was five pounds thirteen ounces, and unbelievably healthy. I smiled as Dr. Carter congratulated me.

Merril called five minutes after Harrison was born. He could hear the child crying over the phone. He professed disappointment at missing his birth. Merril and Barbara came right over to the hospital. Barbara seemed thrilled that Merril had been with her when Harrison was born on our anniversary.

I was beyond caring about Merril Jessop. As I watched him walk away with Barbara I knew my marriage to him was completely over.

I had just given birth to his fifty-third child.

# I Take Charge
# of My Life

**A**fter Harrison was born, I was able to stay home for the first time in a long time and not work. It had been over a year since I'd lived with Merril's family on a regular basis. Now I saw that Warren Jeffs' stamp on the FLDS was becoming increasingly evident.

I'd had a collection of three hundred children's books that I kept in my bedroom. I cherished books. Books were the only real window I had into any other world than my own. I loved to read stories to my children. It was a precious time together, a time of intimacy and tenderness that did not exist in any other area of our lives.

Warren had decreed in 1998 that all worldly reading materials had to be eliminated. While I was away, the family had seized and destroyed my library. My shelves were stripped of my cherished books. I was heartbroken to see that my best books were gone—books such as *Charlotte's Web, Little House on the Prairie,* and *The Indian in the Cupboard.* I made a point to collect books that had won the Newbery Award. They were all gone. The only books left were big picture books of animals.

I felt so violated.

The year I spent in Caliente had spoiled me in one way: I could do my laundry whenever I wanted to. This may not seem like a luxury to most. But to me, it was heaven.

Doing laundry at Merril's was an ordeal. The three automatic washers we had were always breaking down. We had a large, industrial-size washer that was very time-consuming to use. Ruth, for whatever reasons, often would come down and take my laundry out of the washer and dump it on the floor.

I decided I was not going to fight over laundry. My father had a much better machine at his house and had no objections to my doing laundry there. In three hours, I could do laundry for all eight of us.

Merril's wives complained. Merril called me into his office and demanded an explanation. I told him that it was easier than trying to do it in his house and that my father had no objections. Merril said if I was really interested in doing what he wanted, I would find a way to do it in his home. I agreed. But I knew I wasn't changing the way I did the laundry. It was a small step away from his tyranny and oppression, but it was a step.

Linda's clandestine coffee parties were still taking place after nine years. I went whenever I could. It was one of the few places where any of us spoke honestly about what was happening within our community. At one of the early meetings I went to, Linda asked if we had heard what had happened to one of Warren's newest wives when she gave birth to her first baby.

I said that if it was another sewing-scissors-and-dental-floss story, I wasn't sure if I wanted to hear it. "It's worse," Linda said. "This time the baby died." Warren's wife was in Salt Lake City when she went into labor. Warren was in Colorado City. She had been in labor for hours but the baby didn't come. The midwife kept calling Warren and asking if she could send her to the hospital. He refused. Linda said the labor lasted more than a day and the baby finally died. When the midwife called Warren she said his wife would be dead within the hour unless she got to the hospital. He relented, but told his wife the death of her baby was the will of God.

All of us at Linda's fell silent. Someone finally spoke. "If the leader of this community is a man so selfish that he would murder his unborn child, then every one of us is in big trouble." We all picked up our things and started to leave. What more could we say? If anyone heard us talking this way about Warren, we would be in real danger.

I took a detour on the way home and stopped in the park. I sat in the grass, cradling Harrison in my arms. I remembered going to my mother shortly after I married Merril thirteen years before and telling her how unhappy I was. My marriage was so terrible, I couldn't stand it. She told me to be a loyal wife and that I could learn to love my husband. I believed her. For thirteen years I suppressed every emotion I had ever felt. I tried to be at peace even when I knew everything around me was spinning apart.

We had been taught in the FLDS that sometimes marriage between a man and a woman didn't work out on earth. But it did in heaven because in the next life, the couple could see each other for the truly great people they were. Sometimes in this world a man would fail to appreciate the sacrifices his wife was making. But in the next, he'd recognize all she had done and love her. The woman would also appreciate her husband as a god. Once she saw his greatness, all the hard feelings she'd had about him would be forgiven. She'd fall down before him in worship and marvel in his glory.

When I thought that I had actually believed in this, I felt sick to my stomach. For thirteen years I'd tried everything I could think of to make my marriage work, even though my husband was a monster. I'd believed that if I worked harder and did my part, the marriage would improve and Merril and I might be able to love each other.

I'd believed that I was doomed if Merril didn't want me to be his wife in the afterlife. If I failed to please him in this life, he could condemn me to be a servant to him and his other spirit wives for eternity. This would lead me to what we really feared in the FLDS: the second death. The second death happens in the afterlife when a spirit is killed off for the rest of eternity. Such a spirit is cast out with all the other vile spirits to await the second death. A spirit might be forced to endure a thousand years of tortured suffering before the second death actually occurs.

Sitting in the park with my sleeping son, I thought of James— crazy, spooky, rattlesnake-loving James, who patrolled the grounds of the motel all night to make sure Jason would not harm me. I knew I would rather live ten eternities with a man like him that one eternity with Merril.

I had given Merril seven children in thirteen years. My last three pregnancies had been life-threatening. But he still stood up and humiliated me in front of guests in his home and laughed when Tammy told the story of how he wanted to get rid of me.

I had given him all of my paychecks. I cooked his meals and cleaned his house. I had sex with him every week. My reward? Hatred and humiliation. I could not imagine a worse fate than having to live with him and my sister wives throughout eternity.

Nor was Warren Jeffs anyone I wanted to be around for eternity. Hell was a better option for me than anything that existed on earth. I was finished—finished sacrificing my self and soul for Merril Jessop. I was not going to live under his tyranny any longer, no matter what the consequences were.

Cottonwood Park was a peaceful place that afternoon. Harrison was sweetly sleeping. But I had changed. I looked up to El Capitan, the peak that towered over our FLDS community. As a little girl, I had always looked at the peak as a red sandstone curtain that protected us from the evils of an unknown and scary world.

I was still afraid of outsiders and the world I did not know. But El Capitan now felt like a prison wall that trapped me in a world of torture and misery.

I had never before considered leaving my religion, my family, my customs, and my beliefs behind. It was all that I had ever known. Would it be worth it to give it all up? I had no way of knowing. It was frightening even to contemplate a life beyond.

But I did know I no longer believed that Merril would want me with him in the afterlife. If I had nothing with him, I had nothing in eternity. I might as well have the best possible life I could on this earth.

When I got home I went straight to my bedroom. Merril came to my room that night and wanted to have sex. We had not had intercourse for several months because of my high-risk pregnancy with Harrison. I didn't want to have sex with him again. When I got into bed I put Harrison between us.

"If you want me to get close to you, then you are going to have to move that baby." Merril's voice was firm.

I turned my back and rolled over, acting like I hadn't heard him, and went to sleep.

Merril was furious when he left my bedroom the next morning. I was relieved that he was gone. I never wanted him to touch me again. Ever. If I was going to hell, there was no reason to bother trying to please Merril anymore.

I got into the shower and started to shake. In thirteen years, I had never refused to have sex with Merril. That morning as I was scrubbing every inch of my body I realized that it was mine. I had gotten my body back. No man would ever violate me again and treat me like filth. It would be easier to tolerate Merril's abuse if I didn't also have to have sex with him, too.

I got out of the shower and dried myself off. I had never felt more liberated.

Merril ignored me for several months, and it was bliss because the other wives did, too. Tammy had always said, "I'd rather be abused than ignored." I thought that was crazy. Being ignored made me feel happy and safe. When I looked at the vermilion cliffs of El Capitan I smiled at the thought that my prison might not be so bad after all. No one was more surprised than I to realize that my newfound freedom had been purchased by giving up on eternity and settling for hell.

But after a few months Merril returned to my room at night. I ignored his advances and he gave up for the rest of the summer.

It was very common for Merril when he was home to call the family to prayer even after all the children had gone to bed. This would happen between ten o'clock and eleven-thirty. Merril had no concern for his family's schedules or needs or the habits of small children. Sleeping children had to be pulled out of bed, and no one in the family had the right not to come when Merril called.

Prayer time was when Merril terrorized his family.

It began with Merril sitting comfortably on a chair with his wives beside him. The rest of the family would be required to be on their knees. Merril would give a sermon. Then he would invite the family to tell him things he needed to know. Barbara would jump in right away and detail something that a child or wife had done that she was sure Merril would see as disobedience.

Merril would then publicly humiliate and shame the person Barbara had targeted. On this particular day, the heat was on Merril's younger daughters. Merril scolded them without listening to their side of the story. Each daughter was blasted except for Betty. Betty was Merril's little princess. He always made excuses about why she was so perfect.

Ruthie, one of Merril's daughters, pointed out that Betty was as guilty as the rest of them. Merril told Ruthie she was guilty of trying to hide her sins by getting Betty in trouble. Betty was untouchable.

Merril's family stayed on its knees for two hours listening to Barbara's rants about how terrible his children were. He would scold a child until he or she burst into tears. After Barbara ripped through his children, she turned to her sister wives and started a harangue about how slow we were in cleaning up after dinner. We all took our reprimands without raising a voice in our own defense.

Finally, when it was over, I gathered my sleepy children and took them back to bed. When I walked around the corner of the living room I saw Ruthie angrily grab Betty. It looked like she wanted to kill her. I started screaming at her to stop. She dropped Betty's arm and changed her expression to one of polished innocence.

I told Ruthie never to hurt Betty again. This set Ruthie on the warpath against me. She knew that I wasn't going to allow her to hurt any of my children and started running to Barbara with story after story about me.

By fall, the family was pressuring me to go back to Caliente and run the motel. Tammy wanted to quit the motel and return to teaching. I ignored the suggestions. But Merril had no one to manage the motel unless I went back. There was no way I would agree to go back there.

Merril knew I had slipped his noose. He began coming into my room at least once a week. Now he would lie in my bed but not try to touch me. I think his fantasy was that I'd initiate something. Of course I never did. By morning he was always furious.

I would watch him leave my bedroom and think of James' admonition to me: *Sweetheart, you are nothing to that man but a piece of meat.*

But I was no longer a piece of meat Merril could use for sex.

The pressure on me to return to Caliente extended to Merril's children. His teenage daughters began reprimanding me for being disobedient to their father. One said I had no right to be a mother in their home if I remained in rebellion to Merril.

"Well, isn't that interesting," I said to her. "I didn't know that I had ever been a mother in this home. There's certainly never been any respect."

A few days later I walked into the kitchen and overheard Ruth say to several of Merril's daughters, "Father is going to give Mother Carolyn some time to get in line, but if she doesn't get control of herself he is going to put a stop to her rebellion."

I looked at Ruth and said, "This is interesting news. It's nice to be informed about my own rebellion. I should listen more to what you tell the girls."

Ruth turned red and left the kitchen in a huff.

Merril never came right out and asked me to go back to Caliente. He ended up sending Truman, Barbara's second son, instead. Tammy returned to Colorado City and tried to ingratiate herself back into my life with her gossipy ways.

She was close with several of the daughters Merril had married off to Uncle Rulon, and they fed her information, which she was only too eager to pass on. "Did you hear that one of Uncle Rulon's older wives committed adultery?" she asked me one afternoon.

"That's not news," I said. "Everyone knows about her."

"No, that's not the adultery he was talking about," Tammy said. "She committed adultery three times. Twice with her music teacher and then once when she refused to have sex with Uncle Rulon." In the FLDS, refusing to have sex with one's husband was considered to be adultery—as was pleasuring oneself.

The conversation seemed to be headed in another direction. I looked at her blankly, not sure what she meant.

"Uncle Rulon said that if a woman refuses to have sex with her husband she has committed the sin of alienation of affections. This is committing adultery in her heart, which is a sin unto death—as much as having an affair with a man other than her husband."

Now I got it. Tammy knew I wasn't having sex with Merril. If she knew, all of Merril's daughters married to Uncle Rulon knew, too.

Guilty as charged. I had now committed a sin unto death, according to the FLDS, by refusing to have sex with Merril. Forgiveness was impossible. What wasn't clear was why Tammy was telling me this.

A few weeks later I went by the kitchen when Barbara and Tammy were talking. I heard Barbara say my name and then saw her shaking her head. "A woman who thinks she needs a relationship with her husband is a worldly tradition and it's something she needs to give up." I think they assumed the reason I stopped having sex with Merril was because we had no other connectedness. He never acted like a husband to me. They thought actually feeling something for the husband you slept with was one of those "worldly traditions" that needed to be banished.

Merril called me from his office a few days later. "Carolee, how are you doing?" I said I was fine. He went on to tell me the school was desperate for teachers and it would be fine with him if I went back. He'd told them I'd go over and meet with them that day. "What do you think of that?"

I said no. No, I did not want to teach.

*No* was not a word I had ever said to Merril Jessop before. I had refused to have sex and done things my own way, but I had never uttered that one-syllable word to him. How much rebellion there was in simply one consonant and one vowel?

There was silence on the other end of the phone.

I thought that if Merril wanted me to teach maybe he should have protected my charter school.

"Do you want me to embarrass you by telling Alvin that you are refusing to do what your husband has asked?"

I didn't respond. Alvin was the principal who had worked so hard with me to make the charter school a reality. I didn't care what Alvin or anyone else thought. I was finished with Merril and his stupid games of intimidation.

We did not speak of my teaching again. Merril kept coming into my bedroom. I refused to have sex. He took me on a trip with him and made a big point of acting like a lovebird when we were in front of other couples. Merril knew I wouldn't refuse his advances in public.

But once we got back home, his tactics escalated. He became abusive toward my children. He would send them away from the dinner table and say they were not allowed to eat. There would be a pretext about some minor infraction that had occurred during the day. The rest of his wives began targeting my children. They told my kids that since I was in rebellion to their father they were not to obey anything I asked them to do or they'd be punished.

Now I had to sneak food to my own children. I tried to keep them as close to me as I could, but there were times when I couldn't protect them. Sometimes they'd play with Barbara's children and she'd look for any excuse to do something hurtful to them. The cruelty was escalating and I had to find a way to make it stop.

Sex. What else could I try? I decided that the next time Merril came into my bedroom I'd have sex with him and see if that would make the abuse stop. If not, I'd leave.

The next time Merril came to my room I left Harrison in his crib. When he put his clammy hands on me I didn't resist. I hated feeling his breath on my skin. I offered up my body in sacrifice to my children and it worked.

Merril was almost giddy the next morning. A few minutes after he left my bedroom he called me from his office and invited me to come for coffee with his other wives.

Tammy and Barbara were sitting in chairs next to Merril's desk. They were cheerfully sipping coffee. Barbara handed me a cup. I felt like I was being locked into my prison cell again. Merril started making jokes and we all laughed. Ruthie, Ruth's daughter, came into the office and said my son Patrick was not obeying her. She acted as though she'd be doing us a favor if she was abusive to him.

Merril laughed nervously and made an excuse for little Patrick. I sat up in my chair and smiled at him. Without saying a word, Merril and I had an agreement. I'd give him sex in exchange for the protection of my children.

At that point, even though I had given up on salvation, I still felt my children were better off growing up with their half siblings than leaving the community with me for a totally alien world. I felt we were better off in a world with known dangers than one in which everything would be strange, frightening, and new.

But sex with Merril was as far as I was willing to go. I wasn't going to let him work me like a slave. He had pushed me as far as I could go and I think he knew that.

My actions since returning from Caliente had an impact on Cathleen. Merril had sent her to Page to work in his business there by day and run another motel he owned by night. She came home only on weekends for seven years and hated being away from her five children.

At first I think she thought I was stupid for resisting Merril. But then she realized I had something she wanted. I was home with my children and not working. Cathleen had pleaded with Merril for years to let her come home. She was shocked that I managed to get back from Caliente after only a year. Maybe, she thought, I was onto a good thing.

Unbelievably, Cathleen tried to rebel.

One day she came home midweek. When I saw her I asked her why. "I am tired of being abused by Merril and his accountant. I've been trapped between them ever since I went to Page. I quit and came home."

She said she planned to talk to Merril that night.

When I saw her the next morning her eyes were red and swollen. "Did you talk to Merril?" I asked.

"I did. But it was like it always is. I can't talk without crying and that makes him angry. He scolds me until I can't talk."

"So what did he say?"

"He accused me of using my children as an excuse and said I've never done the job in Page the way he wants me to. That's why I'm always in trouble with him."

I had a smirk on my face. "No matter what you do it will never be the way he wants."

"I said I was still coming home." Cathleen looked whipped. "He said I'd be sorry if I did. I told him I wanted to talk to Uncle Rulon. He said I could but it would be something I'd regret more than anything I'd ever done."

"Cathleen, listen to me. What can be worse than the way he's already treating you?"

Merril took Cathleen with him that day to Caliente. Tammy was there managing the motel. The two of them had a long talk with Merril. They asked him why some of the wives in the family had to be out on the front lines, working extremely hard without ever getting any rewards. Other wives, they said, had far fewer responsibilities and got to go on trips.

Merril said it was odd. He told them he never understood why some wives had personalities that were totally in sync with their husband's while others did not. He'd talked to Uncle Rulon about this. The aging prophet had said that some wives worked hard to be a blessing to their husbands but were little more than workhorses. According to Merril, Uncle Rulon said that this is heartache for them on earth but after they die, the hurt they have suffered is instantly healed because the Lord gives their husbands an appreciation for them in death that he never had for them in life.

Cathleen heard this as glorious news. When she told it to me the next day I said I thought it was preposterous. How could any woman endure a life of misery with such a cheap promise of appreciation after her death?

But Cathleen dutifully returned to Page to work she hated and that also kept her away from the children she loved. One night I heard her oldest daughter crying. I went upstairs to the dining room and saw a child sobbing on the floor in a heap. My eight-year-old daughter, LuAnne, came running over to me with big angry eyes. "Do you know what happened? Mother Barbara came up to one of Mother Cathleen's girls and started hitting her on the head with Barbie's extra-big crochet hook."

I grabbed LuAnne and got her away from there. If anyone heard her reporting on Barbara she'd be in danger. Merril walked into the dining room and over to the crying child. He clapped his hands. "Stop this nonsense!"

Having seen her shuddering and crying on the floor a few hours before made me realize that even though I could protect my children somewhat from Merril's abuse by having sex with him, I was helpless to keep them from witnessing the abuse of their other siblings. I was also sickened by my inability to protect the other children. I made sure my children slept in my bedroom again. No one would be able to come into my bedroom and touch them without waking me up.

I was so upset I called Cathleen at Page that night and told her everything I had seen and heard. "Cathleen, you may get a reward from Merril in your next life, but what about the abuse your children are getting in this life?"

The conversation stopped. Cathleen was silent for a long time and then said goodbye. I knew she was terribly upset. But she didn't know what to do to protect her children.

# Harrison's Cancer

I remember walking to the store on a chilly day in early spring when I saw a slow line of cars pulling away from the cemetery. A four-month-old baby had just been buried. I knew his mother. This was her second son, and one who had been born apparently healthy.

But a week earlier he'd started screaming and wouldn't stop. Twenty-four hours later in a Las Vegas hospital, he was diagnosed with a terminal brain tumor. The tumor had grown into an area that controlled his breathing. He was put on life support, but there was absolutely no hope. His parents signed papers allowing him to die.

I could not, would not, even begin to imagine how his mother could cope with the pain from such a catastrophic and unexpected loss. When I got back from the store I found Harrison and held him close.

With long, curly eyelashes that touched the tip of his brows, Harrison was so pretty he could have been mistaken for a baby girl. He was a tease who loved to play peek-a-boo and cuddle and to be held. LuAnne, who was eight when Harrison was born, gravitated to him right away and considered him her baby, mothering him in every way she could think of. He was chubby and an excellent eater. Harrison thrived. He met every developmental milestone on time or ahead of schedule.

His first birthday was coming up on May 17, 2000, my fourteenth wedding anniversary. I marveled at how healthy he was. He bounced back from illnesses faster than any of my other six babies had. Without a doubt, he was my dream baby.

A week later I was mopping the floor. Harrison was sitting nearby and smiling at me. I smiled back at him, then his smile vanished. The right half of his body went into a spasm that lasted for about thirty seconds. I ran across the wet floor and grabbed him. But the spasm had stopped and another smile lit up his face.

I was worried. I called the night clinic and made an emergency appointment for him. He was checked out and everything seemed perfectly normal. But I felt uneasy. I had never seen anything so sudden and so frightening sweep over a child before.

Two days later he had another spasm. I had started working at the grocery story to save money for my escape. Barbara told me about it when I got home. She said it had happened while she was feeding him lunch. But once again, he'd bounced back quickly and seemed fine.

I made an appointment for Harrison in St. George. But the weekend before our scheduled visit he had another spasm, and this time it didn't stop and it controlled his entire body. I was at my father's doing laundry and we called an ambulance.

Several tests were done in the ER, but the cause of the spasm could not be found. He was admitted and the pediatrician did more tests the next day. At one point, a doctor told me Harrison had the hiccups. He was making a sound similar to hiccups, but I knew that wasn't it.

We stayed at the hospital for several days of tests. It was hell for me. This was more terror than I had ever known and it was a terror I was powerless to understand. Test after test came back negative. Merril came to the hospital once to visit us when he was in St. George on business. He seemed concerned but was also convinced that Harrison would get better. After a few days, Harrison was diagnosed with a postviral infection. The pediatrician told me this could last for three weeks.

I didn't know what I would do. Harrison's condition had gotten worse. He was screaming all the time and he slept only with strong medication. At home, it was even more awful. Harrison began vomiting from the spasms. I fed him constantly but had to stop nursing him because when he went into a spasm he bit my breast. He seemed famished—the spasms took a lot of energy. But the more he ate, the more he vomited. And screamed. He screamed nonstop seemingly from terrible, terrible pain.

The pediatrician prescribed some antinausea medication, but nothing gave him relief. She told me this could last as long as three months. I didn't know how we would make it. I wasn't sleeping. His suffering was relentless. I felt so utterly powerless and defeated by my inability to do anything to help him when he looked at me with his big, beautiful, but tortured green eyes.

Someone gave me the name of a holistic doctor in Las Vegas. Linda said she'd take us there. Maybe he'd have an answer that eluded traditional medicine.

I went to find Merril. He'd been ignoring Harrison and showed zero concern. It was obvious to me that he felt Harrison was my problem. I certainly didn't think he'd object to my taking him to Las Vegas.

But Merril turned on me with a vengeance when I told him what I wanted to do. He berated me for having such an idea. I was exhausted after three sleepless weeks. I didn't care what Merril thought and looked at him exactly the way I thought of him—as an unbelievable idiot.

He grabbed my arm and threw me several feet in the alfalfa field. I stumbled over some clumps of dirt but would not let myself fall on my face. I would not give him that pleasure. It took every ounce of strength that I had. I regained my balance and stood my ground. He grabbed me again and threw me as hard as he could. I landed on my feet again but some distance away from him. I looked at him with disgust and defiance.

"Harrison is going to die because of your rebellion. It is your fault that he is sick. God will take him from you because you have been in rebellion to your priesthood head. You can take him to every damn doctor you can find, but no one will be able to heal him. God is going to destroy his life because of the sins of his mother."

His chest was heaving with anger. His cheeks were flushed with anger. And he was almost out of breath.

My eyes were on fire but my words were measured.

"I already made this appointment. Do you want me to cancel it?"

He roared back like an angry bull pricked by the matador's spear. "You know what I want! I have told you it will do Harrison no good to see any doctors as long as your attitude is what it is!"

I turned and walked back into the house. His physical violence had startled me. Merril had never attacked me before. I knew I was no longer safe in his home. I also knew this: Merril wanted Harrison to die to prove that I was in rebellion to God. He had utter contempt for his own son. I knew his real concern was that Harrison could live and not be normal.

When I got back inside I gathered up Harrison and my other children. We had to get away before Merril came back inside. I knew if he attacked me again it would be far worse.

I drove to my father's house, where I knew I'd be safe. I told my mother everything that Merril had done to me in the field. She was outraged and said I should leave him—which was an extraordinary turnaround for a true believer like my mom.

I told my mother that there was no way I could leave with a child as sick as Harrison. But I also knew I would never be safe in his home again, not with someone with his history of violence. I told her that I was finished with the FLDS and that being condemned to hell for eternity was far better than the living hell that stretched out for at least fifty years ahead of me. But there could be no escape until Harrison got better.

My mother and I came up with a plan. I would spend the days hiding out at my father's house and the nights at Merril's. I could not risk getting my father into trouble with the FLDS, which had very strong beliefs against a father interfering in his daughter's marital life, even if he felt she was being physically or emotionally abused. It is a sin for a woman to talk about abuse; if she's being abused, it is because she is not in harmony with her husband. My parents would be considered sinners in the FLDS for listening to me talk about the abuse. Their job was to talk me into being more obedient to my husband's will.

One day when I was at my father's house, he came back from

church and said that Warren had closed the public school system permanently. Everyone in the community had been ordered to educate their children in private religious schools. This affected roughly two thousand children.

As a teacher, I had seen what happened academically when families in our culture home-schooled their children. It amounted to no school. Families were now to band together in small groups and create their own religious schools. There was no uniform curriculum. Warren would tell each school what to teach. Warren didn't want credentialed teachers teaching. He believed we had been contaminated by worldly knowledge. Anyone with an education was seen as a threat because we were too involved with the ways of the world.

It was no secret that Warren Jeffs closed the public schools; it was covered in local newspapers as well as the *Salt Lake City Tribune*. But, inexplicably, there was no public outcry or state action.

Education, which I prized, had almost no value in Warren Jeffs' FLDS. The changes were dramatic but had occurred incrementally. First no one was allowed to get a college education. Then the public schools were closed and those of us who took pride in working there were seen as a threat.

I continued to stay at my father's every day until very late at night. Then we'd return home after everyone was asleep in Merril's house. I would lock my children into my room with me. Harrison would sleep for about two hours and then by early morning we'd head back to my parents'.

Merril cornered me in the family sewing room one afternoon when I was getting some material and patterns to take to my parents' house to make back-to-school dresses for Betty and LuAnne, who were then eleven and nine years old. He insisted on talking to me. All I said was, "I don't want to."

I think this was the first time in my entire married life that I had ever intimidated Merril.

He went to my father and urged him to get me into line. Merril downplayed the situation and said our conflict was relatively minor. My father said he had heard that there had been physical violence between us. Merril tried to brush that off, too. Dad reminded him that I'd been married now for many years and he didn't have any influence with me anymore, nor did he see how he could help the situation.

I knew our crisis had escalated when I heard Merril had talked to my dad. It would be only a matter of time until he went to his buddy Warren Jeffs. I would be in even worse trouble once that happened. I began writing a letter to Warren that told my side of the situation. I wanted to be allowed to live in the community but away from Merril in a space of my own.

I wrote whenever I had a few moments of help with Harrison's care. It took me several weeks, but I finally had a seventeen-page letter that detailed the awful history of abuse that Merril had dealt out to his wives and children. I was building my case to explain to Warren why I was unsafe in Merril's house.

Several of my friends and sisters called me to say they'd seen Merril driving around the community with Warren. I knew things were going to blow. The next Sunday in church, it happened. Warren gave a rip-roaring sermon about fathers who try to interfere in another man's family to protect their daughters. I knew my father faced excommunication from the FLDS if he continued to allow me to stay in his home.

My father called Warren as soon as he got back from church. He explained that there was more to the story than he could appreciate. He said I had a letter that explained why I wasn't willing to go back to Merril. Warren agreed to take the letter and meet with my father and me later that night. We were told to keep the meeting secret and wait until after dark before we drove to Uncle Rulon's house. Then we were to park down the road and knock on the front door at a specific time.

We did exactly as we were told. Warren had one of his brothers waiting for us and took us to a room where Warren was waiting. He seemed irritated that he had to deal with this situation and acted as though it was a lot of nonsense. Still wearing his suit from church, he sat in a chair with his hands folded in his lap. Most of the time he looked down and only raised his head when he spoke.

My father did the talking. I gave Warren the letter. He said he would read it and discuss it with his father and call me at my father's home the next day. He didn't want Merril's family to know that he was talking to me. Warren asked me if I wanted a release from my marriage. I told him I did not because I knew I risked being placed in a worse situation. Warren went silent and cold, but I was not putting myself on his chessboard to be moved around from one marriage to another.

My father asked if he could speak with Warren privately. Afterward, he told me that he'd said he knew me well and knew what I was capable of doing. He told him I had been pushed too hard and that if Warren didn't pay attention to me, I could cause him a lot of trouble.

Warren heard this as a threat, but my father wasn't threatening him. He was telling him the truth. He knew if I was forced back into Merril's abusive household I wouldn't ask for help a second time. I would escape.

Warren called me the next day and said he had read the letter. He told me that I had written only about Merril's sins and confessed to none of my own. Because of this, Warren doubted that I had been truthful. He wanted me to come and meet with him and Merril. Warren wanted to give my seventeen-page letter to Merril. I knew if that happened he'd pass it around to all his wives and children. I asked Warren to keep the letter to himself. Warren agreed Merril could read the letter when we met.

Merril met me at noon the next day. Neither one of us spoke in the car. Warren laid down ground rules when we got to his house. He said he would know which one of us was wrong by seeing who lost control. I knew I would have no trouble staying calm. But it would be a huge problem for Merril.

Merril read the letter and practically stopped breathing. I think this was probably the first time in his entire life that someone had called him on his crap. He took several deep breaths after he read it and then laid the pages on the floor.

Warren turned to me and said that I had confessed Merril's sins and now it was time for me to confess my own. I wasn't that stupid. I knew anything I confessed to could be held against me.

I confessed to a few small crimes. "Well, sometimes I walk past something on the floor and don't pick it up. There have been times after Sunday dinner when I didn't wash the pans that I had used. Once I burned some rolls for Sunday dinner. . . ." My list went on from one small offense to the other.

Warren's face was sober. I couldn't tell if he was enjoying this or not. Merril jumped in at one point and said, "The one thing Carolyn is not guilty of is being careless or sloppy. She irons everything and cooks better than most in my family. She's extremely gifted in home-making and always has been."

Warren was getting impatient. "I wasn't asking for these kinds of confessions. The elements in this letter scream a case of immorality. Merril, has your wife been involved with immorality?" Merril shrugged and then looked at me.

I looked at both of them as if they were crazy. I had never had sex with anyone other than Merril. It was not immoral to complain about abuse. It was just the opposite.

"Before you married this good man were you ever involved with a boy?" Warren's questions struck me as ridiculous. I was not going to play his game.

As a teenager I had kissed a boy when we ditched theology class. He was now an upstanding member of the community, and I was not going to be intimidated into ratting him out.

I had written a seventeen-page letter to Warren Jeffs about Merril's abuse. It was a serious letter that deserved a serious response. It was clear from Warren's question that the tide was turning against me.

He took my silence as an admission of guilt. I felt like a young girl in Salem, Massachusetts, who, if she didn't admit to being a witch, was assumed to be one and condemned to death. Either way I was going to lose.

Warren took a book of Uncle Roy's sermons off his shelf and gave it to me. He told me that one of Uncle Roy's most faithful wives had tried to leave him at one time.

"I want you to go home, read some sermons, be obedient to your husband, and repent," Jeffs said.

I didn't say anything. If he was going to ignore the problem, nothing I could say would make a difference—if anything, it might be spun in such a way as to condemn me even more.

As we were getting ready to leave, Warren told Merril that he wanted to speak to me alone. He said he believed I'd be safe in Merril's house and that it was unlikely that Merril would try anything violent after I'd made such a stink. Warren halfway admitted that Merril had told him he'd wished he hadn't hurt me.

I was outraged when I left his office. Jeffs knew I was telling the truth. But Merril had won. I was labeled an immoral woman and a liar.

My life in the FLDS was over. I would never submit to Merril's abuse again, nor would I go for help to anyone in the community. But Harrison was too sick for me to even think of escape. I would lie low until I could figure out another option.

Merril came to my bedroom that night and we had sex for the first time in three months. With Harrison being so sick I knew I had to sleep with Merril. I couldn't do anything to provoke his anger against me or my other children.

Harrison seemed to be getting worse. My mother and I took turns caring for him at night so I could get enough sleep to hold on. No one in Merril's family would help me.

One night my mother called and told me to come right away. When I got there Harrison was having trouble breathing. Dad told me he was going to have Mom take us to the emergency room at St. George. He said we couldn't call a local ambulance because they would insist on calling Merril for permission to take Harrison to the hospital.

"This is on you and your mother," Dad said. "I will deny that I knew anything about it. You'll both have to take the heat. But if you don't get Harrison to the hospital tonight he is going to die."

Dad told us to be sure we kept our stories straight. Mom was caring for Harrison and he went into a crisis. We rushed him to the hospital on our own. Dad couldn't risk being accused of interfering with another man's family. I could get in trouble for taking my son to the hospital without Merril's permission, but none of us cared.

Mom drove as fast as she could. Harrison was fighting for every breath of air. He was so worn out I thought he was dying. I ran into the ER with him. The nurse took one look at him and buzzed us right in without asking questions. Doctors and nurses sprang into action. The room came to life in a frenzy of activity that was frightening. Harrison stabilized after a few hours, but he was in critical condition. I was told he was too sick for them to consider doing any tests.

The next morning the pediatrician came and told me we were both going to Phoenix on a life flight within hours. The doctors there were alerted and reviewing his case. This was something much more serious than a postviral infection.

I called my mother and told her the news. Since she and my father were already in trouble for helping me as much as they had, she hadn't been able to risk staying with me at the hospital, so she'd dropped me off and left. She said she'd try to bring me some clothes.

Dad called Merril in the morning and pretended he'd only just found out that I was in the hospital. He told Merril we were being flown to Phoenix on a life flight. Merril called me at the hospital. He could barely contain his anger. Harrison was getting the care he needed and Merril was powerless to stop it.

A nurse stayed at Harrison's bedside continually at St. George. When one left, another took her place. I finally felt safe. This was one of the few breaks I had from three months of nonstop crisis with Harrison.

An ambulance was waiting for us when our life flight landed in Phoenix. We were rushed to Phoenix Children's Hospital, where fifteen specialists were on standby. Test after test was done to rule things out. Each time a test came back negative, that specialist was dropped from Harrison's case. After two days of testing the diagnosis was narrowed down to a genetic disorder or cancer. On the third day Harrison was diagnosed with a spinal neuroblastoma, a fatal cancer.

The next day a test was done to pinpoint the location of the cancer. Harrison had a tumor growing next to his spinal cord—but it had yet to invade it. I was told that this was an extremely rare cancer that most children do not survive. The doctors explained that Harrison had been born with spinal neuroblastoma but symptoms don't appear until the tumor begins to grow.

Merril called occasionally and asked a few questions but without much interest. His attitude was that Harrison's death would humble me and then I would learn not to treat my priesthood head with disrespect.

A doctor came into Harrison's room that first night to do yet another test. I was sitting alone in a chair and sobbing uncontrollably. He stood there with compassion in his eyes and said, "I wish I could give you the answers I know you want to hear—that your son is going to be all right. But I can't tell you that, and I understand that this must be hell for you, watching your baby go through something no one should have to endure."

I nodded. I couldn't speak. When he left the room I thought how much kinder and decent this doctor had been to me than Merril or anyone else in his family had. Why was I at the hospital alone while everyone else was home and no doubt judging me as a sinner? In their eyes my son's cancer was proof that I was being condemned by God.

For thirty-two years, I'd believed that every person on the outside of the FLDS community was evil. It was not lost on me that the only people willing to fight for Harrison's life and help him survive were outsiders.

But doctors and nurses weren't the only ones who were kind. A social worker at the hospital came by to make sure I had money for meals and had a change of clothes. Merril never asked me if I had enough money to survive while I was in Phoenix. I'm sure he thought that as long as I was in rebellion, I was on my own.

The night Harrison was diagnosed, I lost it. After the kind doctor left Harrison's room I couldn't stop crying. There was a terrible downpour that night, and I stared out the window into the rain. I could see planes landing and taking off in the distance. Freedom to come and go. There had been no freedom in my life for fourteen years. In the last few months I had been tortured by the screams of my suffering son. I cried until I couldn't cry any more.

My sobs finally subsided. Harrison was quiet and sedated. I kept looking out the window because I was free to do that. It was a peaceful moment. I was tired, weak, and exhausted. But I knew I wasn't broken. Nothing was going to stop me from fighting for Harrison's life, and finally, at Phoenix Children's Hospital, I knew I wouldn't have to do it alone.

The doctors wanted to move forward as quickly as possible. I signed papers the following morning to authorize Harrison's treatment. If Merril had come to Phoenix with us, I'm sure he would have tried to block the surgery.

Harrison was wheeled into the operating room on day five. His tumor was located between two main arteries and was partially encased in one of the veins that fed the spinal nerves. The surgeon explained to me that one of the risks of surgery was that Harrison could be paralyzed for the rest of his life.

It was such a dangerous operation that Harrison was cut nearly in half to open him up wide enough. One of his ribs was removed. The operation lasted for several hours and I got regular briefings from a physician.

The wait for me was agonizing. Merril had come and brought Barbara, several of her sons, Betty, several of my boys, and a few others. Merril was the only one allowed in the family waiting room with me. He told Barbara to watch the others, but she had a seizure and ended up being admitted to the Good Samaritan Hospital. When Merril heard what had happened he left me to stay with her.

As soon as the operation was over, the surgeon told me he felt very confident that he'd removed the entire tumor. He was pleased and felt the operation had been successful.

There was more good news when the tumor was biopsied: Harrison didn't need any chemotherapy or radiation because his cancer was caught so early because of his spasms. The spasms had saved him. Without them the cancer might have progressed to a stage where it was incurable. But his immune system, along with fighting the cancer, was also attacking his nerve tissue. The spasms had been caused by his immune system identifying his entire nervous system as the enemy and launching a full-scale attack on it. The doctors felt Harrison's immune system would now have to be suppressed.

Harrison stabilized a few days after surgery and was started on IV therapy to suppress his immune system. It was critical that his spasms be controlled because they put him more at risk than anything else.

His weight loss was another potentially life-threatening issue. He had a gastric tube, or G-tube, inserted to supply him with nutrition. We wouldn't be allowed to leave the hospital until I knew how to use his G-tube. I learned how to insert it and keep it clean to prevent any chance of infection. Everyone at Phoenix Children's Hospital was friendly and supportive toward me—despite my weird polygamist clothes. Their genuine concern touched me deeply. I couldn't explain to them how strange and abusive my world really was. The claustrophobia I lived with every day had become second nature to me. It had been years since I experienced three weeks in a row of kindness and support, but it felt miraculous to me.

When we were finally ready to go home Merril came to drive us back. It was an awful trip. We barely spoke. Harrison had a hard time. He was still screaming and I had to manage his feeding pump, which was quite a job.

I was so glad to see my six other children when I got home. I had never been apart from them for so long. I was happy to see them looking so well and strong after my three weeks in a hospital, where each child seemed sicker than the next.

What surprised me was that my bedroom was clean and all my children's laundry had been recently washed and put away. This didn't jibe with the fact that no one in the family was speaking to me. I was treated like a wicked woman. The other wives would answer a question if I asked, but otherwise I was shunned. God had spoken loudly to them through Harrison's cancer.

That weekend when Cathleen came home she brought coffee to me in my bedroom before I was up and dressed. I learned that she had cleaned my room and I thanked her for her kindness.

Later I noticed that the family was now acting hostile toward her, too. She was seen as being out of harmony with Merril because she had been helping me. But she didn't quit. For the first time in a long, long time, I felt like I had a friend in my own family.

Harrison did well initially. When we first came home he was able to sleep, with medication, for six hours at a stretch. He never stopped screaming, but I didn't feel he was getting into serious trouble until after we'd been home for two weeks. Something was terribly wrong.

We went back to the doctor in St. George. In the first few weeks after his surgery it seemed we were constantly running back and forth to the hospital. Harrison would either need his pain medication adjusted or he sometimes needed IVs.

Six weeks after the surgery he started turning blue. I called his doctor and rushed him in. She did an X-ray and then admitted him immediately to the hospital. It had seemed to me he'd been getting worse, not better, since his surgery. Now we knew why. His entire chest was filling up with lymphatic fluid. Every lobe of his lungs had collapsed except one, and that wasn't providing him with enough oxygen.

A surgeon was called in to drain some of the fluid from his lungs. Once the fluid was drained we were medivaced back to Phoenix. Harrison was admitted to the ICU for pediatric cardiac care. He was sedated and slept for a long time. I was so terrified that he might die, I rarely left his side. I felt anguished at the level of suffering he must have endured during the past three weeks.

Harrison had an X-ray every day for the next two weeks to make sure the fluid was not filling up again in his lungs. Also, amazingly, we saw that the rib the surgeon had removed was beginning to regenerate. I could see the progression on the X-rays as it grew back into a rib. I asked the doctor if he'd ever seen anything like this before and he said that he hadn't. But he added that he had seen some amazing things happen when it came to healing in children.

Two weeks later, Harrison and I went home again. He had made remarkable progress. When we'd first arrived I was told we might be there for six weeks, certainly at least three. But he was doing better than anyone had ever expected.

The gladness I felt knew no bounds.

# Cathleen Comes Home

**C**oming home with Harrison from Phoenix Children's Hospital the second time was a relief at one level, but at another it was the beginning of an even more intense ordeal. Harrison had survived a complicated surgery, but his regime of pain medication was not working.

Harrison screamed almost nonstop. When he went into one of his spasms, he would bite his arms and hands. It was almost a constant effort to keep him from hurting himself. His doctor prescribed a higher dose of Versed, a potent relaxant and anticonvulsant used to treat seizures and as premedication in some surgical procedures. It's fast-acting and has a short half life in the body.

I could give Harrison three doses of Versed within an hour, but then I would have to wait for two hours until I could medicate him again. He usually calmed down after the second dose, but not always. Sometimes it took three. The IV therapy was finally stopped because the doctors felt it wasn't helping Harrison enough, and his Port-a-Cath—the direct line into his body that was used for his IV therapy—was removed. I was relieved to see that go because it meant one less risk of infection.

Harrison had a hard time sleeping at night. I gave him chloral hydrate, a strong sedative, but it did not always work. In an effort to wean him off the IV therapy, his doctors had given him a drug to control his neuropathy, but it sent him into major anxiety attacks. For weeks, it felt that I was always on the phone with Harrison's doctors, constantly juggling medications, adding here, subtracting there, to try and find the balance that would stop the spasms and his screaming.

One day blurred into the next. Despite his feeding tube, which pumped nutrition into him twenty-four hours a day, Harrison had a hard time maintaining weight. He was switched from a high-calorie formula to a lower-calorie one because he had a leak of his lymphatic fluids. Lymphatic fluids are produced by fat, so with less fat in his system, the leak slowed. The fat content of his diet had to be closely monitored until he healed. But he lost weight with the low-calorie formula. I was supposed to try to wean him off the feeding pump and feed him directly because I could get more food into him that way. But when I tried that he'd get sick and throw up.

I didn't have time to think. I was sleep-deprived and burned out from the relentless stress and fear of seeing my healthy baby boy, who had been just on the verge of walking, reduced to screaming spasms that were stripping him of every ability he once had. His vomiting led to a case of aspiration pneumonia.

*Do I call an ambulance today or not?* That thinking went on for months. The minute it looked like he was having difficulty breathing I called for help. The local ambulance had to come (even without Merril's okay) because Harrison was now known to the system and was being watched. I was on the phone with his doctor all the time, and if the ambulance refused to transport us there would have been an uproar.

Finally, Harrison's doctor in St. George said he needed to go back on IV therapy because he was not improving enough and was still constantly plagued by spasms. With two IV treatments a week, he got a little relief from the spasms. Initially, his doctor felt it wasn't helping him enough to warrant continuing, but finally she realized that any relief at all was a plus for both of us. So we made regular trips to St. George for IV therapy and frequent trips to Phoenix to see his oncologist. Cathleen volunteered to drive me to Phoenix, which was an enormous relief because it was eight hours away.

I was terribly concerned when I had to leave my other children at home to take Harrison to the doctors. This was the first time in my married life when I hadn't also had a full-time job. So I was home more, but consumed by the demands of Harrison's care.

Whenever I could, I would take one or two of my children with me to Phoenix. The playroom at the Phoenix Children's Hospital was wonderful. There were many activities to engage them and wonderful educators who really seemed invested in the kids.

Merril's family would never abuse my kids when I was home, and no one was ever sure when I'd be gone. This worked to my advantage—my children were safer overall than they had been for a long time. I think Merril was also wary of upsetting me too much, and so he, too, had backed off, hoping I would stop causing trouble.

Cathleen had become fed up with managing the Big Water Motel in Page. She quit, moved home, and got a job at the grocery store without asking Merril's approval.

She decided she'd had enough after seven years of being away from her children except on weekends. My success in leaving Caliente made a huge impact on her.

Not only did she move home, she was spending time with me. We were becoming closer after years in which we'd barely spoken. That meant a lot to me but put her in more jeopardy. She was now in direct competition with me for the title of "Merril's most wicked wife."

The warfare among Merril's wives hit new heights that fall when Cathleen did something that was unthinkable: she bought her own washing machine.

This was seen as an act of pure aggression. Cathleen paid for it herself. Unlike Tammy, who gave every dime of her teacher's salary to Merril, Cathleen kept most of her income for herself.

She made no bones about the fact that this machine belonged to her. She put up a schedule over the machine that showed when either Cathleen or I would be doing our wash. No one else.

Ruth was livid. Barbara was outraged. How dare Cathleen think that she and I could have our own washing machine?

Cathleen was called into Merril's office. How dare she bring a washer into his home without first asking his approval? What right did she think she had to restrict its use? Cathleen stood her ground.

"There are three other washers and dryers for the other wives in the family to use. Carolyn hasn't been able to wash her laundry in this home for over a year. We both have the majority of small children in your family. I don't see why this is such a crisis for you."

But it was. It was a crisis because we did not live in a world that was either logical or rational.

Between us, Cathleen and I had twelve children—my seven and her five. The oldest was my son Arthur, who was twelve. Harrison needed care around the clock and Cathleen was the only one in the family who gave me any support at all.

Barbara and Tammy were having long talks every morning over coffee. It was clear to them that we were operating out of their orbit. We did not engage with them and refused to fight. Rather than play into Barbara's power game, we focused on improving our children's lives.

One night after we were both asleep, Merril called prayers. Our children were pulled out of bed and ordered upstairs to pray. Wendell, Cathleen's son, who was not quite two, was asleep in his crib. He was cranky and fussy after he woke up. Merril told Barbara to take Wendell into the next room and discipline him.

Barbara took Wendell into the room where she had beaten Patrick and let him have it. When Barbara beat a baby she would typically spank him until he was blue in the face from screaming. Then she would stop, order the baby to stop screaming, and start beating him again when the hysterical child continued to scream. Eventually the baby would collapse from exhaustion when he was too weak to cry.

Wendell's pitiful screams went on into the night. Everyone at prayers was required to wait until Barbara returned. But when she didn't return, Cathleen's other children were ordered to bed. None of them dared wake up Cathleen to tell her what was happening to Wendell.

Barbara took Wendell into Cathleen's bedroom and laid him beside her.

Cathleen awoke when she heard Barbara's voice. "Wendell will grow up and do what his father needs him to do. Wendell will be a good man some day."

Cathleen bolted up in bed and asked Barbara what she was doing.

Barbara continued stroking Wendell and saying, "Good night, Wendell, you will learn from these lessons how to be a good man."

Then Barbara left the room.

Cathleen looked at her small son and saw how battered and bruised he was. His clothes were still soaked from his tears and sweat. Cathleen awakened her other children and asked them to tell her what had happened. At first they were too terrified to tell. But she persisted and heard about the call to prayer and the attack on Wendell. Her children told her they saw Barbara take Wendell into another room and heard him screaming after she shut the door.

Cathleen walked into Barbara's bedroom where she was relaxing.

"Don't you ever touch one of my children again," she said.

Barbara sat up in bed and shot back. "Cathleen, you are out of order and you know it. I was only doing the will of my priesthood head. For you to question is pure rebellion."

"Barbara, we have nothing to communicate about. I'm warning you that you had better never touch one of my children ever again."

Cathleen left and locked herself into her bedroom. Her room connected to her children's nursery. She locked the door that led into their room, too.

Barbara went immediately upstairs to Merril's office and told him what Cathleen had said. She returned to her bedroom. Merril stood outside Cathleen's room and began pounding on her door.

Cathleen did not respond.

Merril was shouting outside her door. "You're in serious trouble and if you know what is good for you then you will open this door before I break it down."

"Do whatever you want. I'm not going to talk to you," Cathleen replied.

Merril went and banged on the door to the children's nursery.

Cathleen's children were too terrified to refuse their father's commands. They opened the door.

He barged into Cathleen's bedroom and ordered her into his office. "Cathleen, if you are going to challenge Barbara when she acts on my orders, then you will have to face consequences."

Cathleen refused to get out of bed.

"Merril, I'm not going anywhere with you. You better leave now."

Merril grabbed Cathleen and threw her on the floor. Her son, Johnson, was sleeping in her recliner and woke up screaming.

"Leave now, Merril. Get out of here."

Merril threw her back on the floor, but this time even harder.

Her children were screaming from the nursery, "Go with Father, please, please."

Merril grabbed Johnson from the recliner and threw him into the nursery and locked the door. Johnson was a shy child who had always been terrified of Merril. Merril berated Cathleen for upsetting her children. Cathleen's daughters were screaming in the nursery. Wendell, who had fallen asleep, started whimpering again.

Cathleen knew she was out of options. "Merril, if you will allow me to take Wendell to Sara, I will go to your office." Sara was Cathleen's eldest daughter.

Merril screamed at her for hours in his office. He told her that she was never, under any conditions, to sass Barbara. The next morning when Cathleen awakened me for coffee, her eyes were swollen and red. She told me everything her children had told her about what happened to Wendell the night before.

"Carolyn, Merril can batter me and berate me. But I am not going to allow Barbara to hurt my children. I'm going to see Warren."

I warned her against that. I told her about the seventeen-page letter I had given to Warren Jeffs documenting Merril's abuse. I explained how Warren had discounted my charges because I failed to confess my own sins of immorality.

Cathleen latched on to that in the wrong way. She suddenly thought that if she confessed her sins to the prophet, then he would help her.

I felt sick. "Cathleen, that was only an excuse. Warren needed a reason not to help me. The reality is he never intended to. He will do everything he can to cover up Merril's abuse."

She was unshakable in her conviction that if she told Warren the truth about her sins, he would respond to her honesty with help and protection.

"I'm going to ask Warren for help. I do have sins." And she proceeded to tell me about a wrong that she had committed.

I begged her not to confess that wrong to Warren Jeffs. "Cathleen, don't do it. He will eat you for lunch. If you really want to confess, confess to things like not picking up paper from the floor. Don't give him anything to use against you."

But Cathleen was still a true believer. "If I want his help, I need to be honest."

I knew she was doomed. There was no way she would get any help from Warren Jeffs. Confessing to a sin like that would give him power to condemn her to hell.

Cathleen made an appointment to see Warren. He heard another of Merril Jessop's wives talk about his abusive behavior toward her.

Cathleen didn't say much when she came back. She looked spent. She became more obedient to Barbara. Merril told her there would be no forgiveness for her rebellion and instructed her to turn over her small yellow truck to him. She would not be allowed to have her own transportation again. (Some of us had our own cars and vans, but most of us were not allowed to register them and they had no license plates. So if we left the community, we could not travel far without being stopped by the police. Cathleen needed her truck to go back and forth to Page, so hers was one of the few vehicles that was registered.)

Merril also ordered Cathleen to turn over all her paychecks to him. But she told me later she had no intention of doing that. "There is no way I'll put myself at his mercy financially," she said. But I knew Barbara would insist that she did.

Cathleen told me that she was going to make amends to Barbara by working on a project with her: cleaning Merril's office. This was the way they were to learn to love each other again as sister wives.

I told her I thought this was ridiculous. "You have to act like Barbara'a slave to make up to her because she beat your baby?" Cathleen turned and walked away without responding.

The next day I saw Cathleen cleaning Merril's office. Barbara was sitting in a chair barking orders at her. "Cathleen, I want you to clean the window next, and Father likes his windows cleaned a certain way. Don't do them the way you usually do."

Cathleen worked to be perfectly obedient to Barbara. But she still tried to hold on to her money. She was also forbidden to drive me to Harrison's doctor's appointments in St. George. Merril said he would take us, which meant I'd have to endure his abuse during the trip. His cruelty knew no bounds. One time I had a cold sore on my mouth and he said it was because I had been speaking lies. God put sores on my face so everyone could see my dishonesty.

Once on the way home we had a huge argument over something Arthur had done. It was a minor incident and Merril was insisting on giving him a ridiculous consequence. (*Consequence* was an FLDS synonym for *punishment*.) I told Merril that what he planned to do was abusive and that I would not allow it.

"You don't have any control over what I choose to do with my son. If you don't support me, you're only going to get yourself in more trouble," Merril said.

"If you don't quit being abusive to Arthur, I'm taking my children and leaving. I know you think I'm kidding, but I'm not." Merril told me Cathleen and I had already disgraced ourselves with this kind of nonsense. If I needed to go back to Warren and get reprimanded again, it could be arranged.

"I'm not going back to Warren," I said. "Warren had his chance to do what he should have done to stop your abuse. One chance is enough, as far as I'm concerned. The next time I'm taking every one of my children and going to the authorities."

Merril exploded. "If you think of trying something like that, you'll never see any of your children again. The authorities can't help a person like you. All of your children will want to be with their father."

"It doesn't matter what the children want," I said. "The state will give them to me. In a court of justice I'll get the children, not you."

Merril's silence didn't last long.

"Carolyn, you better not start entertaining those kinds of ideas. The consequences you will face if you try something like that will be more than you can endure."

I knew not to provoke Merril any further. If I was going to escape, I couldn't flag my intention again. I had given him fair warning. If the abuse didn't stop, I would leave him when he least suspected it.

Merril reported his fight with me to Warren. Merril was ordered to bring all seven of his wives to a meeting with Warren Jeffs, who was determined to halt the rebellion in our family. Merril's seventh wife was stealing his car at night and taking long trips to Hurricane. She would not come home until the next morning. When she needed money, she got Merril's checkbook and wrote checks for whatever amount she needed. She signed his name, took the check to the store, and cashed it. In ordinary times she would have been severely punished, but Merril and Barbara felt Cathleen and I were a much greater threat.

The meeting took place the following week in Hildale in Uncle Rulon's sprawling house. We assembled in his huge living room with twelve-foot vaulted ceilings and waited there until Jeffs called us into his office. The house was not lavishly decorated; Uncle Rulon was a man of simple tastes. There was some pretty wallpaper and finely crafted woodwork, but for the most part it was functional and plain.

Warren began by telling us we were all married to a good man. If we were interested in salvation, we must remain in perfect obedience to Merril. Barbara asked to speak. "If we see one of our sister wives struggling with her obedience to our husband, what can we rightfully do to help her?" With her sweet voice, Barbara was asking if she could have the right to discipline Merril's other wives.

Warren looked down, frowning. "It is within your right to pray for her."

This was a major defeat for Barbara, who acted extremely surprised that Warren didn't give her more power over us. Then Merril and Warren spoke to each other alone behind closed doors. When Merril opened the door he called me in. I was told to sit in the chair beside him.

Warren looked at me with a sober expression on his face. He seemed sincere and acted as though he didn't want to offend me. But I sensed that he really didn't take me seriously. He said Merril had told him that I was threatening to go to the authorities. He asked me if this was true.

"No, I'm not threatening my husband," I said. "I gave Merril a promise. I will take every one of my children and do whatever is necessary to protect them unless he stops his abuse. What he wants to do is entirely up to him."

Warren Jeffs looked shocked. I don't think a woman had ever spoken to him so directly before. He told me I had no right to mistreat a good man like Merril.

"I don't care if he is a good man and I am a terrible woman," I said. "He has one option. If he wants me to stay in his home as his wife, he'll stop his abuse. If he can't or won't do that, I'll take every one of my children and leave. That's not a threat, it's a promise. This is something that has nothing to do with the kind of person either one of us is."

The color drained from Warren's face. He was not used to someone who refused to be intimidated by him. Merril said now it must be clear to Jeffs how out of control I was and what he had to put up with on a daily basis.

Warren was quietly seething when he spoke to me. "You have the opportunity to become a goddess in this good man's home if he chooses to take you with him in the celestial kingdom. If you persist in wasting this life by offending your husband, you will be cast out as good for nothing and no man will ever want you in his kingdom. You need to repent, keep yourself in perfect obedience, and pray that Merril will find it in his heart to forgive you. If you continue to waste the precious time you have here on earth fighting him, you will have no place in the afterlife."

I was silent for a moment before I spoke. Then I looked Jeffs squarely in the eye and said, "If my reward in the afterlife is being with Merril Jessop, then I'm not so sure going to hell is such a bad thing," I said. "Maybe in hell I won't have to deal with as much abuse as I would in heaven living with Merril."

Warren seemed genuinely at a loss for words. He told Merril to pray for me and then called Cathleen into the room. He used the same sneering tone to speak to her that he had with me. "Are you aware that you will never see Uncle Roy again and will have no chance of being in his kingdom if you keep offending Merril? Merril is the one with the power to recommend to Uncle Roy that you be a wife in his heavenly home." Jeffs could see that his threats were having an impact on Cathleen. He piled on as much intimidation as he could. By comparison, Jeffs had treated me with kid gloves. He tore into Cathleen.

Warren turned to me and asked if I had participated with Cathleen in being rebellious to Merril. I looked at him squarely and said, "Yes, we are both in rebellion to Merril's abuse."

Jeffs told Cathleen she was no longer to associate with me. We could remain in the same house but we were never to speak to each other again.

Cathleen and I left and sat with Merril's other wives until he finished with Warren. The other wives looked at us like we were so stupid and were gloating because we were in trouble and they were not.

In the car on the way home, Barbara asked Merril to lecture to us. "Father, I think all of your wives would be interested in hearing you teach us what obedience means to you. How do you feel about the importance of being obedient? Why would you not be able to have confidence in any woman who can't remain obedient to you?"

I cringed and stared out the window.

As soon as I got home, I went downstairs to do my laundry. The clothesline was next to Cathleen's bedroom. I could hear her crying when I was hanging up my clothes. I snuck into her room through my children's nursery, which was connected by a bathroom to her nursery. This way, no one would be aware of what I had done. I didn't want to get Cathleen into more trouble than we were already in.

Cathleen had a look of desperation in her eyes. It was the violent desperation of an animal who would chew off a limb to escape from a trap.

My voice was barely louder than a whisper.

"Cathleen, I'm sorry for getting you into trouble. I will always be your friend, even if we can't speak to each other anymore."

Cathleen nodded through her tears. I said goodbye and slipped through her room the same way I'd entered.

It was now winter. I hung my wet laundry on the clothesline. The cold wind snapped it around and stung my hands.

I knew that fighting for a life in this community was pointless.

But Harrison was still too vulnerable and screaming most of the time for me to flee. I talked to his doctor at least every other day. He was hospitalized at St. George nearly every week to get his IV therapy. His weight was still an issue, as was finding the right medication for his pain. There was no way for me to run until he was at least holding his own.

Now I had to devise a plan. I would continue having sex with Merril to decrease his suspicions. I would act repentant. Harrison was my inadvertent ally. Merril would never think that I'd dare escape with such a sick child. I knew I could outsmart him. I would wait. And watch.

But I could not get pregnant again. I had to find a way to get birth control. A high-risk pregnancy could cost Harrison his life if I became too sick to care for him around the clock. I couldn't take birth control pills because Merril's other wives and daughters still rifled through my things.

I had to get a shot of Depo-Provera. But how?

# Last Baby

I knew I needed to get a birth control shot, but it became impossible because Harrison continued to go downhill. I was too overwhelmed with his care to do anything else.

The IV therapy he was getting gave him some minor relief for his spasms but did nothing to prevent his nausea. He sometimes vomited several times a day, and as a result he came down with chronic aspiration pneumonia. During the winter of 2001, I called the ambulance far more than I called his doctors.

I also had to start monitoring his oxygen with a pulse oximeter. When he had terrible screaming bouts, I medicated him with Versed. At night he needed Ambien and chloral hydrate to sleep, but sometimes they worked for only a few hours. Now, at twenty months, he could no longer lift his head.

I was devastated. Exhausted, depleted, and wrecked, I had no longer any reservoirs of strength to draw on. I had to keep going. But each day felt progressively worse as it blurred into the next. I did not dare imagine Harrison's future. The present was terrifying enough.

Time after time the ambulance sped us to the hospital in St. George with sirens screaming. The doctors and nurses there fought like hell to keep Harrison alive. Their determination and valor made me realize how much more compassion there was for me in the outside world than there was within my own home.

I knew my future in the FLDS was over. Because of my "rebellion" I had produced a disabled child, disgraced my husband, and brought shame to my family. No one in Merril's family cared about my welfare except Cathleen.

Cathleen had become my rock. Despite Warren's ban on our ever speaking to each other—or maybe because of it—our friendship solidified in ways that gave me courage and strength. We had coffee together every morning and talked about the day ahead. If I went flying to the hospital with Harrison, she looked out for my children and saw that their laundry was done, their rooms tidy, and they were fed.

Barbara and Tammy hated this. They would try to get Cathleen in trouble with Merril whenever they could. But Cathleen tried not to let it get to her. She had a full-time job at the grocery store in the community. She did not turn her paychecks over to Merril. Cathleen had carved out a niche of both obedience and defiance.

Harrison's doctor, Dr. Smith, decided that something more had to be done for him. She felt his spasms might be a long-term condition and that he needed to have a G-button surgically implanted in his stomach as well as a procedure called fundoplication.

The G-button would go directly into Harrison's stomach, instead of the temporary nasogastric tube that went through his nose. A fundoplication prevents vomiting because the upper part of the stomach is wrapped around the esophagus and secured in such a way that it works like a valve to prevent the stomach contents from coming up through the esophagus. This was a huge help to Harrison because he stopped getting pneumonia from all the vomiting and he no longer needed to have the nasogastric tube inserted every day.

The doctors at Phoenix Children's had seen only one other patient like Harrison. That child was still having spasms after three years. Some kids with spinal neuroblastoma stopped having spasms immediately after the tumor was removed. For others, the spasms lasted for years until they finally subsided. I couldn't bear the thought of that happening to him.

I hated that he needed more surgery, but he had to have relief from the constant vomiting. He was always on the brink of starvation because he couldn't get enough nutrition to grow. The emergency trips to St. George were becoming more frequent. Harrison had almost died several times and I couldn't keep pressing our luck. He had to eat, he had to stop vomiting, and he had to be able to breathe. It was hard to imagine his condition getting any worse. Surgery was our only option.

I began making arrangements for his surgery in the spring of 2001. Harrison was almost two and had been having spasms for nearly a year. When I started vomiting that April, I thought it might be the flu. But I didn't have any other symptoms and after a few days I bought a pregnancy kit. I knew what the result would be. I'd missed my last Depo-Provera shot because I was so consumed with Harrison's care.

The test was positive. I was pregnant for the eighth time. If this became another life-threatening pregnancy, it could kill Harrison. No one in Merril's family would help with Harrison's care. We could all die: me, my unborn baby, and my sick son.

Merril's daughter Audrey had moved back to our FLDS community a year before. Dear, sweet Audrey, who had taken me on those long bike rides out to the reservoir when I first married Merril and tried to teach me about the family's dynamics, now became a real ally.

Audrey had worked in the ER at University Hospital in Salt Lake City. She was well trained in critical care and knew that Harrison's condition was a medical problem, not a punishment for my sins.

Audrey herself had fallen ill when she was living in Salt Lake City. As soon as she was diagnosed and treated, she stabilized. Audrey did well.

But Merril's family had shunned her after she got sick. Her illness was seen as a sign that she had disgraced her father by not being in harmony with the husband she never wanted to marry. Even though she eventually married the man the prophet had ordered her to, she was seen as someone who'd been in resistance to Uncle Roy's will. Audrey had also never kowtowed to Barbara, for which she also paid a price.

Harrison had been getting his IV therapy through home health visits. It was always a challenge because of his spasms. I asked

Audrey if she might be able to do this. His screaming was bad enough without the additional trauma of being stuck like a pincushion when he needed his IVs.

The first time Audrey examined him she shook her head. "Carolyn, nearly all his veins are blown. It's because he's needed a lot of IVs but also because they've missed his veins so many times. You can't allow anyone to stick him several times. He won't have any IV access left at all."

Audrey, in her calm and determined way, managed to place the IV line on her first try. From then on, whenever there was an emergency or whenever Harrison needed an IV, Audrey was the person I called.

She was the one I confided in first when I found out I was pregnant.

"I don't know what I'm going to do," I said. "If I get into trouble with this one, we're doomed."

Audrey tried to reassure me and promised she would do whatever it took to help me keep Harrison alive. She said she'd be there around the clock if it came to that. I knew she meant it.

Harrison's surgery was scheduled for June. I had to make arrangements for the trip and also find a way to pay for it. Merril had forced me to go on Medicaid and would give me no extra help. Cathleen volunteered to drive me. She said she could pay for the trip with her own money. Barbara was infuriated at this idea, but Merril did not object.

Merril was relieved that I was no longer threatening to leave him. I had been sexually compliant, even when I was completely wiped out by Harrison's screaming, spasms, and vomiting. When Merril came into my room in the middle of the night and flung himself on top of me I didn't have either the will or the energy to refuse. Sex was the price I had to pay to make him think I'd given up the idea of escape.

Harrison's surgery was a success—at least initially. His post-op recovery was more complicated than we anticipated. Cathleen stayed with me in Phoenix, which was a relief. Merril didn't bother to come. He had no interest in Harrison.

We had been home for only a few days when Harrison's condition plummeted. He developed a high fever and needed larger doses of Versed to control the pain and spasms. The skin around his G-button wasn't looking very good. I decided to give him a bath on our third day home from the hospital, hoping it would settle him before Cathleen came in for our morning coffee.

When I unzipped Harrison's pajamas I almost fainted. There was a gaping hole next to the G-button that opened deep into his abdomen. I sank to the floor at the sight and put my hand to my mouth to keep from vomiting. The room was spinning. I felt as though I could not breathe. But I would not allow myself to pass out.

I pulled myself back up and there was Harrison, his huge, wondering eyes staring at me in his endearing way. He was such a beautiful boy. But he was in big trouble.

He was admitted again to the hospital in St. George. The surgeon in Phoenix had used microsutures that had ripped out because of Harrison's spasms. The wound had become infected and now would have to heal from the inside out. It needed to be packed and cleaned twice a day. But he healed so well he did not need corrective surgery.

Harrison was on a massive regimen of antibiotics to treat his infection and prevent it from spreading. We came home after a few days and had a home health aide to help change the dressings. She taught me how to help her do it. The challenge with Harrison was his spasms. It took two of us to hold him so we could change the dressings to keep his wound clean. But I was vomiting too much to be of much help. I had morning, noon, and night sickness and was as sick as I'd ever been during a pregnancy.

Harrison gradually healed from his surgery. His oxygen levels began to stabilize, but he was still on a feeding pump and he still screamed most of the time unless I was doing something to comfort him. I felt a glimmer of optimism. Maybe we had been through the worst of it. His lungs were improving now that he was free of pneumonia. Maybe, just maybe, he could start to grow and develop again.

I tried to get him to eat food by mouth. It was a battle, but I had some small success. It had been almost a year since he first got sick, and hands down it had been the hardest year of my life.

One afternoon I was in the kitchen making some food for Harrison and trying not to throw up myself when Naomi suddenly appeared—Merril and Ruth's daughter who had been married off to Uncle Rulon when she was still a teenager and he was in his eighties.

Naomi, unlike her other sister wives, couldn't stop talking about what was going on in Uncle Rulon's house. Secrets were not her strong suit. At one point she started talking about her concern over the enormous birth control bills the prophet's wives were running up.

I could not believe what I was hearing. I was so shocked I dropped the blender I was washing in the sink. I turned to Naomi and said, "The enormous *what*?"

Naomi sighed, annoyed that I hadn't heard her the first time. "The enormous birth control bill," she said. "He has to spend so much money on birth control every month it is outrageous."

I was incredulous. "Why is Uncle Rulon purchasing birth control for his wives?"

"He has to because we all have endometriosis and it has to be treated with birth control." Naomi sounded smug.

Uncle Rulon by now had sixty wives. If only a fraction of them were on birth control, the bill would be huge. But I knew there was no way that so many could have endometriosis. It wasn't that common.

Warren Jeffs was the one who authorized all the money that was spent on Uncle Rulon's family. I had heard that his wives who had endometriosis were told to fast and pray. There had to be more to the story than Naomi knew or was telling.

My hunch was that Warren was paying for a cover-up. It was not kept quiet that at least one of Uncle Rulon's wives was having an affair with his son.

Maybe many more wives were fed up with being married to a man at least fifty years older than they were and had started playing around with younger guys—even if they were theoretically their stepsons.

What angered me was that Warren always held up his father's family as a paragon of virtue—the ideal we should all try to emulate.

The thought that these sixty wives had access to birth control when I didn't made me feel sicker than I already was.

I had had three life-threatening pregnancies; this was my fourth. Girls who were married to the prophet were presumed to be living a celibate life since the prophet was an invalid in his nineties. But now Warren Jeffs was paying for their birth control? Something was seriously wrong. Sex in the FLDS was never for pleasure, only for procreation, and since there was no way Uncle Rulon could father any more children, his wives were not supposed to have sex with him— at least not if he practiced what he preached.

Twenty-four weeks into my pregnancy I started to have complications. I started to bleed from placenta previa. At first the bleeding was manageable, but it increased as the pregnancy progressed, and I knew it could be life-threatening if the cervix dilated enough to rip the placenta apart. I could bleed to death in a matter of minutes.

Audrey's husband agreed to let her help me as much as she could during the day. I had to rest as much as possible. Cathleen helped with my other children when she was home by doing laundry and helping me keep their bedrooms clean. I managed to make it through another four weeks until I was finally hospitalized during my twenty-eighth week. When I stabilized, I was sent to Jubilee House, across the street from the hospital. It was a home for cancer patients who needed daily outpatient therapy but lived out of town. It wasn't routinely used for high-risk pregnancy patients, but my obstetrician wanted me near the hospital so I could be closely monitored and whisked into the ER at the first sign of an emergency.

I'd stayed at Jubilee House once before and was able to go back again.

I concentrated on trying to have a healthy baby. It was the best thing I could do for all of us. A severely premature infant would need constant care and run the risk of having disabilities. I couldn't care for two compromised children on my own.

I was given two shots of medication to help the baby's lungs develop. The rest was welcome. I had not had a night of uninterrupted sleep for over a year. I had plenty of food and fluids in the hospital and could feel myself becoming stronger. But it was hard to maintain because I was hemorrhaging more frequently and I lost more blood each time. Sometimes I passed huge blood clots. I would hemorrhage about every three days, and that made me feel weaker and weaker even with the food and rest.

Audrey brought Harrison to see me along with several of my other children, which made me so happy. Harrison was doing better. Audrey's devotion to him was absolute. My other children snuggled in bed with me. It was so sweet, but I was so scared. I didn't know when I could really mother them again because I felt so overwhelmed by the thought of caring for a new baby and Harrison. I felt unstable emotionally because I was so depleted from all the blood loss. Most of time I just wanted to cry.

The three weeks I spent in St. George seemed like an eternity. It was such a dramatic shift for me to be bedridden. Harrison's care had consumed my days and nights for so long. I was too weak even to read, and I slept most of the time. I could not watch more than forty minutes of television before I had to turn it off because the noise was too tiring. I had been quilting some baby blankets before I came to the hospital, but I was too weak to move my fingers enough to sew. Severe headaches—probably from all the blood loss—were a daily problem.

One morning my phone rang. It was Cathleen. "Have you heard the news?" I told her I'd been sound asleep. "Turn on the TV. We've just been attacked. They hit the World Trade Center in New York."

"Who hit the Trade Center?" I asked.

"No one knows yet. All we know is that the towers came down and thousands of people were killed." I don't think she'd seen pictures; no one in Colorado City had a television. Cathleen had heard about it at work from people who listened to the radio. Warren Jeffs' followers were some of the few people in the world who never saw coverage of the 9/11 attacks.

I turned on the television and saw the replay of the towers collapsing. It was beyond comprehension. The images were sickening.

It was hard to watch, harder not to watch. The pictures burned through to my soul. I, like so many others, had thought America was invulnerable.

It was upsetting to me to see Arabs dancing in the streets because of the 9/11 attacks. I had a hard time watching people rejoice over killing and death even though I knew they hated us.

What was worse was the reaction from people in Colorado City. Tammy came to visit me with several of Merril's daughters in the aftermath of 9/11. She couldn't stop talking about how she and all the righteous people she knew saw the hand of God in the attacks. The Lord's people had finally proven worthy enough for God to answer their prophet's prayers. The destruction of the towers was just the beginning. Warren Jeffs had been preaching that the entire earth would soon be at war and all the worthy among the chosen would be lifted from the earth and protected, while God destroyed the wicked.

Tammy's fanaticism was as idiotic to me as the Islamic extremism of the men who'd flown the planes into the twin towers. I had been taught as a child that only the wicked would be destroyed before the beginning of the thousand years of peace. Thousands of ordinary citizens had been murdered on 9/11, and it was impossible for me to see how anyone—even Warren Jeffs—could spin this as an act of God.

Uncle Rulon had encouraged us to pray for the destruction of the wicked. I never could pray for harm to come to anyone else. Watching the smoldering ruins at Ground Zero and listening to the final, frantic cell phone calls of those trapped in the towers made me know in the deepest part of my being that only the wicked could rejoice in a tragedy like this—which didn't say much for my own community.

My doctor was pleased when I made it to thirty-one weeks—nine weeks short of a normal pregnancy. He thought the baby was doing well and said that he'd do a C-section when the placenta finally tore and I started to hemorrhage. Every day that my pregnancy continued made my baby healthier and stronger.

Merril came frequently to St. George. He was thrilled to have finally gotten one of his wives pregnant again. He drove up to Jubilee House several times a week and took me out for a steak dinner and was planning to stay with me overnight, but once when Barbara called, in tears, he turned around and drove back.

I was so frightened being alone when I was sick that it was a relief to have Merril there. He came just as I was beginning my thirty-first week. I awoke during the night in labor. I could feel the contractions beginning to come. I stayed still, thinking that maybe I could will them to stop. But two hours later, I was hemorrhaging massive amounts of blood. Blood pooled around me. Merril called the ER and told them to send an ambulance.

One of the EMTs was a woman. When she saw the amount of blood around me she started shouting orders. "I have to get a line into her while I still can!" In minutes she had two IVs in each of my arms. She didn't start them on a drip, she just opened them up. I sensed how frantic she was beneath her professional calm. She called the hospital and said she was taking me directly to the OR.

I was so dizzy that I felt like I was going to pass out. It was hard to breathe. The last thing I remember was a doctor in the ER trying to keep an oxygen mask over my face. Each time the mask was put over my face I panicked and tried to push it off.

I did not wake up again until I was in the recovery room. I asked a nurse if my baby was okay. She said he had stabilized. I was relieved.

I'd had two previous C-sections, but never before had I been in such penetrating pain. I asked the nurse for more medication. She told me she'd given me as much as she could and that I shouldn't be in pain.

But I was. I was in too much pain for everything to be all right. Merril came in and was extremely happy because our baby was tiny and cute. I told Merril something was wrong. I was in too much pain. He wasn't concerned. When he left the room I lost consciousness.

The nurse tried to take my blood pressure and couldn't find one. I came to and remember my bed being pushed down the hall and people running on both sides of it. An ICU doctor running beside me was trying to put a central line in my neck and had the line placed before the brakes were locked on the bed. I still had two IVs in each arm. The door flew open to the ICU and the room was flooded with people. A bag of blood was being connected to the central line.

A doctor was yelling orders and people were moving fast. I had never been in so much pain. It felt like every cell in my body was screaming for oxygen. I felt such thirst, no amount of water would have quenched it. If the worst pain I'd ever had during childbirth had been a 10, the pain I felt now was at 100. The pain, noise, and chaos were too much.

I decided to let go.

I could hear the doctor's voice in the distance saying, "We're losing her, we're losing her!"

I was slipping under the waves of pain and chaos.

The doctor's voice sounded farther and farther away.

Then it got louder.

"Carolyn! We know you have eight kids! We are not going to let you die. You are not going to die on us!"

At that moment I started fighting to come back.

It felt like sledgehammers were hitting me on all sides. My thirst was unbearable. I started begging for water. I was told I couldn't have any because I was going back into surgery.

When I awoke again I could see the colors of a brilliant sunset through a window in the ICU. I took a deep breath. The sun was setting and I was still alive.

The pain was almost gone now. I still had four IVs and was receiving blood through a central line. My entire body was swollen. I felt like a beached whale.

An ICU doctor came and talked to me. He said they'd almost lost me. A nurse came in with more blood, and I asked her how many pints I'd received. She checked. Sixteen.

The surgeon came in the next morning and told me what had gone wrong. When he took out the baby he'd noticed that the placenta had grown through the scar tissue of a previous C-section. He'd cut around the scar and then tried to repair the uterus. He hadn't done a hysterectomy because he knew about our religious beliefs. He was confident he'd repaired the uterus. But apparently the placenta had grown beyond the scar tissue and into the uterus. When the placenta was delivered, I bled out, and the doctor did an emergency hysterectomy to save my life.

I couldn't believe that after four high-risk pregnancies the reason I'd almost died was because the doctor was trying to preserve my uterus! I was glad it was gone!

A nurse asked me if I wanted to speak with a grief counselor after my hysterectomy. I looked at her as if she were crazy. I loved every one of my children and would never give up a single one. But my hysterectomy felt like a get-out-of-jail-free card. I smiled at her and shook my head. "Eight is enough. Believe me, there's no grief."

Bryson was three pounds ten ounces and doing really well. He needed to be in the hospital for a few weeks, but the pediatrician didn't think he'd have any problems.

Before Bryson was born, the challenges of caring for Harrison had made me think my life couldn't get any worse. After my near-death experience, I knew it could. The nurse brought Bryson from the ICU so I could hold him. He was the tiniest human being I had ever seen. Completely perfect, but on a miniature scale—and born into a world I was determined to escape.

I kept thinking of what I needed to do before we fled. Harrison was in the hospital nearly every month, and Bryson would need a lot of care. I had to get both boys strong. Then I would take my children and run for my life.

My religion had always felt like an unsinkable ship. But Warren Jeffs and his extremism loomed large, like the iceberg that could smash everything apart.

I left the hospital after five days and moved back into Jubilee House so I could be close to Bryson. We didn't go home for two more weeks. I missed Harrison so much. He was my buddy. I was desperate to get back to him. I'd been away from my children for five weeks.

Bryson weighed four pounds when we finally came home and he

was a feisty baby. He nursed easily, but at first I was allowed to breast-feed him only once a day. Breast-feeding is a lot of work for a preemie. A bottle is easier. I expressed my breast milk so he could be bottle-fed. I marveled at my exhausted and depleted body's ability to create food for this tiny boy. It took me months to feel that I was regaining strength.

I now had two more strikes against me in Merril's family. My hysterectomy and near-death experience were further proof to Merril's other wives that God was still condemning me for my rebellious ways. I was thirty-three and unable to bear any more children. For me that felt like a divine blessing rather than proof of a curse.

I would sometimes hear the other wives talking about me. They wondered why I refused to get in harmony with my husband. I should know, they said, that it didn't matter how many times I took Harrison to the hospital. As long as I was in rebellion he would only get worse until he finally died. I had nearly lost my life but still refused to repent. What more would God have to do to make me wake up?

What they did not realize was that I was already wide awake, building my strength, and plotting my strategy.

Cathleen was still my only friend among Merril's seven wives. She welcomed me home from the hospital, helped me with my laundry, and continued to have coffee with me every morning. She bought a few items that I needed for Bryson and Harrison because when I first came home from the hospital I was completely confined to my bedroom.

The other wives treated Cathleen like she was radioactive and shunned her.

Audrey came by almost every day to check on Harrison's and Bryson's vital signs, which was very reassuring for me. If anything shifted, we could respond immediately.

Audrey also faithfully went to church every Sunday. She was as frightened as I by Warren's extremism.

# Harrison's New Port

**D**espite his nearly two years of IV treatment, Harrison still went into daily spasms. There came a point in late 2001 when Dr. Smith ordered that a new port be put in because all of his veins had been blown. I was apprehensive. Every time Harrison had had surgery there was a major complication, but I knew we were out of options. The surgery was done the week before Christmas in St. George and went well. But within days, Harrison's fever spiked to 104 degrees—he had a staph infection. When I couldn't get his fever down, Dr. Smith said to bring him back to the hospital. I called an ambulance and we were on our way. Ambulances were becoming routine.

But it wasn't only Harrison. Bryson was just three months old and still underweight. He came with me wherever I went because he was on a strict feeding schedule. I now nursed him every two hours. While we were in St. George Bryson picked up an infection that developed into pneumonia. So when we finally came home, I was caring for two sick children.

Bryson needed to be on nebulizer therapy to help his breathing. Harrison needed to be on oxygen also because he was having a hard time keeping stable levels in his body.

After I got home and had the two boys settled, I went looking for my other children to make sure they were all okay. Betty was missing. No one in the family would tell me where she was. I'd ask a question and be completely ignored.

The next afternoon she arrived home. I learned she had been staying at Warren Jeffs' house.

It had become common practice for Merril's unmarried daughters to stay at Warren's house for sleepovers on a regular basis. These were wildly popular and like big slumber parties. No sex was involved, but Warren got a chance to interact with these young adolescent girls and think about those he might want to marry when they were a few years older.

Betty was only twelve years old. I couldn't imagine one of my daughters getting married. But I had to ask myself how much longer she would be safe. She was Merril's favorite daughter, and he would be only too pleased to have her marry Warren Jeffs.

Warren's hold over the FLDS kept increasing as his father continued to decline. Uncle Rulon was rarely seen in public anymore, and no one was ever allowed to have an appointment with him. Merril's daughters said that none of his wives was allowed to see him unless Warren gave them permission. The girls also circulated stories that said Uncle Rulon complained that Warren had taken his job away and that he wanted it back. On the rare occasions when Uncle Rulon appeared in public, no one was allowed to talk to him and only a few of the chosen were allowed to shake his hand.

One of the most noticeable changes was that girls were being assigned in marriages at younger and younger ages. When Uncle Rulon first came to power, girls didn't marry until they were over twenty. After his first stroke, the age dropped into the late teens. The sicker he got, the younger the brides in the community became. I remember when Uncle Rulon married a fourteen-year-old girl to her stepfather. Warren had taken the girl's biological father away from her mother and excommunicated him. Then he assigned her mother to another man. Several months later, the fourteen-year-old girl was married to the same man as her mother.

I was determined to protect Betty. But I also knew I couldn't do it and stay in the community. Harrison was still too sick to attempt an escape. Bryson was fragile, but gaining strength. Making them stable and strong was my priority. All our lives depended on it.

Harrison's infection cleared, but a week later he developed another. This went on for months. He would be admitted to the hospital, be discharged, but yo-yo back in a week or two. Dr. Smith thought Harrison would need to have the port out because it was causing his infections. The surgeon felt that we should give it a little more time and see if the condition could resolve itself.

Then Luke had his accident.

Luke was Merril and Ruth's seventeen-year-old son. He was working construction in Page and had a dirt bike—something usually frowned upon in our culture because they're unsafe. Boys who ride them are considered rebellious. So no one in the rest of the family knew about it.

A police officer found Luke unconscious by the side of the road. A life flight took him from the local hospital in Page to the one in St. George. Merril's office was notified that a parent needed to be there soon after Luke's flight arrived to sign papers in case he needed emergency surgery. Luke was in critical condition. His spleen was bleeding and surgery might be the only way it could be stopped.

Merril and Barbara were on their way to his motel in Caliente when the news reached them. Merril didn't want to drive all the way back to St. George, so he called his son Leroy and told him to go to the hospital, check on Luke, and call him back.

Leroy, who was in his twenties, found his brother, who told him he was okay and had nothing more than a bad bump on his head. When this was reported back to Merril, he wondered why he'd been told Luke was in critical condition. A bump on the head was no big deal.

That night Leroy stopped by our house on his way home from work. Ruth had prepared the meal that night and was serving up soup and hot bread when he arrived.

"I just stopped by the hospital to check on Luke like Father asked," Leroy said. "He seems to be doing just fine."

Ruth looked shocked. "What? Why is Luke in the hospital?"

"Didn't Father tell you Luke was in an accident with his dirt bike today?"

She shook her head. "No, I haven't talked to Father today. When did Luke get a dirt bike?"

"I think Father let him get it quite a while ago. But he's doing fine. I'm sure Father would have told you if there was anything to worry about," Leroy said

Ruth cared deeply for her children when she was stable. She picked up the phone in the kitchen and immediately called Merril.

"Father, Leroy is telling me that Luke is in the hospital and that he had an accident on his dirt bike."

There was silence while Ruth absorbed whatever Merril had to say. She continued. "But Father, I think I better go to the hospital tonight and check on Luke. I want to make sure he's really all right."

Ruth listened some more and then hung up. I could see that her hands were shaking. She finished the dishes and told us how worried she was about Luke. "But Father doesn't think that if I go there will be anything to do there anyway. He thinks it's important for me to stay home and take care of the family."

Ruth seemed to be trying hard to convince herself that this was something she wanted to do—even though there were four other wives at home. She was clearly upset and complained the next morning that she had not been able to sleep.

Merril and Barbara decided to go to Las Vegas the following day on business. Merril thought he might make it to the hospital later that day.

Meanwhile, at the hospital, the surgeon monitoring Luke couldn't understand why no parent had yet arrived on the scene. She couldn't operate until the forms were signed. If there was an emergency, Luke's life could be in jeopardy because of his parents' negligence.

The surgeon called Ruth and explained how serious his condition was. While his vital signs were good, he still was not stable. Ruth called Merril and asked if she could go to the hospital. She wanted to do what was right for Luke.

Merril ripped into her and told her he had everything under control. Her only concern, he pointed out, should be to do the will of her husband.

After Ruth called, Merril called his oldest son, Fred. Fred's second wife, Josette, was in the hospital with her sick baby. She went to check on Luke and asked him how he was doing. He said he felt better.

While they were chatting, the surgeon arrived and mistook Josette for Luke's mother. "I'm so glad you finally found a way to get to the hospital," she said. "I've been doing everything I can to get ahold of you!"

"How do you think he's doing?" Josette asked out of genuine curiosity.

The surgeon went through a detailed explanation of Luke's condition, explaining that even though he was holding his own, there was still a possibility that his spleen could rupture, which might require emergency surgery.

After she'd finished explaining Luke's status, the surgeon told Josette that she didn't look young enough to have a seventeen-year-old son.

"Oh, I'm not old enough to be Luke's mother. I'm not his mother."

The surgeon looked stricken. "Then who are you?"

Josette didn't want to say she was the second wife of Luke's half brother. So she said she was just a friend from Colorado City who was in the hospital with her sick baby and had dropped in to say hello.

The surgeon nearly lost it at this point. She was angry and frustrated that she couldn't connect with one of Luke's parents. It compromised her ability to ensure that he got the best care. She saw it as a matter of life and death.

Luke was less concerned. He was getting hungry. Because he might need to have surgery, he was only getting IV fluids.

Merril and Barbara decided at the end of the day in Las Vegas that they were too tired to make the trip to see Luke and postponed it for another day. Merril called Leroy and asked him to go back to the hospital.

When he did, he found his brother watching TV. "I'm so hungry I could die," Luke said.

"Well, a man can't live on no food. Let's go out and get you something to eat." Leroy helped Luke get up and disconnected his IV. He fished his clothes out of the plastic bag in the closet and the two boys walked past the nursing station and out of the hospital. Leroy bought a big steak dinner for the two of them.

A nurse walked into his room and found that the IV had been turned off and that Luke's bed was empty. The hospital went into a panic. Had their patient been kidnapped? The surgeon rushed back to the hospital. Someone called our house and asked to speak to Mrs. Jessop. There were five of us at home who answered to that name. The child who answered the phone asked the doctor which Mrs. Jessop she wanted to speak with.

Luke came back from dinner, got into his hospital gown, and got back into bed. A nurse saw him and ran back to the nursing station to say he'd returned. By this time, the surgeon had arrived back at the hospital. She wanted to know how it was possible that a patient who was in critical condition had disappeared from under their noses.

Then she went to Luke's room. He told her he'd been famished and had gone out with his brother to get something to eat. "Luke," she said, "you have an injured spleen, and although you may not feel sick you could bleed to death at a moment's notice. We can't feed you because if you need surgery and anesthesia you have to have an empty stomach. It's illegal for you to leave this hospital unless you are with a parent. Don't ever do this again!"

Luke agreed to stay put.

The hospital got Ruth on the phone and insisted she come to the hospital immediately to consult with the surgeon. I heard her call Merril.

"Father, I really think I better go to the hospital. This is the second call today. They're insisting I be there."

Merril scolded her over the phone. "Ruth, I have already given you instructions as to what I want you to do. Now, are you going to listen to your husband or insist on having it your own way? You know what will happen to you if you start demanding to do what you want instead of what your husband says is right."

Ruth was practically in tears. "I'm sorry for asking again, but I have been so worried about Luke. The hospital told me today he is in critical condition and if I didn't sign for the surgery he might die."

I could hear Merril shouting through the phone. "Ruth, I have everything under control. Are you going to listen to others rather than a man who has inspiration? I have had numerous people checking on Luke and he's fine. There is no reason for you to run to St. George. I will be coming through there and will take care of things. You need to settle down. There is no reason for you to get crossways with your husband. You're going to get into a condition with me that you will regret."

Ruth hung up the phone and fled to her room crying.

Merril and Barbara got to the hospital the next afternoon and took Luke out for his second steak dinner. Luke apparently told his father that he might need to have surgery, but Merril didn't care. Luke felt his father had more authority than the surgeon because he was inspired by God.

When the hospital staff saw he was gone again, they placed another call to our house, where none of the Mrs. Jessops had any idea where Luke was. That meant another trip back to the hospital for one very angry surgeon.

She confronted Luke again. He told her he'd promised not to leave the hospital with anyone who wasn't his parent, but his father had come. "My father told me it would be all right to eat," Luke said.

The surgeon could not believe Merril had not tried to speak to anyone involved with Luke's care. She had been trying for two days to speak with one of his parents, to no avail.

Merril and Barbara were pleased that they'd been able to take Luke out to dinner. They thought he might be lonely at the hospital, so they decided to ask Leroy to take their twelve-year-old son Tommy to the hospital to spend the night.

When Luke's nurse found him watching TV with his twelve-year-old half brother, she was confused because visiting hours were over. Luke told her Tommy was spending the night because his father didn't want him to be alone.

When she explained that was against hospital policy, Luke said that Leroy had left an hour ago and there was no way for Tommy to go home.

The hospital called Merril, who agreed to have Tommy picked

up. But Merril did nothing about it and went to bed. The next morning, Leroy was sent to pick him up.

The surgeon told Luke the next day that he could go home in another twenty-four hours if he remained stable. The hospital notified Merril, who then sent for Ruth.

"Well, Ruth, the hospital just called and said Luke will be coming home tomorrow. He's doing just fine. All you need to do is listen to your husband and things will work out. I hope this will be a lesson to you. There was no need for you to have kept calling me. God has protected your son despite your disobedience and your constant questioning. You should be thankful that you have a husband God loves who would protect your son despite your rebellion."

Ruth quivered with emotion. "Father, I am sorry for asking to do differently than you requested. I am grateful to be married to you. I am grateful that God protected Luke in spite of my rebellion. Please forgive me and have patience with me for what I have done."

Merril laughed smugly. "Of course, Ruthie. I will forgive you if you learn from this and see that it doesn't happen again."

Ruth spoke softly. "Yes, Father, I have learned to never question you again. Thank you for your forgiveness."

I heard this in Merril's office because he had sent for me. Merril was giving me a "correction." If I would be as obedient to his will as Ruth, God's love would allow Harrison to get better. What Merril was able to manipulate—as if he needed an excuse—was that there was no apparent medical reason doctors could offer to explain why Harrison wasn't coming out of his spasms. The doctors had said that there was a possibility that Harrison could emerge from the spasms and be completely normal again. This was the kindling that Merril used to stoke the fires of his accusations toward me about the consequences of my rebellion.

Luke was discharged the next day. His brothers picked him up and he walked out of the hospital without signing any papers. This created yet another uproar. The hospital called and insisted that Ruth come back, sign the discharge papers, and talk to his doctor about Luke's follow-up care.

Ruth explained the situation to Merril. He attacked her for her impudence and warned her that he might not be so forgiving of her behavior if she couldn't learn to leave well enough alone.

Ruth was practically shaking when she left Merril's office. I witnessed endless episodes of this kind of behavior. Merril would berate her over almost anything, as he did the rest of us. What was different about Ruth was that she was less capable of outsmarting him and defending herself.

The hospital called several days later, this time about the bill. Ruth told them to speak to Merril. He informed her that Luke's bill was her responsibility. "The way I see it," Merril said, "is that you are a single mother with sixteen children and I don't give you any money. So I think the hospital will work with you and help you out."

Child Protective Services informed Merril several weeks later that he was being investigated because of Luke's hospitalization. Merril was warned that he could lose his children if he was found to be abusing them. Merril screamed at the investigator over the phone, "Who do you think you are, calling and questioning me about my parenting? The way I parent my children is nobody's business." He told the man from CPS to go to hell.

But the next day, the investigator showed up at our house. This was a rare occurrence. Child Protective Services rarely came into the community and hardly ever took children away from their abusive parents. Victims were so routinely sent back to perpetrators that people stopped making reports. My experience was that for the most part, Child Protective Services looked the other way at the endemic abuse that was happening in our community because it was easier than investigating large polygamous families.

The minute Merril saw the man from CPS show up, he started screaming at him and told him to leave at once. The man insisted on talking to Luke. Merril refused. Luke heard all the shouting and went outside. He convinced Merril to allow him to talk to the man, and the three of them met in Merril's office. Then the investigator talked to Luke alone.

Luke said that his parents didn't understand the rules at the hospital and that there had never been any ill intent on their part. The investigator promised to write a full report. No one ever heard from him again. I was not surprised.

What did surprise me was that Luke's surgeon, who also took care of Harrison, had a completely different attitude toward Harrison and me when she saw us the next time. The pediatrician felt strongly that Harrison's port should come out because the infection hadn't cleared. But the surgeon disagreed and refused. Her concern was that if this port came out there wouldn't be a way to put another one in. That's because there are only several veins large enough to hold a port. Once those accesses are exhausted, there are no other options. She finally agreed to take it out but made it very clear to me that she would never do another surgery on Harrison and that she was the only surgeon in the area capable of doing a procedure like this. If we ever needed to attempt something like this again, we would have to take Harrison back to Phoenix.

Her attitude toward me seemed harsh. I suspected that she'd put two and two together and realized Harrison and Luke had the same father. She had always been friendly toward me. Now she acted as though she didn't want to have anything to do with us.

I was so upset that Merril put his children at risk through medical neglect. I hated that the surgeon thought I was as neglectful of my children as Ruth and Merril were. Neither she nor my pediatrician knew anything about the polygamous lifestyle that I was living.

We *never* talked about polygamy to outsiders. We lived in fear of outsiders. Even when I had a long relationship with physicians, as I did with Harrison's doctors, I had no way of really knowing if I could trust them. I could not take any risks because if Merril ever found out that I had told the truth about my life to anyone outside the community I would have been sentenced to hell in the afterlife and shunned by my community in this life.

# Warren Becomes
# the Prophet

**B**y springtime in 2002, it felt like I'd been given a reprieve. Harrison's staph infections stopped once his port was removed, and Bryson emerged from his first fragile months into a sturdy and healthy baby. He was nursing so steadily that I had extra milk. This gave me an idea.

I decided to give my surplus breast milk to Harrison. I had read that breast milk was the best nutrition for balancing the immune system. I'd also read that the fat in breast milk could help in repairing the myelin sheath, which is the protective covering around nerves. Harrison's immune system had chewed away at his nerves' myelin sheath, which contributed to his severe nerve pain. I thought my breast milk might help compensate for some of the damage.

I began expressing milk every night and putting it into Harrison's feeding tube. Watching the milk slide into the tube, then into him, I hoped for even the tiniest miracle. Harrison and I had been through so much together and had a wordless, profound intimacy. I loved him beyond measure.

My breast milk was also a potential lifeline for the rest of us: once I got both boys physically strong enough, I could take all my children and escape. Bryson was thriving. The real challenge was Harrison. I had to get him stronger. We were going to the doctor at least once a week and I was constantly on the phone with her. If only my breast milk could make Harrison grow and balance his immune system. If only.

But I also had to teach Harrison to swallow. He'd done it for the first year of his life, but once he got sick and had a feeding tube, he stopped. My goal was to get him to swallow something every day. The initial weeks were hell. I'd put food in his mouth; he'd scream and spit it out. He was a fighter. He fought me with food.

Pizza was my salvation. It had once been Harrison's favorite food. After three weeks, he swallowed a tiny bit of pizza. I was elated. What hope! If he ate and grew stronger, he could save us all.

It took four months, but Harrison finally began to eat different foods, and he became voracious. I was so relieved; he'd been so starved by his cancer, infections, and spasms. Harrison began to seem happier and more stable. There were days when I felt over-joyed, but I hid it. No one could know what I was thinking.

One night when Bryson was six months old I woke up from a deep and dead sleep. Something was wrong. I knew it. I had trained myself to fly out of bed when an alarm sounded on one of Harrison's machines. I raced to his room to turn it off before he awoke. But this time when I got there, everything was silent. The machines were all working, but it was too quiet. Harrison must have stopped breathing! But I looked at the oximeter by his crib and saw that his oxygen lev-els were normal. The feeding pump was working and Harrison's little chest was heaving up and down in a natural rhythm.

Suddenly I realized what was different. Harrison's loud, spas-modic breathing had stabilized. He was breathing normally. Once he was sedated at night his body would not spasm. He was unconscious. But the spasms went to his lungs and made his breathing sound like hiccups.

The hiccups were gone. I sat on the floor next to Harrison's crib. I was shaking all over. He had been on breast milk now for six months and something was happening. For the first time in two years I knew in my bones that Harrison was improving. It was a miracle. My secret miracle.

Harrison began to sleep for longer periods of times. Even with a maximum dose of sedatives, he had never slept for more than six hours. I knew I would need medicine when we fled, so I gradually began to reduce the doses of his drugs—in tiny and incremental ways—and built up a small stockpile. Even when I cut back on his sedation at night Harrison began sleeping for eight hours.

Harrison became so healthy that I took him to the doctor only once a month. He still needed Versed, but much less than before. His anxiety attacks diminished dramatically three months after his breathing improved. Maybe, just maybe, he could come out of those awful and debilitating spasms. Oh, how I wanted my little boy back. His doctor didn't seem that impressed by his small improvements; she was looking for a big change, like the cessation of his spasms. But each small change filled my wellspring of hope. Escape was on the horizon.

One afternoon in early spring I asked Cathleen to help me take Harrison for a walk when she came home from work. It had been another day of constant screaming because of his spasms.

Cathleen told me what people had been talking about all day at work—Warren Jeffs had kicked more than a hundred teenage boys out of the community within the past month.

"It's such a shame that so many mothers are producing so many unworthy sons," she said. "These children are choosing rebellion over doing the work of God and supporting our prophet."

I was speechless. I had been so consumed with Harrison's care that I didn't realize teenage boys were being kicked out of the FLDS in significant numbers. Audrey had told me once about a fourteen-year-old boy and his brother who were told to leave because they were accused of being gay. Homosexuality was seen as an abomination and never tolerated. I'd asked Audrey how the mother of these boys felt when her sons were dumped on a highway and told never to return. Audrey had said the woman was ashamed and heartbroken that she had raised a couple of creeps. She was embarrassed and tried not to think about what her sons had become. But I'd thought that was an isolated incident. I had no idea that boys were being kicked out in significant numbers.

Whatever innocence I had left was wiped out that afternoon during my walk with Cathleen.

It was bad enough that women couldn't mourn the loss of a child for more than a week or two after the funeral. But how could any mother bear knowing that her son was being abandoned into a world he feared and had no skills to face? Since birth these boys had been taught that the outside world was evil. Now, because Warren Jeffs said so, they were hurled out of the FLDS and told never to come back.

Women could show no emotion for these lost boys, who could be kicked out for listening to CDs, watching movies, or kissing girls. Mothers were told to pray to God to show them where they'd gone wrong in raising such children so they would not repeat the mistake with their other children.

When young boys were kicked out of the community, the family didn't talk about it or even admit that it had happened because it was too disgraceful. Women tried to keep it secret. No mother would ever protest the prophet's decision because she believed it was revelation from God—just like her marriage.

Because women were so secretive about this practice, few of us knew the true numbers. The other siblings were told never to speak their brother's name again after he'd been sent away. The outcast sibling had been consigned to the devil, who'd punish him for all his remaining days on earth and seize his soul the moment he died.

No one protested as hundreds of teenage boys were arbitrarily excommunicated from the FLDS by Warren Jeffs.

One night I was doing my laundry when I heard myself paged over the intercom. "Mother Carolyn, you are wanted on the phone." I picked up and heard my sister Linda's voice. "I just drove by your house. Your children are dancing on the tables! I could see them doing somersaults from table to table and dancing around the room."

I couldn't believe it. "There is no way they'd dare do that!"

"Dare or not, they're doing it. Go upstairs and see!"

I left the endless pile of work behind and went upstairs. I saw the show of my life.

Twenty children were dancing. All the lights in the dining room were ablaze. The three long tables were pushed together in a horseshoe and the kids were jumping and flipping from one table to the next. The player piano was belting out something with a jazzy beat. The older children were carrying the babies, and the smaller children danced at their feet. They were carefree and gleeful. I was mesmerized by delight. I had never seen such spontaneous happiness in our family. It amazed me that these little souls still knew how to be carefree and playful.

The fun had begun when Merril and Barbara left for the night. A couple of the boys had a football and started tossing it around. The chandeliers began swinging and the kids squealing.

Unmitigated joy of any kind was diminishing from our lives. Warren Jeffs had our community in a chokehold. I noticed that people's faces now seemed devoid of expression. It was as if they were afraid even to look like they might be thinking. The life seemed drained from their faces. They acted as if emotions had been outlawed. People were determined to "keep sweet" even if it killed them. There was no arguing or questioning. But by "keeping sweet" we lost all our power.

I never knew what was coming next. One day all the dogs were rounded up and killed. This had a harrowing effect on children who were attached to their pets. Oreo was our family dog, a cute black and white mutt that LuAnne adored. When Merril heard that the order had gone out to seize the dogs and destroy them he told one of his sons to take Oreo to Page and put him in the pound. This was devastating for my children even though Oreo didn't die. LuAnne was heartbroken. Merril told the children that tears were not allowed. They should only be concerned with doing the will of the prophet.

The dogs were destroyed after an ugly incident in which a four-year-old boy was killed by his stepfather's pit bull. Warren's decision to kill the dogs seemed completely irrational, like so much else in our world.

One of the most searing incidents of my childhood was seeing Randi, the girl on my school bus with what I'd later realized were burns on her arm and who'd had her long braid hacked off. Her utter agony had broken my heart, and the fear in her face when she got on the bus that day never left me.

Randi was forced into marriage at an early age, and by the time I had my eight children, she already had ten. One day Warren told her she was being assigned in marriage to another man.

Stories like this were becoming more commonplace in the community. Warren would tell a woman one day that she would belong to someone else the next. Her children would follow her and belong to another man. They would take their stepfather's last name. The only way they would be able to continue to see their biological father was if he went to court. But only a handful of men ever did that. Most believed Warren's lie that if they did what they were told there was a chance of redemption. By the time I fled, I knew of fifteen or so women who had been reassigned to different husbands; in the years since, that number has grown to nearly a hundred.

Warren would tell women that their husbands would not be able to offer them salvation in the afterlife and that he was assigning them to a man who could. Our belief was that as women, we could become celestial goddesses only if we were married to a man in this life who was worthy of becoming a god after death. For those who were still true believers, Warren's violent disruption of families was seen as an act of divine inspiration.

Women were not only the ones being torn from their families. Men were, too. It seemed as though I heard about it happening every week. Warren would call a man to his office and tell him he was no longer going to be a part of his family and that he must leave his wife and children, his job, and his community to repent from afar.

Sometimes a reason was given, but often not. A man I knew, Paul Musser, was told by Warren that he was not fit "to exalt his wife into heaven." Paul, who was not in a plural marriage but was devoted to his wife and their thirteen children, believed that Warren's orders were revelations from God.

He went home and told his family that the prophet had told him he was unfit to be their father. The next morning, weeping and sobbing, the family said goodbye to their father and he to them. Paul had no idea of what he had done to fall from favor with God. But he believed Warren knew. Paul's wife and children were given to another man soon after he left. (Paul was eventually able to see that he'd been brainwashed and that what Warren Jeffs did to him was an outrage.)

Two years or so after he was kicked out, Paul's wife was assigned in marriage to yet another man and his children had their third father in less than three years.

One of the ways I could measure the change in our community was at Linda's coffee parties. I'd been too engrossed in Harrison's care for the last year to get to any. I was excited about going back and eager to see what women were talking about.

One woman said she thought all the cell phones in town were bugged. This prompted someone else to say, "Whatever you do, don't drink the punch," a reference to the mass suicide in 1978 in Guyana when nine hundred followers of Jim Jones drank a cyanide-laced grape punch.

Another woman became upset when she heard this. She started accusing us of not following the prophet's will. It had become illegal to say the word *fun*. Warren Jeffs had banished that word from all use. So if we were being silly or lighthearted in any way, we could be reported as being in rebellion to the prophet. This kind of tension was new to me. I'd never been to a coffee at Linda's where women censored themselves or criticized something another woman said. These clandestine get-togethers were the one place we could really be ourselves and talk openly.

I was very confused. When I said something negative about Warren, my cousin Jayne kicked me under the table. I looked at her as if to say, *What's your problem?* Jayne just put her finger up to her mouth. I was at a complete loss. The woman who was upset about the reference to Jim Jones left. We all concluded that those who were upset about the "drinking the punch" comment had already taken a few swigs.

After she did, the conversation became more freewheeling. I learned about secret tapings that had been going on. Men would be called into Warren's office and asked their views on a religious topic or issue. He'd then play a taped conversation in which they'd talked about the same issue, usually in a cell phone conversation. If there was a disparity between what the man said and what Jeffs had preached to believers, he'd be put on notice that he had to get in harmony with the prophet. (Men had also begun reporting on one another to Warren to try to get in his good graces so they wouldn't be kicked out of the community.)

I also learned about how Warren had bugged the meetinghouse of a rival FLDS bishop in Canada. None of us felt comfortable with any of this, but we were not going to bring it up with our husbands because it could get us in trouble if word got around that we were questioning Warren.

Someone else talked about a woman we all knew who was caught having an affair with a young boy after her husband was given a new wife. Because of the affair, she was told that she had committed a sin unto death. Despite the fact her husband had been taken from her, she was still considered his property and he would rule her destiny in the afterlife. Because of her adultery, she was condemned to be a servant to him and his wives in heaven for all eternity.

Warren banished her to her uncle's home, where she lived, in effect, under house arrest. She was not allowed to be a mother to her children and could only see them on short, supervised visits if her husband gave his approval. There could never be forgiveness for her in this life. She was condemned to die the second death and her soul would be destroyed forever.

But women didn't have to commit adultery to be severed from their families. Another woman we heard about was taken in to see Warren by her husband, who felt she was unhappy in his family and he didn't know how to help her. He complained that she was pulling away from him.

Warren condemned her for being rebellious and removed her from her husband. The husband wept uncontrollably; this was not what he wanted to have happen. She was forced to move out of her husband's home and into a small apartment in the community as an example of what could happen to a woman who wasn't "keeping sweet."

When we talked about this at the coffee party we all felt that she should have taken her children and left the community. But women risked so much in standing up for themselves. If Diane had stood up to Warren, her husband never would have allowed her back into his home. He loved her and hated losing her, but he loved the prophet even more. It is hard for someone on the outside to fathom, but men would have died for Warren Jeffs. Jeffs was also cagey; he'd often hint at the possibility of eventual forgiveness if they did what he wanted them to do.

What was most unsettling was that families could be torn apart for no reason—or reasons Warren would never reveal. We knew that he could turn on any of us the way he did with the others. A man who wanted to get rid of a wife could now march into Warren's office and know that even with the flimsiest complaint or accusation he would be likely to get a fresh start with someone else.

Cathleen and I were still having our morning coffee together when an episode with a Canadian bishop came up. Cathleen was critical of those in Canada who were defying Warren Jeffs and refusing to follow the newly ordained bishop. I could not believe her unquestioning support for Jeffs.

"Cathleen, Warren can't upset the leadership in Canada just because he is in a bad mood one day and think there will be no consequences." She looked at me in disbelief. Cathleen still thought that Warren Jeffs was a god despite what he had done to her. She got up and left. We never had coffee again and she rarely spoke to me.

Ordaining a new Canadian bishop was one of the rare instances when an action backfired on Warren Jeffs. Uncle Rulon was so incapacitated that he had no real power anymore. It had all been ceded to Warren—except that the old man had a few tricks up his sleeve. We saw this play out in Warren's feud with the Canadian bishop of the FLDS, who had always been close to him.

Warren saw him as becoming a threat to his own power and tried excommunicating him from the FLDS church. The bishop had thirty wives and more than a hundred children. He told his family what had happened and said they could leave if they liked, but everyone chose to stay.

Warren felt the bishop was in total defiance and appointed the bishop's half brother as his successor. The half brother refused to take the position. Warren bullied him until he finally relented and came to be ordained.

The story that circulated around the community was that when it came time to ordain him, Uncle Rulon, who was so demented he didn't even recognize the man, put his hands on the man's head and did far more than make him a bishop. He made him a high priest, apostle, patriarch, first counselor, and finally bishop. Then he topped it off by giving him the keys to the priesthood and, in his final blessing, making him the prophet of God.

This made him more powerful than Warren, which of course Warren could not stand. He told the new bishop to forget about everything he'd been ordained to beyond bishop. The new bishop told Warren he was a complete fraud.

One day I was on the phone talking to someone about Harrison's physical therapy when Merrilyn came into the kitchen crying. I asked Cathleen if she knew what the problem was.

"Warren has sent her back to Merril because Uncle Rulon never wants to see her again. She's Merril's problem now."

Merrilyn and I were both thirty-four. For nine years, she'd been married to a man sixty years her senior. I hadn't wanted to marry Merril, but I cherished my eight children. Merrilyn had no children. My sweet, innocent classmate, who had once tried to charm our teacher at the pencil sharpener, had been forced to spend the best years of her life in an old man's harem. Now she was cast out.

Merril banished her to his motel in Caliente. After several weeks of cleaning rooms, she decided to leave her father and her religion and fight for the life she'd never had.

Merrilyn found a ride into St. George and hooked up with the party circuit. The following week she went to Cedar and tried to get her own apartment. A boy who was still in the FLDS was helping her try to get settled. After three days, Merrilyn had a job.

But then Merril came and required that she come home. The next day he took her to see Warren Jeffs.

I was looking out the window when they came home. Merril looked disgusted. Merrilyn was crying and walked straight to the garden. I went out on the back deck of our house and watched her. She was sitting on a stump in the garden and sobbing. After a few minutes, her sister Paula arrived. Paula had been married off to Uncle Rulon, too. She must have snuck out of his house to come to see Merrilyn. She threw her arms around Merrilyn, who was in tears, and held her close.

The next day I heard Tammy talking to someone on the phone about Merrilyn's punishment. The boy who had tried to help Merrilyn in Cedar had been excommunicated. Tammy said that Warren had told Merrilyn she would spend the rest of her life as a slave. She would never be allowed to have children or anything of value in life. The devil would be waiting for her as soon as she died and would instantly destroy her.

Warren told her the only way she could be spared from this fate was by the blessing of blood atonement. If the priesthood granted her this blessing, she might be able to remain as a servant to Uncle Rulon through all eternity.

Blood atonement meant Merrilyn's throat would be cut from ear to ear.

Warren had begun preaching about blood atonement. In his sermons he said that Jesus Christ died on the cross in atonement for the sins we commit unknowingly. The sins a person commits *knowingly* can only be redeemed through blood atonement, but it is not a sacrament an individual can choose for herself. It can only be mandated by the priesthood.

In all my years in the FLDS I'd never heard a prophet preach blood atonement. I was well aware that Warren Jeffs was taking the community in new directions. I'd never thought murder would be one of them.

Several months later I learned that Warren had spoken to Merrilyn and warned her that if she didn't change her ways, she would have to pay with blood atonement.

Three weeks after Merrilyn was kicked out of Uncle Rulon's home, the old prophet finally died, on September 8, 2002. He was ninety-four years old and had more than sixty wives and more than seventy children.

Warren proclaimed himself prophet almost immediately and married his father's wives. Now he was in absolute control over all our lives.

No one vocally challenged his right to succeed his father as prophet. There were no other apostles in the FLDS, and Warren had been effectively running the community for nearly six years before Uncle Rulon died. He had managed to quell any dissenters or competitors within our ranks. Nevertheless, word circulated throughout the community that Warren had a hit list of over a hundred men he intended to kick out to ensure that any opposition to him was eliminated.

At Uncle Rulon's funeral, I heard Warren Jeffs preach that the prayers of the community had been answered. We had been ordered to pray for the last year that the invalid prophet would be lifted up and renewed—which we thought meant in *this* life. Now Warren was saying that our prayers had been answered; he'd been renewed, but after bodily death. Warren also preached that the faithful among us could count on the same thing.

This was frightening. We were going to be the next to die? I was always listening for something that pointed in the direction of a mass suicide. Warren was crazy enough to try something like that—and I knew many in our community who believed it would be a privilege to die for Warren Jeffs.

In the weeks following his father's death, Warren began preaching that Uncle Rulon was God and that he had come to usher in a thousand years of peace. Warren began making subtle suggestions that, as the prophet's son, he was Jesus Christ.

His words were frightening enough, but the blind obedience of people I had known all my life was even more disturbing. They had lost any capacity to think for themselves.

Warren went crazy making prophecies. No one in the community was allowed to have any access to outside information, so he even began predicting the weather. I still had access to a computer because of the small Internet business I'd started. I'd often go online to see how closely Jeffs' forecasts matched what I found online. They were identical.

Warren also began preaching about how the armies of the world were gathering in the Middle East and that World War III had already begun. I still had a radio in my bedroom and would listen to it when I knew I would not be caught. Radio was strictly forbidden. I heard about the war in Iraq and knew enough about what was happening in the Middle East to know that Warren Jeffs was lying.

Warren continued to preach about how it was time for God's chosen to have a temple to do the work God had planned for us. This frightened me because we had always been taught that we would not begin building a temple until after God had cleared the wicked from the earth and we were living in the thousand years of peace. Warren's temple talk scared me. We'd been taught that every blessing we needed for our salvation could be done without a temple—except for blood atonement. I feared where Warren Jeffs might be leading us.

Merrilyn was sequestered at the motel in Caliente. Her half brother Truman, the little boy who had been left behind at the gas station on our bizarre honeymoon trip to San Diego, was assigned to watch over her. As far as I know, Merrilyn never tried to escape again.

Loretta, who'd been the first of Merril's daughters to marry Rulon, returned to Merril's house. She had refused to marry Warren Jeffs and was sent home until she was ready to repent. The rest of the family—with one exception—condemned Loretta for her disobedience just as surely as they condemned Merrilyn for her adultery.

Oddly enough, it was Ruth who took Loretta's side and told me that she felt Loretta was a victim. This was strange—many of Ruth's daughters had been married off to Warren, and she'd always been a true believer. I felt disgusted by the cruel way Loretta was condemned but knew to keep my mouth shut.

Audrey and I still talked almost every day. She'd come over on the pretext of checking on Harrison. Both Audrey and her husband were concerned about the vitriol and extremism coming from Warren Jeffs. I avoided going to church, but Audrey went regularly and filled me in on what Warren was preaching. He kept mentioning the "Center Place" and how he would be sending people to Zion. But the catch was that there could be several Zions. Anywhere the prophet sent us was considered Zion.

I told Audrey that I thought Warren was planning to separate us in remote areas like concentration camps. He needed to be in absolute control and couldn't risk letting us live freely in the community. Once we were split up we'd never be able to escape because we'd undoubtedly be separated from our children.

I knew I had to get out fast. But I couldn't run the risk of fleeing when Merril was at home. I had to wait until he was out of town and all my children were home. Arthur worked on construction jobs and was often out of town. I needed a window of opportunity, and the second I got that window, I'd jump.

My mother beat me to it. She'd become so infuriated with Warren Jeffs that she told my father she was leaving with her two youngest children. She was upset not only with Jeffs but also with the community of believers who were blindly supporting him. Mother felt they were completely ungodly.

I was not surprised that she decided to leave. I knew that for several years she'd hoped life would change, but she only saw it deteriorate.

Mother had become my defender. She'd been shocked when Warren condemned me after I reported Merril's abuse. She'd told my father that if he didn't get me out of my marriage, she'd leave him.

I think my mother finally realized how betrayed she'd been by her religion. She knew my father didn't love her. She'd buried one daughter and felt like she'd lost two others who fled the FLDS. She saw me lost to a life of abuse and degradation. How could any religion that created so much harm be of God? It was an obvious question that few asked.

Mother had been so proud of our faith and culture. Seeing what it had become made leaving the only option. My father did not try to stop her. Unlike almost every other man in the FLDS, he felt that my mother had the right to choose how she wanted to live her life. He told her to pack what she wanted to take with her and he'd have a truck come by early one morning and move her out.

My mother and my two siblings, Jennifer, sixteen, and Winston, nine, left on April 19, 2003. She walked away from the only life she'd ever known for fifty years. Once she was out of the community she filed for a divorce and ended her thirty-eight-year marriage.

When my mother left I felt unbearably alone. We had grown closer over the years and she helped me so much—especially with Harrison. I know the day she drove us to the emergency room it broke her heart not to be able to stay and see us through the crisis. But that was too risky because she'd taken us to the hospital without Merril's permission. Those moments cut her to the quick.

I kept quiet about my plans to flee, but others in the community were discussing the option for themselves. Audrey and her husband were planning to quit and move to northern Idaho. I was losing the people I was closest to and afraid to confide in those who were still left. I never knew if some offhand remark of mine might be reported back to Warren Jeffs and create problems for me. I was determined to maintain a semblance of normalcy.

I never gave a hint to any of my children about my plans. But as I'd learn later, LuAnne began to have dreams about our escaping. In her dreams she'd see us all together in a house outside Colorado City. All her brothers and sisters were crying and saying they wanted to go back to their father and half brothers and sisters. Betty was pleading with me to take everyone home. LuAnne's fear in the dream was that we were all going to hell and she was scared and crying. As she'd explain later, it was a relief when she awoke and found that she was still with her father's family. But her dream kept recurring. Betty was the only person she confided in, and she told LuAnne that the reason she kept having the dream was because she didn't say her bedtime prayers.

I did not make waves within the family. Bryson and Harrison were a shield for me because they still required so much care. I dutifully had sex with Merril to keep up the façade.

It was a tense and unpredictable time. Anything could happen at any time.

Three days after my mother left, my moment arrived.

# After the Escape

The trip to Salt Lake City was pure hell. Betty was literally hitting me in the car and screaming, "Uncle Warren is going to find out what you are doing. You'll be in so much trouble! He'll never let you get away with this!"

Darrel had to lock all the car doors. My other children would have enjoyed the adventure and the ride if Betty hadn't been so hysterical. She kept acting as though I was going to kill every one of them.

"Mother, you are taking us out into this wicked world to be destroyed! Father will never allow it." Betty was upset for a reason. Warren Jeffs had been condemning Salt Lake City as one of the most evil cities on earth because of the Winter Olympics. His real agenda was to get the FLDS members who lived in Salt Lake to move to Colorado City in order to consolidate his power. But to my daughter Betty, if we were in Salt Lake when God erased the wicked from the earth—which Jeffs was preaching could happen any day—she and all of her brothers and sisters would be wiped out instantly. My other children were scared into silence.

Arthur tried unsuccessfully to calm her down. Darrel finally screamed at her to shut up. But she wouldn't listen and she didn't stop. It was five hours of pure hell. Harrison was also screaming because traveling made him so uncomfortable.

While we were driving, Darrel got a call on his cell phone from my mother. We had a place to stay. Mother—who escaped just three days before—had contacted Dan Fisher, a prominent dentist and former FLDS member who agreed to let us stay on his property near Salt Lake City.

Dan had been born into the FLDS. At one point he'd had three wives. But he quit shortly after Rulon Jeffs came to power and began living with just one wife. Dan became extremely successful after he invented one of the best tooth-whitening systems and other dental products. He still had many relatives in the FLDS and knew how bad things had become. For years, Dan has tried to help people who wanted out of the cult. His willingness to help me saved our lives.

When we got into Salt Lake City we made a quick stop at my brother's to let the children use the bathroom. Moments after we left, Arthur's house was surrounded by trucks from the FLDS. The hunt was on. My brother's construction shop was surrounded by Merril's posse before we even got to the city. They'd beaten us to Salt Lake.

On our way to Dan Fisher's I noticed that my son Arthur was watching the road closely. I thought he might be planning to run the moment he had the chance. He wasn't acting out like Betty, but I could tell from his body language that he was furious with me.

Dan has five guest houses on his property. His wife, Leenie, welcomed us with enthusiasm and gentleness. She couldn't have been expecting a woman with eight children to land on her doorstep that morning, but she seemed delighted that we had.

Leenie took us to the largest guest house. With four bedrooms and a large living and dining area, it felt like heaven. I started to think about getting my children fed and making sure that Arthur didn't bolt. Leenie's daughter Sarah had come over and said she'd get them some Happy Meals while Dan talked to me in the main house.

Dan was waiting in the dining room with a glass of wine in hand. He asked me a few questions to get a grasp of my situation and background. He was impressed that I had a bachelor's degree in education and that I'd taught for seven years. But when I mentioned that I was married to Merril Jessop, he stopped pacing around the room, put his wineglass on the table, looked at me, and said, "Wait— did you say your husband's name was Merril Jessop? *The* Merril Jessop?"

I looked at Dan, somewhat surprised by his reaction. "Yes, Merril is my husband."

"You mean I have Merril Jessop's kids on my property?"

"Yes. Actually, you have eight of them."

Dan's face paled.

"Carolyn, when people come to me for help I don't usually go to the authorities. Generally, I don't recommend it. But if Merril Jessop is your husband, you're not going to have even a remote chance of getting out unless you go straight to the top for help. I feel it's urgent to get the attorney general's office involved today as soon as possible!"

"I'll do anything to protect my kids."

Dan left immediately. I don't think either of us understood the danger we were in.

My head was spinning. I hadn't slept for twenty-eight hours. I was running on adrenaline from the stress and tension of our ordeal and there would be moments when I felt weak and ready to pass out. Everything was happening so fast. When I got back to the guest house I did a head count and discovered that Arthur was missing. I guessed that when he was watching the road he'd been looking for the nearest pay phone so he could run back and call Merril.

Arthur didn't have any money, but boys who worked on construction crews always had phone cards in case they got into trouble. I ran back to Leenie's house and told her what happened. Her daughter Jolene had just arrived to help.

Leenie called Dan, and he said it was too dangerous for us to remain on his property. He said we'd be safer at Jolene's. I started rounding up my children to take them into hiding again and gathering up the black plastic garbage bags with all our clothes.

Betty started screaming again. "I'm not going with you! What are you doing? Where are you taking us?"

I found out later that before he left, Arthur had told Betty that he was going to call Merril and that she would have to get the children into the truck the minute he arrived. I pulled her into the car while she was fighting and kicking me as hard as she could.

Fortunately for us, Jolene had just graduated from dental school, and few in the FLDS even realized she was back in town. She had a beautiful house not too far from her father's. Jolene carefully explained to my children that there was an alarm system and if anyone opened a door or window from inside, an alarm would go off and the police would come.

Shortly after we settled in, Sarah arrived with Arthur. She'd found him a few miles from Dan's.

Arthur had unwittingly saved our lives because when he fled, I knew our cover was blown and we had to leave Dan's immediately. I found out that Merril had arrived at Dan Fisher's house five minutes after we left for Jolene's. He had learned where we were staying even before Arthur called because, as I'd later find out, my stepsister betrayed me. If he had found us there before I had a protection order, there would have been no legal way I could have stopped him from taking my children. I would have had to go to court to fight for custody. It would have taken years.

Arthur's five-mile run was a godsend.

I also learned from this episode not to talk to anyone. Merril had tracked us down because Darrel had told his wife where we were after he dropped us off. She mentioned it to my stepsister, who called her mother in the cult, who then called Merril.

Jolene insisted I go to bed for a few hours. She ordered pizza for my children and sent me upstairs to crash with my two youngest. I nursed Bryson to sleep and put Harrison in bed beside me.

After a few hours Jolene awakened me. Someone from the attorney general's office had come over to question me so he could file for an emergency order of protection. He asked me for the name of someone in the community to call to tell them that the attorney general was now involved in this case. I gave him Sam Barlow's name. He was a close ally of Warren's, and I knew he would see to it that the word got around. I was sure Merril would still keep hunting for us, but at least he would be answerable to the law once the protection order was in place.

After he left, I went to check on my children. Betty and LuAnne were sitting on the couch. "I'm not eating another thing until I can go back to Father," Betty said. LuAnne said she was on a hunger strike, too.

Jolene said that not eating wouldn't get them anywhere. Moments later, her husband came in and put on the movie *Shrek*. It was the first movie my younger children had seen since Warren Jeffs banned them in the community. They were enchanted. I took Bryson back upstairs to bed. Arthur followed me into the bedroom.

"Mother, I know you have been living in hell," he said quietly. "But I can't back you in this. I don't want to live in Salt Lake. I want to be in Colorado City with my brothers and sisters."

I just listened. I knew he needed to feel he could tell me everything.

"I have never lived in a big city before and I don't want to. I want to be in a small town."

"Arthur," I began cautiously, "you're fifteen. In a few years you can live wherever you want. But until you're eighteen, you'll be with me."

Arthur was not a boy who showed his emotions. But suddenly he began to quiver, then shake. "Mother, this has been the worst day of my life. I watched the road going to Dan's house. Once we were there, I got the address and ran to call Father. When Father answered his cell phone I could barely speak, I was so out of breath. I told him where you were. I was going to run back and meet him there but Sarah showed up and stopped me."

By this point, Arthur was sobbing. "Mother, I gave Father my word. I told him I would meet him at the address that I gave him, but I didn't do it! I always keep my word to Father."

It was awful to see my son in such agony.

"Arthur, I don't expect you to understand what I am doing. But there's no way your father ever would have let me leave peacefully. Escape was our only option."

"I don't want to be pulled into this fight between you and my father. I don't want to have to take sides. What you did this morning seems crazy. But I will do whatever is necessary to protect my brothers and sisters. You can't ask me not to."

I was proud of Arthur because he was such a responsible son. He had been completely indoctrinated by the FLDS and I didn't expect this to be easy for him. We'd always been very close. He never saw much of Merril. But he had been taught to fear and respect him.

Now he was in an impossible situation. He didn't want to turn against me, but he also wanted to keep his word to Merril. I knew this was tearing him apart, but at the moment there was nothing I could do.

When we finished talking and I'd helped Bryson get back to sleep, I went to check on the rest of my children.

Everyone except Betty and LuAnne was bathed and ready for bed. Jolene had gotten them ready. It was one of the strangest moments of my life. In seventeen years, no one had ever helped me get my children ready for bed before. Never—not even when I was sick and confined to bed during my worst pregnancies.

Merrilee bounced into the bedroom. "Mama, look at me!" Her eyes sparkled. She was, for the first time in her life, wearing little-girl clothes. "Look, Mama!" She pulled up her nightgown to show me her underpants. "See the roses!" The panties were trimmed with rosettes, and this was the most miraculous thing Merrilee had ever seen.

She'd had a bubble bath and shampoo and her hair smelled fragrant. Jolene had a daughter Merrilee's age, so her clothes fit my daughter perfectly. Merrilee had never realized such pretty clothes existed. After wearing long underwear 24/7 through all the seasons, she was experiencing herself in a way she never had before.

All of my children were euphoric. Even Betty seemed happy and engaged. This was an unimaginable adventure. They could eat as much as they liked, drink sodas, and watch television and movies. For the first time in their lives, I think they felt like the center of attention because they were not competing with dozens of siblings.

Arthur asked if he could work with my brother the next day, and I agreed. I felt that I could trust him, and I knew my brother would keep close tabs on him. When my brother came to pick him up the next morning, he took me aside.

"Carolyn, I don't think you know how much trouble you have created for yourself. The entire city is crawling with men from the FLDS. They are scouring every possible place you could be hiding. I was afraid to come over here because I was sure I'd be followed. Things are really crazy. I know you went to the attorney general's office, but Merril is not afraid of the law, not under these circumstances. I'm worried about your safety. Getting out of that religion might just not be possible."

I looked directly at him. "The truth is I have nothing to lose. I would rather be dead than live that way another minute. I'm going to protect my children and do everything I can to get out."

Arthur started to laugh. "Yes, I imagine you will. I don't know anyone else who would try such a stunt. Your van was so out of gas we couldn't get it off the trailer. You took a van that had almost no gas, loaded it with children who didn't want to go, and now look where you are! Actually, you've gotten farther than anyone else could have."

Then he got serious again. "Carolyn, you took the children of one of the most powerful men in the FLDS. They will hunt you down for that and plow over anyone who gets in their way. There's no way the FLDS is going to let you escape with Merril Jessop's children. This is one fight I don't think you can win."

# A New Life Begins

The next morning Dan Fisher came over to Jolene's and told me the emergency order of protection was in place. Now if Merril grabbed the children he'd be in a lot of trouble. Dan said if I felt I needed still more protection, I could move into the battered women's shelter in West Jordan. But he added that he and Leenie would be delighted to have us return to their residence.

This was a no-brainer for me. My children had been too traumatized by our escape to go into the shelter system. I felt we would be safe enough at Dan's. He sat down and had coffee with me. We were sitting around Jolene's table with her husband, Neil Jessop, who was a relative of Merril's—although not close to him. Dan was telling me about the crimes he was hearing about in the FLDS and said I was right to get my children out.

"I never knew what this country's Founding Fathers fought for until I left," he said quietly. "Even so, it took me a few years to grasp what it really meant and how deeply it mattered.

"You have a real fight ahead of you," he went on. "It might mean testifying against Merril and Warren. Neither of these men is going to let you take your children without a fight."

I knew what Dan Fisher was saying was true. But it terrified me. I was willing to fight for my freedom, but I had not realized that might mean testifying against Warren in court. My fear was that I knew so much about him he would never let me be free. I had witnessed him marrying an underage girl—my stepdaughter Millie, who was seventeen when she married Warren.

I remember Millie going through the motions during her wedding in a robotic way. I knew this wasn't what she wanted because the day Merril told her she had to marry Warren, she broke out in hysterical sobs. I was just coming into the house and went into Merril's office to see what was wrong. Millie threw herself into my arms, crying and crying. Merril kept telling her to be brave. It was one of the most helpless moments of my life. At that point, Utah had not passed a law that banned underage women from polygamist marriages. Millie went on to become one of Warren's favorite wives.

What I later learned was that Warren mistakenly thought Millie was my oldest daughter. This lit a fire in me to do everything I could to protect Betty so she would be spared a similar fate.

Dan said that my best hope of overall protection was to go into the attorney general's office and tell everything I knew about Warren Jeffs. Bryson started to fuss as I was taking in all that Dan was saying. I was trying to quiet him while I was shaking all over.

"I know what you are saying is right. I will tell them everything I know. But backing out of the FLDS is only one of my concerns. How am I going to take care of my children and support us all? Harrison needs twenty-four-hour-a-day care, and my other seven children are traumatized and afraid of the outside world. My work at home is cut out for me, but I still have to find a way to feed us."

"Carolyn, listen to me. Of all the women I've helped, you are in the best shape of any of them."

I wasn't sure what he meant. It seemed impossible to believe that this was true.

"It might take some time to get on your feet," Dan said, "but at least you have a college education and you're very intelligent. Most of the women I see have less than a seventh-grade education and no life skills. You're in a different category altogether."

Dan and I talked for nearly an hour that morning. He said he would try to get an investigator from the attorney general's office to meet with me and listen to what I knew about Merril and Warren's crimes. Dan told me to take it a step at a time so I would not get overwhelmed.

He also reminded me that I was now in an environment with checks and balances. A judge could rule on the evidence in my case rather than condemn me as an immoral woman. I could tell a courtroom about Merril's abuse instead of having to talk to Warren Jeffs, another perpetrator. I was thirty-five years old and had never been in a fair fight or had anyone on my side. This was going to take some getting used to. But I was not backing down. That was one of the few things about my life I did know.

Dan left, and I went upstairs and started gathering up our things for the move back to Dan's. My sister Annette came over to help me move. She'd also fled the FLDS. Several years later she met Merril's half brother Robert—who had also quit the FLDS. They dated for several years, then married and had four children. After living in several different cities, they returned to Salt Lake to be closer to other family members who'd left. Annette and I laughed about the black garbage bags we relied on for suitcases. She had escaped with one; I, with many.

It was a relief to go back to Dan's guest house. I immediately started doing laundry because we didn't have enough clothing. My children went outside to play, and I'd never seen them more excited or happier. This was a great adventure for them. Little did they know they were never going back. For the second night in a row I put eight happy children to bed. It felt like a miracle. Betty kept up her threatened hunger strike and claimed she would never eat. But I put food in her bedroom at night and when I went up in the morning, the plate was empty. Arthur was quiet now but concerned. I think he understood what I was trying to do and why. But he was afraid I couldn't pull it off.

Harrison awakened me the next morning with his crying. I gave him a bath and then took him outside to pull him around Dan's reservoir in a wagon. The morning was silent with a shimmer to it. Dew was still on the grass as the sun was beginning to rise. I watched two Canadian geese fly low toward the water, then skid across the surface of the reservoir before gliding to a stop.

The world looked brand-new. I was seeing life in color again. For seventeen years I'd lived in a blur of terror and fear. It had taken all my energy to survive my life. I'd noticed a sunset here and there, but there had been no time for beauty, wonder, or marvel.

It hit me all at once. I could suddenly see beauty in an ordinary day: the bright green grass, the emerald pines, and the red, red roses on Dan Fisher's rosebushes. The forbidden color looked especially brilliant to my grateful eyes.

I took Harrison out of the wagon and sat with him in the grass. I looked up and saw that the gates at the entrance to Dan's property were locked and a security guard was stationed outside. For the first time in longer than I could remember, I felt safe. Harrison went into a spasm, and I held his body next to mine to quiet him.

When I looked up, I saw a black truck on a hill above Dan's property. It was an FLDS truck. I was being monitored. My sweet moment vanished. I put Harrison in the wagon and headed back to the guest house. Once inside, I realized I was still safe. The only power the person in the truck had was the power of observation.

The next day I went with an attorney to file more paperwork for my order of protection. I also got a call from my father, who tried to convince me to stay out of the courts. He said he was sure Merril would help me work things out and that I didn't need to make such a big fuss.

"Merril and Warren already had their chance to work things through with me, and they both refused," I said. "If Merril was interested in working with me, he would have done it three years ago."

"But Carolyn, he didn't realize you were so serious then," Dad said. "He doesn't want his children living outside the community, and he wants you back. He's willing to let you have your own house."

"Dad, Merril has never kept one promise he's made to me. Why should he change now?"

My father told me I didn't need an attorney. He and Merril could find one for me if I was determined to continue in the courts. I could not believe what I was hearing.

"Dad, do you think I'm that dumb? I'll be keeping my attorney," I said. "I am not going to live with Merril's abuse any longer. I have a clear claim on my children and I'm going to fight for custody." I had never stood up to my father before. It felt good.

My father was still a true believer and did not feel I had the right to leave and take my children with me. He was helping Merril on principle: in my father's eyes, Merril owned me the way he owned his car. Dad felt Merril was wrong to abuse me, and he'd never doubted me when I told him what was happening. But he felt now that Merril understood how serious I was, he might be less abusive to me if I came back.

For my father, my salvation was at stake. If I broke the covenants that I'd made with God, I would relinquish all claims to any kind of salvation. So Dad was thinking of the big picture, and within that context, he genuinely believed he was acting in my best interest to encourage me to return.

When Merril's pressure on my father couldn't get me to roll over, he turned to my son Arthur. He kept badgering Arthur to make me talk to him. I had been gone for only a week, but Linda told me the things Merril had already started to say about me in church.

Merril accused me of being the worst kind of apostate and said I had turned traitor to the work of God by going to the authorities. He said I planned on destroying his children, and he even accused me of betraying my grandmother, who had stood faithful during the raid on Short Creek in 1953. During that raid, it was said that if one woman turned against the work of God, then every woman could lose her children and the men would be imprisoned. Merril put me in that category of being the one woman who would destroy the work of God in the last days and turn traitor to the prophet.

I told Arthur that now that I knew what Merril was saying about me behind my back, there was no way I'd speak with him. Arthur told his father I'd heard what he had said about me in church. Merril was furious that someone had ratted him out.

Two weeks later, on May 17, 2003, was our seventeenth wedding anniversary. To mark the day, I got a babysitter and went to a salon to have my hair cut and styled. This was the first time I had ever had my hair cut professionally. Annette took me there and we looked through books and magazines to pick out a hairstyle. It felt weird to be looking at all these different and forbidden ways to comb my hair and to know that I could have any of them I wanted!

I had always worn my hair in the FLDS style, which meant a big wave in the front and then pulled tight in the back. Sometimes we wore long braids wrapped around our head. A woman's hair could never be loose. Sometimes I'd rolled my hair up and put a lace hairnet over it. Now I was overwhelmed by the choices when I looked at all the styles, and had absolutely no idea what would look good on me. Trying to be pretty was such an alien concept. Annette helped me pick a cut that was soft and easy to comb and style. I got a professional perm—which I'd done once before in the FLDS as an act of sheer rebellion—and the stylist taught me how to comb it to match the picture. It felt so strange to me to wear my hair down and without a big wave across the front that was anchored in place with hairspray.

When I got home, I was in the midst of making dinner for my children when a big bouquet of carnations and other flowers arrived from Merril. *Much joy for a pleasant day,* the card read. *Pleasant* was one of Barbara's favorite words, so it was obvious to me that the flowers were from her.

My children were so excited by the flowers that I couldn't throw them away immediately. I just left them on the table and proceeded to make dinner. Harrison had been born on my anniversary, so we were celebrating his fourth birthday that night. I had bought a cake and candles for him, which was a novelty for all of us. In the FLDS, birthdays were rarely celebrated.

Early the next morning, while everyone was still asleep, I took the entire vase of flowers to the dumpster and threw them in. I could hear the glass shattering. It was liberating. The oppression was over. My life was my own, and no one could take my freedom away from me now.

I had another immediate fear to conquer: driving. I had avoided it as much as I could since the accident on Black Ridge. Compounding the problem was that I wasn't used to driving in a big city. But I had to be able to buy groceries and drive Betty and LuAnne to their counseling sessions. LuAnne was in school but Betty and Arthur were not yet ready. (My other three school-age children were in public schools, but Dan made arrangements for their transportation there and back.)

My freedom didn't mean much if I couldn't drive. Still, it terrified me to get into a car again. My heart raced and my mouth went dry. I couldn't let the girls see how scared I was, so I took a deep breath and turned the key in the ignition. It would be a year until I felt comfortable driving again.

The biggest challenge I faced was financial; this was not a surprise. I had no expectations of getting any money from Merril. He'd even refused to contribute to Harrison's care before I escaped, since he believed Harrison was my punishment from God.

But I had made one really smart move before I fled. In planning for my escape, I knew I had to do something about money, and the one option I had was getting Social Security benefits for my children. Harrison was getting $100 a month in SSI benefits, but that never covered his monthly costs.

When Merril had retired, he applied for Social Security benefits for two of his youngest children, Harrison and Wendell—Cathleen's son, the one Barbara beat one night at prayers. This was dishonest because he claimed that the boys' mothers weren't able to care for them. But scamming the government for benefits, whether food stamps or welfare, was routine in the FLDS. It was referred to as "bleeding the beast." Merril was smart enough not to put more than two children on Social Security—he knew he'd be investigated if he claimed he was raising dozens of children by five mothers. The children had to be living with him if he was to collect the money. It was credible that he could be raising two children from separate mothers.

I calculated that if Social Security knew about my other children, Harrison's benefit would jump to at least $400 a month. So I applied.

But when I did, I was turned down because Merril claimed my other seven children were not his and that we'd never been married. I had just almost died giving birth to Bryson, and I was infuriated. But in denying my claim, Social Security gave me a long list of items I could send in to substantiate his parenthood, so I at least knew what I needed to get this turned around.

Between nursing Bryson, coping with Harrison, and trying to get my stamina back, I was not exactly in the mood to take on a big bureaucracy, but what choice did I have? I was thinking big picture. I needed a steady income, no matter how small. And I had to find a way to prove that my children were Merril's without his knowing it.

I knew that there was documentation in Merril's office; he had birth certificates and tax returns. But how to get it was the challenge. Merril's office was closely monitored when he was away. It was off-limits to anyone else in the family, but the door wasn't locked. What I decided to do was wait until Merril was out of town and sneak into his office when everyone else in the house was asleep. I set my alarm for 2 A.M.

I never went through more than one file at a time. It was too big a risk if I was caught. And I always brought something of Harrison's with me—such as the dishes I used to feed him that I might be returning to the kitchen—so it would look like I was up because of him.

I'd take a flashlight and would lock myself in Merril's office. But I attempted this only when I knew Merril would be away for two nights, because once I took anything, I had to copy it the next day, then sneak it back into Merril's office the following night. But I found a treasure trove of documentation.

There were tax returns in which he claimed my children as deductions and a letter to the attorney general's office explaining that he couldn't pay his medical bills from his heart attack due to his large family. Then he listed all his underage children. I made about eight trips over two months collecting all the documentation I might possibly need.

Once I submitted the documentation, all of my children received benefits. Merril knew about this but not how I made it happen. I dutifully turned over the $700 a month I was receiving to him. Little did he know how masterfully I'd outsmarted him.

But on my first day of freedom, I called Social Security and told them I had a new address so the money would come directly to me and not to Merril.

I also applied for state benefits in Utah, but that was slow going. It took several months, and there was one goof-up after another. Even though the state acknowledged that Harrison's situation was critical, there was nothing to do to speed up the process, which was agonizingly slow.

Harrison and I went for a walk at sunrise every morning after his bath. I pulled him in the wagon down to the reservoir. That black truck was still perched on the hill like a menacing shadow. I felt like I was trapped between a world of freedom and a world of slavery. The truck remained there for several weeks.

A few days later when Dan Fisher returned from a business trip he asked to meet with me. There was a problem. Merril was in hiding and the police had not been able to serve him with the order of protection. In truth, he said, I didn't have much protection until Merril was actually served. The police wanted me to lure him into a trap.

In the three weeks since my escape I had tried to face every fear head-on. This felt like the ultimate challenge. I didn't think I could do it. The thought of seeing Merril again made me shut down.

Dan said that since Merril was still hounding Arthur about seeing me, we had an easy way to make this happen. He urged me to set this in motion. I trusted Dan and finally agreed.

We talked it through. The key was that I could only meet Merril in a public place. There would be undercover cops there, so I'd have some protection. But that didn't make me feel safe. I had lived under Merril's tyranny for seventeen years and had seen how hard he had come down on wives who disobeyed him.

I had embarrassed him in the eyes of the entire community. Now everyone knew he did not have his family under control. Trained to be terrified of him for seventeen years, I found it excruciating to stand up to him, let alone trap him. But I knew Merril was a coward at heart. What I feared most was what he would try to do to me after our confrontation—not what he might do or say during it.

Other women had fled the FLDS, but I was unaware of any who had made it out with all their children, nor did I know any who were ever granted full custody in court. No one had ever fled from a man as powerful within the FLDS as Merril Jessop. In taking on Merril, I knew I was taking on the cult.

Most women who fled would willingly leave all their children behind, or just take the smaller ones and leave the older ones at home with the understanding that if they were allowed to take half their children, they wouldn't fight for the rest. I did know of one woman who got all of her children out, but when the FLDS came after her, she sent all of them back and relinquished custody. Another woman escaped with all of her children and won temporary custody. But then she died suddenly from a brain aneurysm in the grocery store and all of her children were sent back. We were told her death was sent from God as punishment.

I had made it further than any woman I'd ever known. If meeting with Merril was the next price I had to pay for our freedom, so be it.

I told Arthur I would meet his father in the produce section of Smith's the next morning. Arthur made all the arrangements and came with me. When we walked into the store, I was approached by one of the undercover police. He told me not to worry, I'd be safe.

Arthur lit into me. "What are you doing? You set a trap for my father!"

"Arthur, your father gave me no other option."

"I am not going to let you do this to my father," he said as he headed toward the entrance of the market to warn Merril.

Every nerve in my body was electrified.

When Merril walked into the store he met Arthur and the police. He was served with the protection order. Merril insisted he be allowed to speak. The police agreed under the condition that they be close by.

Merril kept his voice low. His eyes were on fire.

"What you have done is inexcusable," he said. "You'll never get away with this. If you know what's best for you, you'll stop right now."

I knew better than to argue with him. I let him rant.

He insisted that the custody case I filed in Utah would be thrown out of court or transferred to Arizona. "You'll never win because the children don't want to be with you. They all want to be with me. You have yourself in a position where you'll never see your children again."

I felt calm in the face of his wrath. I knew that more than anything else, he wanted to feel my fear. I would not give him that pleasure.

"Merril, I think a judge will look at this whole case and not just your side."

This made him even angrier.

"Carolyn, your very existence is on the line with the course you are pursuing."

"I would rather be dead than live one more day like I did for the last seventeen years."

I could see him stiffen. He attacked me for trapping him. "It's not very smart of you to play these games. I came here thinking you had enough character not to do something like this."

I didn't care how long he went on. The police were watching his tirade and finally told Merril he had had enough time.

"She's blown this all out of proportion. There's no reason for an order of protection," he said.

"You can make that case in court in two weeks," the officer said. "If it's not necessary, it will be removed."

Merril lashed at me again. "See what you've done! We can't talk to each other for two more weeks!"

I had no intention of ever speaking to him again. But I was concerned that he might succeed in getting the case transferred to Arizona.

Two weeks later Merril and I faced off again in a Salt Lake City courtroom. Merril had retained Rodney Parker, an attorney who had made his fortune defending the FLDS in court. Parker acted as though this was all a big joke, and maybe to him it was.

But I think I caught him off guard when he looked at me for the first time. I didn't look like some wack job. Women who fled the FLDS were always portrayed as totally insane and under the influence of the devil, and while Parker could tell I was scared, he also realized I wasn't crazy.

The judge read the complaint. I think she felt like the circus had just rolled into her courtroom and was unfurling its tents.

Rodney Parker argued that Arizona should have jurisdiction over this case. The judge corrected him and said that Arizona could release it to Utah and she would request that. Parker did not seem prepared for this. He started arguing about the order of protection.

My attorney made a motion to speak with the judge. He told her Merril had threatened me by saying my "existence was on the line" in front of three police officers standing nearby. Parker looked stricken and turned to Merril and started talking. He hated being unprepared in court, but Merril had obviously not been completely forthcoming with him.

A few days later I learned that my case would be heard in Utah. A big win.

Dan Fisher helped me get my children into public schools. (Bryson was too young and Betty and Arthur weren't emotionally ready.) We both thought that even if it was only for a few weeks, connecting with other children and wearing normal clothes would help normalize them. It also would help me gauge where they were academically and what grade would be appropriate for them come fall.

Betty and Arthur refused to give up their FLDS clothing. Betty was incensed that her siblings were going to dress in worldly ways and go to worldly schools. She interfered whenever possible. She was angry, argumentative, and mean to me. I finally asked my younger sister Karen to let her stay at her house. I couldn't handle the stress or problems Betty was creating for the rest of us. Karen was ten years younger than I and my full sister. She was in an arranged marriage but she and her husband both fled.

I felt that I was finally standing on solid ground—until my attorney told me that Merril should be allowed to have visiting rights with my children. I didn't like the idea, but Doug told me that Merril had rights as their father and if I kept him away, it could work against me in court. That might have been true in a more normal case, but in reality, Merril was a danger to my children. I should have pushed harder.

Doug White had been recommended by a group called Tapestry Against Polygamy. He had represented women pro bono in polygamy cases, but the stakes had not been nearly as high as in mine. Most of the women he'd worked with were from smaller polygamist communities that were afraid of the law. Often when these women fled, that was it. No one came after them. Those who ended up in court often found that the men didn't show up. Most of the cases he won, he won by default. But he had never handled a case like mine.

I later learned that White's view was that a man should always be allowed to see his children, no matter what he's done. If I'd known that at the time, I would have found another attorney.

Arrangements were made for Merril to see the children for an hour in a nearby park. My brother-in-law Robert agreed to supervise the visitation.

By now it had been six weeks since we'd escaped. One might think that since he was fighting so hard for custody, he might have spent some time with the children. But that was not the case. Merril never cared about our children. He cared about making an example out of me so other women didn't make a break for freedom the way I had.

Merril arrived at the park with Barbara. She pranced around the picnic table, seemingly delighted. Merril shouted at Robert for the entire hour, attacking him for his role in helping me settle into my new life. "If you knew what was good for you, you'd send her back right away and stop participating in this nonsense," Merril said.

I was pushing Harrison in his stroller and walking around the perimeter of the park with my sister Annette. "Barbara is thinking of all the ways she can punish you when she gets you back in her clutches," Annette said.

"She should save herself the time," I replied. "I'm never going to be under that bitch's power again."

Barbara was watching us walk around the park. I think she finally realized that she had no power over me anymore. "She can't stand it that you're so happy right now and she can't hurt your children," Annette said.

I realized she was right. Barbara couldn't hurt my children or me—not that day, not ever.

When Merril said goodbye to the children he told them to "stay faithful."

He didn't kiss or hug them, but he never had.

Several days later one of Dan's friends drove into his yard and saw several of my children playing. He stopped the car and asked ten-year-old Patrick how he was doing. Patrick's face lit up in a big smile. "We're living in hell!" he replied automatically. His words said one thing, his smile another. Patrick, like my other kids, was having the time of his life. Leenie kept a cupboard full of cookies and snack foods. Her freezer was loaded with ice cream. The day we first arrived she said my children were welcome to help themselves anytime they were hungry. She also told them when they came over for a snack that they could give her a hug.

This was a gift Leenie gave both to my children and to me. I had to learn how to hug my children again after we escaped. In Merril Jessop's family, it was against the family laws to hug and kiss our children, so nobody did it. When Arthur was a baby, I hugged and kissed him constantly. But his older brothers and sisters taunted him about this until he started to cry. My hugging and kissing him was causing him so much pain, I stopped. When Betty was a small child, she would never allow me to hug or kiss her because she knew her other siblings would mock her.

It's hard to explain how routine an abnormal life can become. But over time, I simply stopped hugging and kissing my children. Of all my eight children, I probably held Harrison the most because when he was in a spasm it was one of the few things that helped. I held my children when I nursed them and felt the miracle of that bond, but once they became toddlers, our physical contact stopped. For a time that broke my heart, but then so much of life crushed down on top of me that this one loss got buried under the rubble and I never gave it much thought until Leenie told me how important it was to show affection to my children. Holding them again helped reconnect me to life in a tender way.

Dan and Leenie invited us to join them for a week in San Diego, where they had a beach house. My children had never seen the ocean and were excited at the thought. Betty refused to come with us because we were being so wicked and because we told her that she couldn't wear her FLDS clothing on the beach. So she stayed behind, but it was okay because she was actually doing better at Karen's house. It seemed to be a relief for her not to feel responsible for keeping all of her brothers and sisters in line with FLDS doctrine.

Dan arranged to have some of his family and friends who were coming on the trip take turns driving my family. That made it much easier on me. He even had someone to help me with Harrison. Dan's continual kindness to me was miraculous. When we got to San Diego we had two rooms in a hotel that was down the beach from Dan's home. The kitchenette was stocked with food, so I wouldn't have to shop. One of the rooms had a sliding glass door that opened directly onto the beach.

The moment we awakened, we put on our swimsuits and my kids raced through the soft sand to splash and play at the water's edge.

Merrilee and Bryson ran up and down the beach chasing sea gulls. They were still at that wondrous age when they believed that if they just ran a little faster they could wrap their arms around a big bird.

Bryson was almost two. He couldn't talk a lot, but one of the words he said very well was *ducks*.

He toddled up and down the beach on his chubby legs, waving his arms and shouting, "Ducks, ducks, ducks."

Merrilee was busy building princess sand castles. She was just about to turn six and princesses were her new discovery. The week we escaped she watched a *Cinderella* video for the first time. Merrilee watched it so many times that the tape finally broke. Everything in her life now revolved around being a princess.

Patrick and Andrew used their imaginations to build forts out of sand and play games on the beach. They were still scared of the water because in the FLDS you are not allowed to go near it. None of my children knew how to swim, so they'd only wade up to their knees.

I spent three relaxing days with my children on the beach and at the hotel. At night I'd go up to Dan and Leenie's beach house to be with the adults. It was wonderful to be able to drink wine, laugh, eat, and talk. I hadn't socialized like that before. Dan and Leenie brought a lot of their married children along on the trip, so their beach house was happy, noisy, and fun. Arthur, who was fifteen, and LuAnne, who was eleven, spent most of their time there with the older children. These were the most carefree days of childhood they'd ever had.

I had never known this kind of happiness was possible.

# I Meet the Attorney General

Shortly after we returned from San Diego, Merrilee turned six and we had a princess birthday party for her. It was the first party she had ever had in her life.

Even though birthday celebrations were practically taboo in the FLDS, over the years I'd given my children small presents on the sly. When my older children—Arthur, Betty, and LuAnne—were young, I was able to get away with making them a birthday cake. But none of my kids had ever had a genuine birthday party that celebrated their being who they are. As the cult became more extremist, anything that even hinted at making someone feel special on his or her birthday became strictly off-limits. Even compliments were banned. Warren Jeffs taught that it was unacceptable to acknowledge compliments. A person had to rebuff the praise or say something like, "It's all because of my priesthood head."

Dan's wife, Leenie, had the same birthday as Merrilee, so the celebration was even more of a bash because it was for both of them. Their house was decorated with balloons and streamers. There were tables full of food and piles of presents. Jolene had found a princess gown among her children's Halloween costumes. Merrilee was ecstatic. This was unimaginable joy for her, and for my other children, too.

We all sang "Happy Birthday" before the candles were lit. One side of the white cake with pink frosting had candles for Leenie, the other for Merrilee.

My daughter was radiant and opened her presents in amazement. My children had never been in toy stores. The younger ones had been so stripped of worldly things such as dolls and stuffed animals that these presents were unbelievable not only because of what they were but also because Merrilee knew they were for her.

This was an unforgettable moment for me. My daughter was happy. Every adult in that room cherished her. I had never been able to experience what would be an ordinary joy to most families: a six-year-old's birthday party with family and friends. Laughter, singing, and silliness washed over me like a stream of love. I could simply enjoy watching my dear little girl get to be a fairy-tale princess. I was free to be happy. I could do things for and with my children that I'd never been allowed to do before in their lives.

Merril was furious when he learned about Merrilee's birthday party from Betty. He was unhappy because he did not have the power to prevent me from taking the children to San Diego. It was remarkable, though, to feel how much space opened up inside me when I didn't have to fear Merril's punishment anymore. I was so accustomed to being afraid that I had no way of gauging how much of me that fear consumed.

For the first time in my life I could put my children to bed at night and know they were safe. No one could wake them up and make them go upstairs for prayers and then abuse them. I could feed them breakfast in the morning and not worry that later, when my back was turned, someone would punish them for eating.

Merrilee's birthday party opened my eyes to something I'd been trained not to do: have fun with my children. Every time I did something enjoyable with my children in Merril's family, I was criticized for it or told it had created a problem. This went on for seventeen years, whether I took my children to the park, baked cookies, or played games with them outside. I was conditioned to believe that if I did anything fun with them, I'd be made to pay and pay and pay. As the years went by, I ceased doing the things that would cause trouble.

But I was free now. I made myself do things with my children so I would learn how to break out of the cycle of fear that had been cemented around my soul.

Someone gave us some McDonald's dollars, and that, as simple as it sounds, was a challenge for me. I knew I could do it—no one was going to punish me for this—but I was still afraid. I had to keep telling myself, "Carolyn, it's okay, it's okay, you can do this."

We did it. We went to McDonald's. But when I got home I was a nervous wreck. My reaction shook me up. I put my kids to bed and stood in a hot shower to calm down. My body, my reflexes, and my instincts were all programmed for fear. I could not undo overnight the damage that had been done to my psyche over many years. The only way over was through—I knew that—but it was still debilitating and stressful. All I could do was face the fear and keep going.

But fear was still all around me. My family had to pay a price for my freedom. My sister Linda almost paid with her life. Someone in the community must have known I went to her house the night before I escaped and assumed she was in some way complicit.

Some weeks after my escape, she took her family hiking in a remote location in her truck. On her way there she lost her steering. This was surprising because she was driving slowly and the road was clear. Fortunately, she was able to maneuver her truck off the road without any of her five children being hurt. When the mechanic came he told her someone had tampered with the steering wheel.

I had to face off against Merril again in court in June. But his attorney was prepared this time and managed to deftly turn the tide against me with the help of the lawyer I thought was going to protect me.

The issue was custody. Merril's attorney presented him as the good and steady all-American guy on *Father Knows Best*. Yes, he had a lot of children, but he cared about them all.

The two attorneys asked the judge if they could meet to try to work out a deal. I didn't quite know why that was happening. The judge put a time limit on their meeting and the rest of us sat and waited.

When my attorney, Doug White, came back, he told me they'd

reached a deal. I would get temporary custody, but Merril was going to get full visitation rights. The protective order would remain in place. Merril agreed to pay for counseling for his daughters—which he'd opposed—but only if the therapist was neutral about polygamy. In other words, the therapist was to be an advocate for the children and keep whatever feelings he or she had about polygamy out of the counseling sessions.

I felt blindsided. My attorney had rolled over and handed Merril nearly everything he'd demanded. I told Doug I didn't need as much protection as my children did. He said that I didn't have any grounds on which to prove Merril should not be allowed to see his children unsupervised.

"I have fought these cases before," my attorney said, "and men will work hard to get the right for visitation, then once they get it they drop the whole thing and never see the kids. It is not something that is worth fighting for because it really isn't an issue."

It was an issue to me—I felt we had been sold down the river. At the time I was unaware that I had the right to reject the deal my attorney made. I had lived so long without rights that I didn't understand the ones I now had.

The attorneys outlined their deal to the judge. She asked me if I was in agreement with this. I was in such a state of shock that I stood before her feeling numb and dazed. I had no idea I could converse with the judge, so I just said that yes, I agreed with the deal.

What I learned later was that the judge discounted my allegations of abuse against Merril because I agreed in court to let him have unsupervised visitations. This made me look like either a bad mother or a liar. My credibility was shattered. Legally, I could now lose my children.

A guardian ad litem was assigned to this case, but that had the potential to work against me because at this point all my children were saying they wanted to return to Merril. They believed there would be terrible repercussions against them if they sided with me. They knew that in FLDS society their father held all the power, and in their eyes that made me powerless. I hadn't been allowed to parent them in a traditionally loving and nurturing way when I was living with Merril. They knew I was their mother, of course, but they had others.

When the first meeting with the guardian ad litem was a few days away, Merril pulled out all the stops. Two of his older daughters, Esther and Merrilyn, found a way to get onto Dan Fisher's property and find my Betty and LuAnne. They took them for a walk down the road and showed them how to give themselves hickies on their arms. Two days later when they met with the guardian ad litem they said the hickies were from my hitting them. The guardian knew it was a lie. I found out about this when Patrick and Andrew showed me how Betty had taught them to put hickies on themselves. She said that Esther had taught her how to do it on Merril's orders. He wanted all of the children to give themselves hickies and then tell the guardian ad litem that I was hurting them.

As the weeks wore on, I became distraught about what was happening in the custody case. I knew Merril would spend unlimited sums of money to destroy my credibility in court and convince a judge that I was an unfit mother—the only way he could win sole custody in Utah.

Dan Fisher was upset that my case was going so badly. He knew that unless I got a first-rate attorney, I would lose custody of my children. We looked at one of the major family law firms in town. The attorney we spoke with was blunt: the firm did not want to take on a cult. The FLDS had been in court before and won their cases by financially wearing out their opponents. "This cult will dump a million dollars into this case before they'll walk away from it," the attorney said. "Carolyn is a hole in the dike for them, and there is no way they will ever let her get these kids."

Dan said he'd pay my legal bills. But then we got a big break. Utah's attorney general, Mark Shurtleff, agreed to meet with me. I had been meeting regularly with the investigator from Shurtleff's office about the extremism and abuse that had taken hold in the FLDS. But Dan and I both felt the attorney general needed to become more actively involved. Now we had our chance.

Dan and his brother Shem came with me. I brought a two-page

list summarizing the abuse that was occurring in the FLDS because of Warren Jeffs. I organized my thoughts and composed myself. I did not want Mark Shurtleff to think I was some insane woman who'd grabbed her children and fled in the middle of the night.

When I shook his hand I looked him directly in the eye and asked him how much time I had. "Thirty minutes," he said. We sat around a table in a conference room. Dan said we were here because of the human rights violations that were taking place within the FLDS community. He said he felt the attorney general's office had to intervene.

I began by giving each person at the table a copy of my two-page list of abuses. It delineated the numerous marriages I had witnessed among under-age girls and the emotional devastation this had caused. I described how women were taken from their husbands and arbitrarily given to other men.

I told how young boys were trained as spies to go into FLDS homes and report back to Warren. I explained how Warren had terrorized young children by having animals tortured to death in front of them. I told them about the day all the dogs were destroyed and how Warren taught that a society that treated animals humanely was corrupt and had turned away from God.

It was chilling to recount what had become routine in my life. I talked about the teenage boys who were kicked out of the cult, dumped on highways, and told never to return. In a polygamous culture, boys are disposable, I told the attorney general. Sometimes they'd be kicked out on trumped-up charges—exposure to CDs or movies or kissing a girl. More often than not, they'd simply be told one afternoon that they had to be gone the next morning. (Dan Fisher's foundation for these boys knows the names of four hundred who have been summarily expelled.)

The attorney general was riveted. He asked me question after question, seeking more detail and specifics. We were there for well over thirty minutes; every so often he would ask his assistant to cancel his next appointment.

I explained that for seventeen years, I was married to one of the most powerful men in the FLDS community. I knew Warren Jeffs and how he behaved. He was consistent, predictable, and to my mind very dangerous.

Two and a half hours later, when our meeting was finished, Mark's aloof, professional demeanor had shifted to one of sheer outrage. He stood up and addressed everyone at the table.

"This situation is really serious, and it has the potential of becoming a mass suicide. We have got to pull more help in on this situation immediately. We need to collaborate with the state of Arizona and pull in the feds."

The meeting was ending and we hadn't even talked about my custody case. Dan jumped in and insisted we focus on it. I was the first woman who had ever taken the FLDS to court for custody of her children. Most of the time, if a woman left, she did so knowing she might not be able to get all her children out. The reality of abandoning some of her children was the price a woman had to be willing to pay for her freedom.

Dan told Shurtleff that Merril had hired one of the highest-paid attorneys in the state to fight me. Dan and I knew that if Merril could win his case against me, no woman would ever again try. A representative who was at the meeting from Child Protective Services agreed completely.

Shurtleff shook his head in disbelief. Then he said that my case was going to be a high-profile one and he would find an attorney smart enough to protect my children. He was true to his word and moved fast. A few days later he put me in touch with a former judge, Lisa Jones, who had done custody cases for years and knew family law inside and out. She was now working for a major law firm and agreed to take my case pro bono.

Mark Shurtleff is a Mormon but has no ties to fundamentalism. He later told me that for years people had come into his office complaining about polygamy. But state officials had always warned him that if he went after polygamists, it would cost him his career. Even though polygamy is a felony, he would be perceived as persecuting religion.

Mark also told me that he didn't sleep much the night after our meeting because he knew there was no turning back. He knew he had to deal with polygamy. Now when we give speeches together he says, "After I talked with Carolyn, I realized that I had been elected to do a job and I couldn't ignore my responsibilities, even if it resulted in costing me my career."

His involvement was a turning point for my custody case. Mark began collaborating with Arizona's attorney general. I met with investigators from that office, too.

I met with Lisa Jones a few weeks later. She's a small woman with a big presence. With her short red hair, she can come across as a firecracker. But the truth is that she's much more of a heat-seeking missile that aims right at her target and rarely misses. While she's tough, she was easy to work with and became my rock. Lisa told me at our first meeting that she didn't believe in coincidences. She had planned on doing some writing and asked her firm to reduce her workload. She'd just managed to free up her schedule when Mark Shurtleff called and told her about me. Lisa said that after she spoke with him she understood that the way had been cleared for her not to write but to take my case.

Merril's attorney, Rod Parker, knew he'd be playing hardball now that Lisa Jones was involved. She was no pushover. When Lisa called Parker and reported another case of Merril's abuse, Parker told Merril to cut it out—he could not pull these stunts any longer. Parker knew that with competent legal representation I would win in court. Merril and his minions began to back off.

It began to feel as if the tide had turned in my favor.

# Shelter

**N**ow that Merril had visitation rights with my children, it was easier than ever for him to fill them with more lies. He began telling them that Dan Fisher was an immoral man who wanted to have sex with me until he was sick of it and then would throw me into the streets. This was terrifying to them because they believed if that happened, I'd return to their father.

By this point, my children liked being with me but were still afraid of living in the outside world. They didn't think I had the ability to take care of them. I reached out to Lisa, and we agreed that my kids had to feel like our new life was for real and that it could be maintained. The key to this would be finding a place of our own to live.

The quickest way to accomplish this was to go through the shelter system. The battered women's shelter in West Jordan was my jumping-off point. The social workers there knew all the options for assistance and would help me find permanent, subsidized housing. I put my name on the waiting list and was told it would take about a month before we could move in. Dan supported me fully.

I enrolled my younger children and Betty in summer school to help them start catching up. They were seriously behind academically.

What sabotaged my hoped-for achievement of normalcy were Merril's visits. He was permitted to take the children every other weekend. He'd collect them for the five-hour drive to Colorado City on Friday night. It seemed to take my children two weeks to unwind from the visits to Colorado City. They'd be tense and argumentative when they came home. On Sunday when they returned they sat down to the huge meal I'd made—roast beef, potatoes, gravy, hot rolls, vegetables, and dessert. But no one touched a thing. I knew Merril didn't feed them well and couldn't imagine what was wrong. I put the food in the refrigerator.

Merrilee finally told me what was going on: Merril had ordered them to fast and pray all day on Sunday that they'd be returned to their father. I called my attorney and made a complaint. Under the visitation rules, the children were not to be dragged into the custody fight. Merril wasn't even supposed to talk to them about our case.

The next day, Betty and LuAnne launched a verbal attack on me. They accused me of having bad feelings toward my sister wives and said I needed to learn how to forgive. I was told that I was trying to drag them to hell and see them destroyed only to satisfy my own self-ish emotions. Both of them accused me of being the abuser and claimed it was I who had always been abusive to them, not their father. They said I'd told the court that Merril had starved them for several months. This was news to me, because it was untrue. There was plenty of abuse to report in court; I didn't need to make any up.

"You're an apostate, owned by the devil!" Betty said. "He wants your soul and he wants ours."

"You can't be our mother because you put yourself under the power of the devil," LuAnne wailed. "None of us wants to be with you!"

It was awful to feel them lash out this way. I called Lisa again to make another complaint. She told me to write down everything they were saying. She also called Rod Parker, Merril's attorney, and com-plained to him about the fast. Parker was put on notice that if Mer-ril's abuse toward the children did not end, he'd be called back into court.

Parker said that Merril was eager to have Bryson for visitations, too. Bryson was nearly two. If I didn't allow him access to Bryson, Parker said I could expect to be back in court. I was still nursing Bryson and planned to do so until his second birthday. I usually nursed my babies for eighteen months, but Bryson had been so premature that I wanted to give him an additional boost. Since I was still nursing him, I couldn't send him off for those weekends with Merril. Being deprived of him infuriated Merril.

We were at the shelter for five weeks. The breakthrough came when a woman who knew what we were up against, Rhoda Thomson, raised some money to help me get a roof over our heads: two trailers that combined to give us five bedrooms and four bathrooms. We had a beautiful front yard and space out back where the children could roam and play.

When Merril heard about our new living arrangements, he was furious. I think he hoped that I'd be forced from the shelter into the streets and then back to him. He couldn't have been more wrong.

# Our First Christmas

**M**aking ends meet was tough. My monthly income from Social Security and SSI was $1,500, which after I paid my rent left $150 for gas. The homeless coordinator who was helping me gave me $60 a month in gas vouchers. I had $700 a month in food stamps to feed the nine of us. I had $80 in state financial aid each month to use for everything else. I could stretch a dollar from a dime and I made the best of it, but we often fell short. Despite the frustration and hardships, though, I finally was living in my own place.

My brother, Arthur, paid the insurance on my van and for my cell phone. I wore donated used clothing, and the Rotary Club spent $100 to buy clothes for my grade-school children. I was still waiting for my Section 8 voucher to come through to pay for housing; I was told that could take up to six months.

Christmas was coming, and we had never celebrated as a family before. I remembered how my mother had once had a renegade Christmas that my father came home and ruined. I hadn't planned on doing anything special until one of Dan's daughters-in-law, Tammy, said she wanted to help me with our first Christmas.

The whole idea of spending money to decorate a tree struck me as a little weird, but I was certainly willing to give it a try. Several of the people Tammy knew who were going to help provide presents came over to get a list of my children's names, ages, sizes, and ideas for gifts they'd like to have.

I know it sounds strange, but I was at a complete loss when they asked me what my kids wanted. My children rarely ever asked for anything. In Colorado City, I wasn't allowed to give them anything beyond absolute necessities. The women were surprised that I was so clueless about what my own children wanted. They helped me come up with some ideas.

A few weeks before Christmas vacation, my children went to Colorado City for three days. When they came home, I knew instantly that something was different. They seemed more agitated and upset. There was a lot of anger and fighting among them, which is always a sign that something's wrong. Betty was acting smug and self-righteous. Merrilee finally blurted out, "Mother, we were not allowed to eat anything the entire time we were at Father's."

I froze. "Why?" I asked.

"We had to fast and pray for three days. We want you to die so we can go back to Father." Merrilee and Andrew were allowed to eat a few crackers and one apple during the three-day fast, but the older children were allowed only water.

My outrage knew no bounds. I called my attorney and made another complaint. Merril's attorney denied that my children were being made to fast and pray for my death.

At the time, none of the other kids would talk about praying for my death, but they did later on and now speak openly about it. Back then, however, they accused Merrilee of lying. Poor Merrilee told me that she was scared because she knew Betty would get her in trouble with Merril. Betty and I had a big fight over that.

I called Child Protective Services and reported Merril's abuse. A caseworker came over to our house and questioned the children about their visitation. I was not present. They were all willing to talk except Merrilee, who was afraid of the caseworker. But no one told him the truth. Betty insisted that I was beating all of them, not their father. She claimed they were only safe with their father and that he would never starve them.

The caseworker sat down with me afterward. He told me he was sure I was telling the truth and that my children had been deprived of food, but they were too frightened to admit it. The caseworker did not believe I was abusing them. The catch was that he was allowed to write his reports based only on what he *heard* and *saw,* not on what he *believed.* So he felt that under the circumstances, it was in my best interest if he wrote nothing about the interviews. He said that if the children had shown signs of starvation it would be a different matter, but they all looked healthy and well fed, so there was nothing he could do.

My children had left for another visitation when I went into the pantry to get something to feed Harrison. When I opened the small walk-in closet that served as a pantry, I found it was empty. It had been well stocked with snacks and donated canned food. All of the snack food—crackers, pretzels, and chips—was gone. It all had left the house in my children's suitcases.

I sank to the floor in sobs. Anguish rolled out of me in waves. I pounded the tiles of the floor with my fist. I had no way to protect my children. Merril could take them, starve them, and hurt them. I had taken huge risks to win our freedom, and yet my children were still at the mercy of a monster. This was the lowest moment of my life. I had no way of making it financially. I had left friends and family who would never speak to me again. I felt like I had nothing to show for all that I'd endured. I felt absolutely powerless. It was one thing to be subjected to Merril's reign of terror when there was no access to outside help. But now I had legal representation. I'd been to court, and yet I was still powerless to protect the children I loved beyond life. They were all I had and all that mattered to me. Despite everything I had done, Merril could still ruin their lives, confidence, and promise. My outrage reached the stratosphere.

When my children came home right before Christmas Merrilee told me they were forced to fast again. None of the food they'd taken came back in their suitcases. It was all gone. I called my attorney, but she said there was nothing she could do if the children insisted it hadn't happened when the court-appointed guardian asked them about it.

The kids had just been back for a few hours when the family who was doing our Christmas called. When could they bring presents and put them under the tree? My children were so tense, I thought the presents might provide a happy focus, so we did it right away. In the FLDS, we never celebrated Christmas, so this would be a happy first for them.

When the doorbell rang, Santa Claus entered in full regalia with one of his elves. He walked into our small living room with his bells jingling. "Ho, ho, ho," he said. "I've been looking for you children for all these years, and I've finally found you!"

My eight children were mesmerized. Even Harrison seemed transfixed. Betty was off to one side, but she was clearly taking in everything. The little ones were wide-eyed and beaming.

Santa had more to say. "You have all been such good children, so I had to be sure I brought plenty of gifts to make up for all the gifts I didn't bring you when I couldn't find you!"

Santa invited the younger children to sit in his lap and tell him what they wanted for Christmas. They didn't have any idea of what to say. None of us had ever been part of a world where wishes were acknowledged and sometimes dreams came true. Being cherished or feeling special was not something we'd experienced.

Santa explained that he had brought so many presents that he only had room to bring along one elf and Mrs. Claus to help him. And the reindeer had had to stay back at the barn because he needed to come to our house in two cars instead of just his sleigh.

Mrs. Claus began bringing in bags of presents from the car. Santa told my children they could help put the gifts under the tree. Merrilee's eyes looked like they were about to cartwheel out of her head with excitement. Patrick and Andrew were fascinated and incredulous. Even Betty began to get interested in the presents when she saw how many were arriving. She started to help Santa make extra space for them. When Patrick thought no one was looking, he grabbed a big plate of sugar cookies that Santa had brought and wolfed them down. I noticed that Patrick kept his eyes on Betty, wary that she might catch him eating. Merril had instructed the children to fast until the next day. But Betty stayed engaged with Santa, and Patrick finished the cookies.

As soon as Santa left, my children began clamoring to open their presents. I told them Santa had come early to our house because he had so many packages for us, but that we were going to wait for three more days until Christmas before opening them. My strategy was simple: I wanted to extend their excitement and anticipation as long as I could to help counter the trauma of their visitations.

Betty was outraged about our Christmas tree. We never would have had such a thing in Colorado City. Every time she came into the room, she turned off the lights on it. "Christmas is a lie. You just planned this to make us want to be with you and not our father." Then she told her brothers and sisters that I was trying to buy their loyalty and that they should go ahead and open their presents.

I was very firm. Any present that was opened was going back to Santa. I didn't argue with Betty, I just laid down the rules. I knew that unless I stood up to her, she would continue to sabotage me the way Merril had. It got easier with time, and Christmas was a help because the other children were so eager and excited about their presents. That undercut Betty's power.

That night I put eight very happy and excited children to bed. Although she never would have admitted it, Betty was as excited about getting Christmas presents as everyone else. There were piles of presents beneath the tree waiting to be opened. Our house felt festive and warm.

The three days before Christmas were full of anticipation. My children spent every moment sitting around the tree, looking at presents, shaking them, and imagining what might be inside. "Just one gift, can't we open just one?" I smiled but remained resolute. No presents until Christmas morning.

On December 25, at 6 A.M., we unwrapped the first present. But that sounds more orderly than it was. Christmas morning was the happiest chaos of our lives. When I went into the living room, the kids were ripping into their presents. I didn't know so much happiness could exist. Our little family had never shared such boundless joy. There were smiles and shrieks and laughter and exclamations—"Oh, wow, look at this!"

Betty was very excited about her presents and shocked that she had received so many. Merrilee got more princess-related gifts and was ecstatic. There were a lot of presents for Harrison, which he couldn't open by himself, so each child took a turn helping him open something.

It was miraculous. Hope was alive again inside me and triumphed over the despair I'd felt when I broke down in sobs and pounded on the floor, wondering if we were ever going to be better off than we had been before.

Yes, we were. I had risked all our lives for freedom. My gift that morning was the knowledge that it had not been a mistake.

# Last Custody Case

**B**efore Christmas vacation was over and my kids were back in school, I got sick. It felt like the flu on top of all the morning sickness I had ever had. I was so weak and disoriented that I could barely walk across the room. I was vomiting and running fevers.

It was almost impossible to marshal enough energy to cook for my family.

Betty decreed that her brothers and sisters could not help me. She insisted that since I'd taken them away from their father, I was responsible for all the work. My sickness was proof to her that God was answering Merril's prayers. I think that her strategy was to make things so difficult for me that I would have no choice but to cave in and return to Merril.

I was sick for a month. There was no way I could keep up with the laundry. I still cooked simple things for Harrison but came to rely on prepared foods for everyone else. Taking my children to six different counseling appointments each week in addition to Harrison's doctor and therapy visits kept me on the run. It was also becoming a full-time job staying on top of the paperwork required to keep our welfare checks coming.

I was sinking fast. Life on the outside was so hard.

I had started seeing a therapist myself after leaving the shelter: Larry Bill, who worked with domestic violence victims. We talked for a while about my history. I told him that everything would be a lot better if I could just shake this flu.

Larry looked at me. "Carolyn, you don't have the flu. You have post-traumatic stress disorder." I had never heard of PTSD before. He told me what it was. Physical and mental symptoms can develop that last for years. It's common in combat veterans, survivors of sexual trauma and domestic violence, and anyone who has endured relentless stress or been through a natural catastrophe such as a hurricane, earthquake, or floods.

Larry asked me if I was having nightmares. I said they'd started the third day after I escaped and never stopped. They were often about Merril or Barbara or someone in the family attacking my children. Other times the focus was on my being forced to do something in the cult I didn't want to do. Nightmares are a classic component of PTSD. Larry said it was a chronic condition that could be managed and treated but would never completely go away.

I felt blindsided. PTSD on top of everything else? How could I take care of everyone if I was sick? I asked him how I was supposed to cope.

He told me to stay as functional as possible. He couldn't tell me when I would get better because every case was different. But he stressed that the more I surrendered to PTSD, the worse it would get. I had to fight this and it wouldn't be easy, but he made it clear to me that he'd be by my side.

For six weeks I had been crawling to the bathroom to vomit. What kept me going was the thought that in a few more days I'd be better. Now I was being told I had a long-term condition with no end in sight.

My head was spinning as I walked to the parking lot. I tried to put the key in the ignition and was shaking so badly the keys dropped to the floor. I was coming undone. My biggest fear was that if Merril learned I had a mental disorder I would lose custody of my children.

I had barely been making it when I was well. Now this. Without my health I could lose everything. If I lost my children there would be no reason to remain on earth.

Then an image came back to me. I remembered being in the accident on Black Ridge, feeling frozen and close to death. I remembered being claimed by a fatigue so deep that I wanted to lie down in a snowdrift and sleep forever. What had kept me going then was that I knew if I did, I would never see Arthur again.

If I could find the strength then, I could find it again. Beneath everything, I still wanted to live.

I had to get hold of myself. I would do it five minutes at a time, fewer if necessary. The big picture was too scary. Minutes were not as bad.

I vowed to tell no one about the PTSD. No one. Everything I said to another person found its way back to Merril. I couldn't risk him finding out I had PTSD.

A plan formed. I would get my children to school and ferry them to their appointments. If we all showed up for everything, no one would get suspicious. I could cook and clean in five-minute intervals, then rest.

I picked up my car key from the floor and turned on the ignition. It took several tries. I took a few more breaths and started the car.

As soon as I got home I started my five-minute plan. Cook for five minutes. Rest. Clean for five minutes. Stop. It was slow going, but when I went to bed that night I felt I had at least tried.

PTSD was a reality I could face five minutes at a time. But another reality slammed into me hard and fast: I was out of money. I learned that the Section 8 vouchers I needed for housing costs were now on an eighteen-month hold because of limited funding. I was out of cash. The money I had saved while I was living at Dan's was gone. I knew if I went to him he would help me, but I hated asking him for everything I needed, and I didn't want to run to him every month. I was determined to do everything possible before going to him. But I could not pay my utility bills and didn't know what to do.

One morning after I dropped my children at school, Patrick and Andrew came right back out and said there was something for me in the office. The boys stayed with Harrison while I went in. Patty, a woman in the office who always gave Merrilee lots of hugs, handed me a card and said the children's teachers wanted to do something special for me. I thanked her and asked her to thank the teachers. I walked to the van, card in hand.

Inside the card was close to two hundred dollars with a note from the teachers saying that they all admired my courage. Shaking with joy, I went right to the post office to mail my utility bill. The next hurdle was a notice from the welfare office that my case would be closed the next day unless I returned several forms to them within twenty-four hours. All the forms had to be signed and dated by someone at each of my children's schools—all five of them.

A storm had moved into the valley and it was starting to snow on top of the few feet of snow we already had. I called the welfare office and said I had a handicapped child and a toddler and I couldn't do this in twenty-four hours by myself. I asked for an extension. I was told there was no way. If I didn't make the deadline, my case would be closed. Then I would have to reapply. I figured it would take months to get my benefits again.

The next day I cancelled every appointment I had and headed out into the snowstorm with Bryson, Harrison, and Harrison's wheelchair to make my rounds. I was still struggling with PTSD. My five-minute plan wasn't much help on a day like this.

Harrison's immune system was compromised from his hormone therapy. I worried that he would get sick. It was blindingly cold. At each school I had to take the wheelchair out, set it up, settle Harrison into it and bundle him up, and then get Bryson from his car seat.

When I got to my brother's to fax in the paperwork, I was shivering so much my teeth would not stop chattering. When I woke up the next morning I had a hard time breathing. I had a fever and knew I had pneumonia. I couldn't get out of bed. LuAnne started taking care of Harrison once she realized how seriously sick I was. Betty even started making meals and doing some dishes.

For the first time, my kids were worried. By Monday morning, I was still burning up with fever. I was too sick to call anyone and too afraid that if I did, someone might find out about my PTSD. Merril was already accusing me of being mentally ill. I knew that some women who tried to flee polygamy ended up locked into mental institutions and had their children taken away from them. I would risk anything to avoid that fate.

I told my children I was too sick to take them to school. I didn't even have the strength to call and cancel my appointments. Amazingly, Betty and LuAnne started bringing me tea. I was able to sip the tea, but I couldn't eat.

Tuesday morning was no different. But Betty didn't want to miss any more school. She was worried about keeping her grades up and called Mitzi, the PTA president who had taken Merrilee, Patrick, and Andrew under her wing.

Mitzi took the children to school and said she'd do so as long as I needed help. Then she made me a big batch of chicken soup. I tried to sip some every two hours. Mitzi also bought me some over-the-counter medicine and a vaporizer, all of which helped. By the time the weekend was over I knew I was strong enough to take my children back to school.

The next time Merril had visitation, he didn't bring the children back. I called my attorney on Sunday night, and she called Rod Parker. He said Merril was too sick to drive. I knew this was a game. I was also told my father was too busy. When I called him he said he couldn't bring the kids back that week and he was sorry. I didn't believe him, but I let it go.

The next day I called the schools and explained why my children were absent. My van wasn't in good enough shape to make the trip. Mitzi said she and her husband would drive down to Colorado City. I couldn't thank her enough.

Merril went nuts when he found out Mitzi would be driving his children back to Salt Lake. I had called his bluff. Moments later, my father called. He said he'd drop everything and drive the children back. I told him to forget it. Merril had already broken the court order by not returning the kids on Sunday, so I'd made arrangements for their safe return.

Merril's family went ballistic. No one knew who Mitzi was, and they tried to claim they had no way of knowing if the children would be safe with her. My father returned with the children after all. Mitzi and her husband had made the six-hundred-mile round-trip for nothing. But Merril never tried this trick again.

Word found its way back to me that Merril had married five more wives since I'd left. Each had been married to someone else until Warren Jeffs had ordered her to marry Merril Jessop. I knew that some of the families who had joined Merril's had a history of physical and sexual abuse among their children.

I told my attorney that I didn't feel safe sending Merrilee into that environment. She was too young and too vulnerable. I feared she'd be molested by one of the older boys that were now part of her "family."

We moved to get the case back into court as soon as possible. Lisa agreed with me that the situation for Merrilee was too dangerous.

My children's therapists were frustrated by Merril's behavior. They were trying to help them heal, but after every visit to Colorado City they came back injured and lost ground. The violence was always reported to Merril's attorney. Rodney Parker began pushing to keep the case out of court and got three postponements. When he tried for a fourth, my attorney objected and stood her ground. A date was set. Parker said he had a conflict, and another conference call was scheduled among the lawyers and judge. But Parker wasn't in his office, so the judge said the date would stand: June 24, 2004.

With no hope of getting subsidized housing for at least eighteen months, I knew that all of my income was going to be used for rent. I started every month knowing I didn't have any money to pay utilities or purchase anything except food.

Patrick was having a play at school and needed a sword. I promised him I would try my best to figure something out. But this was going to be hard to pull off. Patrick got more and more agitated as the days went by. After two weeks his counselor took me aside and said that the sword was a big emotional issue for him. The counselor said she felt that the sword would make Patrick feel more secure about his life and my ability to take care of him. I told her I didn't know where to get one and didn't have the money. She said I could pick up a sword at Wal-Mart for five dollars.

I had six dollars to my name. I'd been saving that for laundry soap, but now I realized the sword came first. We stopped at Wal-Mart on the way home. We bought the sword. Patrick acted as though the weight of the world had disappeared from his little soul. It had been fun to buy it for him. But now what did I do for laundry detergent?

The next day, Connie, the homeless-shelter coordinator who'd helped register my children in school, stopped by to check on us. She brought along a box of laundry soap samples that she'd picked up from the shelter. "I knew with all your children you could probably use this." Connie also gave me some gas vouchers. What a relief.

I could do my laundry, but I was still not going to make it through the month. Then Leenie called me and said a costume director from HBO was in town and was looking for someone who could help design clothes for the series *Big Love*. Leenie thought I could make some money by sewing at home. I leaped at the opportunity and got hired to sew several pairs of long underwear. I sewed like mad and finished the order in a few weeks. The job was a godsend. It gave me enough money to pay my utilities through the summer.

On the appointed day, I arrived at the courthouse at 9 A.M. I was scared but also hopeful. Rod Parker was not going to be there and had arranged for a substitute attorney to take his place. The guardian ad litem was not there, either. But my attorney was, and the small courtroom was filled with my supporters. Merril looked a little taken aback. For once he didn't act as though he was holding all the cards.

Lisa argued that Merril should be allowed to continue to see our children, but in Salt Lake City. She made a persuasive case for why it wasn't good for the children to be forced to travel to Colorado City every two weeks. The fill-in for the guardian ad litem admitted she didn't know much about the case but said she didn't see why the children couldn't travel back and forth.

Lisa was brilliantly prepared. She outlined in great detail the incident that had happened, the stress and anger the visits caused, and why this was damaging to the children.

When the judge finally issued his opinion, the courtroom fell still. Our lives were on the line. He spoke deliberately and in an even tone.

"While I believe it is important for the children involved to have a relationship with their father, I find there is enough evidence to support the need to have the visitation restricted to the Salt Lake City area."

My heart stopped. I'd won. We were safe. I knew Merril would never put the effort into coming up to Salt Lake City. The fight was over.

It was a huge win. I had proven that it was not in my children's interests to ever be in Colorado City. We were finally and truly free.

This was a groundbreaking case at many levels. If I could get my children out of the cult, any woman with enough determination could, too.

The absolute power the FLDS had over women had been cracked. I had proved that a woman could not only flee and live on her own but also win custody of her children.

It was a proud day.

# Brian

After I won custody, I went home to gather up all my children to take them to the zoo. We were going to celebrate! Betty refused to go with us and Arthur was very upset. The younger ones were confused and felt they should be angry, but they were too excited about the zoo to muster any anger. We all had a great time, and when we got home we had pizza and root beer floats. It felt like the weight of the world had been erased from every aspect of my being.

The school year started and life began to feel more normal. I was feeling stronger and less debilitated by the PTSD. It wasn't such an ordeal getting the kids out the door. I was stronger and more optimistic than I'd been since the escape.

Merril came through Salt Lake City one night and took the children out to dinner. He was heading home from Canada with a new wife. Merril had married a young girl, Bonnie Blackmore, who was a Canadian citizen. He introduced her to my children as their new mother. Bonnie was barely older than Betty.

Two weeks later, he wed another young girl. Ally Barlow from Hildale, Utah, was the next in his marrying binge. In less than a year, he'd married seven new wives. He was sixty-eight years old with thirteen wives and more than a hundred children now, including many stepchildren. I think he needed to prove that he could still have any woman he wanted.

When Merril wasn't marrying more wives, he was liquidating assets and building housing in Texas on Warren Jeffs' compound in Eldorado, which spanned nearly two thousand acres. A few months after he married his under-age brides, he moved them to Texas and destroyed all traces of their ever having lived in Colorado City, presumably so there would be no evidence that could be used against him.

I knew I had to find a job to enable me to pay my utility bills that winter. With Harrison and Bryson, it was impossible to work a regular 9-to-5 job. I ended up going to work for a small locksmithing business run by a couple I'd met over the summer who'd once been part of another polygamist community with no ties to the FLDS. Paul and Lodeen had fourteen children and needed help with their bookkeeping. Paul said it was fine to bring Harrison and Bryson with me to work. There was a room downstairs where Harrison could sleep and Bryson could watch cartoons.

I took the job with delight. I have a good head for numbers and was put in charge of collecting past-due accounts. Lodeen gave me a big stack of invoices, some of which went back two years. I tracked down phone numbers on the computer and made an endless stream of calls. Payments started coming in.

I was earning enough money to pay my bills. There wasn't a lot left over, but this was the highest ground I'd managed to reach. Once I got the children off to school in the morning, I went to work with the boys. In the afternoons I shuttled kids to one appointment after another.

After an appointment for Harrison one afternoon, the ignition on my van froze. I couldn't turn the key and start it. I called Lodeen to see if anyone was in the shop who could come over and help me. Paul came by.

Paul and I had an easy relationship and a lot in common because of our polygamist pasts. That afternoon he told me he had never truly given up the idea of living polygamy but felt the right person had never come along—until he met me.

I was stunned. He told me that I would probably never find a man willing to take on a woman with eight children. In his view, polygamy helped solve this kind of problem. He and Lodeen had worked hard and were now in the position of being able to help me. Why should I have to live alone because I'd been dealt a bad hand?

I told Paul I had no problem being alone and that there was no way I'd ever consider polygamy again. I'd fought hard for my freedom and I knew I might have to fight hard for the rest of my life, but there was no way I'd go back to polygamy. Paul wanted me to look at the positives. But frankly, I didn't think there were any.

I told Paul I appreciated everything he had done for me. He and Lodeen had offered me a hand up instead of a handout, and I was deeply grateful for that. But that was it. I wasn't interested in anything else.

For the first time in my life, a man respected me when I said no. Paul said he still needed my help at his business if I was willing to continue. I didn't really want to work for someone who wanted to marry me, but I didn't know what else to do. My job was enabling me to survive. I continued working, and he never said anything about marriage again.

The job went so well—I brought in $30,000 in past-due accounts for them—I realized my abilities hadn't been wiped out by the trauma of the last year or my PTSD. What I knew I needed was work I could do from home. There was no way I could support my family on a teacher's salary.

I decided to become an accountant. I could do that from home and make my own hours. I looked into graduate school at the University of Utah and realized I needed to pass the GMAT test in order to apply.

I signed up for a GMAT prep class and started going on Saturday mornings. It was hard to find the time to study, but I was thrilled to be using my brain again and doing something for myself.

One Saturday I started getting dressed for school but didn't put any energy into it. I just didn't care. When I looked in the mirror I thought I looked awful. I was wearing black jeans and a big heavy sweater. My hair was frizzy from a new perm. But so what?

Then a strange and unfamiliar feeling came over me. I had a

sense that I was going to meet the love of my life that day. I wasn't looking for the love of my life! That was what was so unsettling. I knew everyone in the class already. I was running late and brushed the thought off as something crazy.

That day we had a substitute teacher. He introduced himself as Brian and said he had an MBA from Harvard. That got my attention. I'd never met anyone who'd gone to an Ivy League school. He was good-looking and clearly very fit.

I noticed during the class that he paid a lot of attention to me. Why was he looking at me? Was it my imagination? No, I realized it wasn't. He'd ask the class a question and stare at me.

He told us we were going to go down the rows and answer the questions in the book. I was second in line. I read the question, answered it, and then looked up. Brian was staring at me but didn't say anything. Had I gotten the question wrong? I must have looked puzzled, because he snapped out of his reverie, commented that my answer was correct, and moved on to the next student.

As the class continued, Brian kept encouraging me to participate. I felt confused by his attention, so I stayed quiet.

During our break, Brian said to some of us that he'd send us a study guide for the GMAT class that he'd prepared if we'd give him our e-mail addresses and phone numbers. We all signed up.

On another break, I overheard Brian telling someone nearby that he was divorced. After class, several of the students went to the front of the room to chat with him. I felt shy, but I didn't want to pass up the chance to talk to someone with a degree from Harvard. I drifted up to the front along with everyone else. Brian had his eye on me.

But then the dean of the business school came in and invited Brian to lunch. I could see that waiting around to talk with him was a waste of time, so I left and did not look back.

It turns out that Brian told everyone he had to leave. After making apologies to the dean, he jumped in his car.

Brian could see me walking down the sidewalk on the right. If he left campus, he'd have to turn left. Left meant never getting to know me. He had taken a new job in San Francisco and was already working there. Turning left was the safe decision. But he'd been making those all his life. He turned right.

Brian pulled up to me in his BMW and rolled down his window. "Carolyn, I know you don't know me and this may seem sudden, but would you like to get some lunch with me? You can ride with me or follow me in your own car. Whatever you're more comfortable with. But I would really like to get to know you."

My heart nearly came to a halt. What a surprise. What a *happy* surprise. But what should I do? Should I say yes and go to lunch with a total stranger? The safe thing was to say no. But I didn't. "I'd love to get some lunch with you," I said, and got in his car.

Now what? There I was sitting alone in a car with a strange man. What a weird feeling. I had never felt so shy in my entire life. Ever. I was thirty-six years old and on my third date. (My first two dates were awkward non-starters.) This was the first date I'd ever had with someone I found really attractive.

Brian mentioned something about his son. I looked at him and said, "Oh, you have a son?"

"I do. Two boys, in fact. What about you? Any kids?" he asked.

"Yes, I have eight."

Brian started laughing. He thought I was joking.

I looked at him because I didn't get what was so funny.

Then it was his turn to look surprised. "You have eight children?" I nodded.

Brian looked like he was choking on something. "Seriously, you do not look like you even have any kids. I thought you were joking. Is a sports bar okay for lunch?"

I'd never been to a sports bar in my life. I said that sounded great.

The mention of my eight children broke the ice. Brian came from a family of six. He said his mother was very beautiful. "Like you. You remind me of my mother in a lot of ways," he said. Well, that seemed all right.

Brian admitted that he had begged off having lunch with the dean so he could try to catch me after class. He said if that had failed, he would have called me with the number he had from the study guide sheet.

"You made up the study guide thing just to get my number?" I said, shocked.

"No, not exactly. I'm e-mailing everyone a study guide. I just didn't need their phone numbers." He smiled.

Over lunch I told Brian how I'd ended up with eight children and about my escape and the seemingly never-ending custody battle I'd finally won. Talking to him suddenly felt as easy as breathing and as natural as blinking. No man had ever listened to me as intently as he had.

Brian had just gone through a divorce, and in talking we realized we'd both been married for seventeen years, almost to the day—he was married three weeks before I married Merril and divorced two weeks before my escape. Both of us had been divorced for eighteen months, and neither of us had dated seriously since.

Brian later said he realized at lunch he wanted to have a relationship with me even though he knew it would turn his life upside down. He was scared but didn't let that stop him from saying, "Do you want to go see a movie tonight?"

"Sure," I said.

"I work in San Francisco but I come to Salt Lake every two weeks to see my sons. I'd like to date you when I'm not seeing my two boys."

I smiled. "Sounds good to me."

He took me back to my car and kissed me goodbye. Really kissed me.

We never got to the movies that night because Brian wanted me to meet his friends. All of them had degrees from prestigious schools. A few had Ph.D.s. I'd never socialized with such educated people before. What a difference. It was stimulating to be around such vitality. The next day I met more of his friends at breakfast and lunch. By the time Brian went back to San Francisco, I'd met almost every friend he had in the city and I was in love for the first time in my life.

Brian began calling me every day from San Francisco. After two weekends of dating in Salt Lake, Brian began begging me to fly to San Francisco with him. I pulled out all the stops to find a babysitter and did.

For years I'd lived a nightmare. Now I was living a dream. I could not believe someone like Brian cared about me and wanted to introduce me to his family. His dad had been career military and Brian had been an army captain. Part of what attracted me to him was that he'd worked hard for everything he'd achieved but still remained open and caring in a strong and natural way. He gave me hope that I might be able to pull myself out of the bad place I was in. It was easy to be with him but still so unreal. What a joy to be able to laugh with a man.

I had been to San Francisco with my father several times. But I'd never seen how beautiful some of the outlying areas were. We stayed with Brian's sister, who lived in a house on a cliff that looked over the ocean.

I remember standing with Brian on the edge of the cliff and feeling the deepest peace I'd ever known in my life. I thought that when I escaped, I'd gone over the edge—the edge of everything I had ever known.

Freedom was something I had always been able to imagine. It was the opposite of oppression, slavery, and degradation. But love?

I had never known what it felt like to be loved by a man—to have the love that says, *You matter,* the love that says, *I adore you, I believe in you, and I want you by my side.*

Love was brand-new. The thrill was, I wanted Brian, too.

# Better and Better

**M**y children stabilized more each month. Betty was still the wild card in the family and ran away a lot. Calling the local police department was becoming a regular part of life.

I thought I was doing well, too, until I was knocked down again by PTSD. I had a fever and chills and felt completely debilitated. That's when I learned what caring meant. Brian was on the phone to me several times a day. I had never been protected before, never known what it felt like to really matter to someone. I had never been more than property to Merril. Now I was not only a person but a cherished one at that. I could feel emotions that had been cut off and cauterized coming back to life. Even when I was sick, I was more alive in spirit than I had been during my seventeen years of marriage.

The fever and chills spiraled into pneumonia that winter. One Saturday I found I couldn't breathe very well and I thought I'd stay in and try to get better. I went to find LuAnne to help with Harrison and found that Betty and LuAnne were both missing. It had been several months since Betty had last taken off, because I think she and Merril both knew it wasn't working to their advantage. This was the first time Merril had tried to take more than one of my children, however.

The first thing I did was call Brian. I told him I was too sick to call the police. I was sure the girls were in Colorado City. Brian pushed me to call the authorities, walking me through it step by step. I promised him I would. Then I remembered that Arizona law enforcement had put an investigator in the community in 2004 as an outsider to help people like me. Gary Engels worked out of a trailer he shared with social service workers from Child Protective Services. The idea was to give women a place to turn to for help—but very few used it. This was the first time there had ever been any real law enforcement in the community—all the other police were FLDS members who looked the other way. The local police followed him with guns whenever he moved about the community.

"There is nothing like this in America," Engels told the Southern Poverty Law Center, which tracks hate crimes in America. "It's like a fiefdom. Everyone lives and survives by the will of Warren Jeffs. He can take away your family, your business, and your home. What king ever had that power?"

The Southern Poverty Law Center characterized the FLDS as a hate group in 2005, putting it on a list with the Ku Klux Klan and the Aryan Nation, among others. In doing so it cited statements such as this from Jeffs on race: "The black race is the people through which the devil has always been able to bring evil unto the earth." Jeffs' hateful speech is not limited to just race. Homosexuals were a frequent target: "The people grew so evil, the men started to marry the men and the women, the women. This is the worst evil act you can do, next to murder. It is like murder." On violence, there is this statement from Jeffs: "I want to remind you what the prophets have taught us, that whenever a man of God is commanded to kill another man, he is never bloodthirsty."

When I called Gary and reported that my daughters were missing, he said he'd investigate immediately. The police in West Jordan, Utah, faxed orders to the Mohave County, Arizona, office to go pick up Betty and LuAnne. None of the local officers wanted to go into Colorado City late on Saturday night, but Gary insisted. The orders were there; they were required by law to act. Extra police officers were called in from Arizona to accompany them.

The doors were locked at Merril's. A young girl answered Gary's knock and slammed the door in his face. Betty and LuAnne had only been in the house fifteen minutes.

The officers circled the house. Through the windows they could see a large group of people standing in a circle and talking. The police were worried about a stand-off. The house had not been surrounded very long when the FLDS police officers told Gary that was not Merril's house. This was a lie. They told Gary he should stop harassing innocent people and leave.

Gary said he had orders stating that Betty and LuAnne were at this residence. If they weren't, he said, why did the people inside refuse to talk to him? A search warrant was in the works, and Gary said that the moment he had it he was going inside.

Shortly thereafter, Merril called Gary and lit into him. He insisted that this was not his residence and he had no right to be there. Merril said he had no idea where Betty and LuAnne were. "Carolyn is only trying to cause trouble for innocent people because she is unable to control her daughters." This was a lie and Gary knew it.

Gary did not back down. Merril called him again with more threats. Gary said when he had the search warrant, he was coming in. The girls would be taken into custody and Merril would face charges.

Merril called back with an offer. He admitted that Betty and LuAnne were inside, and he said that if they could stay the night, he would see that they got back to my house the following day.

Gary called me and said it was up to me. He'd move if I told him to. I wanted my daughters back as peacefully as possible, so we agreed to accept the deal. I could not risk someone getting hurt during the stand-off or when they went in with a search warrant.

Betty and LuAnne came home the next day, and Betty never took off again. I think Merril realized what the consequences would be if he tried kidnapping any of his children again.

Merril continued to liquidate his assets. He sold his Big Water Motel, which had sixty rooms, and another smaller one. He sold his rodeo arena, which was the largest in northern Arizona, and most of the equipment from his construction and trucking companies. His cement company was closed, and so was the motel I used to run in Caliente. Merril was liquidating hundreds of thousands of dollars in assets, and not a dime went to child support.

We never reached an agreement because I was collecting a small amount from his Social Security, and he did not want to pay child support. He only wanted to pay the Social Security money. My attorney refused that offer because we knew Merril was lying about his income. Legally he owes me child support based on his assets and income. But I have to prove he still has hidden assets and is profiting from them. This would cost a tremendous amount of money in investigative fees, and even if I proved that Merril had unreported assets, there's no guarantee that Merril would ever pay what he rightfully should.

My dad owned a third of the motel in Caliente. Merril wanted my father to give that money to Warren. My father refused, saying it was going to my mother to help her buy a house after their divorce. Merril was furious and told Dad that he had no obligation to my mother. After thirty-eight years of marriage, my father felt differently. Merril said God would take care of him legally if he was doing God's will. Dad wasn't buying it. My father was excommunicated from the FLDS by Warren Jeffs and ordered to return to Jeffs his two wives and the more than ten children still living at home.

Gary Engels estimates that more than three hundred men have been kicked out of their families by Warren Jeffs and excommunicated. The men are told to repent from afar by sending Jeffs long letters detailing their sins. If their list of sins is identical to the list of their sins Warren Jeffs has received from God, they will be allowed to return to the FLDS. That, of course, never happens, but Jeffs has used this tactic to accumulate a massive amount of detail about what men considered their worst deeds and most shameful secrets from men desperate to reunite with their families.

Jeffs sent some of his goons to my father's house to tell him that he had been kicked out of the work of God. He was no longer to manage the local grocery store, which he'd done for more than eighteen years. His home was to be turned over to the FLDS.

Jeffs' emissaries told my father to delineate all his sins in a letter to the prophet, leave the community, and repent. He was instructed to pray constantly for God's forgiveness and with sweetness in his heart thank God and the prophet for their grace in allowing him to repent.

My father asked the men if they would give Warren a message for him. When they agreed, my father said, "Could you sweetly tell Warren Jeffs to go to hell?"

The goons looked scared. How dare my father speak like that to the prophet of God! Didn't he understand the risk of eternal damnation? His complete disregard for Warren Jeffs was like a body blow to them.

Merril was soon on the phone to my father to say he was taking over the store. My father had no objections to that but told Merril he was planning to take his retirement money with him. During his years running the store my father had accumulated a substantial retirement account. Merril told my father the money should go to Warren Jeffs. My father refused and said Jeffs would have to fight him in court.

Warren had ordered my fathers' two remaining wives, Rosie and Muriel, to turn themselves in for reassignment to other men. My father told them they were free to do whatever they wanted. He said he'd never owned them; he had become their husband through a covenant with God that he was still prepared to honor. The choice was theirs.

My father had raised thirty-six children in his life, eight of whom were stepchildren. Unlike Merril, his children mattered to him. So did their mothers.

Rosie decided she would stand by my father and had no interest in becoming a pawn in Warren's sick games.

Muriel decided she could not risk her salvation and surrendered to "the will of God." She placed herself and her four children at the mercy of Warren Jeffs. I do not know if she's been reassigned in marriage. I do know that women who were ensnared in Jeffs' web did not fare well. Several women whom I knew had been reassigned as wives more than once, some to as many as five different men. One woman said she felt like she had become a "priesthood prostitute."

My father's heart was shattered. He wept for days. His family was torn apart. Warren Jeffs had made a mockery of the faith and community my father loved.

There were leaders in the community who had tried to block Warren Jeffs and protect the values we had had. Key among those was Uncle Fred Jessop, who had been the leading FLDS bishop throughout my lifetime. Uncle Fred was widely admired and loved. He had been investigating Warren for fraud. Now in his nineties, Uncle Fred worried about leaving a crook and criminal in charge after his death. Secret meetings were held with other men, one of whom was his stepson, William Timpson Jessop. William turned traitor and went to Warren and told him everything Uncle Fred was planning.

Warren had Uncle Fred sent to another compound and told the community the Lord had removed him as a bishop and appointed William in his place. The other men who had been part of the secret meetings were kicked out of the cult. This is how opposition to Jeffs was eliminated—swiftly and surely. Uncle Fred was too beloved for Warren to have excommunicated him. His ploy was to make it look as though Uncle Fred was too old and deserved to retire.

Uncle Fred disappeared from the community in late December 2003. A few weeks later, in January 2004, Warren Jeffs made what would be his last public appearance when at a town meeting he kicked out of the FLDS twenty-one men whom he called "master deceivers" and reassigned their wives and children to other men. The men were told to keep sending money to Jeffs and work on their repentance from afar.

Jeffs had always been private, secretive, and somewhat paranoid. After his father's death, he never went out into the community without security guards. At the time of that town meeting, no one knew that he was going into hiding. But as months went on, that meeting became the last time anyone could remember seeing him in public. He still sent tapes into the community and did sermons that were piped in over the phone.

In July 2004, a civil lawsuit was filed in Utah against Warren Jeffs and two of his brothers by his nephew, Brent Jeffs, who accused Jeffs of sodomizing him when he was a student at the Alta Academy, a private school in Salt Lake that Warren ran.

Brent's lawsuit was motivated by his brother Clayne's suicide in

2002. Clayne shot himself in the head after disclosing that he had been abused by Warren Jeffs. Brent had never told anyone about his own abuse until after his brother shot himself.

In his lawsuit, Brent Jeffs said Warren told him that he was doing "God's work" when he assaulted him and that if he ever disclosed the abuse, "it would be upon pain of eternal damnation." Brent Jeffs said he was routinely sodomized from the time he was five or six years old.

Jeffs refused to appear in court to answer those charges. Federal charges were filed against him for fleeing to evade prosecution. With armed zealots guarding him, plenty of money, and a network of FLDS safe houses in the United States and Canada, Warren Jeffs managed to conceal his whereabouts. Federal and state authorities were also wary of triggering another Waco and did not want to move on Jeffs in a situation where many others might die.

Even though he was in hiding and on the run from the law, Jeffs still wielded power through tapes, phone calls, and messages he relayed back to the community. From time to time he would appear to perform a marriage. But these were rare and secretive moments that people learned about only after they had occurred.

By the time he dropped off the radar, Jeffs had effectively wiped out any opposition to his reign. Those men who were left behind— men like Merril—were total disciples. Merril's devotion to Warren Jeffs had never wavered over the years, even as the community sank to deeper levels of extremism.

During the winter of 2005, I was driving home with Betty and Merrilee on a snowy day. A car in the opposite lane swerved into mine. I turned my van to the side of the road to avoid a collision, but the car still crashed into the back of my van.

The children weren't hurt, but I had terrible back and shoulder pain as a result. I went to see a chiropractor, who said that area was too tight to work with and adjust. He sent me to a massage therapist, Lee Bird, who turned out to be a godsend.

Lee was learning Feldenkrais massage, which is based on a belief that new connections can be formed between brain and body that can help retrain the nervous system. During the course of my treatments, I told Lee about Harrison and how hard it was for me to still lift him.

Going on a hunch that Feldenkrais might help Harrison, Lee offered to treat him for free. I was desperate to find more help for Harrison. He had improved greatly during our first two years in Salt Lake but now seemed to be on a plateau.

Harrison began seeing Lee three times a week, and within months he began crawling correctly. A few months after that, Lee had Harrison on his feet. He couldn't walk alone, but he could take a few steps if he was well supported. This felt miraculous. Harrison had always screamed in the past when he was placed in a standing position. Now not only could he crawl, he could climb. His newfound mobility made him happier and easier to handle.

Brian remained a steadfast and joyful presence in my life. I experienced a kind of intimacy and tenderness I'd never known before. Brian taught me how to dance, took me to see the Utah Jazz play basketball, and introduced me to the life he said I would have been living if I hadn't been born into polygamy.

Sometimes we'd just hang out and watch movies. I had never seen a lot of the classic films we enjoyed watching together. Brian is Jewish and he took me to his synagogue and taught me about some of his beliefs and traditions. It was interesting to me, but at the moment I'm not in the market for another God.

Brian has a deep respect for women and had a hard time listening to some of what I'd been through. I didn't tell him a lot of things because I knew they would be too painful for him to hear. We went for long walks in the park together and he got me interested in running. Brian had done the Boston Marathon five times and the New York Marathon once.

When summer began, Brian gave our family season passes for Lagoon, an amusement park for children that's like a mini Disneyland. It also has the best water park in the valley. Brian said I was always doing things for my children but that I rarely got to do things *with* them.

Betty was furious that we were going to be riding on the roller coaster, going through the haunted house, and banging around in bumper cars. She tried her best to sabotage us by telling the younger children not to go. The FLDS believed water was the devil's domain, and Betty tried to convince her siblings that I was throwing them into the devil's lair.

Individually, the children were doing well, but as a family we were still in the throes of the cult mentality. We went into counseling together. After a few sessions the therapist said that she wanted to work one-on-one with Betty. I was so grateful when Betty said she was willing to go.

I went back into therapy with Larry Bill. He told me that I was hurting Betty by allowing her to terrorize the family and that I was jeopardizing everyone else. It was hard for me to accept, but I knew what Larry was saying about Betty was true. We needed a time-out.

I talked to my brother, Arthur, and he agreed that Betty could come to live with his family for a few weeks. Betty was livid and accused me of throwing her out. I said two years of struggle was enough. She could come back when she was willing to behave.

So Betty moved in with Arthur. She actually seemed relieved to be able to lay down her arms. Her father could no longer use her as a weapon, which I think had been a terrible burden for her—something I didn't appreciate at the time. She still maintained contact with Merril, but she wasn't spying on us for him.

Merril went ballistic. He insisted that if Betty wasn't living with me she should be with him. I made it clear that Betty's move was only temporary and that she just needed some time and space of her own.

Patrick and Andrew did well in counseling and told me they wanted to take karate. I thought that was a fine idea and found a six-week program nearby. I asked for and received a reduction in tuition from $20 a child to just $10 for the whole six weeks, because I was still strapped for cash. My job with Paul had ended and I had not figured out something else.

Hill Dalde, the karate instructor, was a fourth-degree black belt. On their first day he told me that Patrick and Andrew were going to be his top students. I thought he meant for the six-week class. He meant long-term: he saw great potential in both my boys.

We found a way to continue karate—another godsend. Patrick and Andrew made great progress, moving up four belts in their first year. It was one area in their lives where they had total mastery of their bodies and their environment. Hill developed a mentoring relationship with my boys and would take them to the movies as they reached new goals.

Patrick and Andrew had never had such a positive role model in their lives. Brian had met my children, but we were taking it very, very slow with respect to introducing him into our lives.

After the first year of karate, Hill agreed to teach Betty, LuAnne, and the little princess herself, Merrilee. Betty did very well because she's very disciplined. LuAnne is athletic, and although she's not as motivated as the boys, she's done fine. Merrilee is determined and persistent, which serves her well in karate. She's also a natural athlete and has been steadily moving up with her belts.

Despite all the help I'd been given, I still had trouble asking for it when I needed it. I was so used to doing what I was told and never asking for help. Dan Fisher thought his foundation was paying my rent when I left the battered women's shelter and was upset when he found out that hadn't happened. He could not believe how much I'd struggled without asking for more help.

As my children felt safer and more secure, I began to hear more stories about Merril and Barbara's abuse. One of my daughters told me about being molested by her half brother. Patrick told me about the night Barbara beat him so hard, he thought he was going to die. He was even afraid after he told me what happened because he didn't want his half brothers to hate him for telling. It was one abuse story after another.

The kids continued to unload stories for about a year. It was painful for me to listen, but I knew that their mental health depended on my ability to hear and validate what they'd endured.

After two and a half years of waiting, the Section 8 housing voucher came through in November 2005. I went on an orientation to learn the details, and when it was over I sat in my car and cried. I was only going to have to pay $70 a month for rent. For the first time in my life, I had breathing room. No longer would all my money have to go to housing expenses. Knowing I'd have $500 left over after I paid my utilities and other expenses felt like an unbelievable windfall.

By Christmas, I learned that Merril had moved his entire family into Warren Jeffs' compound in Texas. At that point he had fourteen wives and about forty children who were still young enough to be living at home. The one person who was left behind was his wife Faunita, who was put in a mental institution in Flagstaff, Arizona. She was told she was unworthy to participate in the kingdom of God.

In the spring of 2005, the state of Utah seized the assets of the FLDS, which were worth $110 million. The assets—all in real estate—were part of a trust called the United Effort Plan, or UEP. It has been set up by the FLDS as a charitable trust. The UEP owned all the homes in the community.

Warren Jeffs used the trust to his advantage by putting assets in the names of his cronies, who would then sell them and give Jeffs the money. Since there was never really any oversight until the state went after it, the UEP was like a personal ATM for Warren Jeffs.

Jeffs, who had been in hiding for more than a year, did not try to defend himself when Utah went to court to gain control of the UEP trust. He knew if he showed up, he would be arrested on the state and federal charges that had been leveled against him.

Once the court gave control of the trust to the state of Utah, legally Warren Jeffs was cut off at the knees. Utah, Arizona, and the FBI were all pursuing him, and his assets were unavailable to him.

But thousands of brainwashed believers still clung to him as their prophet and leader. This was further proof of what many had grown up believing: that evil outsiders were always poised to attack and persecute those who were doing God's work.

So Jeffs still exerted power. He ordered his followers to withhold the state tax they would normally pay on their houses that were owned by the U.E.P. This is a substantial amount of money, about a million dollars a year. None of Jeffs' followers paid taxes. The administrator of the trust responded by going after Warren's brother Lyle with an eviction notice. After he was forced to pay his taxes, others in the FLDS did, too.

Rumors circulated in the community that Jeffs now had the ability to be transported directly by God from place to place. He would show up in the twinkling of an eye and disappear just as magically. Jeffs' fanatical believers were convinced that this was why the authorities had so far been unsuccessful in capturing him. Jeffs fed into their perverse worldview by sending back stranger and stranger communications. He took full credit for the tsunami off Thailand that had killed hundreds of thousands in December 2004 and said that more disasters would befall those who were trying to stop the work of God.

Warren's response to what seemed like the beginning of the end for him was to marry and marry and marry again. The rumor was that he was up to 180 wives. He was marrying younger and younger girls—one of whom was my former second-grade student Jennet Jessop, who was fourteen at the time.

What was also disturbing was the number of people who disappeared. Entire families would be moved out of the community during the night. To this day, no one knows where they are. Winston Blackmore and his first wife, Jane, lost their daughter, who disappeared with her husband.

Since Brent Jeffs filed his civil suit in 2004, over a hundred young boys and girls were interviewed by the Utah attorney general's office about their allegations of sexual and physical abuse by Warren Jeffs.

The media became more aware of Warren Jeffs as the hunt for him continued. Stories were written about the men who'd been excommunicated and the hundreds of "lost boys" whom Warren Jeffs had arbitrarily banished from the FLDS.

Johnny Jessop, one of the "lost boys" Dan Fisher has been supporting, can't find his mother, Sue, and has filed a lawsuit against Jeffs to reveal her whereabouts. There have also been rumors that children were being taken from their mothers and sent to the FLDS compound in Texas—which is called the YFZ Ranch, which stands for "Yearning for Zion." These were children who belonged to men Warren had kicked out of the cult. We heard that they were being sent away to be raised the way Warren wanted them to be raised.

I began to see that we'd made it out just in time. But I was sickened by what I heard about people who had been part of my life.

When Faunita was eventually released from the mental institution in Flagstaff, she hitched a ride from someone and returned to Colorado City and stood alone on the doorstep of our old home. She tried to open the door, but it was locked. When Merril moved to Texas, he gave the house to Nathan, Faunita's son. But since Faunita had been excommunicated, Nathan's family wouldn't let her in. Faunita stood in the rain while her grandchildren stared out the windows at her. Ruth and Merril's son Wallace finally came and picked her up. Wallace told her she couldn't stay in the community, drove her to a motel in Hurricane, and left her there.

In the end, one of Faunita's grandsons, Merril III, who had been kicked out of the FLDS and was a "lost boy," came and rescued her. He rented her a little place and bought her groceries. But he was a teenager trying to survive on construction jobs and not making very much. With little education, he could barely survive himself.

Faunita was also a diabetic, so her health was perilous. One day she was found wandering, delirious, in Wal-Mart. After forty years of living with Merril's abuse, Faunita was badly damaged and very sick. A few women who had been on the other side of the religious split that divided the FLDS started helping her buy groceries. Her situation was particularly heartbreaking to me.

But a year later, quite unexpectedly, Faunita, her daughter, Audrey, and son-in-law, Merlin, dropped in to see me. I was as delighted as I was stunned. I never expected that anyone from Merril's family would want to see me again.

Faunita looked happier than I had ever seen her. She hugged me and laughed joyfully. She said she wanted to apologize for not helping me more when Harrison was so sick. Faunita was close to tears when she told me how sad she felt for me then. But she said she was too sick herself to reach out to me.

I never expected Faunita to make such a turnaround. Even though she is alone much of the time now, she is removed from the constant cruelty and abuse she endured for decades as one of Merril's wives.

Brian moved back to Utah in the spring of 2005. He wanted to be closer to his two teenage boys, and to me. One of the things I love about Brian is that he is a devoted father. His sons anchor his life.

Some of Brian's friends chided him about dating a little Mormon schoolteacher with eight kids. He told them I was the most amazing woman he had ever met, and he introduced me with pride when we went to parties. It felt surreal—happily so—to be dating a man who was a corporate executive. But most of all, I welcomed being included, for the first time in my life, in a world where ideas, culture, and education were respected.

Once the UEP trust was in the hands of the state of Utah, an advisory board was created to suggest how its assets could be best utilized to benefit those still in the community and requesting help. Thirty people applied for the board and six were chosen. I was one of them. This was more than an honor for me, it was a vindication. After years of trying to protect myself from the evils of the FLDS, I was now aligned with those who were going to fight to undo the damage it had done to children and families. Even though Warren Jeffs was in hiding, his power was gradually being shut down.

Arthur turned eighteen on December 20, 2005. Merril ordered him to leave everything he had and return to the FLDS. Arthur refused and told his father the religion had turned into something weird. Merril denied that it had, but Arthur held his ground. His life was going in another direction now. Merril was outraged. No son of his had ever stood up to him before.

Arthur graduated from West Jordan High School on June 6, 2006. It was one of the proudest days of my life. Arthur had been on the honor roll for three years. During his senior year he was taking a full load of classes, including the ones he needed to make up for the year he had missed. He was also taking flying lessons and working part-time for my brother.

At an awards dinner before commencement, Arthur was the recipient of a special award and a $500 scholarship given to a student who has overcome adversity. The principal didn't list everything that Arthur had endured, but what he highlighted was enough to make the audience applaud. Two days later he received another $500 scholarship to the college of his choice from the Chamber of Commerce.

When graduation day came and Arthur walked across the stage to receive his diploma, I leaped to my feet the moment his name was called, and clapped and cheered for my son. My heart was exploding with happiness.

# End Game

**E**arly in May 2006, Warren Jeffs' name was added to the FBI's Ten Most Wanted list. He was charged as an accomplice to rape in Utah, on two counts of having sexual contact with minors in Arizona, and for unlawful flight to avoid prosecution. The FBI felt that national publicity might help to bring him in, and a reward of $100,000 was offered for his capture. "I have a corner of my state that is worse than [under] the Taliban," said Utah's attorney general, Mark Shurtleff, after Warren Jeffs became one of the Ten Most Wanted.

Warren, who had been in hiding now for two years, had long preached that he would be taken like Christ and crucified. But the end, when it came, on August 28, 2006, was far less dramatic. The car that he was traveling in was pulled over on a routine traffic stop because it lacked adequate registration. Inside were wigs, dozens of cell phones, and $50,000 in cash.

Warren Steed Jeffs, fifty, was under arrest.

My beautiful stepdaughter Naomi, one of Ruth's daughters, was with him. She was taken into custody that night with Warren and his younger brother Isaac, but charges were not filed against the two of them.

I was stunned, thrilled, overwhelmed, and surprised that he was caught so soon after he went on the Ten Most Wanted list. The fact that he was caught driving a red car—a color he had banned—

amused me. Warren had always been a complete hypocrite. He forced the community to live under rules he ignored.

I had just gotten home from taking my children to school when the news broke. The phone didn't stop ringing. I talked all day to friends and family. We were so glad he was finally behind bars. When I saw him on television for the first time, my heart began racing and it felt hard to breathe. I hadn't realized how much of a hold he had on me and how even just the sight of him could send fear streaming through my body again. It was hard to think that such a meek-looking man could impose so much terror on so many. Seeing him walk into a court in custody was an unbelievable milestone for me.

While there was tremendous relief that Warren was finally in jail, there was still a mountain of questions. Who was going to take over the FLDS now that Warren was behind bars? What was going to happen to the families that had been split apart on Warren's orders? Would men be free to return to their wives? Could the "lost boys" come home? Would people realize how betrayed they had been and insist on justice and change? Was this the beginning of the end for the FLDS?

Warren's arrest was not the end of his power. After his capture he was still seen as the prophet, albeit a persecuted one. The message he sent out was that God wanted him to be captured. For FLDS members living with almost no exposure to the outside world, this was believable. They were not going to abandon their loyalty to him overnight because he was in the hands of the wicked. The word around the FLDS was that the authorities didn't have anything on him and it was just a matter of time until they would be forced to let him go. He always found a way to stoke the fires of his fanaticism for a community of his brainwashed believers whose faith in him continues. They believe he is being poisoned in prison.

It's hard to know what to believe about Warren Jeffs. He apparently confessed to his brother Nephi Jeffs that he was the most evil of men and had worked his way up through the FLDS only because he wanted power. Jeffs said he hadn't upheld the priesthood since he was twenty. He asked his brother to convey his "confession" to the community. Then he changed his mind and told him not to.

Somehow after his capture he sent word back to his followers to close all the private religious schools. Children were to stay at home and out of school. This is still in effect today.

Jeffs' mental competency was an issue initially, but a judge found him competent to stand trial. A trial is expected to begin in the fall of 2007 on the state charges in Utah against Warren Jeffs for being an accomplice to rape. There are other charges against Jeffs in Utah and Arizona. He faces federal charges for evading prosecution. I was told that he has been placed on a suicide watch and is wearing paper clothes.

Warren Jeffs is both a problem and the symptom of a problem. The FLDS has created a lot of Warrens, men who are intoxicated with their own power, believing they need at least three wives to get into heaven and wanting to dominate women and children. Generation after generation of believers have been conditioned to equate obedience with salvation. People who have never been taught or allowed to think for themselves don't suddenly change. Change is too frightening. Unlike other cult members who have lived a prior life outside and know other values, the FLDS is the only life Jeffs' followers have ever known.

There are currently no government programs in place to help the "lost boys" who have been kicked out of the cult. Dan Fisher still does what he can, but these boys need massive support, education, and training. One of the lawsuits against Jeffs has been filed on behalf of the "lost boys." The hope is that a financial settlement against Jeffs can be used to set up a foundation to provide them the continual help and support they need to successfully adjust to their new lives.

There's now a federally funded Safe Passage program in place to help women trying to extricate themselves from polygamy. But it meets only a few of their needs, and much more comprehensive assistance is needed. Its funding runs out sometime in 2007, and if its grant is not renewed, it will cease to exist.

Utah and Arizona officials have talked about trying to make a determined effort to put law enforcement officers in Colorado City and Hildale who have no ties to the FLDS. The problem is that the police there don't want to leave and will claim they are being discriminated against because of their religion. But I believe there is proof that some of the officers were funneling money to Warren when he was a fugitive, and that might cast their claims of discrimination in a different light. Until this situation is resolved, it's still frightening and risky for a woman who wants to leave because she cannot trust local law enforcement officials to help.

I often get updates on Merril's family. Ruth had a nervous breakdown in Texas and was sent back to Colorado City to repent. Tammy also made it out of Texas thanks to her son, Parley. The child Tammy had been so desperate to conceive was sent to work on construction crews as a twelve-year-old and forbidden to see his mother once she went to Texas to live. He was not allowed to go to school and had no money to live. He started to steal from his older half-brothers and got into trouble with the law.

Here the system worked. Once he was arrested as a juvenile, counseling sessions indicated that his problem was simple: Parley missed his mother. A judge told Tammy she could leave Texas and take care of her son or lose custody of him. Tammy decided to be a mother and last I heard she and Parley were doing well.

Betty graduated from high school with honors and turned eighteen on July 2, 2007, and says she plans to return to the FLDS. Two days after her birthday, on the Fourth of July, Betty left our home after an anguished goodbye. She hugged all her siblings and told them she loved them. But when she came to me, she put her arms around me and sobbed and sobbed. She thanked me for all I had done for her and said she loved me. I told Betty I loved her, too, and would always welcome her home. My heart was breaking in ways I could not have imagined and was not able to explain. I knew this day might come, and when it did it was shattering in its devastation.

All of my children were terribly upset that Betty was leaving us. They all told her that they couldn't understand why on the day that celebrates America winning its freedom she was relinquishing hers.

I sensed in Betty a deep conflict about returning to the FLDS. Her decision means she will no longer have access to us, and I think that will be awful for her. When she left, she promised to call, but none of us have been able to reach her by phone since her departure.

I wonder if Betty—stubborn, independent, and quite capable of thinking for herself—will be able to stay in the FLDS. One of the reasons I stayed as long as I did in the FLDS is that I had nothing to compare it to. I had no sense of what it meant to be free and have the power to make my own decisions about life. Betty has friends who love her, and she's become a passionate defender of those she perceives as underdogs. This kind of outspokenness will never be permitted when she is back in the cult.

Nor do I think Betty can appreciate how the tide might turn against her. I'm sure she will be seen as contaminated by worldly ways and her worldly education. I have great fears about her return to a culture of abuse and degradation. I don't think she will do well there. If she decides to leave, I will always welcome her back. Betty and I have had our struggles, but she's my daughter and I will always love and protect her.

Arthur has his pilot's license and is a full-time college student at Salt Lake Community College. He's the first of Merril Jessop's sons ever to go to college. His dream is to become a commercial airline pilot.

LuAnne has her green belt in karate and is just finishing her sophomore year in high school. She's poised and beautiful and determined to go to college.

Patrick and Andrew are still passionate about karate and now have earned their brown belts. Arthur is a real role model to them. They both want to go to college. At a recent highly competitive karate tournament, both boys won medals.

Merrilee has finally decided there might be more to life than becoming a princess. She's a Girl Scout and devoted to her karate lessons like the rest of her siblings. She dreams of becoming a veterinarian.

Harrison, who's almost eight, still works with Lee and is on the verge of walking.

Bryson is starting kindergarten in the fall. He's bright, with a happy and well-balanced personality. His teacher says he is always smiling at school and has great social skills. Bryson is very athletic and eager to play soccer. Bryson was a year old when we fled and the only child I've been able to parent one-on-one in a nonpolygamist environment.

I am never far from terrible reminders of the awful world we escaped. On April 7, 2007, eighteen-year-old Parley Dutson, one of the "lost boys" who was kicked out of the FLDS two years before, allegedly put a gun to the head of his fifteen-year-old girlfriend, Kara Hopkins, at a party, pulled the trigger, and then sexually assaulted her. He's been charged with murder. Police say drugs were involved. Desperate people do desperate things. His cry for help was a gunshot blast. It shouldn't have to come to that.

Two weeks later marked the fourth anniversary of my family's escape on April 22, 2003. Brian had taken me out to dinner the night before. I never could have imagined when I fled in a panic with my children that four years later I'd be dining in a fine restaurant with the love of my life.

We celebrated as a family the next day—except for Betty, who said she had too much homework to do. We went to see a movie, Meet the Robertsons, and had dinner at a Chinese restaurant. It was the most ordinary of evenings. But not to me. My children and I now know what it means to be safe. Freedom is extraordinary, and love a miracle.

# Afterword

September 25, 2007 was an unforgettable day, a day I never dared dream could really arrive. I had been watching the trial of Warren Jeffs closely. I was even flown to St George as a potential witness before the defense rested its case but I was not put on the stand.

A week later, the jury of five men and three women began deliberating. I held my breath. The jury asked for clarification on one point and then sent word back the next day that it was deadlocked on the second charge against Jeffs. The judge told them to continue their deliberations. The following day, a female juror was replaced by an alternate. No one had any idea of what had happened, but I was not optimistic.

At best, I thought Jeffs might be convicted on one count. I also knew that there was a strong possibility he could be acquitted, but it was too disheartening to contemplate. Abuse against women in the FLDS will not stop until women's voices are not only heard, but believed.

Warren Jeffs still controlled the lives of many people I knew and some that I loved – none more so than my own daughter, Betty. I didn't want her to live under his tyrannical rule and I felt her future hung in the balance. The suspense of waiting for the verdict made me tense.

If Warren was acquitted I knew other victims would be silenced, too afraid to come forward. FLDS members distrust outsiders and certainly have no faith in the justice system. I worried that if Jeffs were acquitted the State might not go forward with the other cases it has pending against him. Would the public lose interest in the issues raised by polygamy? Would the crimes polygamy can cause continue to rip into the lives of another generation of families?

Brian and I were finishing lunch when I heard that a verdict had been reached and the jury was returning to the courtroom in thirty minutes. Brian and I went to his office so I wouldn't be alone when the verdict was announced.

My cell phone rang moments later and it was Laura Palmer, the writer I've worked with, calling from New York City. The suspense was too much for her, too. She was logged on to the *Salt Lake City Tribune*'s website. Neither one of us thought there was any way Jeffs could be convicted on both counts. We braced ourselves and said that even a partial verdict would be a significant victory because of what it would symbolize. I told her how afraid I was about hoping for anything more. Brian was trying to load a news page onto his computer when Laura suddenly said, "Warren Jeff was convicted on both counts! Oh, my God, Carolyn, he's been convicted...on both counts!!!"

I sank into a chair shaking with emotion and feeling dizzy. Justice had prevailed. The system worked. Warren Jeffs could be sentenced to spend the rest of his life in prison. Guilty. Convicted on two counts of being an accomplice to the rape of a fourteen-year-old girl.

Other victims could believe that if they found the courage to come forward, justice might prevail for them, too. Every polygamous group now would know that crimes against minors are going to be prosecuted.

It's too soon to know what the future of the FLDS will be with Warren behind bars. We can all make predictions about what might happen, but I'm far more interested in finding ways to help those victimized by polygamy and his crimes. I would rather work toward making changes than predicting them.

The morning after the verdict I awoke and felt like I was living in a brand new world. I escaped to freedom four years ago, but on Wednesday, September 26, 2007, I felt finally and completely free.

# He just wanted a decent book to read ...

Not too much to ask, is it? It was in 1935 when Allen Lane, Managing Director of Bodley Head Publishers, stood on a platform at Exeter railway station looking for something good to read on his journey back to London. His choice was limited to popular magazines and poor-quality paperbacks – the same choice faced every day by the vast majority of readers, few of whom could afford hardbacks. Lane's disappointment and subsequent anger at the range of books generally available led him to found a company – and change the world.

*'We believed in the existence in this country of a vast reading public for intelligent books at a low price, and staked everything on it'*
**Sir Allen Lane, 1902–1970, founder of Penguin Books**

The quality paperback had arrived – and not just in bookshops. Lane was adamant that his Penguins should appear in chain stores and tobacconists, and should cost no more than a packet of cigarettes.

Reading habits (and cigarette prices) have changed since 1935, but Penguin still believes in publishing the best books for everybody to enjoy. We still believe that good design costs no more than bad design, and we still believe that quality books published passionately and responsibly make the world a better place.

So wherever you see the little bird – whether it's on a piece of prize-winning literary fiction or a celebrity autobiography, political tour de force or historical masterpiece, a serial-killer thriller, reference book, world classic or a piece of pure escapism – you can bet that it represents the very best that the genre has to offer.

## Whatever you like to read – trust Penguin.